Iran and the U.S.
2017 - 2023

New Atlantic Media,
an Imprint of ProseWorks Media
Chapel Hill, NC
2024

Iran and the U.S.
2017 - 2023

Observations
of an
American Journalist

November 25, 2017 - September 18, 2023

Martin Love

Iran and the U.S. 2017 - 2023
Copyright © 2024 by Martin Love
All Rights Reserved.

Book Design by Tim Hubbard
New Atlantic Media, an imprint of ProseWorks Media
Chapel Hill, NC
NewAtlanticMedia2002@gmail.com

10 9 8 7 6 5 4 3 2
ISBN 979-8-218-42169-4 (paperback)

Printed in the United States of America

Also By Martin Love

The Girl From Ha Giang

CONTENTS

Preface 1
Illusion and Disillusion with Trump
    Nov 24, 2017 3
Exceptionalism and Magnanimity
    Dec 4, 2017 7
The U.S. is no beacon of Democracy
    Dec. 16, 2017 11
Moral objection valid Dec. 19, 2017 15
Ali Salameh
    Dec. 25, 2017 19
Objections may be constructive
    Dec. 31, 2017 24
Wealth moving from West to East
    Jan 6, 2018 27
One view from afar
    Jan. 13, 2018 30
Ibn Khaldun's insight centuries ago applies today
    Jan. 20, 2018 33
An American looks at mandatory hijab
    Jan. 27, 2018 36
Exhibiting confidence and strength can be a delicate dance
    Feb. 4, 2018 40
Woe to leaders mired in the credibility trap
    Feb 8, 2018 44
Pence and the troubling prospect he is
    Feb 12, 2018 47
Iran tops in the "human development improvements since the revolution
    Feb 13, 2018 51

THE CHARGES AGAINST RUSSIA ARE MICKEY MOUSE FEB 20, 2018	53
THE ZEALOT AT HAMRA CHECKPOI FEB 26, 2018	56
THERE IS HOPE IN ENLIGHTENED INDIVIDUALS IN ANY CULTURE MARCH 14, 2018	60
THE CHALLENGE OF U.S. GOVERNMENT LOSING ITS MARBLES MARCH17, 2018	63
PSYCHOPATHS SEEM TO HAVE GATHERED OF LATE APRIL 6, 2018	66
AMID CHAOS, PATIENCE IS A PRIME VIRTUE APRIL 15, 2018	69
AMERICAN SEDUCTIONS ARE DANGEROUS BALDERDASH APRIL 23, 2018	72
ACTRESS PORTMAN IS NOW ESSENTIALLY A DE FACTO BDS SUPPORTER APRIL 25, 2018	75
SUMMER 2018: A BIT OF FEAR AND LOATHING ARE NATURAL MAY 9, 2018	78
THE ONUS OF IDIOCY ON IRAN COULD BE VANQUISHED MAY 13, 2018	81
ACHING FOR POSITIVE RESOLUTIONS TO FRIGHTFUL QUESTIONS MAY 19, 2018	85
WHO DOES POMPEO THINK HE IS KIDDING? MAY 23, 2018	88
U.S. MAY BE HOISTING ITSELF ON ITS OWN PETARD MAY 26, 2018	93
NO ONE WILL BE ABLE TO CRUSH IRAN JUNE 8, 2018	96
TAKE HEART: THE NEXT 100 YEARS WILL BE BETTER JUNE 28, 2018	100

Iran is not alone in these difficult times
    July 10, 2018..103
Let's hope Ocasio-Cortez has real guts
    July 18, 2018..107
A litmus test of sanity: the fate of Iran and Assange both
    July 23, 2018..110
The U.S. has become a threat to itself, too
    July 29, 2018..114
Iran may need reforms but the U.S. is absurdly regressive
    August 4, 2018 118
Perils could actually herald positive change
    August 9, 2018 121
Can the U.S. do without friends in the long run? No
    August 19, 2018 125
Geopolitical and economic transitions are painful
    August 25, 2018 128
Saadi's words from the 13th century are worth remembering right now
    August 29, 2018 132
No, it's not the strongly cruel who survive in the longer run
    Sept 2, 2018 135
Overreach and arrogance are the curses of every empire
    Sept 5, 2018 138
Faint stars in a blackened heaven exist
    Sept 10, 2018 141
Not an easy time at all and no thanks to the U.S.
    Sept 16 2018 144
Change is coming, but when is the question
    Sept 24, 2018 148

Banality and crudeness on display in Washington
Oct 3, 2018..151
Those who are temporariily losing badly often do win
Oct 7, 2018..154
The beginning of Trump's unraveling may be at hand
Oct 15, 2018..158
Human pigs find pleasure in fights so avoid them when possible
Oct 21, 2018..161
So many questions, so few answers so far
Oct 23, 2018..164
A general overview of this era of discord
Oct 27, 2018..168
Ignorance is the bane of humanity
Oct 31, 2018..171
Some Arabs increasingly look like abject pansies
Nov 4. 2018..175
The world prays for the wisdom and cool of Iranians
Nov 10, 2018 178
The recent liberalized scene at Azadi is purely good, smart anodyne
Nov 17, 2018 182
U.S. policy errors mount with Trump's banalities and delusions
Nov 25, 2018 186
Bold counter moves even if naïve are worth examination at least
Nov 28, 2018 189
The loss of the American empire is baked in the cake
Dec 5, 2019 193
What dooms nations can be surprising, and it resides internally
Dec 14, 2018..197

At bottom, what ails the U.S. looks like mental illness
Dec 21, 2018..201
U.S. may be bumping up against the limit of its "empire" schemes
Dec 23, 2018..204
Trump may have begun a serious turn for the better in the Middle East
Dec 29, 2018..207
For Iran as with Syria, a determined mass of unified and determined citizens will defeat aggressors
Jan 5, 2019 211
A random litany of potentially better news for Iran seen for 8000 miles
Jan 8, 2019 215
The U.S. wants to incite Iranians and this must be rejected
Jan 12, 2019 218
It behooves largely Muslim lands to avoid becoming like Saudi Arabia
Jan 19, 2019 222
In U.S. one NYT columnist just made a serious impact
Jan 26 2019 226
Trump may get his personal donnybrook, but in Venezuela
Jan 29, 2019 229
You cannot put lipstick on a pig and make it pretty
Feb 2, 2019 233
Rarely has the world been so challenged by U.S. hubris
Feb 4, 2019 237
Respect warranted for at least two bright Americans
Feb 13, 2019 240

Coexistence between Sunnis and Shias must be a primary goal
Feb 17, 2019 243

Maybe it is always darkest, like now, before any dawn
Feb 23 2019 247

The U.S. may have created a pool of quicksand...and jumped in
Feb 26, 2019 251

Muslims can be proud of Omar and Tlaib in U.S. Congress
March 6, 2019 254

A wild theory about Trump is a sign of natural despair and desperation
March 13, 2019 258

Pity any nation that has veered from the moral messages of Christianity and Islam
Apr 6, 2019 262

The aggravation of Trump's lack of vision is the world's burden
Apr 8, 2019 266

The U.S. under Trump and his crazed Neocons aim to tyrannize the entire world.
Apr 25, 2019 269

Trump's one opportunity to survive with any positive legacy: dumping his Neocon, Zionist advisors
Apr 27, 2019 273

U.S. undermines itself clinging to hegemonic notions.
May 4, 2019 276

Trump's "threat" administration is a one trick pony so far
May 11, 2019 280

Whether more U.S. sparked chaos or real accord is the question that haunts the world
May 18, 2019 284

Iran, whatever it further suffers, is going to win in the longer term
May 23, 2019 288

There are good reasons why Iran won't fold to U.S. extremism
May 28, 2019 291

Iran's potentials despite economic sanctions must be realized eventually
May 29, 2019 295

Iran deserved credit and attention for trying
June 3, 2019 298

With U.S. President Trump, money Trumps all
June 8, 2019 302

Nothing is so dangerous as a wounded beast backed into a corner by itself
July 14, 2019 305

Iran is wisest not to damage burgeoning favorable public opinion
June 19, 2019 309

Trump has a moment of sanity that begs for continuance
June 24, 2019 313

Cry not for hapless Trump: he created the current mess
June 30, 2019 316

Iran will have the world's respect, and prevail
July 9, 2019 319

The Jeffrey Epstein case could sink U.S. elites and induce real change
July 14, 2019 323

Demand that the Mideast become a nuclear free zone!
July 20, 2019 327
Is Biden up to the challenge of wise governance...?
Jan 9, 2021 331
If any country has erred this century, it's the U.S.
Jan 6, 2021 334
Cruelty and Stupidity are the hallmarks of U.S. moves this century
July 27, 2019 337
Iran's strength lies in continued patience
Aug 6, 2019 341
Occam's razor may be useful in explaining Jeffrey Epstein
August 13, 2019 344
Crises everywhere and Trump and supporters are vapid
Aug 20 2019 347
Crises everywhere and Trump supporters are completely vapid
August 20, 2019 351
Iran is wooing and winning sympathizers, the U.S. is not
Aug 25, 2019 354
The dangerous Mideast logjam requires lubrication by the U.S. for its release
Sept 1, 2019 358
Trump and fellow gangsters look increasingly foolish
Sept 7, 2019 362
Absolution from crimes by deflection and deceit is never successful
Sept 20, 2019 368
The U.S. has evolved to "Inverted Totalitarianism"
Sept 29, 2019 371

Reasons to be optimistic and steadfast in Iran
  Oct 11, 2019 375
A speculation about the Trumpian core
  Oct 14, 2019 378
A short rant after a personal visit to Syria
  Nov 1, 2019 382
Iran actually is managing misfortune with aplomb
  Nov 9, 2019 385
The coup in Bolivia shines yet more dark light on America
  Nov 13, 2019 388
U.S. stupidity, as now, followed by worse stupidity
  Nov 22, 2019 391
Little to no intelligence at the top of U.S. media and government
  Nov 28, 2019 394
U.S. has no right to slam violence (it has helped promote or executed) anywhere
  Dec. 6, 2019 398
A search for counters to U.S. imperialism is necessary and hard
  Dec 9, 2019 402
Boris Johnson, an unhealthy choice anywhere
  Dec 16, 2019 407
If it had a soul, America may have lost it
  Dec 21, 2019 410
Let the ICC do what it alleges it will
  Dec 29, 2019 414
Trump may have given Iran an unintended assist
  Jan 4, 2020 418
It must be always emphasized: Allah's mercy and compassion
  Jan 10, 2020 421

Protesters in Iran may be bolstering U.S. imperialism
Jan 13, 2020 424
Dignity, smarts and grace: that's Iran's performance of late
Jan 13, 2020 428
The U.S. now: widespread thuggery
Jan 18, 2020 431
Iran's one strike may have changed Mideast forever
Jan 24, 2020 434
The "Deal of the Century" is DOA, period
Jan 29, 2020 438
Iran, under extreme pressure? Superb responses so far
Feb 5, 2020 441
Iran may be more "democratic" than the U.S. nowadays
Feb 14, 2020 444
Black Swans if not dangerous raptors are everywhere
Feb 15, 2020 447
America has not been helping itself
Feb 21, 2020 450
America is not immune
Feb 28, 2020 453
Javad Zarif's brain should be duplicated at the U.S. State Department
March 4, 2020 456
With solidarity, Iran will pull through
Mar 9, 2020 460
Trump, it seems likely, is finished politically
Mar 17, 2020 463
Earth's non-human species enjoying diminished human activity
Mar 24, 2020 466

American society suffused with anger and violence: analyst

April 16, 2020 469

Trump could "not have been more wrong" on coronavirus: analyst

April 18, 2020 472

U.S. exceptionalism is fading at warp speed

May 11, 2020 478

The U.S. movement from prosperity to utter decay

May 25, 2020 482

Martin Luther King was right : the earth does bend towards justice

June 29, 2020 485

An assassination has made a dark Mideast darker than ever

Nov 30, 2020 489

The U.S. and allies have done little but inflame West Asia

Dec 5, 2020 492

Sustained and rare, honest goodwill by the U.S.D is its only salvation now

Dec 23, 2020 495

A view of the fractured U.S. by a non-neo liberal

Jan 19, 2021 498

It's a wonder Iran has not ditched the JCPOA

Mar 9, 2021 502

Martin Love: Pardoning Blackwater killers inexplicable

Mar 12, 2021 506

Biden ain't cutting it so far

Mar 26, 2021 508

Huge whiffs of desperation in Washington now

Apr 4, 2021 512

Zionism is the Ebola virus of American political afflictions
  Apr 16, 2021 515
War is not the solution but patience is
  Apr 27, 2021 519
Escalations in Palestine designed by Netanyahu to keep him in power: analyst
  May 18, 2021 522
Imagine what Gaza could become if the siege were lifted
  May 26, 2021 526
Zionists are a one trick pony called VIOLENCE
  June 9, 2021 530
A roundup: America continues to lurch from bad to worse
  June 30, 2021 533
America is still headed for a material collapse eventually
  August 5, 2021 537
The U.S. empire is slowly disintegrating
  August 28, 2021 540
Something like Astana can be helpful for Afghanistan: analyst
  Sept 2, 2021 543
As the U.S. "empire" frays, there is Zubeidi and his colleagues
  September 15, 2021 548
U.S. is stuck in post 9/11 power politics: analyst
  October 18, 2021 555
Weep or not, America is beginning to hurt seriously
  October 24, 2021 559

A VIEW FROM THE PEANUT GALLERY IN THE U.S.
 NOVEMBER 14, 2021...562
IN TRUTH THE U.S HAS BECOME A WEAK AND THEREFORE
 DANGEROUS COUNTRY
 DECEMBER 5, 2021 566
S. ARABIA AND ISRAEL BECOMING WORLD PARIAHS: ANALYST
 JAN 28, 2022 569
THE U.S., ASIDE FROM CRIMINALITY, MUST BE SIMPLY JEALOUS
 OF RUSSIA
 JULY 16, 2022..574
MAYBE, JUST MAYBE, REAL CHANGE CAN HAPPEN
 AUGUST 2, 2022 577
U.S. OBJECTIONS TO ANYTHING IN IRAN ARE AT BOTTOM
 SELECTIVELY HYPOCRITICAL
 SEPTEMBER 18, 2022 580
RETRIBUTION IS COMING
 DECEMBER 2, 2022 584
SOLEIMANI WAS A GREAT MAN. PERIOD.
 JANUARY 3, 2023 588
"THE DIE IS CAST" FOR THE U.S.
 JANUARY 21, 2023 591
SUCH RIDICULOUS PANIC OVER A DARN BALLOON!
 FEBRUARY 8, 2023..595
DID SY HERSH'S JOURNALISM SPARK AN ALIEN INVASION?
 FEBRUARY 15, 2023..600
SOMEDAY A DAY OF RECKONING FOR CRUELTIES
 MARCH 1, 2023 603
DANGEROUS TIMES AMID SERIOUS GLIMMERS OF REAL AND
 HUGE, POSITIVE CHANGES
 APRIL 2, 2023 610
AMERICAN INFLUENCE IS FAST CRUMBLING
 APRIL 9, 2023 614
RUMINATIONS ABOUT THE CHANGES UNDERWAY
 APRIL 16, 2023 617

THE U.S. IS ON A SUICIDE MISSION
APRIL 23, 2023..620
GREED IS THE DOWNFALL OF WESTERN AND U.S. POWER
MAY 19, 2023..623
COUNTRIES CAN ROT LIKE FISH OUT OF WATER — FROM THE HEAD DOWN
JUNE 7, 2023..627
LITERALLY FREAKISH TIMES IN THE U.S. AS DECLINE ACCELERATES
JUNE 17, 2023..630
INIMICAL TO U.S. HEALTH, THE GREATEST POISON IS THE NEOCON CABAL
JULY 2, 2023..633
ALL THE EARTH IS AT RISK
JULY 10, 2023..637
AVOID MORAL DECLINE BECAUSE THE RESULT IS FAILURE
JULY 17, 2023..640
THE U.S. MAINSTREAM MEDIA IS DESPERATE WITH LIES
JULY 23, 2023..643
ONE NOTABLE PALESTINIAN SEES NO CHANGES FOR NOW BUT "SAMUD" WILL PREVAIL
JULY 30, 2023..646
DESPERATION THREATENS THE ENTIRE WORLD
AUGUST 8, 2023 649
U.S. IMPERIALISM REMAINS VERY STICKY AND TERRIBLY TRAGIC
AUGUST 16, 2023 652
GOP DEBATE MATTERS AND TWO "WINNERS". FOR NOW: TRUMP AND RAMASWANY
AUGUST 27, 2023 655
AMERICANS: PREPARE FOR LIFE IN A FUMBLING THIRD WORLD PARIAH!
SEPTEMBER 10, 2023 659
NUCLEAR WAR CAN BE AVOIDED IF THE U.S. GETS WISE
SEPTEMBER 18, 2023 662

Preface

Martin Love is an American journalist who for several years wrote frequent columns for Iran's primary English language newspaper, Tehran Times. Love wrote each column addressing his concerns over issues unfolding at the time of writing whether in the U.S. or overseas. Not a single word was edited or cut, including some measured questions about Iranian policies occasionally. A decades-long observer of the Middle East, he discovered that he could write freely for Iran's media where he could not write freely in the U.S. mainstream media, particularly about the Middle East and especially Israel/Palestine. Love, now in his late 70s, worked long ago as a reporter at several U.S. newspapers, and also Forbes magazine. He has graduate degrees from the University of North Carolina and Yale and is also a graduate of Columbia's graduate school of journalism in New York. He is also a writer of a novel, one based on having worked in Hanoi at Vietnam News for several months in 2007 as an editor. Widely traveled in West Asia, his first exposure to the region occurred in 1969 when he spent a summer picking bananas at an Israeli kibbutz in the Jordan Valley.

Iran and the U.S. 2017 - 2023

Illusion and Disillusion with Trump

Nov 24, 2017

Let's make one thing clear right off the bat. I did not vote in the 2016 presidential election. I would have voted had Bernie Sanders won the Democratic Party nomination, but Hillary Clinton rigged the primaries to give herself the nomination to run against Trump.

It's no secret what happened. I and many other observers have no doubt Sanders would have become President, beating Trump. But above all, in the past election, myself and others did not want Clinton to win. Her mendacity and her policies as Secretary of State were and remain abhorrent to millions of Americans.

Trump on the campaign trail made a lot of noise about revamping U.S. foreign policy, making it more benign. He even talked about friendly relations with Russia, not demonizing that country, and say what you want about Vladimir Putin, I admire him for going in to Syria and helping shore up the Assad government and Syria as an intact state against the mercenary terrorists sponsored by the Saudis and some of the Arab states on the Persian Gulf and, of course, the Zionist entity that calls itself "Israel".

In my view, and in the view of other sage Americans who really understand what America is now (more on that later), I believe Trump since last winter has largely betrayed many who voted for him even if many may refuse to believe it until the next economic downturn. Particularly the so-called "middle class", the many millions of voters in the "flyover" states between the Atlantic and Pacific coasts. For one thing, he and the Republican Party have proposed a tax overhaul that benefits "the rich", really a small minority of oligarchs at the top of the U.S. food chain. Whether the proposed tax overhaul passes the U.S. Congress remains an open question. If it does, expect a widening of the fiscal deficit, already out of control.

Trump's foreign policies also don't look very positive so far. His administration has given tacit support to the Saudi war on Yemen, and many there face starvation, even cholera, and many innocents have been murdered. It's an abomination. Also, no question, Trump has thrown his hat into the ring with Netanyahu's Likud government in Israel. People in his administration has threatened to move the U.S. embassy to Jerusalem. His administration is attempting to force the long suffering Palestinians to reengage in "talks" with the Zionists towards some kind of "peace" deal, but we all know how that goes and has gone for decades. The U.S. has not been a fair arbiter, and Trump hasn't the courage, given political considerations at home, to force the Israelis to make a fair deal, and meanwhile the so-called "two state" solution is virtually impossible now. It's a mess like few others. Trump's support and alleged current "friendship" with Saudi prince Muhammad bin Salman does not look promising, too, and I could go on about such postures which do not, by the way, point to benign actions or changes that promote peace in the Mideast and beyond. But there remains the matter of hope. Hope that somehow Trump wises up. But there is a much larger matter to consider, in my view, and that is the question of what the United States seems to have become in the last three or four decades.

But before trying to identify what the U.S. is now, let me say directly that even if the mainstream media in the U.S., and that includes the major newspapers and network broadcasters, has largely become a mouthpiece for the state, we here still enjoy press freedoms and freedoms of expression that have not yet been entirely curtailed, and as a journalist off and on for many years, I am not a "mainstream" voice in spirit even while, occasionally, I have seen some work published in establishment journals. It can be difficult to tell the truth, in any case, as perhaps it is in some other countries. I rely on the shared views of intellectuals and other writers like myself who have at least attempted to get a grip on the American scene, such as it has become. One such intellectual, for example, is the now retired Princeton University political science professor Dr. Sheldon Wolin. In general, Wolin believes that the U.S. has become a state of what he terms "inverted totalitarianism". This is a state which does not rely on the existence of a political "strongman", but rather a state that on the surface maintains the institutions and norms of a "democracy" but really is no longer a true democracy where ALL the citizens have an equal voice in the formulation and conduct of policy. Democracy has become an illusion.

We have now the appearance-- the illusion -- only of two major political parties alleging to have different views and aspirations, but really both are beholding to the same special, narrow interests, and this is largely why we get the same old policies year after year, whether internal or foreign, no matter who wins an election. (This includes the same old, stale attitudes towards Iran.)

What, then, are these powerful "interests"? They are, by and large, major U.S. corporations and the oligarchs who run big business and the Wall Street banks, powerful lobbies like

AIPAC, and even the U.S. mainstream media. Laws have been enacted to make these various interest groups the supreme arbiters of policy, even environmental policy. For this, in my opinion, the U.S. is struggling with outright decline and weaker influence worldwide. Struggling in such a way that makes attempted maintenance of influence and power and hegemony dangerous, as we see in the myriad U.S. military interventions overseas, perhaps starting with the Vietnam War. It's a game that cannot be played indefinitely, if for no other reason but that the U.S. national debt is beyond redemption, and money printing is no path to prosperity, or has never proven to be such historically.

Thus, many Americans wait in a state of suspense and suspicion. What, we wonder, is coming next, and yet there remain too many citizens, the relatively uneducated, who fervently want to believe that the government under Trump is working in their interests, and often vehemently refuse to believe otherwise, if only because it comforts them in a time of confusions and unease. If, for example, the economy cracks once again as it died in 2008-09, and it well may sometime ahead, then the country faces a day of reckoning – as many more citizens become more disillusioned and outraged. The wealth disparity in the U.S. has never been greater, and poverty is becoming rampant. And people always finally point to what bad policy has done to their living standards.

Exceptionalism and Magnanimity

Dec 4, 2017

There is no reasonable justification for citizens anywhere to consider themselves or their country necessarily "exceptional". When one is talking about particular governments pushing the meme of "exceptionalism" (rather than, say, humility) in some grandiose way, watch out.

Some in (and others influential with) the U.S. government have crowed "exceptionalism" in recent decades to, well, justify policies, particular overseas policies or actions that have included rampant war-making, even the torture of foreigners deemed "enemy combatants" -- often with scant evidence they are – and other so-called "crimes against humanity" that have resulted in the murder of millions of innocent people.

Here, one may be dealing with the worst demonstrations of some aspects of human nature. I don't like it, many other American don't, too, and those who simply are not aware would not like it, if only they knew better. However, the majority often have their heads down trying, in some cases desperately, aiming to tend their families and survive to the exclusion of broader concerns.

Researchers at Princeton University have recently demonstrated that the odds, if an idea is proposed and supported by the bottom 90 percent of Americans, has almost nil chance of passage into law by the U.S. Congress. However, if legislation is proposed by the top (most powerful, wealthy) 10 percent of Americans, representing special interest lobbies and corporations and the billionaire class, it has vastly greater odds of becoming law. The U.S., some have suggested, is the most powerful military force the world has ever seen, and why not with a "defense" budget of almost $1 trillion, surpassing the next 10 countries combined? But overseas the U.S. has not literally "won" any wars, not many "hearts and minds", and aside from the costs or because of them, the U.S. has become an exceptionally mediocre country since the Vietnam War, which constituted imperial overreach on steroids just as further militarism since then has seemed like fruitless imperialism.

Various comparative statistics dealing with a variety of issues, even comparative healthcare results and metrics and educational effectiveness, can be cited to support this claim of "not exceptional".

Internally, the majority of Americans have been neglected. Real Democracy, which the U.S. has claimed to advocate as rationale for its military adventures overseas (remember Iraq in 2003), has even been neglected at home.

Consider a recent study by Princeton University. The creeping abolition of "Democracy" in many respects is a serious problem. Consider:

Researchers at Princeton University have recently demonstrated that the odds, if an idea is proposed and supported by the bottom 90 percent of Americans, has almost nil chance of passage into law by the U.S. Congress. However, if legislation is proposed by the top (most powerful, wealthy) 10 percent of Americans, representing special interest lobbies and corporations and the billionaire class, it has vastly greater odds of becoming law.

This has especially been true since 2010 and the ruling by the U.S. Supreme Court upholding the infamous "Citizens United" legislation, but in fact many have noted this phenomenon for the past 40 years.

In essence, the "average" American has very little influence as a voter. There is no more appropriate word for this phenomenon except, simply, corruption. Researchers note that in an ideal "democracy" any proposed legislation, if it is supported by 50 percent of the population, OUGHT to have a 50 percent chance of becoming law, and so on. But we know anyway that an "ideal" government probably does not exist anywhere yet. But at the same time, a government anywhere that aims to become incrementally more "ideal" or representative, at least, is certainly one worthy of support.

Time and again government in the U.S. has had tremendous opportunities. And then blown them. For example, right after the 9/11 attack on lower Manhattan, there existed worldwide empathy for the U.S. IF the aim of the government is generally to garner support and allies overseas, even to capitalize on the empathy post 9/11, it might have asked humbly for the world to join with the U.S. and track down the perpetrators, those behind the attacks, those who had helped plan them. The word "magnanimity" comes to mind.

But the U.S. did the opposite: not only did the official investigation of the attack fall short, leaving a host of unanswered questions, but the U.S. government went to war in a blind rage of apparent vindictiveness, ultimately losing goodwill in the Islamic world especially.

In essence, the "average" American has very little influence as a voter. There is no more appropriate word for this phenomenon except, simply, corruption. And this loss has been ongoing since. It has not escaped many thinkers that 9/11 itself, or something like it, might have been a foregone conclusion, giving the U.S. cover to attack many countries. Many Americans have asked an important question: Cui bono (who benefits?)

I can think of only two beneficiaries: The U.S. corporate Military Industrial Complex, which President Eisenhower warned against in 1960 as he was leaving office, and Zionist interests, which before 9/11 had a plan, using the U.S., to attack various largely Islamic countries in sequence called The Project for a New American Century, and before that the Yinon Plan.

The infamous Neocons were behind both. It's no longer a secret. And many of the original Neocons remain as drivers of foreign policy. Trump's refusal to re-certify the nuclear deal with Iran is an example of Neocon influence. And it's shameful.

If one could offer wise advice for current adversaries of the U.S. and its allied overreachers, it might be something like this: Be patient. Internally, make your countries stronger, support democratic representation, build your economies (even if under U.S. economic sanctions) and wait. Externally, remain vigilant on defense but also confident and relaxed and as inoffensive as possible, and wait.

The various, largely corporate and military, powers in charge of U.S. policy are slowly hacking away at the foundations of their own power. Unease and anger among the powerless, the many who have little if any voice, is growing. U.S. economic clout and the exorbitant privilege of having the world's dominant reserve currency are waning.

The so-called "petrodollar" is at risk, even in Saudi Arabia, if only because their largest petroleum customer is now a growing China. There will be real change, change beneficial to the entire world, eventually. It is inevitable and patience is a virtue that rewards.

The U.S. is no beacon of Democracy

Dec. 16, 2017

I am pleased now and then to write something for the Tehran Times from the U.S., more honored than I would be to write, say, a regular column for the New York Times or the Washington Post, both of which are at the heart of the corporate print media complex in the U.S.

And I have never even been to Iran, nor, admittedly, do I have direct knowledge of the country except of its deep history, and that as a civilization Iran has produced art, architecture and literature of almost inestimable quality in all of its evolution from one polity to another over many centuries.

I also can't speak with any authority whatsoever about the Iranian media. To be frank, that's not my business, and even if it were I would not dare to try the analysis for fear of simply being wrong, not knowing enough, and anyway how can anyone who has never lived in Iran or even visited have a legitimate voice about such matters?

One thing is clear, though. Many "establishment" journalists in the U.S. who do write anything about Iran don't really have a clue, and anyway almost the entire media establishment in the U.S., if not a small minority of respected journalists still around, is, in my opinion and that of many Americans, hopelessly corrupted now.

Consider that, if you look closely enough, various media outlets in the U.S. operate as extreme forms of predatory capitalism, using information aimed at capturing control, influence and wealth for the few at the expense of the many. Now, in the U.S., six behemoth transnational corporate conglomerates virtually own the entirety of the mass media, including newspapers, magazines, publishers, TV networks, cable channels, Hollywood studios, music labels and popular websites: Time Warner, Walt Disney, Viacom, News Corp., CBS Corporation and NBC Universal. (Even in the UK, some 70 percent of UK national newspapers are owned by a mere three companies, while 80 percent of local newspapers are owned by only five companies.) Today, the world's largest media owner is Google, closely followed by Walt Disney, Comcast, 21st Century Fox and Facebook. Together, Google and Facebook have captured some 20 percent of global ad revenue. And all these corporations control and manage the bulk of what many in the West read and watch, including to a lesser extent on the Internet. They define much of the erroneous understanding of the world in the U.S. And that understanding of many other countries, such as Iran, is sorely lacking. To say that the media has been "captured" by special interests could be an understatement.

To cite just one example of "reporting" that was erroneous by the absence of full assessment is a recent column by none other that than the Washington Post's David Ignatius, who writes a foreign policy column twice a week in that newspaper and who has several times visited both Syria and Iraq. Ignatius, whom I know personally but not well, wrote a piece about how ISIS was defeated in Syria by massive U.S. military firepower --- and failed to mention who actually defeated ISIS and deserves the most credit for it: the Syrian Arab Army with the assistance of the Russians, Hezballah and Iran! We know from reports outside the mainstream media in the U.S. written by reliable journalists that the U.S. government may actually have been supporting ISIS and other mercenary terrorists groups in Syria with money and weaponry. It's incredible that someone like Ignatius, who has been at the Post for decades, can get away with crowing about how it was the U.S. military that did the job.

On a more positive note, it's no surprise that many of these media companies, including the Washington Post, are beginning to lose influence with the "average" citizen in the U.S., and their business models are not looking all that healthy in terms of the sponsorship and readership they have. Many in the U.S., if not horribly confused by or with the information they receive, just don't trust the corporate media like they formerly did, because it caters to special, narrow interests. But so does Trump and the U.S. Congress. Take Trump's plan, announced December 6th, to move the U.S. embassy from Tel Aviv to Jerusalem, a plan which has been condemned virtually worldwide. With regard to this, consider who is pulling Trump's strings: Likud Israel of course, but in the U.S., billionaire donors to Trump's election last year. People like Sheldon Adelson, Haim Saban, Paul Singer and a few others, plus AIPAC and the Christian "evangelical" community. Yet a recent poll suggests that some 65 percent of Americans are against this embassy move. This may be all anyone needs to know: that U.S. foreign policy is not much representative of majority sentiment. And it has not been for a very long time, and many are aware of this discrepancy. Democracy, which the U.S. claimed to be bringing to countries it has destroyed, such as Iraq and in part Syria with its paid proxy terrorist groups that entered Syria from outside, and other countries such as Libya, no longer really exists in the U.S. Just ask other notable journalists like Pulitzer Prize winner Chris Hedges, who left the New York Times when he was told NOT to question the war on Iraq in 2003, and even some foreign journalists such as Australian-born John Pilger.

There are many others, but you won't find them at major U.S. newspapers or broadcast media right now. But here's the positive: Americans ARE becoming smarter, and it would be beyond foolish for the U.S. government to ignite another war in the Middle East on predominately Muslim countries, including Iran. Not only has the U.S. lost credibility at home and abroad with the plan to move the U.S. embassy to Jerusalem, but what's left of that credibility, if there is any, would be lost forever with further war making. This is virtually guaranteed and as a result, the U.S. would LOSE. And a revolution of some kind would likely occur inside the U.S. But the big changes will happen anyway in time, because the bursting the financial bubbles ahead may have the same effect, impoverishing millions as the fiat dollar drops like a rock and the U.S. debt burden becomes impossible to manage.

China and Russia and even Iran stand to become countries that could very well lead the world to a brighter future.

Moral objection valid

Dec. 19, 2017

This is part personal, it is passionate, but it is nonetheless fully substantiated by facts and long study, experience and observation, real time objective observation, over decades. And after a while, if a person has half a brain and heart, one stops mincing words and throws caution to the winds and tries hard to tell and write truths that some others don't want to hear and they, the others, try to squash such truth telling. But here goes, from an American journalist no less writing gladly for an Iranian newspaper.

There is nothing on earth so abominable as right wing Zionism (except maybe ISIS) and current day "Israel". That country, and its U.S. supporters, especially the Neocons in the U.S. government and in various administrations past and in so-called "think tanks" in Washington, have led the U.S. and its Western "allies" into murderous wars and crimes against humanity. Millions have died as a result. In this century criminal actions have decked or tried to destroy various countries in the Middle East, such as in Iraq, Afghanistan, Libya, Syria and others. One looks hard for reasons for such criminal actions, and I certainly have.

One must ask a simple question. Who has benefitted? Has the U.S. benefitted? No. But who? Only the Zionists and their supporters in or outside of Israel have benefitted inasmuch as

Iran and the U.S. 2017 - 2023

Israel has managed to steal the West Bank and the Golan, to turn Gaza into the largest open air prison on earth, and deny if not entirely obliterate the basic aspirations of millions of Palestinians. Zionism, a colonial enterprise, has been a threat to neighboring countries. This is no secret. It is certainly no secret to Iran and Iranians. And it is no secret to many Americans now, too. The world at large looks on aghast and the primary question that screams for an answer is simply this: when will this stop? When will justice be served? Well, in truth, it will one day be stopped, we just don't know exactly when, nor how many lives will be lost between now and then.

I am one journalist who has been horrified for decades. I was in Gaza for six weeks at Jebalya refugee camp in 1975, and again in 1993. I had the story way back then. I have the story now. I was living in the West Bank in 2006 for months with a Palestinian family. I have that scene firmly in memory, too. I have written about Palestinians, and sometimes seen reports avoided or abandoned by even such newspapers as the New York Times, which has rarely if ever allowed objective reports about many issues in the Mideast to appear in its pages. But none of this is news to most Iranians. Nor to the best journalists anywhere now.

A reasonable person must admire Iran for its long stand against the depredations of Zionism. And here's exactly why one must admire, in my view. If Iran as the Islamic Republic were or even seemed to be a grossly self serving, offensive player in West Asia, starting wars with its neighbors, trying to grab more territory and resources it does not already have, and at the same time slammed Israel's actions, then Iran would not have, I think, the credibility it has, or ought to have, on these matters as a largely Islamic country. But the history I have read tells anyone who bothers to study that

Moral objection valid Dec. 19, 2017…

Iran has not, purely on offense, attacked any other country in centuries. This is critically important, because it means Iran's objections to injustice have been based on morality. This is precisely why I am not alone in admiring Iran and Iranians. It is why I am honored to have any connection with Iran, and some smart friends there.

Lately, I asked several hundred people I know, primarily U.S. based, and whose own opinions I have read, to respond to a question I posed to them. I asked: "If you had an opportunity to address the Iranian people directly, what would you say to them?" Quite a few responded. Some of them wrote merely about how they wanted to visit Iran, admired its literature, its art, its architecture, its landscape and its civilization in various iterations over thousands of years. A few others wrote back in a deeper vein. Here are three examples of that:

I would wish to convey the fact that a growing number of Americans are not fooled by the heavy-handed propaganda and lies against Iran that is repeated in our main press outlets. More and more people are aware that what is printed in American newspapers is selected to prepare the people to fear Iran. This government needs the population to be fearful for one reason: to distract from the fact that their own government is corrupt to the core.

Sadly, the American people are wilfully ignorant. They know nothing, and don't want to know, about the CIA's overthrow of Mosaddegh, the Shah's brutality, the U.S. military shootdown of passenger Flight 655. This ignorance was, perhaps, excusable in 1990. But not in the Internet era, when a few clicks of a mouse will reap the same information that once took hours or days of painstaking research through library stacks. The 9/11 false-flag event destroyed, along with the WTC towers, every good instinct Americans once had. We are now a nation of sniveling cowards. A Mordor. Even our culture has become a sham. Frightened silly of Muslims, though we don't know the difference between a Shia and a Sunni, a Salafist or a Sufi. We see scary men chopping off heads. We hide our eyes and close our ears, because the truth is unthinkable. Yes, there are a few Americans who see the truth. Our votes are a meaningless joke, but it doesn't matter, since the U.S. government supports war and militarism. My advice is to never trust the U.S. government. Keep building your military defenses. Remember the lesson of Ghaddafi, who gave up his chemical weapons and attempted to work with the West. Keep strong, Iranians, and know that there are at least a few Americans who know that you are not our enemy.

I would like to thank them for all their sacrifices and support in standing up against inhumane Zionist imperialist warmongering and occupation. I would like to tell Iranians that they have my utmost respect and send them my love as a fellow human being. I know that Iran is not a perfect nation, as no nation on earth is, but they are certainly a nation that deserves to be honored for their righteous stand on behalf of oppressed people.

It is thus warranted, I believe, to say to Iranians that they need not be paranoid over threats by the U.S. under the Trump administration, nor over threats by members of the U.S. Congress. A continuance of a principled, moral, non-offensive, non-aggressive stand against aggression by other countries is important. It is real leadership, Islamic leadership, in a world that often has lost its moral bearings. When Trump on December 6th declared unilaterally Jerusalem, a city equally revered by three faiths, the capital of

Israel to where the U.S. Embassy may relocate, he violated UN resolutions, international law and common sense, and went against all diplomatic efforts to bring peace to the region. He also provoked the ire of at least 130 countries. What if, say, even U.S. allies, particularly European ones, finally say "enough" and begin to peel away from support of the U.S. and find new friends, particularly in Asia? Frankly, I think that's coming and that the future is in the East.

Ali Salameh

Dec. 25, 2017

He came from a most depressed place at age 18 and made a good life for himself in the U.S. and has been able to help his family in Gaza enormously for decades as a result. He is among the fortunate few Palestinians.

'Ali Salameh, is now 65, and one of several children of Miryam and Yusuf, Palestinians made refugees in 1948 during the Nakba by Zionist terrorists when they were driven from their village, Iraq es-Suweidan, in Palestine, to Gaza. His parents wound up at Jebalya Refugee Camp, the largest refugee camp in Gaza, where 'Ali was born.

It all happened for 'Ali because a journalist in North Carolina happened to write an article about the Middle East in a newspaper in 1970 after a summer with visits to Israel, Lebanon, Jordan and Syria. An elderly man of 80, one Emmett White, who once had headed the International Red Cross and was well traveled and based in Baltimore, Maryland, was visiting his sister in North Carolina and happened to read the newspaper article and wanted to meet the young reporter over lunch. He imagined they had something in common, as both were disturbed about the ongoing treatment of Palestinians, whether Muslim or Christian.

White had a book with him: "The Unholy Land" written by a Canadian Christian minister named A.C. Forrest. In this book in the preface, Forrest wrote about an unnamed teenager who "had no future" and worked with his father, the manager, in a citrus grove in Gaza, a walled grove ("bayyara" in Arabic) owned then by the Near East Council of Churches. So this young journalist and Emmett White, over lunch, hatched a plan. Why not find out who this unnamed youth was and sponsor him to come to the U.S. and attend college and live? It was a fine idea and a year later, in 1971, 'Ali appeared at John F. Kennedy Airport in New York City. He had never been outside the Gaza Strip before.

It was a sudden, dramatic change of venue for a teenager like few others ever will or can experience, especially coming from Gaza.

Ali soon was in Greensboro, North Carolina, a modest city at the time of some 150,000 people, and not long after that he was studying at a local community college and had a job, too, for a construction company. He was assisted by the young journalist's family in Greensboro, and though he lived alone initially, he adapted quickly and he was often at the journalist's mother's home for a meal or just company. A few years later, he married a pretty American girl and they settled down to raise a family. They now have two adult sons, both in their 30s. 'Ali owns a few convenience/grocery stores now and has been a modestly successful businessman. His wife also ran a restaurant for many years, but of late she has been working as a wildly popular and beloved, elected public servant in Greensboro.

Ali has developed over the years many American friends, of all races. As a Palestinian Arab and Muslim, he straddles the social worlds of African Americans and whites, and is a beloved friend to both races. He helped found a mosque with other Arab and Muslim friends in Greensboro, too, and attends Friday prayers there regularly. Muslims in Greensboro, and there are a few hundred from various countries in the Middle East, are a tight knit community.

For the American journalist who helped him come to the U.S., there has long been the pleasure of a deep and abiding friendship. But more importantly, 'Ali and spouse and their two children have visited Gaza and 'Ali's parents and siblings from time to time. And 'Ali has contributed to his family's welfare with moral and financial support. He built his family members in Gaza a home near the center of Jabalya Refugee Camp where his mother still lives at age 96. Yusuf, his father, passed away a decade ago.

The young journalist, now a much older man, also made two trips to Gaza because of his friendship with 'Ali. The first in 1975 and the last in 1994. (Back then one could take a taxi to al-Quds from Gaza on occasion for Friday prayers at the Haram esh-Sherif, but no longer and not for many years.)

He will never forget walking to the "bayyara" as a young man in 1975 with Yusuf and there sitting, as if in the Islamic "janna", in winter sunshine and sampling all sorts of citrus until the sweet juices ran down his neck under his shirt. It was a taste of heaven, the best citrus, and the hospitality and warmth of the poor refugees in Gaza remain one of his fondest memories.

'Ali today does not know what's going to happen in and to Gaza, but he is fearful for the safety of all the people imprisoned there by the Israeli military, and under frequent bombardment by Israeli warplanes and the IDF. It is a bizarre situation for a Palestinian to be living in relative safety and comfort in a country, the U.S., whose economic and military support underwrites crimes against Palestinians.

Perhaps the sole relief, so far, is that Palestinians know that a great majority of the world's people empathize with their plight and condemn Israeli actions and postures. (Just this month a huge majority of United Nations member countries condemned the U.S. president, Trump, and his plans to move the U.S. embassy from Tel Aviv to al-Quds, even as Trump and his Ambassador to the U.N., Nikki Haley, threatened to withdraw financial aid to countries opposed to the plan.)

'Ali understands that violent opposition to Israel occupation by Palestinians, as in the past, could be met by even greater violence by the fourth most powerful military power on earth. "Every time that occurs," 'Ali says, "observers around the world wake up more to what we as a people are dealing with."

He is hopeful, and believes that the non-violent "BDS" (Boycott, Divestment and Sanctions) program under the leadership of Palestinian Omar Barghouthi and others, including even some notably courageous Jewish intellectuals, writers, and academics who live outside Occupied Palestine or Israel, by choice, is currently the best tool to force change and further discredit the Zionist regime. (This kind of action eventually led to the end of Apartheid in South Africa and

Nelson Mandela's freedom from decades of imprisonment there, and interestingly, it was the U.S. that long supported the Apartheid regime in South Africa and even claimed that Mandela was a "terrorist" until he was freed.)

In general, most Palestinians and also Muslims in the U.S. like 'Ali know that they may suffer if they speak out in support of Palestinian rights, or against the Zionist regime, even if they are fairly well integrated in to U.S. society. It isn't that Americans don't empathize with the Palestinians under occupation, if they know anything about conditions in places like Gaza and the West Bank.

One serious problem is that too many Americans don't know anything much about the Middle East, and part of the reason for this is that the mainstream U.S. media parrots misconceptions and propaganda pushed by the government inasmuch as it support the Zionists and disallows full reporting about the Palestinian suffering.

America may be a "powerful" country, but relative to most citizens of other countries, U.S. citizens still are not well educated about other cultures and countries, especially in the Middle East. Geography plays a role in this lack of knowledge, too.

But "nothing lasts forever," 'Ali correctly says, especially when it involves gross injustice.

As the famous Black leader Dr. Martin Luther King said decades ago before he was gunned down in 1968 in his long battle against racial segregation in the U.S.: "The arc of the moral universe is long, but it bends towards justice."

One must not forget that the struggle for justice in history in many countries and societies has often taken far longer and been frustrated far longer than ever desirable. Racial equality in the U.S. remains quite incomplete, despite the changes leaders like Martin Luther King advocated and at least partially succeeded in gaining.

Note: The main character's name 'Ali Salameh has been changed in the story to protect his identity.

Objections may be constructive

Dec. 31, 2017

Go to an Internet search engine and type: "What has Iran done to hurt the United States?" And guess what? Little to nothing comes up to suggest Iran had ever done anything to "hurt" the U.S., aside from the hostage crisis during Jimmy Carter's presidency. Carter cut diplomatic relations with Iran, and so it's been ever since. Sadly.

But what did appear were myriad commentaries about what the U.S. has done to damage Iran. And the lists are substantive and the items don't even overlap entirely. A sane person can kinda understand why the hostage crisis occurred; so much pent up frustration in Iran suddenly released with the downfall of the Shah. For Iran, it was a sudden kind of expression of freedom and an almost spontaneous outburst of sheer, youthful anger at a meddling U.S. Meddling for decades, too.

One can cite all sorts of Western or U.S. meddling: As far back as 1872 Nasir al-Din Shah, Shah of Iran from 1848-1896, sold Baron Julius de Reuter the right to operate all of Iran's railroads and canals, most of its mines and forests, and all future industries. (Back then Iranian oil resources were hardly even known.) Outrage was so intense at this insane "sale" that it was soon rescinded. The American and British coup against Mosaddegh in 1953 was a nightmare for Iran and soon enough the U.S. was training the regime's secret police in how to interrogate Iranians with methods based on Nazi torture techniques. Saddam Hussein invaded Iran in 1980 and Iraq went all out (with U.S. help) trying to make biological, chemical and nuclear weapons, and actually used chemical weapons on Iranian soldiers. Saudi Arabia was even funding Saddam Hussein's nuclear program with billions of dollars and the U.S. knew it and did not care. And there have been a myriad of other outrageous actions by the U.S. The shoot down of an Iranian civilian airliner. Other threats, including nuclear, even from morons like Sheldon Adelson, a Jewish billionaire with deep tentacles and money influence in a corrupted U.S. government, including that of Donald Trump.

One could go on and on citing ways the U.S. has been cruel to Iran, but the prime question is why, aside from the influence of various foreign lobbies and fifth columnists inside the U.S.? In my view it comes down to this: Iran, by opposing U.S. Mideast policies and imperialism exercises a CONSTRAINING influence or effect on U.S. strategies in the region. And this is an important point, because it suggests than animosity is not the result of some core, fundamental cultural dissonance between, say, the American or Iranian people, and maybe even not especially political, too. But rather because a major country with 80 million people, Iran, wants to be left alone, does not want to be threatened, and does not appreciate

U.S. meddling – for selfish gain – in neighboring countries, and these objections alone create a fair bit of obstacle to U.S. or Western hegemony in the Mideast.

It's not only a good thing for the Mideast, but also it's good for the American people at large. The U.S., as even former Congressman and Presidential candidate Dr. Ron Paul said in December, could well crumble as the Soviet Union did in 1990. He has suggested it could happen to the U.S. most anytime. Frankly, I am not placing bets on this happening right away, but stranger things have occurred.

Objections to U.S. foreign policies are potentially good for the American people because it's difficult to discern what recent U.S. administrations have done to boost longer term prospects for the U.S. generally. The infrastructure is crumbling, the debt is out of control both personal and governmental, poverty is rising fast, the two major political parties are dysfunctional and despised by most Americans, and the monetary system is at grave risk of dissolution. And why? Because, in large part, of overseas military interventions since the Vietnam War and other costly attempts to create a world where mere objections, including Iranian objections, are not heard.

And meanwhile, Average Americans who fail to demand fair representation in government and refuse to believe how narrow and corrupt representation has become, and who fail to try to put a halt to warmongering by the Military Industrial Complex and its cronies in government, and who fail to recognize injustices perpetrated overseas, are setting "THEIR" country up for failure eventually, as well as their own prospects, as Dr, Ron Paul suggests. Trump would have those who voted for him believe that he is delivering the country back to the average citizens as a result of his victory last year, but this is not the truth, and the tax "reform" legislation bears that out, as well as his insane view of what "national security" mandates (more of the same hegemonic blather).

Wealth moving from West to East

Jan 6, 2018

Protest and turmoil. Social or political or economic or all three. Some turmoil has been happening in Iran of late.

The attention of news outlets in the West turned to it, thanks to the corrupted mainstream media, particularly in the U.S. The same old responses, as with other states that have undergone unrest to a greater or lesser degree. The U.S. is "with the People" of some country, but against its government, it claims. A government it wishes were subservient to the U.S.

But what's interesting is that the mainstream media in the U.S. has not reported on massive protests in Israel against Netanyahu, and against Israeli corruption. And the same media rarely suggests that protests in the U.S, which are frequent enough in recent years, is due both to political and social discontent. Real protests, sometimes frequent, in the U.S. are snuffed out by what amounts to an existing U.S. police state as bad as anything the former East Germany erected with the Stasi, and as bad as anything the former Shah erected with the Savak in Iran before the Islamic Revolution.

And even worse, the U.S. government does not give a damn about "the People" in some country that is witnessing some unrest. Any statements suggesting it does are, frankly, a LIE. Did the U.S. give a damn about the people of Vietnam 50 years ago? No. The people of Iraq or Libya or Syria in this century? No. The people of Yemen or Somalia or Afghanistan now? No. Let's get real. The U.S. government today, controlled by oligarchs and the Military Industrial Complex, does not much give a damn about the American people, too. This is fact and more and more people in the U.S. are figuring this out, but too slowly some believe. The U.S. government, unfortunately, cares hugely about maintaining its POWER, economic, political and military, and that of its "allies" such as Israel or Saudi Arabia to name two undemocratic allies. Trust this statement, Iranians.

So, if for whatever reason as an Iranian you have a beef about YOUR government now, don't let discontent play into the unfriendly machinations of the U.S., or of the Saudis or the Israelis and others. Please! Continue to support Syria as an intact, independent country. Continue to support the Palestinians and justice. Continue to support any country or party that resists succumbing to the diktat of Washington and which stands against injustice and oppression. And many Americans support you, too, in this. Never forget that. Even if you don't hear of this support very often. The world needs multipolarity. A unipolar world with the U.S. in charge has been a disaster since myself and 500,000 or more Americans marched several times against the Vietnam War forty plus years ago in Washington. Vladimir Putin of Russia has insisted on multipolarity, too. And that brings up Russia as partner with and neighbor to Iran.

WEALTH MOVING FROM WEST TO EAST …

As the recent discontent is partly economic in Iran by all accounts, and the country is suffering with too much inflation relative to economic growth rates, consider that the future still looms ever brighter. And this despite U.S. economic sanctions which the U.S. under foolish Trump and his Zionist masters may augment. Iran is allegedly going to join the Russian-led Eurasian Economic Union this year, for one thing.

While Washington threatens further sanctions on Iran and on Russia, too, these two major Eurasian economies, are moving closer to de-dollarize their trade flows and to lessen the impact of any Western sanctions. Washington reacted the last time a major country, Ukraine, in 2014 opted to join the EEU and then was the target of a CIA-led coup d'etat. This time the U.S. will not have its way. The geopolitical map of the world is changing rapidly and in ways Washington seems not to grasp.

Quite a few other countries also want to de-dollarize trade and get out from under U.S. control. Furthermore, China's Belt and Road initiative will tie together countries in Asia like never before in a peaceful accord, and present an insurmountable rebuke to U.S. and Western imperialism. The U.S. anyway is so deeply in debt now, having missspent on costly and ludicrous wars, that it will never succeed in climbing out of its deep financial hole. All this will, in time, boost Iran's economic prospects enormously and help all Iranians. It's the coming thing, a huge shift of wealth and prosperity from West to East.

Speaking with Dr. Vladimir Golstein last week in Providence, R.I.,, Golstein said enthusiastically that Russia and Iran are "natural allies" and have often been so allied for centuries. "Iran joining the Eurasia Economic Union this year is a sure step to greater prosperity for Iran and partners," he asserted. Golstein is one of the world's top experts on Russia and neighbors from his post at Brown University in the U.S. He believes that Russia will not abandon increasingly close ties with Iran, and the economic union will bind partner countries together peacefully even further.

It would seem, anyway, that as the West, the U.S. especially, expends and exhausts itself in efforts to dictate to the rest of the world, the aforementioned wealth transfer from West to East will happen and Asian economies will shine, including Iran's, while Iran in the meantime focuses on securing itself further with a government responsive to the concern of all its citizens.

ONE VIEW FROM AFAR

JAN. 13, 2018

I know a thing or two about protests. But the last real protest I was amidst, for a few days, was in February, 2011, in Maidan Tahrir in Cairo.

I was there as a reporter for a U.S. newspaper, but I was also a participant because the crowds, especially when Mubarak fell, were ebullient, friendly and peaceful and in that sense I was with them in spirit. Sometimes not peaceful were Mubarak's "mukhabarat" and the police. They sealed Mubarak's immediate fate at the time. Violence discredits anyone, including any government.

This reporter had the impression the Egyptian Army was there to offer a moderating influence, a kind of warning to both sides. I found the soldiers disciplined, professional and unprovocative during those winter days in Cairo. And I loved the primary chant: "The People Want the Fall of the Regime" (or specifically, in fact, the fall of dictator Hosni Mubarak) and in Arabic that chant was stirring. But again, the most important thing was that the protesters were almost entirely non-violent… as far as I could tell as a witness in Maidan Tahrir in central Cairo.

It is first important to mention that Iran's leader Ayatollah Khamenei is correct. Khamanei has noted that police in the U.S. have in recent years murdered nearly a 1,000 people annually, most of them innocents, and has used any means possible to suppress protests. Law enforcement in the U.S. often shoots first, and often enough, no one is really mounting any kind of threat against law officers. In fact, far fewer police personnel in the U.S. have been killed in recent years than ever before in the past half century or more. How many people died in Iran's recent protests? Less than 30, I have read anyway, and we here in the U.S. don't even know who exactly was responsible for that.

And then in the mainstream U.S. media, uncritical organs of the State these days more often than not, we have major newspapers like the Wall Street Journal publishing commentary by the head of the terrorist organization Mujahadin-E-Khalq claiming that the current Iranian government is "unstable" and ill supported by most Iranians. That Maryam Rajavi got space in the Wall Street Journal says a lot about current establishment and Trumpist views in the U.S., and there's never been any question the MEK is nothing but an ugly terrorist organization responsible for tremendous mayhem in and near Iran for decades.

On a more positive note, those governments that stood behind and endorsed the nuke deal with Iran, thanks to the efforts of former U.S. Secretary of State John Kerry and former President Barack Obama, are utterly appalled with some members of the U.S. Congress and the Trump administration for failing to stand firmly in support of the deal, which Iran has adhered to completely and sincerely by all responsible accounts. And the U.N. has lately been adamant that the U.S. NOT interfere in the internal affairs of other countries. And also live up fully to the deal itself. It's about time.

But no right minded person can claim any government anywhere is perfect and is fully addressing the ideal of "democracy" and the needs of its people. The U.S. in recent years certainly is a gross offender in this regard, and U.S. citizens are irate about this fact. A recent poll, for one thing, showed a big majority of U.S. citizens are firmly set against further U.S. military adventures overseas. Will they be heard? One can only hope. Consider that every government over time anywhere, like the human body itself, ossifies, ages, becomes rigid and maybe even riddled with some corruption that results in the neglect of average citizens and their needs or demands for representation and reform. At such times change is warranted. Iran is no exception. Iranians, engaged in active protests or not, must show the world through peaceful actions it remains a civilized nation, one that understands and wants democracy, that can learn from the past, and that can be hopeful about the future. The revolutionary Iranian chant of "Marg Bar" may be superseded by "Nang Bar" with respect to addressing grievances. That would seem to make sense.

Ever since the Iranian Revolution in 1979 that overthrew the Washington installed dictator, the U.S. in spite has been trying to regain control in Iran. Now, the Trump Administration seems to be at work, along with the Zionists and the Saudis, against the Iranian people, not merely the Iranian government. Foreign agents, if they exist in Iran or anywhere, should never be permitted to attempt the overthrow of a government. The Trumps and Nikki Haley's and Netanyahu's of this world are loudmouths who admit they use bribes and insane threats against other countries. These clowns could well destroy American power and influence in the world. If that happens, it will be well deserved and can't come soon enough.

Ibn Khaldun's insight centuries ago applies today

Jan. 20, 2018

NORTH CAROLINA - Dr. Franz Rosenthal, was a Jewish man and scholar of great wisdom and repute. I happened to take a couple classes of his at Yale University in the U.S. in the early 1970s. Though deceased now, he was the top Western scholar of Islam, Islamic history and Semitic languages in his day, and also one lucky Jew who as a young man before World War 2 managed to exit Nazi Germany, but many of his elder relatives who never escaped in the 1930s died.

Rosenthal knew what caused the rise and fall of Islamic (or most any) polity. He was a translator in to English, for one thing, of Ibn Khaldun's magnificent and groundbreaking 14th century historical theories about the rise and fall of political dynasties summarized in the famous work called the "Muqaddimah". Rosenthal laid out Islamic history and Islam itself for his students at Yale in great detail, and lovingly. He considered Islam, as Muslims do, the "final" revelation of the monotheistic tradition earlier established by Judaism and then Christianity, and he did indeed consider it an improved manifestation of the tradition and Arabic, the language of the Qu'ran, the most expressive of languages. Had he not been born Jewish, I gathered from knowing him, he'd have been Muslim. He had a profound, enduring respect for Islam and its achievements over the centuries since Muhammad's death in the seventh century.

Given the demonization of Islam by some in the West, and particularly in Washington, for NO other reasons but that the Islamic Republic,, to cite the prime example, officially abhors and rejects Western imperialism and its demands for control and hegemony in the Middle East, as well as Iran's valid rejection of Zionism and its cruelty to the Holy Land's natives, the Palestinians, one has to be concerned.

Another attempt to take down a country by the U.S. and allies, as happened with Iraq and Libya and Syria especially, could well be catastrophic and lead to a third world war. Given this potential threat, anyone sympathetic with Iran's posture and empathetic about the difficulties of economic sanctions and other hostile moves, as one such as Dr. Rosenthal (I am reminded here) certainly would be if he were alive, suggests a desire, anyway, that whatever internal discontent there may be in Iran be minimized as much as possible, and NOT by forced suppression.

If in fact there are reasons for internal discord in Iran, those of us in the West who admire Iranians and the country's accomplishments over many centuries, feel obliged to hope fervently that the current Iranian government will correct whatever matters that exist that may be causing discontent, especially among young Iranians, who are Iran's future.

One big reason for this hope is that the U.S. or any country supportive of U.S., hostility be deprived of reasons to condemn Iran's governing authorities, even as Iran rightly maintains its rejection of imperialism and Zionism.

Consider, for example, how bad things have become in the U.S. with this microcosmic anecdote: At a local school board meeting a teacher in a mid-sized city in the U.S. engages in a conversation with a school broad member, but the conversation is interrupted by a policeman. The young teacher wants to know why the board members are voting themselves a huge pay raise but nothing for teachers? Then the police show up, the young woman is slammed to the floor and put in handcuffs and then carted off to jail. The teacher did nothing wrong and broke no laws, but someone did not want her challenging the school board at all. This in fact is an accurate picture of what is widespread in the U.S. today: it is corruption, obviously, backed by force. It involves entrenched authorities serving themselves rather than their constituencies. And these are the seeds of mass discontent and maybe, eventually, revolution, which under the right circumstances can happen in the U.S., just as it did in Iran in 1979.

Having never been in Iran, I do still know that there is wide gap between the haves and the have-nots. I know that the economy has been weak and there is high unemployment, maybe 30 percent, among young people. This is also true in the U.S., where the percentage of the population is not so skewed to young people as in Iran. In the U.S., real reform is badly needed. This is also probably true in Iran. Can the current government leaders in either the U.S. or Iran be flexible enough, and unselfish enough, to permit real reform, and even to allow protest as a normal occurrence in a more open society? No one knows yet. But one thing is certain: by failing to allow evolution and reform in either country, however different the two cultures may be, instability can be expected and at some point events might spiral out of control.

It was Ibn Khaldun's genius in the 14th century (that Franz Rosenthal at Yale recognized), that identified what Ibn Khaldun called "'asabiyya", an Arabic would that roughly translates into the term "group solidarity" as the defining foundation of a strong, unified society. Every Islamic regime Ibn Khaldun studied that had fallen apart (and there were several in the North Africa of his day centuries ago) or become weak, had lost its "group solidarity" because leaders failed to address the needs of the governed and the society had become fragmented, even though it remained Islamic to the core. One only needs to reduce this to families: families are strong only to the extent that members support one another and cohesion among members remains strong, because fair dealing exists and internal corruption has been reduced or eliminated. Proper ongoing reform, as evolving circumstances warrant, is a vital task in virtually any country on earth.

An American looks at

Mandatory Hijab

Jan. 27, 2018

Iran's most visible leaders to writers like me in the U.S. seem to support the rights of Iranians to protest some mandates they may not like. Consider the delicate matter of women having to wear the hijab if they are out and about in public. Certainly lots of women in Iran probably prefer to wear a head scarf. What might be uncomfortable is not the scarf itself, but occasionally getting arrested if they are seen without hijab, as noted recently in an article about Iran here in the U.S.

A couple decades ago, teaching at a college in North Carolina, I had a 20-year-old Iranian woman in one of my classes. She was not only a very good and attentive student, but also a delightful person, and even while she was studying and living in the U.S. she wore the hijab, even though she did not have to. I once asked her what the hijab meant to her, why she bothered with it in the U.S.? Her answer was clear, rational and unequivocal. And she was clearly quite beautiful, too, one could discern, despite the hijab, as Iranian females are almost universally claimed to be, at least outside of Iran. "I want people to pay attention to me as a person, a whole person," she said, "and not merely to how I look, as some kind of object. Besides, it's mandatory in Iran and I'm used to the hijab. I find it affords a sense of protection from unwanted attention."

Fair enough, and a superb answer, I thought, she gave.

The entire question of mandatory modest dress is rather fascinating, from an American distance. In the Qu'ran, inasmuch as I am familiar with its magnificent revelations, there are just a few verses related to dress, and they endorse modesty in attire for females, that it is highly desirable. There seems to be no specific mention of the hijab for women out and about in public, as required since after the Iranian revolution in 1979. There was warranted euphoria about the revolution, but few at the time ever imagined having to worry about the implementation of compulsory hijab. It is an alleged fact that when Ayatollah Khomeini decreed mandatory hijab, many Iranian women protested, but Iranian men did not offer them much support because the focus was primarily on solidarity with the new government in order to show a united front for and with the nascent revolution. It has been claimed, I have noted, that the woman question was not initially a part of the revolutionary political agenda. But since 1979, Iran has apparently made hijab an emblem of its religious identity, a visual symbol of both the government and the ideal type of Iranian woman.

What's even more interesting is that in the West or at least in Europe, some countries are forbidding Muslim women from wearing the hijab, at least in public, suggesting that they are preserving Western culture by denying Muslim women freedom of expression – their freedom to wear hijab if they want to. This makes no sense, and seems highly hypocritical. Here in the U.S. I see Muslim women frequently wearing hijab, many of them, and one must be pleased to know that the U.S. at least is not telling anybody what they have to wear, as long as they are clothed in public. This is not the case at all in what one ought to consider the deeply repressive, undemocratic societies in the Arab world, such as in Saudi Arabia, which quite embarrassingly is a U.S. ally.

Indeed, compared to some Arab countries, Iran is a bastion of tolerance and multiculturalism and religious freedom, relatively. It is utterly disgraceful that Iran is not fully portrayed as such a society, particularly in the U.S., and that the U.S. ever supported terrorists like ISIS and other groups aiming to bring down secular Syria, to cite just one country targeted by U.S, Israeli and Saudi hypocrites, to name three. Women under ISIS control have rarely been treated so badly by anyone, anywhere ever in history, and we did not see the U.S. protest. In fact, the U.S. government has supported ISIS and lied about clearing them out of most of Syria to date. It is a fact that the Syrians, Iran and allies such as Russia and Hezbollah defeated ISIS, not the U.S. Well, anyway, Iran is not a secular country, but it is damn closer to being one in practice than some odious Arab countries I have visited and written about, such as Saudi Arabia.

But there is still a nagging question over mandatory hijab from this American's perspective.

If hijab is an important symbol of identity for Iran's Islamic government, is it a GOOD, effective symbol? And I mean by "good" does it help Iran to portray itself as the society it really and truly is (one of the best in the Middle East at least) to the West, which seems to have insanely seized on mandatory hijab as a symbol of gross repression, which in fact it probably is not, even though one imagines that many Iranian woman might prefer it not be mandatory? It's neither mandatory nor forbidden in the U.S. But still, Muslim women in the U.S. often prefer hijab in public, for reasons similar to those of the young Iranian woman whom I taught two decades ago. It's a way of expressing personal, even religious, identity and maybe even offers some sense of protection for those preferring to wear hijab.

In the long run, of course, I prefer as an admirer of Iran and Islam that Iran presents NO ammunition whatsoever to Western and especially insane U.S. critics of Iran and Iranians. These critics know nothing, it seems, but we do know what that criticism really is: political. Because Iran opposes U.S. meddling and imperialism, for one thing, in the Middle East. And rightly so. However, there may be other more effective, more important ways to celebrate and portray a Muslim and Islamic identity, and one may very well be giving half a country's population at least some leeway to choose whether to don hijab in public and not literally arrest them if they strip it off. These are perilous times, and many Western societies, including U.S. society, are falling apart, at least not looking so good with all the sabre rattling and hegemonic political demands, as if that offers some salvation, when in fact it offers nothing good for anyone at home or abroad

Exhibiting confidence and strength can be a delicate dance

Feb. 4, 2018

Fiction or not, and it's probably not at all, there is this term floating about regarding who really runs the U.S. government called the "Deep State".

This entity, assuming it is something fairly organized and real, consists of institutions like the CIA, and NSA and perhaps even the big players in the mainstream media such as the New York Times and the Washington Post and the big network broadcasters. And it may include major so-called "think tanks" as well, this latter staffed by pundits, alleged intellectuals, writers and policy promoters in or around what Donald Trump in 2016 characterized as "the Swamp", denoting Washington. Well, one thing is for sure, the U.S. is now a democracy in name only, even with elections, because many of those who manage to become candidates for public office have already passed a litmus test and if their views diverge too far from this Deep State (it would seem), they never manage to become acceptable candidates, even if they claim they are.

One case in point is that of Chelsea Manning, a former U.S. soldier, who blew the lid off war crimes in Iraq in 2010 when he gave Wikileaks classified documents and videos detailing some of the military abuses in the Middle East. Manning, a transgender, was imprisoned and ultimately sentenced to decades in prison until Barack Obama pardoned him. Now, Manning is apparently going to run for the U.S. Senate in his current home state of Maryland. Most people think he hasn't a chance of winning any election, but stranger things have happened and his campaign ahead, whatever it consists of, will at least be interesting to watch.

Now, in the U.S., huge efforts are underway to limit public exposure to the ideas and reports of dissenters on Facebook, Twitter, the Internet and other social and informational media platforms. And we already know billions of dollars have been spent to keep tabs on not just Americans but a good portion of the entire world by vacuuming up e mails, telephone conversations and more. It's like nothing ever seen before, in part because the technology is available, and it would put past totalitarian or repressive regimes like, say, East Germany with its Stasi apparatus, or perhaps even the reign of the Shah in Iran with his Savak goons, to shame for having nothing so intrusive and objectionable.

Meanwhile, regarding Iran, we see the Trump administration and others attacking the JCPOA, a good agreement addressing the non-proliferation of nuclear weapons based not on trust but on tough verification procedures. But here's what is especially galling. That whenever one reads reports in the U.S. from academia or the mainstream media about the JCPOA and its merits or demerits, the almost universal presumption is that Iran was aiming to have nuclear weapons, or eventually build them. And yet Iranian authorities have at bottom said that such weapons are anathema to Islam and Islamic values, and that Iran never had any serious intention, at least as the Islamic Republic since 1979, to build them, even if Iran developed some rudimentary capacity to do so. You really can't get any clearer if Iran, as the ISLAMIC Republic, declares nukes verboten to Islam. Otherwise, Iranian authorities could be treading into a supreme hypocrisy that undercuts the very ideological foundation of the revolution and the current state! So, one must ask, why the presumption in the West? Why can't Iranian authorities be believed?

I really don't think the non-belief is about nukes, or the gripes about Iran. One reason is simply that it makes NO sense for Iran to have nuclear weapons, because they would not be a real deterrence against attack by the U.S. and Israel and maybe other countries. The nuclear arsenals of the U.S. and Israel would ever be far superior and more dangerous, and Iran might only invite a preemptive attack that would be disastrous for the entire Middle East. Netanyahu for one has been itching to attack Iran for decades and drag the U.S. into a joint campaign. Frankly, we now know from recent history that countries that wind up as alleged or implied enemies of the U.S. land in such an onerous position because, quite simply, they won't align themselves with U.S. "empire" or hegemony, which anyway is very slowly melting away. Remember what happened to the USSR in the late 1980s. It exhausted itself trying to maintain military might, and in Afghanistan, too. This, I believe, this exhaustion is ahead for the U.S. It seems inevitable and patience is required to see it play out, and then, perhaps, a more peaceful world, one would hope or dream.

But some observers in the U.S. like me wonder. Iran must try to do its part and try to appear magnanimous to some degree, to obviate criticism from the U.S. and so-called "allies" like Israel. The latest suggestion by Mohammad Javad Zarif about setting up mechanisms for real dialogue between countries on the Persian Gulf is a fabulous idea. We see, for example, the two Koreas attempting to do just this, an effort which in some respects makes tremendous sense and excludes the U.S. from pretending it is "protecting" that part of Asia when, in fact, it's mostly looking after its own narrow interests. The same might be accomplished, say, between Iran and other Mideast countries.

Obviating Western criticism of Iran may also be inherent in much smaller matters, such as perhaps going easier on some Iranians who have been in the West and then imprisoned in Iran when they returned to their native country. Whatever the charges against them, some of them (if not all) may not truly be serious "threats" to Iran and letting them go could improve Iran's standing from a PR perspective. Again, the matter of handing the U.S. "ammunition". Magnanimity and forgiveness, which seems to be a deeply forgotten concept in the U.S., really is or can be a real, convincing sign of confidence and strength whether one is talking about an individual OR an entire country such as the U.S. or Iran. We certainly don't see magnanimity in the U.S., not with any government in several decades, although Obama did do a good thing in letting Chelsea Manning out of prison for revealing truths, even if they were "classified".

Woe to leaders mired in the credibility trap

Feb 8, 2018

What's really going on in the U.S.? Why is there internal political and social turmoil and division? Why are groups and so-called leaders at each other's throats and why is the general populace so apparently discontented?

Why do things seem to be falling apart in some respects and the finger of blame has been improperly pointed at other countries and their leaders such that the U.S. vilifies Russia and Iran and Syria and North Korea, to name four, and other countries and sometimes with deadly military consequences? And woe to other countries that finds themselves in the same straits, for it will have landed there not because of some twist of fate, but rather because internal systems of checks and balances have been badly abused and compromised in the U.S. And interestingly, there is a name for this state of affairs, when reform and healthy change become virtually impossible. It's called the "credibility trap".

So what is this, this "trap"? It exists when the regulatory, political and informational functions of a society have been so badly damaged by a long term, lambent corruption in vital spheres that they can no longer address any meaningful correction or reform without also, at least incidentally, implicating those who point it out. The status quo in such a society has at the least and for too long tolerated the corruption and fraud, and probably those in power also profited and continue to profit from it, such that the society's power brokers have become susceptible to blackmail. The net result of this is that failed or failing policies are often sustained, because the admittance of failure is just not an option, and it has become almost impossible to dislodge the perpetrators even if, on the surface anyway, there still exists "democratic" or other mechanisms that ought to be capable of ridding the society of them.

If this concept called the "credibility trap" seems like a lot to take in, read the above paragraph again. It makes sense, and it is precisely where the U.S hangs now, and maybe some other countries, too, that have lost their way.

Consider, for example, U.S. military engagements in various foreign countries. As "powerful" as the military may seem, with some 800 or more bases spread all over the planet, and U.S. defense all told costing $1 trillion a year of printed, fiat currency generated with piles of debt, no "wars" have been won, and not even the Vietnam War decades ago. The war in Afghanistan has dragged on for almost two decades, and nothing has been "won" but enmity. If, say, a top U.S. military person were to come right out and declare the failures, that person would essentially be indicting themselves as a failure strategist or commander. So the Pentagon literally pretends and claims that military progress is being made to justify the costs. (It does keep a lot of people employed.) And the mainstream media goes along with this, with many of the top mainstream journalists extolling the false successes. It's a vicious circle. Washington depends on creating enemies to sustain the fear necessary to justify the so-called "defense" budget of about $1 trillion annually.

And Trump, campaigning in 2016 for the Presidency, promised differently. He literally claimed the U.S. was going to back off from hostile engagements overseas, that there may be a "peace" dividend almost three decades after the end of the original Cold War. The Nunes memo suggesting FBI abuse and the corruption of the surveillance system in the U.S. was not an issue, until it became one for the Republicans for political reasons, and war hawks on both sides of the aisle in Congress used the (by and large false) charges against Russia to create animosity among average Americans to keep the money flowing into "defense" coffers and, ultimately, to some extent, into their own pockets. But without a complicit mainstream media (New York Times, Washington Post, MSNBC, Fox News, CNN, etc), the U.S. might have been on the road to reform.

Last week I sent a note to the top foreign policy international columnist at the Washington Post, one David Ignatius, whom I have known marginally for decades. I suggested that he retire eventually (he's approaching 70) in a blaze of glory by writing his final book: an expose of why and how he and others, especially the so-called Neocon pundits and writers, have often been in thrall to government, rather than serving as effective checks and balances to corruption and misdeeds in government, as was the case during the Watergate scandal in the early 1970s. Such truth telling, as he could accomplish, given all that he has seen and knows, would make him a rich(er) man with huge sales, too. Sadly, he snubbed the idea. But this snubbing is the "credibility trap" in action. Because if this writer exposed as much as I suggested in a personal memoir, he'd have at the same time discredited some of his past work as dishonest and partisan. Meanwhile, the Washington and Wall Street gravy train rolls along without a hitch, until it doesn't. And someday it won't.

Pence and the Troubling Prospect He Is

Feb 12, 2018

I enjoy a number of news sources about Iran here in the U.S.. This is the wonder of the Internet.

Some of these sources are Iranian dissidents in the West; Iranians who likely would not be welcome in Iran. I feel bad for them in this regard, but this in nothing new. I can't think of any country that welcomes all its past and current citizens, whatever their current or past views. Some countries, like the U.S., have even assassinated American citizens overseas, even children, in drone strikes and other horrific actions. And like anyone with half a brain, it is at the least annoying when I read about, say, Iranians with dual citizenship, and some of them notable people, who have been imprisoned in Iran. The Western mainstream media makes a big deal of such action. It's always looking for a reason to vilify Iran, because Iran rejects Western/U.S. imperialism. But Saudi Arabia, for example, chops off heads willy nilly, and the U.S. calls it an "ally" and says nothing about the chops. Sickening.

Israel, another example, tries to eject entire classes of people or at the least puts them in virtual prisons under threat, such as African "Jewish" refugees. Israel jails its own Arab citizens, and of course many thousands of native Palestinians who have no rights at all, including hundreds of innocent children, and charges few of them with anything, and even if it does bring charges, most of them are baseless or absurd, and the punishment rarely fits any alleged "crime". I have not read of a single instance of Iran jailing children.

At any rate, it can be useful to look at countries that some may call socially or politically oppressive, and to compare them with countries that claim they are democracies that also allegedly abide by the rule of law internally and internationally. Personally, I believe in the separation of church and state. I believe that one's religious convictions might better be a private matter, but that's just my opinion. Theocracies, wherever and whenever they have been instituted, don't often work out very well in the long run. This is a simple, historical fact.

Many Americans don't look hard enough to discover the truth, so busy they are waving flags at football games and imagining that a "Support Our Troops" mantra is all that's required to be a patriot.

What's interesting about Iran is that while one can posit some "human rights" abuses, they are nowhere as bad as some in the U.S.. No other country has incarcerated so many people, and many of them Blacks and other minorities, and the numbers may outstrip that of even the old USSR. Many in U.S. prisons, if you were to look really hard, are either "political" prisoners who as prisoners can no longer cast a vote, or just poor people who, unlike some well-known politicians, just don't have the clout or money to buy their freedom from prosecution. Moreover, the rule of law nowadays is frequently violated by the "elite", by politicians especially, and even by the two political parties. But also by U.S. banks, Wall Street, corporations, etc. And the violations have increasingly been ignored by regulatory bodies and the courts. It's all about power, or the maintenance of it, in the hands of the few. In the international arena the U.S. is anything but law abiding, at least as far as longstanding international laws are concerned. Think Iraq, Libya, Syria and many other countries, including Iran as far back as Mossadegh's overthrow by the CIA. The U.S. currently is occupying oil rich parts of Syria, and recently murdered over 100 Syrian soldiers. These are war crimes, and meanwhile in recent decades U.S. presidents have gone to war without, as demanded in the U.S. Constitution, the formal assent of the U.S. Congress. Such matters would be unbelievable were they not facts, even if many Americans don't look hard enough to discover the truth, so busy they are waving flags at football games and imagining that a "Support Our Troops" mantra is all that's required to be a patriot.

As far as theocracies go, history speaks of relatively benign and nefarious ones. And also the same regarding countries alleged to be "democratic", like the U.S. today. But what's weird is that it may be the case that the U.S. is a heartbeat away from becoming a theocracy (a Christian one) itself, if not in name, to some extent in fact. Consider Vice President Mike Pence of Indiana.

Pence may be good reason to hope Trump serves out his term, and the potential next one, in the White House. Pence is, in the words of a journalist friend, "both a Christian fundamentalist and a dispensationalist, which means that he thinks every word in the Good Book (Bible) is literally true and that Christianity is going through phases or dispensations that will lead to the rapture of true believers into heaven followed by the wrath of God descending on those who refuse to see the light." You can't make up this garbage! Trump, incidentally, is no real Christian and never was at least if you gauge that by his deeds, but Pence maybe is, if you fall in line with an estimated 20 percent of the U.S. electorate, the evangelicals and their embarrassing kin. Trump did indeed choose Pence as his VP running mate in 2016 because he knew such a ticket would easily capture this big chunk of voters, whether they deemed themselves Republicans or Democrats.

Pence in any event is smooth, a better talker than Trump, and absolutely convinced of the rectitude of his ideas. He is even such a "Christian" as to forbid himself to dine alone with any woman who is not his wife, so as to avoid even the possible temptation of a sexual liaison outside his marriage. Does this make him a "good" man. No. It makes him a blind man.

Take the matter of Pence and the Zionist state, Israel. To him, Israel's creation and survival are part of some (un) godly master plan that will lead to the end of the world. He's so blind he cannot see that the "end" of the world is not at all a good plan for anyone on earth, including his loved ones, and especially not for Jews, who won't, by the terms of the plan, ever get to heaven, dead or alive. His views on the Middle East were strikingly obvious when he visited Israel not long ago. He even damned Iran in a speech before the Knesset, after Arab

Knesset members were evicted. He claimed to "stand" with Israel absolutely, seemingly unaware that most Americans have never been anything but ambivalent about Israel and don't themselves "stand" with the Zionists. So as misguided as many think Trump is, particularly about the Mideast, one would have to say that a person like Pence, who as President could potentially affect many aspects of billions of lives across the globe, is downright crazy. On that note I fervently hope, in the absence of another VP, that Trump remains in office. Pence would, it seems, manage the U.S. like some kind of frightful and odious theocracy. Being forewarned may be a step to being forearmed.

Iran tops in the "human development improvements since the revolution

Feb 13, 2018

Western countries like the U.S. and Middle Eastern ones such as Israel and Saudi Arabia like to put the Islamic Republic of Iran down as some kind of medieval state that presents a threat to the region and, at least from the standpoint of the U.S. government, the world, but it's all a big lie unless "threat" literally means an Iran that has or is becoming a relatively more prosperous and powerful country that internally at least has been improving the lives of its citizens.

Consider the latest published report (2016) by the UN which addresses what it calls "human development" in all the member states of the UN. According to this most recent published report, between 1979 and 2016, Iran overall has enjoyed the greatest growth in the Human Development Index of any country in the UN. Since 1980 life expectancy since birth has rocketed up 54 to 76 years. Expected years of schooling has climbed from less than 10 years to almost 15, while mean years of schooling has gone from 2.3 to almost 15 years, to cite just a couple items.

So what is "human development"? According to the UN, "human development is about the freedom to realize the full potential of every human life, not just of a few, nor of most, but of all lives in every corner of the world – now and in the future".

Relatively, Iran has seen more progress in this regard than any other country in recent decades, claims the UN report. Iran falls in the rank of all countries at number 69. (Norway is number 1, the U.S. is ranked at 10.) In the Middle East among Arab countries, Saudi Arabia is ranked at 38, Bahrain at 47, Kuwait at 51 and Oman at 52. But consider that these Mideast countries are not nearly the size of Iran, and because of resource wealth can generate for their relatively small numbers of citizens considerably higher per capita incomes than Iran, with over 81 million people. No other Mideast country is ranked above Iran but these four above, and among all the countries ranked, 188 of them, Iran stands just below the top third in the rankings.

The charges against Russia are Mickey Mouse

Feb 20, 2018

If it were not simply insane, you'd have to laugh: Months of investigation, many millions of bucks spent, and U.S. Special Counsel Robert Mueller, a former head of the FBI, announces last week an indictment of 13 Russian nationals and three Russian entities, accusing them of interfering in the 2016 presidential election and operating fake social media accounts.

After such scrutiny, THIS is all he's got to condemn Russia for? These are Mickey Mouse charges. Not one of the Russians indicted is a member of the Russian government, for one thing. Putin and government colleagues had nothing to do with this "criminal" case brought to accuse Russia of trying to influence the 2016 Presidential election and boost Donald Trump's prospects of winning by criticizing Hillary Clinton and supporting not just Trump, but also Democratic Senator Bernie Sanders.

The defendants reportedly worked hard to pump out messages into Facebook, Twitter and Instagram, controlling social media pages that targeted a range of issues, and they allegedly used servers inside the U.S. to hide the Russian origins of the various accounts. In fact, anyone who happened to disparage Clinton during the election process may also have been a "collaborator" of some sort.

It appears that the U.S. may be doing a good job of destroying itself with such hypocrisy and self-deceit and psychosis. In fact, the only known instances of American politicos teaming up with Russians involves operations between the Democratic Party National Committee and the Clinton campaign along with U.S. "intelligence" services like the FBI and the CIA, which altogether helped pay for an incredible document of dubious content called the "Steele Dossier" claiming that Russia hacked the e-mails of Hillary and her campaign staffers. Robert Mueller has yet to examine this, and may not, and it involves misconduct of a number of senior people at the usual suspects such as the CIA, FBI and NSA. And meanwhile, the interminable witch hunt about Russian collusion in the election processes is making it difficult, if not impossible, for the U.S. to deal with much more important and dangerous issues such as a financial system that seems to be headed towards the most horrific train wreck in the history of the U.S. Of course, the Trump Administration and GOP morons in the U.S. Congress have set this in motion with the recent tax cuts that are bound to result in trillion dollar fiscal deficits for many years into the future. That alone is probably going to derail Trump if not the entire government, while the vast majority of Americans will be desperately trying to keep their heads above water in a very different humbled and hobbled economy.

The U.S. is near bankruptcy if it hasn't already arrived unrecognized. The current fiscal and monetary set up will not last, and when it implodes, the U.S. will have no options but, for one thing, the closure of the mechanisms of overseas interference, such as the many hundreds of military bases overseas, and maybe much of the federal government itself. But here's what's really galling and evidence of such massive hypocrisy as to choke a horse, or an entire herd of them.

The charges against Russia are Mickey ...

Carnegie Mellon University has put together a database concerning U.S. interference in elections of other countries. It's been a common practice for decades. The database cites 81 instances of U.S. interference overseas between the end of World War II and just the year 2000. You can bet that if the database were expanded to include the years since 2000, the numbers would go up dramatically. The interferences cited were also largely carried out in secret. Only a third of them were public, and in some 60 percent of the interventions, the candidate(s) that had received U.S. assistance won the election even though the action swayed the actual vote by an average of just 3 percent.

Since 2000 "interventions" have been far worse, including "regime change" by military means which everyone knows about, especially some seriously damaged, if not destroyed, countries in the Middle East and I need not name them. And millions have been murdered as a result. Back in 2006 Hillary Clinton, in an interview, argued that just allowing elections in some overseas locations was a mistake. She said, for example, that Palestinians should not be permitted to hold elections "unless the U.S. did something to determine who was going to win". (There were elections in Palestine and Hamas candidates did quite well. They were even monitored by one of the few former Presidents in recent decades who seemed to be a decent, moral person – Jimmy Carter).

What possible solace can be derived from the unpleasant, depressing and unproductive actions and hypocrisies of the U.S. government and military overseas now? Maybe there's only one: that it can't continue very much longer, and this is why I have suggested or counseled patience and endurance to beleaguered friends or any kind overseas. The U.S. is near bankruptcy if it hasn't already arrived unrecognized. The current fiscal and monetary set up will not last, and when it implodes, the U.S. will have no options but, for one thing, the closure of the mechanisms of overseas interference, such as the many hundreds of military bases overseas, and maybe much of the federal government itself. Governance will become much more local and rational in the U.S., too, and real democracy where the average citizen has a say in how things are managed may blossom like the fruit trees and the abundant flowers in Spring that Iranians love and tend so beautifully.

The Zealot at Hamra checkpoi

Feb 26, 2018

Twelve years ago I found myself at a place called Hamra Checkpoint deep in the West Bank at the western edge of the Jordan River valley.

I had flown from New York to "Israel's" Ben Gurion airport near Tel Aviv, and there a Palestinian driver met me and took me to Hamra Checkpoint along a circuitous back road route that avoided the primary highways upon which only Israeli vehicles are permitted to travel in the West Bank. The driver could go no farther than Hamra. There, some 20 Israeli soldiers were guarding a military gate of sorts preventing travel up to my destination, the town of Tubas in the lovely, rolling hills overlooking the Jordan Valley. And 100 meters farther on, on the other side of the checkpoint, stood an elderly Palestinian gentleman, my host in Tubas and the headmaster of a school that had recently been established by a Palestinian native of Tubas who lived in the U.S. and who had made a fortune as a medicinal drug developer and businessman. He was giving back to his hometown with the new school, and he had had wanted me to go to Tubas and evaluate the school and stay for a couple months with his parents and siblings, too. It was an invitation I readily accepted.

The school's headmaster was waiting patiently for me beside his dilapidated car beyond the checkpoint. My driver from the airport departed and I was alone, almost, at the checkpoint but for the soldiers and a few Palestinian workers trying to get somewhere themselves. It was a cold February morning with clear skies, and waiting with my bag in the middle of the road I was questioned by a couple of the soldiers. Where was I going and why? But I had a couple questions myself for them, especially for a porcine Israeli soldier whose English was excellent. I asked him where he was from. He said "Israel". But I knew better, having looked him over and heard him speak, and I asked forthrightly: "No. Where are you REALLY from?" Perhaps I had startled him, because he did blurt out an answer and said: "New York". He was, in fact, just another young Jewish immigrant to "Israel" from the U.S. serving out his mandated time in the IDF. I wanted to tell him he had no business there and to return to New York, but did not. I wanted to move on.

And then I noticed someone else standing alone on a hill beside and overlooking Hamra. He was clearly neither a Palestinian nor an IDF soldier, and he seemed to be, by his posture, cradling a weapon and wearing civilian clothes, something I figured out fast enough: a Jewish "settler" living somewhere in a nearby illegal Jewish "settlement" in the West Bank. He also seemed to be the primary authority at and around Hamra Checkpoint, because a while later he spoke from a distance with the soldier I had queried, but in Hebrew, and then he seemed to wave the muzzle of his rifle in the direction I wanted to go.

Yes, after an hour's delay, I was permitted to join my host and travel on to Tubas. Perhaps I should have been grateful to this apparently authoritative civilian that I could then head to Tubas, but I was not. It dawned on me that this settler (and many others like him) completely dominated the Likud government in "Israel", and the illegal territorial expansion of the state was THE prime motivation of the Zionists and their government. And not just a "settler" he was, but an extremist and religious zealot that, if more organized and funded, was every bit as malevolent as the terrorists who just a few years later flooded in to nearby Syria, supported by the U.S. and the Saudis and some other Persian Gulf Arab regimes, aiming to topple the Assad government and sow further chaos in the Middle East.

And later, I thought, oddly enough, of something called "Exter's Pyramid", an inverted one, that in the world of finance pictorially represents the financial risks of various asset classes. At the very bottom of this pyramid, representing the least risk, is Gold. (At the top, the unfunded liabilities of governments, such as those in the U.S., as the most dangerous in terms of default) If one were to create a similar pictorial image of various entities representing the greatest danger and malevolence geopolitically, one might readily rank Jewish settlers like the man at Hamra Checkpoint as the worst, with the U.S. Military Industrial Complex a close second. (Up among entities of little risk to humanity in general would have to be Iran, even though the corrupted Western mainstream media would have you think otherwise.) It seems that Jewish settlers, anyway, because they control the actions of "Israel's" government, and "Israel's" leaders grip and feed U.S. foreign policy in the Mideast, that these "settlers" may, to an gross extent, hold the fate of the world in their hands: Because the Middle East is more combustible than ever with both Russia and allies and the U.S. and allies in a face off, particularly now in Syria, that could erupt in to World War 3.

I have never forgotten the weapon toting Jewish civilian "settler" at Hamra. I had had an encounter there with a religious zealot who represented, when you boil the equations down to their essences, the purest threat to world stability one can now encounter, I believe.

I did, 12 years ago, enjoy weeks with peaceful and oppressed Palestinians in Tubas at the new school, which sadly no longer exists. I can't ever forget that, too, as I ponder with astonishment Trump's vilification of Iran. And that vilification seems to be based solely on the fact that in 1979 in Iran there was a revolution that threw off a largely U.S.-British puppet regime that no one in Iran was happy with. Iran, we know, has never offensively attacked ANY country in centuries, and plans solely to try to defend itself if attacked. It's a demonstration of how twisted and moronic any Western hostility to Iran is, and if it were to abate, geopolitical sanity might prevail as well as political sanity in the U.S.. But we remain a long way from it.

There is hope in enlightened individuals in any culture
March 14, 2018

Plato, perhaps the most notable Western philosopher who lived in Athens some 2500 years ago, wrote: "Those who are able to see beyond the shadows and lies of their culture will never be understood, let along believed by the masses."

This certainly is one sad truth that applies to every culture that ever existed since there is never perfection in human affairs and organizations, but the "shadows and lies" in different places and at different times vary in size and intensity so as to render some cultures qualitatively better than others. Regarding those who do have the vision to see dangers and hypocrisies, however, they can be better understood and believed, but this usually comes at a time when the culture itself is in a state of dissolution and crisis, and only complete morons could fail to figure out they have been delusional.

What is especially remarkable about the "culture" in the U.S. currently is that the "masses" are especially delusional about the notion of American "exceptionalism" touted by those in the U.S. government and those influential with it. This concept is nothing more than an invitation, it appears, to wreak havoc and chaos militarily around the world. To threaten, bribe, harm and intimidate others. And the delusions about the wisdom and rightness of American foreign policies are in part, at least, a factor pushed by the mainstream media in the U.S., which is beholding to corporate interests and oligarchs. But the U.S. is hardly alone in its presumptions,

THERE IS HOPE IN ENLIGHTENED INDIVIDUALS ...

and its alleged chief "ally" in the Middle East, Israel, may be even worse with its delusional policies and actions.

But there is cause for some hope and it can arrive, as it always does in any culture, by way of an enlightened individual who is not afraid to speak out and challenge the status quo.

In the case of Israel, I am speaking of Avraham Burg, who back in 2000 even served as interim President of Israel. I recently heard and saw Burg on public TV in the U.S.. He has been in the U.S. promoting a book, being interviewed and even speaking at synagogues in cities like New York and Boston, and often to applause by Jewish audiences. But what is most striking about Burg is his apparent warmth and humanity, his ability to project what seems to be genuine optimism about the possibility for reform and change in Israel's society and "culture"... and thus at least a lot more "peace" in the Middle East eventually. He has said that Israel's future is a choice between becoming a fundamentalist Jewish state or a bi-national Jewish-Arab federation with open borders and part of a regional union. He has called for the boycott of products from Israeli settlements in the West Bank. He has denounced while he confirmed the existence of nuclear weapons in Israel. He has called for a reduction, if not the elimination, of the Zionist "Law of Return". He thinks that "Zionism" is not a sound basis for Israeli culture any longer.

And you might think he is not at all welcome among his fellow Jews and that he might already have been targeted by extremists, as Yitzhak Rabin was, in Israel. But this is not the case. Perhaps it's wishful thinking, but Avraham Burg seems to have the uncanny ability, given his warm personality and intelligence, to say all sorts of things that Zionists extremists deplore without provoking extreme reactions.

The immediate question is whether Burg is having a positive impact among his fellow Jews in the U.S.? How has he been received at the synagogues where he has spoken and promoted his latest book? Reports suggest that his appearances have been without incident, without displays of temper or hostility. In fact, no discord at all, except that at one synagogue on New York's West Side someone suggested, very lightly and with a smile, that Burg was a "troublemaker." But given the reception he has enjoyed, the question has also arisen whether anyone really cares what Burg thinks, and Burg has not presented his views in a "political" way, but merely as an author (again, his fine persona) who has some ideas worth exploring. Still, even if there is a paucity of "care" about his specific ideas, with audiences secure in their notion of "exceptionalism" within the meme of radical right-wing Zionism, one has to imagine that Burg's ideas do have, or will have, some impact. Especially as the crimes of the Likud government and its supporters in Israel become increasingly apparent to the world.

Iran must be lauded for its longstanding posture against the extremists in Israel and for justice for Palestinians. And against Israeli militancy, which has created chaos, in partnership with the U.S., in the Middle East. The reaction to this posture is that the Israeli government claims it "means" that Iran wants to wipe out millions of Jews. Netanyahu recently made this claim again. This is dishonest hyperbole. One must not forget that Iran has the largest Jewish population in the Middle East outside of Israel and these Jews do not want to move to Israel.

The challenge of U.S. government losing its marbles

March 17, 2018

Any watcher of the international scene, and especially the Mideast, has to be dismayed, bewildered and even, for that matter, a bit frightened. Growing complications and threats abound.

At the top of the threat list of late is Donald Trump himself, who seems to have abandoned entirely the promises he made during his election campaign in 2016 to reduce U.S. belligerence overseas and the nasty games of regime change overseas, successful or not. And meanwhile, truths are emerging.

To cite just one, a Ukrainian member of Parliament, one Nadezhda Savchenko, has come out and stated that the current Speaker of Ukraine's Parliament and other current officials in Ukraine led snipers to a hotel overlooking the Maidan in Kiev to fire on and kill their own citizens and virtually ensure the overthrow of the elected government in 2014, escalating mass protests into an armed coup. The entire violent coup was thus, apparently, a "false flag" event, staged with U.S. support, not to mention the "false flag" chemical weapon attacks in Syria by terrorists trying to topple the Assad government.

But worse must be Trump's recent sacking of Rex Tillerson as U.S. Secretary of State and his replacement by former CIA chief Mike Pompeo. Pompeo was replaced as CIA chief by a known criminal, the three decade plus veteran CIA operative

Gina Haspel who once managed a CIA torture site in Thailand after 9/11 and later, when called upon to cough up records of U.S. torture activities, destroyed them, another felony for which she was not called to account. They have long called her "Bloody Gina" inside the CIA.

Tillerson has been called a "realist", whatever that actually means, but we know what Pompeo is: an ideologue and friend of the largely Zionist Neocons who ought to have been entirely discredited after the Iraq debacle. Pompeo's elevation to America's top diplomatic post is a win for those who want to destroy the Iran nuclear deal.

Tillerson wanted to maintain the JCPOA, Pompeo does not. Neocons, against any logic, practical or moral, are back in the saddle. (At least junior U.S. Senator Tom Cotton did not get the CIA post, as earlier it was suggested he might someday, but now John Bolton, former perennially warmongering ambassador at the UN, may be in the running to become Trump's National Security Advisor, a post for which any Congressional confirmation is unnecessary.) Says Joseph Cirincione, head of an NGO trying to halt the spread of nuclear weapons: Trump is destroying the moderate camp in his Administration.... Tillerson's firing...weakens American credibility.... It's almost as if someone is paying Trump to do it." And meanwhile, the mainstream media refuses to look at the ways the Israeli lobbies such as AIPAC have corrupted BOTH political parties. Israel is the ONLY country in the entire world trying to smash the JCPOA, and the question has to be: Why? There is no good answer to this question, except that "because they, the Zionists, can" through its corrupted control of U.S. policymakers. And because the Zionists want a different government in Iran. Nothing new here. But let's shift gears.

The challenge of U.S. government losing ...

I was recently at my doctor's office for a check up and checking in at the front desk. To verify my identity the lady behind the desk checked my driver's license. She asked me a few questions. One question was: "Are you employed?" I told her "sometimes" and that I was occasionally editing copy for a foreign newspaper. Curious, she asked where? I told her in Iran. She frowned. I could tell she did not have a good opinion of Iran, no doubt influenced by U.S. criticisms in the mainstream U.S. media. I shot back: "Iran is quite a wonderful country that hasn't attacked anyone on offense for over 200 years." That was not what she was thinking about, and she said: "The way they treat women, making them wear head scarves." This, in fact, was virtually all she knew about Iran and the sole reason she had frowned. I explained the utility of the hijab for many women, Muslim or not, even in the U.S. among some Muslim females. She shrugged with disinterest. And this exchange got me to thinking.

I don't think there is any question that Trump and minions will abrogate the JCPOA in May. What happens next, I don't know, but of course I would hope the other signatories to the deal will try to continue to uphold it and split from the U.S., and not just on the matter of the nuclear deal. This is quite possible. The world is getting fed up with U.S. diktat in most every respect. Trump looks increasingly like the loose cannon he is, along with the U.S. Congress.

And there are hopeful signs, even inside the U.S. This week, for example, a young, fresh Democratic Party candidate in Pennsylvania in a heavily Republican district that voted for Trump won a special election for the U.S. Congress touting views and policy positions inimical to Republicans. This suggests, if it does not guarantee, that the Democrats may capture both houses of Congress later this year. Americans are getting fed up, too, with Washington and Trump.

Psychopaths seem to have gathered of late

April 6, 2018

A message from a friend this week, writing: "Martin, perhaps you are one of the few Americans who can actually broadcast to the Iranians that we, the mass of the people here in the U.S., do not see them as enemies."

This statement is quite true, at least among Americans who know something or other about the Middle East and Iran. Unfortunately, I cannot say this about the Trump Administration as it this month has been rejiggered with new appointees such as Mike Pompeo and Gina Haspel. I wrote on March 17th in the Tehran Times that it appeared Trump was aiming to appoint Neocon warmonger John Bolton as his National Security Advisor.

That happened on March 22, a day of infamy in my view. Bolton is such a dangerous figure that when he was U.S. ambassador to the UN during George Bush's term as President he is said to have stated that if the top 12 floors of the UN building in New York City were destroyed by a missile, it would not make a whit of difference. On that statement alone Bolton belongs at Guantanamo as a "terrorist".

Worse, the prospect that the U.S. will attack Iran increases enormously with Bolton working in the White House. According to reports, he has been obsessed for many years with war on Iran, and called for bombing the Islamic Republic repeatedly when interviewed on Fox News. He is a total supporter of the right wing Zionists, too, as would be expected with such demands. He does not at all understand the consequences of such an attack, and moreover, he has been one of the prime influences on Trump to tear up the JCPOA. He has also danced to the tune of the primary financier behind both Trump and Netanyahu, casino magnate Sheldon Adelson.

According to journalist Gareth Porter, when Bolton was working at the State Department, he initialed a "devious strategy aimed at creating the justification for an attack on Iran" by seeking to convict Iran internationally of having a covert nuclear WMD program. He used propaganda and loads of fabricated evidence, most of that created by Mossad. There was no such covert program, as everyone knows.

He was working for Dick Cheney in fact, and with the Israelis, not for his boss, Colin Powell, at the State Department. Just before the war on Iran began in 2003, Bolton is said to have promised the Zionists that the U.S. would destroy Syria and Iran as well. But allegedly the Pentagon was cautious about these subterfuges 15 or so years ago, and allegedly again, the Pentagon REMAINS cautious about any moves to plan or execute an attack on Iran.

One can only hope that caution, which seems real, is strong and remains so. Perhaps Trump will be impeached? That would be in my view a welcome event at this point for a

Iran and the U.S. 2017 - 2023

President who has rejected virtually all his campaign promises in 2016.

But let's conjecture a bit. Muhammad ibn Salman has been feted in Washington in recent days, and reports are circulating that Israeli warplanes have actually been training with the Saudis and possibly the Emirates air forces, too. And we already know that Trump has given the Zionists carte blanche, what with the move of the U.S. embassy from Tel Aviv to Jerusalem.

Netanyahu has also been in Washington this month. One has to wonder if there has been an unannounced conclave between the Zionists, Saudis and the U.S. to discuss and coordinate war plans on Iran as well as on Syria and Hizballah. Allah help us because it's possible this coming summer could be very hot indeed.

No doubt Iranian authorities know about this nexus of warmongers appearing in Washington this past month and come to some speculations themselves about what it all means. I don't think with Bolton in Trump's ear the JCPOA has a chance of surviving. Whether other signatories to the deal have the spine to stand up to the U.S. is anyone's guess at this point, but I can't imagine European signatories or Russia, for examples, can stand by and allow the Saudis, Zionist and U.S. to attack Iran. What's in it for them?

Nothing that I can imagine but yet more subservience to a U.S. government that has gone rogue and quiet possibly, desperately, insane. The U.S. is by the way threatening European countries and companies that want to see the Nord Stream II gas pipeline completed to Germany.

The U.S. aim is simply to undercut Russia's energy sales to Europe and replace Russian supply with more expensive LNG gas shipped from U.S. sources. Few are happy about this, and it may be that this will inspire countries like Germany and France to object to threats or actions against Iran. One can only hope.

I know that many American friends, like the one quoted above and myself, too, are frightened and appalled at what could be taking shape in Washington, Israel and Riyadh. And above all we do not see Iran as any kind of "enemy". But what can we do? If we had the ear of Iranian leaders I know we would say to pull your allies and friends and possible friendly countries in close and together figure out strategies to fast obviate hostilities to Iran or its allies by creating more "caution" in the Pentagon. In fact, such enormous caution that Trump and minions are discredited and shunned as psychopaths.

Amid chaos, patience is a prime

virtue

April 15, 2018

Even if you have the best possible sources to try to figure out what's happening and where it is going in the U.S., it's virtually impossible to know exactly given the daily frantic, frenetic shifts of alleged action and policy.

Front and enter, of course, is the Trump administration's attack on Syria with Britain and France. All this fomented by an alleged chemical weapons incident in Douma that quite possibly did not even occur, and if it did, the so-called "rebels" likely did it. There still is not a single coherent voice I can see within the administration, and they are all apparently squabbling with each other as they move the Doomsday Clock ever closer, and closer than it has ever been, to midnight.

As a young teenager I lived through the Cuban Missile Crisis. My family lived 100 miles from Havana at the time in Florida, and it created a panic in my family such that my mother packed us up and moved 800 miles away. But at least then JFK was in the White House, the Neocons as Zionists did not exist, and much wiser heads ran the government in Washington and persuaded Krushchev to pull Soviet missiles out of Cuba. But the current situation in the U.S. is far more problematic now, and while there are a few sane voices in Washington, they are not being heard. Why?

Because in the U.S. there exists a huge industry that seems to desire a war with Syria, Iran and even, possibly Russia and China. And this thing called the Military Industrial Complex by Dwight Eisenhower in 1961, which then was miniscule in comparison to what it is now, that thrives on money and war related businesses and now has a wide political aspect that includes a majority of those in Congress who receive campaign funding that allows many to stay in office without challenge. Also, there exists hundreds of so-called "think tanks" whose primary interest is promoting war, and they are cheer led by a complicit mainstream media that any real, serious journalist would reject ever working for. Self interest and not national interests prevails with all of them.

Trump may have better instincts, but every time they emerge, like his recent claim of wanting the pull the U.S.

out of Syria, pressure from the Zionists and the corrupted Congress forces him to back away. Does he not know that he would be a hero to the entire world if for once and finally he said NO to these blood besotted elites both foreign and domestic? What about a heroic legacy, rather than one of abject cowardice and selfishness? Does Trump not know that the vast majority of people in the West and East do not want another war in the Mideast, especially now that the current seven year long Syrian war has been winding down? But then the refusal to listen makes sense, too, since the U.S. is in fact no longer a real democracy, and neither is Britain. As the great diplomat Henry Cabot Lodge said decades ago: Nothing is so dangerous as a fully armed country that is also bankrupt. And I would add, not just monetarily with fiat green paper printed in the trillions, but moral bankruptcy, too.

Meanwhile, Iran is experiencing a currency crisis with devaluation, especially to the U.S. dollar. The country runs a trade surplus, but no matter. Getting dollars for goods sold back to Iran has been a problem, allegedly, as overseas banks are loathe to cooperate with or operate in Iran, no doubt under malign U.S. influence. But here's the positive in this misery: the dollar will in time be shunned and lose its status as world reserve currency. Those countries give away real goods and services for pieces of green paper backed by absolutely nothing but military power is a recipe for eventual failure, and with that the demise of U.S. capacity to humble and hobble other nations. The March launch of the Petroyuan oil futures contract by China is one step towards the castration of the Petrodollar, and actions by the U.S. and other Western countries to hurt Iranian commerce as well as Russia's in particular is only going to hasten the move away from the dollar, which really is the lynchpin of U.S. economic power overseas. We may view the ramped up U.S. hostility to both Russia and China and Iran this year to the nascent establishment of means to bypass the buck in international trade. Patience and fortitude by countries such as Iran is what's required as the U.S. "empire" slowly slips towards irrelevance. And one more thing aside from patience: a bit more social liberalism for Iranians in general because that helps ease people through hard times.

Actually, if any Iranian really wants to sock away REAL money, exchange Iranian currency for gold and silver. I can promise that with patience investors will be rewarded handsomely.

American seductions are dangerous balderdash

April 23, 2018

An American journalist can't be unaware of protests in Iran against some aspects of the status quo. However much this may be falsely and crudely amplified in broadcasts via the usual channels such as Twitter by unhappy Iranians outside Iran I don't know, but it is hard to not see some commentary and even videos of this.

Such tells me a lot that is positive about Iranians generally: that Iranians are not afraid to speak their minds against whatever they object to, that inside Iran there is lively debate about a host of issues despite whatever countermeasures may be taken by the Iranian "establishment", and that Iranians are more aware about what's happening than, for example, Americans seem to be now. Yes, I recall my youth in the 60s and early 70s of the last century when the U.S. was awash with protests against the Vietnam War and the Civil Rights struggle against racism was rampant, and at least at the time, more or less effective. I also know that Iran, since the revolution in 1979, has not reached its full potential (which is huge) yet, and as a result there is at least economic distress in the country with a population that has grown enormously since 1979, but I attribute that largely to U.S. –led sanctions against Iran and the reluctance of foreigners to invest in Iran's economy and growth potential despite the vibrancy and smarts of Iranians.

But here's my central problem with dissidents I read about in or outside of Iran. If they think allowing U.S. or "Western" interests to gain ascendancy constitutes some sort of salvation or solution to current woes in Iran, they are badly mistaken. To the extent that the U.S. is some sort of "empire" now held together by militarism, and creating chaos to maintain it, Iranians would be well advised not to presume the U.S. government and its elites really give a damn about Iran, and the U.S., having descended into a kind of totalitarianism where real democracy is kaput, is itself headed in to serious trouble both domestically and overseas.

This will all be revealed in the next economic recession, which may occur sooner rather than later, and with such all the skeletons of mismanagement and dishonesty are going to emerge from the closet. In some ways I look on the Iranian situation the same way I do the allied Syrians under Assad. For now Assad has "won" the war there, and seems to be more or less popular for having done so and driven many of the crazy terrorists to defeat. Sure, Assad is not a "perfect" leader (and he is a dictator of sorts), just as no country, including Iran, can claim perfection of governance. But anyone who slanders Assad seems not mindful of the fact that over time it will be the Syrian people who will ultimately decide Assad's long term fate, based on his governance in a Syria that may no longer be under such strident attack by Western and Saudi and Zionists interests. The same can be said for Iran: Iranians themselves will ultimately decide the continued evolution of the Islamic Revolution, and this can best be accomplished without Iranians presuming the U.S. and its proxies care about Iran generally except to gain control of its people and resources for largely selfish ends. I simply insist that Iranians keep up their opposition to Western and Zionist imperialism until it has been hobbled, and it will be in time.

For now, the "West" is engaged in a huge effort to maintain hegemony, and the moronic recent attack on Syria by May and Macron and Trump seems to be mostly war making over the "right" of the U.S. to do whatever the hell it wants without abiding by international law, facts on the ground and even common sense. And all the while many countries are actively seeking ways to explore other options and literally creating a fresh, alternative, multi-polar world, which is exactly what Russia's Putin has been demanding for several years along with other leaders. Regarding Putin, it is quite remarkable that Time magazine, which 50 years ago had a vast readership, reportedly and recently published a list of its 100 most influential people worldwide, and Vladimir Putin did not make the list. I am quite sure no Iranian leaders made the list, too. No one can or should trust the mainstream media in the U.S.. I am under the impression that Iran's media seems more "open" to diverse opinion and fact.

Actress Portman is now essentially a de facto BDS supporter

April 25, 2018

Natalie Portman has refused to accept an Israeli prize worth $2 million. She is an Israeli citizen but lately she has been "disturbed" by the killing and maiming of Palestinians, including women and children, inside the Gaza border by IDF snipers, and for some time has not been a fan of Netanyahu.

Well, good for her. Some in the Israeli government are threatening to rescind her Israeli citizenship and calling her an "anti-Semite". You have to wonder if she is not further outraged by the reaction to her refusal. But there's been near unanimous silence by the U.S. mainstream media over the horrors in Gaza, and very few in the U.S. government have dared to speak out, notable Democrat Bernie Sanders among the few who have.

As a journalist, I have marveled at how many decades the Zionist state has enjoyed impunity by the U.S. and Western allies, and this specific impunity has been the sole factor that has permitted Israel to launch and expand the settlements on stolen land, to continue the occupation of the Golan, and to turn Gaza for over a decade in to the largest open air prison ever conceived. I, for one, started visiting the Middle East as far back as 1969, and writing about impressions and experiences there. It took about two successive summers in Israel to figure out that the Zionist program was nothing but an immoral, hyper nationalist program that was going to do, in partnership with the U.S., untold damage to the people and countries in the Middle East.

In 1975 I visited Gaza for a month, the first reporter to write an intimate and lengthy report about the Palestinian refugees there. I took the report and photos to the New York Times, which expressed interest. They held it for a year, leading me on, and then literally threw the report at me when I went back to inquire. I was dismayed. I've had other stories, apolitical ones, based on educational survey in the West Bank accepted by some magazine or other and then killed shortly before publication. I wrote a well-praised (by a few other writers) novel set in Vietnam eight years ago. It was published, but by a tiny publisher with no marketing funds, and it languishes at Amazon Books.

One day it will be a minor classic, but I'll probably be dead. But no matter. It surveyed Vietnam now, but also the Zionist project, since one of the characters was an evil Mossad agent who was up to no good in Vietnam. Big publishers were interested in the story, but demanded I eliminate the Mideast material. I refused. A few years ago I was writing op-eds for a major newspaper in New England, and then made a cardinal mistake in a column wherein I suggested that the U.S. "normalize" relations with Iran…and Israel. (Another way of saying fair and balanced policy, and this was just before the JCPOA was initialed.) More dismay as I was called an anti-Semite, too, for what I considered a common-sense suggestion. But I have seen this action time and again over the last 40 years, and other well meaning journalists, the best of the best, have also been marginalized if not eliminated from mainstream U.S. media, which to be quite honest, is under the thumb of monied Zionists and corporate owners like never before. Anyway, when a journalist has solid arguments, any fear of defending a position is gone, and when governments lack solid arguments and their narratives crumble, they begin smear campaigns as we are seeing now. Julian Assange as journalist, however unconventional, is probably the victim of the biggest smear campaign ever mounted against reporters, and his situation remain perilous, even to his health there in the Ecuador Embassy in London.

I mention this not to object on a personal level, because I know right from wrong and am proud of that, but simply to point out how deeply inimical to any overall objective of world peace and harmony this frightful muffling of information and expansion of propaganda has become. But if there is truly an objective of world peace among so-called leaders, it hardly has been honestly expressed. Even Trump, in a phone call this week with Netanyahu, actually asked him whether he wanted peace at all.

Good question! Meanwhile, many news outlets still are failing to question the Skripal narrative put forth by the British establishment, while anyone who reads much knows it was a false flag to set up the missile strike on Syria by the U.S., Britain and France. Same goes for the alleged chemical attack in Douma by Assad, another false flag, actually a staged incident, which has been pointed out clearly by independent journalists like Robert Fisk who have visited Douma. If Americans can't now figure out how much they have been misled by the mainstream media, then perhaps there is no hope for peaceful resolutions to all the various crises around the world and particularly in the Mideast, a region I love for its diversity and cultures and people, excluding the Zionists but not smart Jews like Natalie Portman seems to have become as a result of the continued carnage in Gaza.

Iran and the U.S. 2017 - 2023

Summer 2018: A bit of fear and loathing are natural

May 9, 2018

A bit of fear and a bunch of loathing mark the days of intelligent people anywhere, and I'm hearing this from Iranian friends in Iran and in the U.S.. It seems that this summer may be like no other in recent memory: either good sense and rationality will somehow prevail, or the world, and particularly the Middle East, will be plunged into some sort of all or nothing conflict to tie up loose ends of U.S. and Zionist and Saudi imperialism.

Assuming World War 3 does not erupt. That's the fear part, and I cannot even get my mind around all the moving parts embedded within this outrageous situation foisted upon the world, literally, by a Trump Administration that has become totally subservient to the influence of the so-called Neocons, most of whom happen to be Zionists, too. You'd have thought these same old tired psychopaths who fomented the absurd "War on Terror" and the disastrous attacks on Iraq, Afghanistan, Libya, Yemen, Syria, etc, would have been at least entirely discredited by now, if not in jail.

Consider the ultimate outcome of U.S. foreign policies just since 2003. The latest estimates of the victims of post 9/11 aggressions by the U.S. and Western allies are that about six to seven million people have been killed as a result of the unnecessary wars waged along with the destruction of six countries, especially in the Mideast. Maybe the true number of deaths is only five million, but it could well be more than seven million, too. And in addition, the latest tally doesn't even mention the further millions of people whose lives, loved ones and bodies have been shattered irrevocably by the wars. And the true numbers of people killed is still believed to be only in the tens of thousands by the general publics of the U.S. and Britain, as if that was not bad enough. The mainstream media disinformation continues with fabricated crises this year such as the highly suspicious Skripal poisoning and the unproven and well discounted chemical weapons gas attack in Douma, Syria.

Meanwhile, it has been reported at least that President Rouhani, whatever the Trumpists do, wants to keep alive the JCPOA with those other nations that originally crafted and endorsed the deal. One can only hope those other countries ascribe to this reported desire by President Rouhani, and at the same time drive a big fat wedge between the U.S. and its alleged allies that widens over time and fully reveals just how "rogue" and dangerous the U.S. has become to the entire world and any prospects for peaceful resolutions to the various extant conundrums and conflicts worldwide, which are in fact based solely on the U.S. desire to remain hegemon, as it has arguably been since the end of the second World War. A blessed turning point may come when more countries turn away from the U.S., particularly in Europe, and fully understand their long-term interests and prospects are not being served by the U.S..

For Iran, it appears that Trump will reimpose economic sanctions against the Islamic Republic, further damaging Iran's economy and its people, who have all the more reason to call upon Russia and China especially to try to reduce the impact on Iran of such sanctions. The isolation of the Saudis, the U.S. and the Israelis may be productive of real change, but who knows?

Let's assume just for the sake or argument that the pain, economic and otherwise, foisted upon the Iranian people does in fact result in some sort of "regime change" which reduces clerical power and which the U.S. has been trying to foment since the 1979 revolution. (The U.S. did foment such in the 1950s with the overthrow of the duly elected Mossadegh and Iran's desire then to fully control its own resources.) Everyone knows that Iran's currency has lately collapsed. Everyone knows that Iran has witnessed protests over economic grievances in recent months. Everyone knows that Iran's government has imposed some difficult measures to try to halt the economic erosions, to no avail so far. Everyone knows that the immediate pain felt by many Iranians is being blamed on the government by some of the protesters, and that "regime change" could occur. But the blame, such as it may be, is misguided IF many Iranians believe that the end of clerical rule offers real salvation. Sure, a more "pro-democracy" governance inside Iran may be welcome, just as it is or would be welcome in ANY country with a population as vibrant as Iranians always have been. It was that very vibrancy that brought about the end of the Shah's puppet regime in 1979 against considerable odds!

But the U.S. and the Zionists, who are wagging the tail of the U.S. dog and have been for several decades with regard to Mideast foreign policy, seem to be making one huge mistake IF they imagine that some kind of material change in Iran's governance will result in a material change of disposition towards the U.S. and "allies". That huge mistake is simply believing that the Iranian people, in my view, will somehow become disposed favorably in any aftermath to the U.S. and the Zionists, who would be blamed, or should be blamed, for any suffering and chaos that may accompany internal change in Iran.

The U.S. government does not honestly give a damn about Iran's people, just as it never gave a damn about Syria's or Iraq's or Libya's or Afghanistan's or Palestine's, to cite just a few examples. Six million dead in U.S. led wars proves this. Same goes for the people of the Korean peninsula. The historical record has made this all too obvious. The U.S. corporate state does not even care much about the American people in general, but primarily does care about the maintenance of its own unilateral power both within the U.S. and overseas by any means necessary, and more Americans, at the margin, are (too slowly) waking to this fact.

The onus of idiocy on Iran could be vanquished

May 13, 2018

My 25 year old car, albeit an old BMW, would not start yesterday and I had to call for assistance, including a tow and a visit to my local auto mechanic shop here in North Carolina, U.S.A. No big deal, but I took a poll with everyone I encountered, some seven people, all of them very "average" Americans without much sophistication or any serious "education", asking them what they thought about Donald Trump's move against the JCPOA and any hostile reimposition of sanctions on Iran.

I doubt half these folks could have easily located Iran on a map, but not a single person thought Trump's action made sense and they seemed to know vaguely that Iran had abided by the terms of the JCPOA since inception. I might have been shocked and surprised, but I was not, and although I did not ask, the people I queried were probably the kinds of people who voted for the orange haired, now Neocon captured deal breaking liar in 2016. Indeed, these people seemed quite concerned and they probably had voted for Trump because he had promised disengagement from overseas wars and hostilities during his Presidential campaign against Hillary Clinton.

During an otherwise depressing day and week past, this informal poll contained some good news indeed. But still, these people and myself have little or no recourse against Trump and minions, except perhaps to look forward to midterm Congressional elections in a few months and at the least the reasonable chance of unseating GOP candidates and incumbents, not that that will do much good, but it's a start. There is, for what it's worth, disgust and revulsion towards further war by the U.S. government and its fake "allies" on the Middle East, on Iran and its supporters like Syria and Iraq.

Trump lied for the umpteenth time and claimed Iran was "on a quest for nuclear weapons" as the alleged "world's worst sponsor of state terror" which is a horrible joke and lie if ever there was one. Where's the proof? Of course there is none, just as there was no proof, just fabrications, that Saddam Hussein had any WMD. If Iran is on a quest for nuclear weapons, why did 17 U.S. "intelligence" agencies in 2007 and 2011 declare that Iran had no weapons program, all must ask rhetorically? If it's any consolation for Iranians, efforts ARE underway to prevent the Trumpists from dragging the U.S. or anyone else into war on Iran and its allies. The Europeans are apparently insisting that Iran and the U.S. abide by the terms of the JCPOA. They know Iran has been so abiding all along. They want to keep the deal alive, it seems. And this while the U.S. has abided by nothing but falsehoods, fabrications and lies.

Even worse is Trump's stated claims of empathy or something with the Iranian people under the current clerical government, but if that empathy were real and honest, Trump would not be planning to reimpose draconian economic sanctions on Iran, which ultimately hurt average Iranian people more than anyone else. So we know what this all means: that this madness has very little or nothing to do with WMD, but rather "regime change" or just simply creating upset and potential chaos in a proud country that more than any other in the Mideast has long rejected U.S. imperialism and Israeli apartheid.

No doubt President Hassan Rouhani, who twice defeated more hardliner candidates, could be in trouble, but I hope not. The JCPOA, his greatest achievement, could be seen by Iranians as the failed gamble of a man who trusted the now obviously untrustworthy U.S.. In my view, any effort by Iran to replace moderate leaders inside Iran could be seized upon as a pretext for war. Talk about a difficult and delicate situation for all Iranians, but there you have it! And no one wants further war in the Middle East. Neither Syria nor Iranians in Syria, nor Hizballah in Lebanon, which after recent elections is now leading Lebanon. Nor do the Russians want to see all their hard work in Syria demolished, but Putin is not likely to sit idly by and watch further strikes on Syria, or overt military attacks on Iran. However, it's worth noting the Netanyahu was in Moscow this past week and he may have persuaded Vladimir Putin not to supply Syria with S300 defensive missiles. This is a mistake, but Russia's relationship with the Israelis is "complicated" by the presence of an estimated million "Israelis" who formerly had been Russian citizens. In any event, I hope both Russia and also China make an effort to help ring fence Iran with additional defensive capacities as a clear warning to any potential attackers.

What I am saying here is no secret to Iran's leaders, and what happens next is difficult to forecast, but if it's any consolation to frightened and besieged and respected Iranian friends, understand two things: 1. This unilateral abrogation of the JCPOA appears to have been condemned worldwide, and I mean that literally, and especially by JCPOA signatories in Europe. Whether various countries in the West have the smarts and wherewithal going forward to assist Iran in circumventing economic sanctions effectively, in essence giving the well-deserved middle finger to both Trump and Netanyahu and Muhammad bin Salman, and to maintain the JCPOA absent U.S. participation, is anyone's guess at this time. But if this circumvention were successful, and the effort solid enough and permanent, and the threat of U.S. sanctions against those who don't cooperate with U.S. sanctions on Iran prove to be mostly ineffective, too, then we have the makings of a huge sea change against arbitrary, illegal, and destructive U.S. influence and imperialism worldwide. The bullies, and they are simply bullies, will be reduced to irrelevance and wide contempt. It could mark the END of many decades of malign U.S. "power" overseas, the end of the Neocons and maybe even the end of Zionist capture in Washington as well as any respect towards the U.S. that still may exist. 2. Iran, if it can somehow summon the strength the get through this difficult time with dignity and without inviting additional hostility from outside the triad of the Trumpists, the Saudis and the Zionists, could ultimately be freed to develop as it ought to without the onus of idiocy, especially by the U.S.. I hope to God I am not dreaming.

Aching for positive resolutions to frightful questions
May 19, 2018

Remember the Sharpeville massacre in South Africa? Probably not because it was long ago, in 1960, when South Africa was suffering apartheid and a crowd of some 7000 protesters gathered in this town in what is now Gauteng.

The South African police opened fire on the crowd and 69 people died. Claims are that the police opened fire when the crowd started advancing towards a fence surrounding a police station. Sounds familiar, what with the massacre in Gaza when some 62 people died from Israeli gunfire near the border fence just this past week, and many hundreds of others wounded, many of them maimed for life. You can't get any uglier than what happened in Gaza, though, because the shooting was premeditated, not spontaneous as a result of some real, immediate threat. South Africa anyway is no longer an apartheid monster, and one should remember that the U.S. supported the apartheid regime in that country to the bitter end of it, when Nelson Mandela was released from prison and then became president of the predominately Black country.

The U.S. seems rarely ahead of the curve, almost without exception siding with particularly repressive, unprogressive, states like Saudi Arabia that applies a medieval internal rule of

Islamic jurisprudence that outstrips, it seems, anything Iran's clerics have instituted since 1979. (And turned holy Makkah into what looks like a kitsch Disneyland.) The U.S. seems incapable of recognizing right from wrong, and especially while Trump's administration like never before narrowed its entire foreign policy to fit the demands of the Likudniks in Israel, and as sage Paul Craig Roberts, former editor of the Wall Street Journal, has claimed, Israel is arguably the most "evil" nation since 1948. It is more than merely astonishing, and it smacks of a vile desperation, like a petulant, spoiled child determined to have its way exclusively and going whole hog now to get its way in one last (I think) huge attempt to maintain Anglo Zionist hegemony over much of the world. The U.S. abrogation of the JCPOA reflects this, too, and it appears, at least on the surface, that its abrogation has been almost universally condemned.

And moreover, to paint Iran as a real threat to the U.S. or the Israelis makes no sense. If there is any threat, it is ideological, not military. Relatively speaking, Iran's GDP is comparatively minuscule at around $400 billion, and its military expenditures are similarly minute, while the U.S. spends almost a trillion dollars on its grossly offensive "defense". Meanwhile, I frankly think that the negotiations between the U.S. and North Koreans will fail, if they occur at all. Why? Because the U.S., before it unwinds sanctions, is insisting that North Korea's nuclear program be irrevocably dismantled first. The one thing that seems to be, for the moment, protecting Kim Jong Un's government and forcing the Trump Administration to seem vaguely "friendly" and open minded is the existence of North Korean WMD. The U.S. anyway is untrustworthy. The destruction of Libya is just one example. Another, of course, is the U.S. action against the JCPOA, but there are many instances of betrayal.

The question, obviously, is what can Iran do if European signatories, China and Russia fail to preserve the JCPOA without the U.S. and also ensure that U.S. sanctions against Iran don't further damage Iran's already suffering economy and people going forward? Reflexibly, there is the possibility that Iran will ramp up its nuclear research and uranium enrichment activities once again. If North Korea appears to cow the U.S. even marginally, one can imagine that some of Iran's leaders may wish it had a nuclear deterrent, too. As heretical as this may be, one could almost wish another country, say Pakistan, would literally GIVE Iran a couple nuclear weapons, or say they would if Iran were about to be attacked militarily. You'd have to wonder that U.S. and Israeli sabre rattling might be halted? But it's hard to know. And here's another idea: Trump had allegedly embraced talks with North Korea, face to face. If he had any sense he would at least suggest a summit between the U.S. and Iran to calm tensions and institute a semblance of serious dialogue, and further suggest open talks between Iran and its regional rivals like Saudi Arabia, as Javad Zarif has suggested. However, the great barrier to anything like this is quite obvious: it is Israel primarily. As long as the U.S. does Israel's bidding, the threat of war will remain unless the EU fully splits from the U.S. on foreign policy and aligns itself with the preservation of the JCPOA come what may. For example, if the U.S. applies sanctions on European companies wanting to maintain and expand business and economic ties with Iran, why wouldn't the EU similarly apply sanctions on the U.S. in retaliation? Sanctions on the U.S. have never been suggested or applied, to my knowledge. Europe's choice ahead may be obvious: continued vassalage or sovereignty and national independence. O, so many questions and so few ready answers!

As tragic and destructive as the killing of innocent protesters in Gaza by IDF snipers has been this Spring, the world now has fully seen the depravity of Likud Israel, which is the world's nemesis at this time, and increasingly seen as such. It's about time, for the fundamental racism and cruelty of the Zionists has always existed. Hell, they invented terrorism! Had the Zionist been handed an unpopulated piece of land, okay, but they were not. Can Israel continue to exist as it is with so few friends and admirers? Secondly, can the U.S. literally afford another war in the Mideast? Who will support war except a parasitical Israel? Answers will certainly appear over the course of 2018 to many questions, and in the meantime admirers of Iran's principled and wholly, truly Islamic stand against injustices will remain, especially if the Islamic Republic also opens more to its citizens and becomes increasingly more democratic, more tolerant and more eager to address and eliminate any corruption within Iran. It's a challenge, for sure, but one definitely worth consideration in these difficult times.

Who does Pompeo think he is kidding?

May 23, 2018

Mike Pompeo, the new U.S. Secretary of State in the Trump administration, has this week made radical demands upon the sovereign and significant and thousands of year old state of Iran (or Persia, as you will) and its 90 or so million people that, in effect, can either make a sane and reasonable person do one of two things, or both: Be rolled with uncontrollable laughter and/or curled up into a ball of lachrymose despair. And I alone, as a U.S. citizen, am not alone in thinking so inside the U.S.

What Pompeo's recent speech literally reflects is just about every dangerous ailment of disposition and judgment that has infected U.S. policy since perhaps the Vietnam War and as well led to untold and tragic military aggressions outside the U.S. upon other peoples and countries. There are many adjectives to characterize the essential nature of Pompeo's pronouncement on May 21, but the one that comes most readily to mind literally fits Pompeo's name: Pompous. And even if the Islamic Republic fulfilled all the weird demands, some of which are completely uninformed and senseless, what does it get in return? Not much: A new agreement or treaty or something like JCPOA Iteration Two around any and all development of nuclear expertise in Iran. Pompeo offered nothing else such as, for examples, bilateral diplomatic relations with the U.S., respect and friendship, a complete evisceration of sanctions, economic aid and trade. Let's take a look at the various demands.

Declare to the International Atomic Energy Agency (IAEA) a full account of the prior military dimensions of its nuclear program and permanently and verifiably abandon such work in perpetuity.

Stop enrichment and never pursue plutonium reprocessing, including closing its heavy water reactor.

Provide the IAEA with unqualified access to all sites throughout the entire country.

End its proliferation of ballistic missiles and halt further launching or development of nuclear-capable missile systems.

Release all U.S. citizens as well as citizens of U.S. partners and allies.

End support to Middle East «terrorist» groups, including Hizballah, Hamas and Islamic Jihad.

Respect the sovereignty of the Iraqi government and permit the disarming, demobilization and reintegration of Shia militias.

End its military support for the Houthi rebels and work towards a peaceful, political settlement in Yemen.

Withdraw all forces under Iran‹s command throughout the entirety of Syria.

End support for the Taliban and other «terrorists» in Afghanistan and the region and cease harboring senior al-Qaeda leaders.

End the Islamic Revolutionary Guard corps-linked Quds Force‹s support for «terrorists» and «militant» partners around the world.

End threats against its neighbors, many of whom are U.S. allies, including its threats to destroy Israel and its firing of missiles at Saudi Arabia and the United Arab Emirates, and threats to international shipping and destructive cyberattacks.

Comments in no particular order of importance.

It's never been actually and conclusively verified that Iran ever really had a "military dimension" to its nuclear research activities, unless one simply believes that any expertise at all in nuclear technology is by definition inclusive of a "military dimension". That, in essence, any country that simply has learned and mastered the various potentials and applications of nuclear technology "must" also be ineluctably and invariably involved in hostile military machinations. This makes no sense whatsoever.

Stopping uranium enrichment completely by Iran, even if it applies to some peaceful use of such in practice now or eventually, is unfair UNLESS the same demand in made of every other country on the planet, including the U.S. and Israel, to name just two. Reciprocity is critical IF the U.S., as it should, seriously desires to eliminate the threat of nuclear war across the globe. In my view, yes, Iran ought to agree to this stoppage but only if other countries, some of which like Israel have extant nuclear WMD, also verifiably dismantle their own centrifuges. No exceptions, including no exceptions for the country, the U.S., that has deemed itself "exceptional". IAEA inspections must similarly be applied across the board to those countries in possession of the expertise to make nuclear weapons.

Regarding the demand about Iran's ballistic missiles, such that they exist, it's obvious that to whatever extent they have been developed at all, they comprise, or literally can only comprise, little but a purely defensive capability that every country is entitled to, particularly when any country has been so threatened by military attack as Iran has been. I am sure Iran would eliminate its missiles if the U.S. and Israel, and any other hostile country, did so, too.

Pompeo is flatly mistaken, also, to suggest that a "heavy water reactor" is currently operable in Iran. Who did his prior research in preparation for his speech? Suggesting that Iran did not effectively destroy its alleged reactor, given reports by outsiders that it had, is nothing but propaganda designed to smear Iran.

Iran has long been the sworn enemy of al-Qaeda (and ISIS and an-Nusra and many other terrorists organizations, and was completely appalled and empathetic to the U.S. when al-Qaeda was alleged to have been behind the 9/11 attack in New York. So I have no idea what to make of Pompeo's claim that Iran is harboring any al-Qaeda leader(s). Yes, Iran has been assisting Hizballah, which is a deep part of Lebanon's government, so is Pompeo also set to declare that Lebanon is a "terrorist" state? I think not if Americans want to maintain any presence in Lebanon at all.

As for Iranian presence in Iraq, and particularly in Syria, nothing needs be said but that the governments of both countries apparently invited the Iranian presence to assist in the eradication of truly terrorist entities such as ISIS. Also, I know of no instance where Iran has actually fired missiles at Saudi Arabia or the UAE. This claim by Pompeo seems to be another bit of misleading propaganda and indeed, if Iran had so fired missiles directly across the Persian Gulf, I daresay that Iran and these Arab countries would already have been engaged in full-scale war with Iran. Javad Zarif has, however, fired unqualified appeals for dialogue with the Saudis and the UAE.

It's difficult to imagine whom Pompeo thinks he is kidding. His address and demands are so bizarre, based on inaccurate information, and so completely Israeli-centric that you have to wonder that Netanyahu wrote the address, along with John Bolton. It is simply hoped by many that the other signatories to the JCPOA sees these demands for what they are, a clear attack on Iran's sovereignty and underneath, an attempt to foment chaos and "regime change" within Iran. Above all, the Iranian people must stand tall, stay cool and work with those countries who also don't buy Pompeo's, or Israel's, BS.

U.S. may be hoisting itself on its own petard

May 26, 2018

The Chinese suggestion that "May you live in interesting times" is now fulfilled, it appears. Who made current times most interesting, in some respects like never before since World War II, is a lame minded Donald Trump this Spring, plunging the thoughts of many across the world into chaos and trepidation.

In a complete about face to many of his campaign promises in 2016, which arguably got him elected, he has, particularly with regard to the Mideast: Withdrawn the U.S. from the JCPOA, opened a U.S. embassy in Jerusalem, completely ignored grotesque Zionist carnage in Gaza especially, threatened Iran on several fronts, adopted Muhammad bin Salman (who threw in his fortunes with the U.S. and Israel and may have recently been shot, or perhaps he is dead?), may be planning to officially recognize the Israeli occupied Golan as Israel's, occupied parts of eastern Syria and also attacked Syria with missiles, ramped up support for the Saudi War on

Yemen with the installation of Army Green Berets near or in Yemen, is planning massive "sanctions" against Iran and even may be planning, with the Pentagon, a military attack not just on Iran, but also on Syria and Lebanon, too. He has also threatened Europe with sanctions if Europe attempts to maintain growing business with Iran. More could be cited, but this list is quite enough for now. So, what does it all mean exactly?

It means, first of all, that the U.S. had lost, and had been losing, control of the Mideast like never before…and imagines that control can be re-won with the moves he made this Spring in concert with the Saudis and Israelis. The extreme nature of the moves tells the world that the U.S. is desperate, failing and flailing. It is hardly any kind of evidence of strength.

For example, remember 9/11? In the immediate aftermath, the Islamic Republic strongly empathized with America, even though enmity had existed between the two countries for decades. Iran's response was exceptional, and without any gloating whatsoever: President Khatami at the time condemned it, as did Ayatollah Khamenei. The mayor of Tehran even sent a message to the mayor of New York, and this was the first public, official contact between the U.S. and Iran since the 1979 revolution. Sixty thousand spectators allegedly observed a minute of silence during a soccer match in Azadi stadium, and candle-lit vigils spread across Tehran, and all this should have informed the U.S. about the real character and substance of the Iranian people and their government.

So what did the U.S. do? Rather than take the responses in Iran and elsewhere as opportunities to open up dialogue with alleged enemies, it went on a vengeful military rampage that has continued to this day. A rampage that the U.S. believed would forever cement its control and hegemony in the Mideast. And all this while the official explanation of who was behind 9/11 in New York was never sufficiently uncovered, and left the entire incident full of unanswered questions that have never been officially probed. Had the U.S. truly been a "strong" country, not a shallow military behemoth with little else in its arsenal but anger, it would have literally banked on the goodwill and empathy of the world by reaching out itself to mend divisions, including the divisions with Iran that was extending a gentle hand to an aggrieved America. This must be mentioned because to whom was the U.S. primarily in thrall right after 9/11, aside from the so-called Neocon cabal in the U.S.? Netanyahu and Likud Israel, who pushed the U.S. vehemently to attack Afghanistan and Iraq for starters. Thus, it can be said that:

The same driver of U.S. foreign policy in the Mideast remains Israel, and given Trump's complete adoption of Netanyahu's obsessions and Israeli demands like no U.S. President before him, the U.S. has merely tripled down on policies that have quite literally failed since 9/11 in both spirit and substance. And despite what carnage and suffering the Trump administration with Israel and perhaps the Saudis could possibly this year inflict on Iran and Iran's people, the coming failures could be magnified like never before. To put it simply, the U.S. government under Trump is about to hoist itself on its own petard like never before, but as it does so, it also unfortunately harms not just Iran but many other counties as well as its European allies. This is no solace at all for anyone, but it may, just may reorder and remake the world into a multipolar globe, which it definitely has not been since the dissolution of the USSR. Imagine, for example, a much more unified and ultimately prosperous Eurasia, including Iran, and an America humbled, the U.S. dollar humbled, its war oriented economy humbled, and with far fewer allies. It's possible that unless and until the U.S. makes amends, even – I daresay – apologizes for the last few decades, it may remain what it seems to be becoming -- a pariah.

No one will be able to crush Iran

June 8, 2018

One has to speculate: What is America's overseas cause now? In World War II it was the defeat of Adolf Hitler and the Nazis, and also of Japan, which had attacked Pearl Harbor.

Later, it was the defeat of Communism and the USSR, and a victory in the Cold War. Now? Hard to imagine there is a cause at all but maintenance of an "empire" of sorts with a misguided toolbox of military threats, economic sanctions, aspersions against foreign cultures, breast beating and crude assertions of "democracy" at a time when in fact it has faded significantly inside the U.S.

The U.S. is a "police state" more or less now, and Washington a vast bureaucracy of surveillance of citizens and corporate control hiding behind a huge façade of alleged democratic values as thin as rice paper and bolstered by mainstream media propaganda. Policy lies are hidden by false advertising and bizarre, misleading names. If anything, it seems Orwellian and much of it remains unbeknownst to "average" persons, saddled with debt like never before and trying to maintain some semblance of a "middle class" lifestyle. The military holds sway, and easily, with the recent budget allocation of well over $700 billion annually.

Take something as minor but popular and seemingly innocuous as sports in the U.S., in particular NFL football, where many players are Black and some in recent years have refused to remain standing on the field for the national anthem before a game, sensitive to racial discrimination, never completely abolished despite decades of struggle. It used to be that players stayed in the locker rooms during the national anthem, but no longer since 2010.

They have been forced onto the field, and taking a knee has been essentially forbidden while the government is spending many millions of taxpayer dollars to put on grandiose, "patriotic" displays inside stadiums and other sports venues. It's all one big "as if": as if the government gives a damn, as if it is really defending the interests of the multitude, as if it really cares…when it patently does not., or not much.

The U.S., supposedly the most "developed" country on earth, and unlike many other Western countries in Europe, sports a third world infrastructure, the absence of affordable healthcare and higher education (both of which are free in many countries), debased industry outside the Military Industrial Complex and rotting cities. The rich get richer and the poor poorer.

To cite just one statistic, CEO's of many U.S. corporations take home pay many hundreds of times larger than average employees. Fifty years ago the ratio was double digits, and in some cases even single digits. One could go on with various comparisons of all kinds to describe the descent of social sense, but any reasonable person gets the picture of a country that has lost its way and is no longer worth emulating.

Meanwhile, in my adult lifetime wars of choice have been launched and millions killed on the flimsiest of pretexts, or none at all. Those benefitting from the aggressions, starting primarily with Vietnam in the 1960s, have narrowed with each successive decade since, and now, who? Alleged beneficiaries are U.S. corporations embedded in the Military Industrial Complex and their shareholders, and associated oligarchs, U.S. banks and Wall Street (which profit on discord), all representing a tiny slice of an American population that overall has seen the "middle class" decimated while public and private debt has accumulated like nowhere else in history ever has, threatening the foundations of the fiat monetary system itself.

As dystopian as one can paint aspects of the U.S. now for a majority of its citizens, one also has to be well aware that on the surface anyway, the U.S. remains one of the "richest" resource rich countries on earth. So-called living standards, albeit supported by unsustainable debts of all kinds, remains relatively high, the façade intact for now and capable of lulling too many Americans into complacency. The question that at bottom remains is this: for how much longer? I don't know and neither does anyone else.

But one might discern that U.S. militarism around the world may suggest a tone of desperation in Washington. So what does this mean for the Islamic Republic that the Trump administration, catering to Neocons and Zionists almost exclusively, has obviously put in its crosshairs for "regime change", pretending it cares about the welfare of the Iranian people?

No one will be able to ...

Well, first of all, Power in the U.S. cares for almost nothing but itself. And it seems fairly clear that, as with Syria, the ultimate aim is not necessarily better or more liberal government for Iran, but simply and mostly chaos, the breaking up of Iran's diverse population into competing factions virtually at war with each other such that, as a unified country, Iran would no longer exist. (This gambit did, of course, fail in Syria thanks to Russian and Iranian assistance and the fight and spirit of Syrians. In Iran's case, I know of no particular expatriate group that the U.S. emboldens but the terrorist MEK that, by most accounts, is despised by most all Iranians.

But let's say that with radical economic sanctions ahead from outside and other pressures, protests in Iran against the mullahs and demands for change reach a critical point, as they did in 1979 against the Shah. What then? I don't know, but as an outsider who has never been able to visit Iran and knows far less than I should, one would simply pray that any evolution at all proves to be positive and positively enduring.

And as an outsider, I frankly don't care who is in charge in Iran as long as those in charge are positively responsive and responsibly serving all Iranians as best they can and hold that service out as the primary goal, including the maintenance of the demand that Iran not become a vassal to rapacious U.S. or Western interests, and as well keeps up opposition to Zionism.

One positive thing that did cross my desk this past week is a recent statement by Ardashir Zahedi, former Iranian ambassador to the U.S. just prior to the revolution, long exiled in Switzerland. In this statement, he slams the U.S. as a bully. He declares that Iran's "noble people" in the face of outside threats always manage to stand together. He supports invited Iranian aid to Syria's elected government.

He is disgusted by the war on Yemen. He says that the JCPOA remains a valid and binding document, and prays for the diplomatic maturity to keep it alive. And he adds that the social situation inside Iran will evolve and he has tremendous confidence in Iran's youth. He says unequivocally: "No one will be able to crush Iran."

What I take from Zahedi, whatever his current standing may be in Iran, is simply this, and it is encouraging: Iran will continue being an independent, proud nation, subservient to no bully, come whatever "evolution" that may occur, despite the U.S. and its minions.

Take heart: the next 100 years will be better

June 28, 2018

Occasionally it makes sense to stand back and take a look at history from a long-term perspective, and in this regard I am talking about the last 100 years, which really have not been kind to the Middle East, its diverse people, and even to Islam.

As a youth, one of my favorite books for its sheer descriptive beauty was "The Seven Pillars of Wisdom", written by TE Lawrence, about the Arab Revolt in World War I against the Ottoman Turks, who for centuries had governed over Greater

Take heart: the next 100 years ...

Syria and Arabia. A British soldier and scholar, Lawrence, along with the Hashemites, led the revolt of Arab tribes in Arabia against the Turks, promising full "independence" and self governance for the Arabs. But at the same time the French and British signed the secret Sykes-Picot agreement to carve up the Levant and the Middle East after the war into colonial domains. As well, the British issued the infamous Balfour Declaration in 1918 that "looked with favor" on handing the Zionists a colonial "homeland" in Palestine. The war period really was the beginning of 100 years of Western aggression and colonialism, by direct method or proxies, on the Islamic world, and it largely rested on the recognition of vast petroleum discoveries in the Mideast and the greed of Western governments to control it. As for Lawrence, it remains an open question whether he knew during the war of the coming Western betrayal of the Arabs. I think he probably knew enough, and ultimately regretted his role during the war.

Despite all the twists and turns, and horrors, of history in the Middle East over the past 100 years, Western aims and intentions, particularly American and British in the recent half of this past 100 years, have not abated. The so-called "War on Terror" is nothing but a colonialist operation at bottom by the U.S. Betrayal has been the order of these times, most recently and glaringly, the abrogation of the JCPOA by the Trump administration. And I recently heard from a young Iranian friend and famous photographer who wrote: "The U.S. has ruined our lives and prospects." Her words crushed me, and in fact, many other friends, both American and Iranian. Yet there must be hope, for without that, there is nothing in these sad times. Where can it be found?

I believe this is the last, loud gasp of American aggression on the people of the Middle East, and that of the Zionists, too. Very slowly, subtly or not, the world is reorganizing itself. This century will turn out not to be the "American century", but Asia's, and perhaps especially Eurasia's, which includes Iran. Aggression tends to reach a crescendo when it is most apt to be in the initial phases of failing, and the crescendo itself pushes that failure faster than it would otherwise occur. The U.S., even if so few recognize it for now, is economically spent and faces some sort of fiscal bankruptcy and monetary crisis ahead, which will dethrone the ultimate lynchpin of U.S. power, the dollar, which has allowed for U.S. militarism.

Just this past Spring, for example, a magazine I once wrote for, Forbes, uncovered Pentagon files revealing that the Pentagon cannot account for an added $21 TRILLION in spending since the 1990s. This could well hyper-inflate the buck to death and kill the American "empire" and its 1000 or so military bases spread all over the planet. In the view of a number of astute economic observers, the "dollar" is doomed, and the question is not if but when. Also doomed is the so-called Petrodollar. China and Russia and other countries have lately been disgorging themselves of U.S. bonds, too, and buying gold hand over fist as a preferred financial reserve. There is some indication that both China and Russia, too, may issue a gold back currency eventually. Meanwhile, Iranians now suffer horribly as their own currency has been steeply devalued since the U.S. scuttled the JCPOA in early May. Unfortunately, gold has become terribly expensive in Iran of late, but it has been a salvation to some citizens of other countries such as Venezuela who have managed to corral the asset. But there are other factors also that point to the demise of U.S. power and aggression.

Another important factor is simply that more and more people, including Americans and Europeans, are appalled at the immorality of U.S. foreign policy and the neglect of needs here at home. Poverty in the U.S. has grown tremendously this century, and the engine of prosperity, the "middle class", has been nearly destroyed. The gap between the "rich", the "one percent" and all the rest of citizens is wider than it ever has been. This does not bode well for the U.S. economy, nor for the criminal U.S. government. The next economic downturn or recession will be like no other in the U.S. As the billionaire Warren Buffett has opined, we get to see who has been swimming naked as the waters recede. And recede they will. As well, with upcoming midterm elections later this year in the U.S., new faces are appearing as candidates, and some of them are speaking out against the U.S. government's overweening support of "Israel", to which the U.S. gives roughly $10 million fiat a day. Like never before, these fresh candidates are showing they are not afraid of the Zionist lobbies in the U.S.

So, here is some hope for real, substantive change, however long it takes. Iranians should find some relief in this and remain patient and wise. O, yes, and congrats to Team Melli for a brave showing at the World Cup. The next 100 years will become Eurasia's and Iran's, too, inshallah.

Iran is not alone in these

difficult times

July 10, 2018

Iran and the U.S. 2017 - 2023

Iran has been "Iran" for a long time. Yes, I have read Herodotus and other historians about ancient Iran, and other historians in periods since. So while full condemnation of whatever forces are keeping Iran in the 21st century from reaching its full potential economically or as a society or both is perfectly justified, one ought not to worry about Iran longer term.

Iran will be Iran with a clear Iranian identity a lot longer than the United States will remain an intact nation, and in fact, even now, there are people in parts of the U.S. that would like to become independent of Washington.

And so would many countries in Asia and Latin America be pleased to witness the diminution of U.S. economic and military power which, particularly during and since the Vietnam War has wreaked such havoc and carnage across the globe.

It is anyway difficult to pinpoint exactly when the U.S. began to stumble badly as a generally beneficial actor on the world stage. We know, for example, that the U.S. played a key role in the defeat of Nazi Germany and imperialistic Japan and their allies during World War 2, and this was all to the good, despite the unnecessary use of two atomic bombs dropped on Japan. After the war the U.S. helped rebuild Europe, and eventually Japan, too, but not with unselfish motivations. During the Cold War with Russia that country was eventually obliged to withdraw from Eastern Europe. Communism was more or less defeated while Russia had to hunker down deeply and repair itself to reemerge, as it has to some degree, as a world "power" under Vladimir Putin. But the handwriting was on the wall as early as 1953 with the U.S. and British plot that brought down democratically elected Iran's Mossadegh, and reinstalled the Shah. Until the Revolution in 1979, Iran was a firm "ally" of the U.S., and in general the "alliance" of almost ANY country with the U.S. was thereafter based on one thing alone: not any kind of give and take of competing interests, but complete subservience to U.S. economic and military power or else any country balking as such subservience would be branded an enemy ripe for sanctions, economic warfare and even war itself. So it has been for my lifetime so far, but where, really do things stand now?

Even while the U.S. is at the apex of its military power with its vast spending, the foundations, particularly the economic foundations to sustain power, are slowing rotting away. When former President Richard Nixon took the U.S. fully off the gold standard in 1971, he opened the door to an ungoverned spending spree with "money" conjured from thin air the likes of which the world had never seen before. Current debts are unsustainable, and unfunded liabilities ahead in the U.S. may top $200 trillion. Deficit spending under Trump, and the recent tax cuts, suggest deficits above $1 trillion every year for the next decade at least. This will likely trigger a monetary crisis where the dollar is deeply devalues and loses its "exorbitant privilege" as the world reserve currency. The two core government programs, aside from the military spending, benefitting Americans have long been Social Security and Medicare. They are also a big hit to the U.S. financial situation, and current estimates say both Medicare and Social Security will be bankrupt or insolvent within the next 15 years. Take either away from Americans and political upheaval, even some sort of revolution, is likely.

In fact, what we see now in the U.S. with the erosion of civil liberties, surveillance of citizens, the rejection of

Constitutional mandates and more, is little more than the efforts by the "elites" to forestall a political upheaval or revolution by the bewildered U.S. masses who are sinking deeper into relative poverty, just as many other countries, including Iran, suffer economically because of U.S. power. Meanwhile, in the Middle East, both Saudi Arabia and Israel, the prime allies of the U.S. in the region, are increasingly on shaky ground both economically and morally. But what does this mean for Iran?

Iran is in for a rough(er) patch going forward, for a while, and so are many other countries both in the Middle East and elsewhere such as Latin America and Asia. Iranians ought not to feel alone is this difficult time of transitions. So are U.S. citizens facing hard times ahead, and Iranians should not condemn Americans generally, I daresay. Many in the U.S. feel powerless and afraid, too, because of Washington's and Wall Street's insane policies to control and maintain the narrative, along with its corrupt allies like Saudi Arabia and Israel. Fortitude and unity must be paramount, particularly in Iran. But this means that Iran's "elites" must also be willing to accede to the wishes of Iranian citizens generally, and use this difficult period to self-reflect and shore up internal support not with batons and bullets, but with a genuine willingness to vanquish corruption and above all listen attentively to all Iranians. If Iran's leaders can do this successfully, and foster internal unity and support, then in time, the current difficulties will abate and Iran, as a vital part of a rising Eurasia under Chinese and even Russian leadership, will find itself in much better shape than it currently is as a resource and culturally rich country that deserves far better than what an imperial U.S. has been meting out for decades since World War 2.

Let's hope Ocasio-Cortez has real guts

July 18, 2018

A comely 28 year old restaurant employee with a Latin name and background from the Bronx, New York City, knocks off the multi term Congressman in a primary election who may ultimately have become the Democratic Party leader in the U.S. House of Representatives, displacing Rep. Nancy Pelosi (who really is no leader at all). This is heady stuff, and she arrived on the political scene with a slate of progressive ideas, including calls for an end to U.S. warmongering and universal healthcare for all citizens.

Even more notably, Alexandria Ocasio-Cortez a month ago, before her win, was tweeting that she opposed the U.S. embassy move to Jerusalem, rampant Israeli human rights abuses, and what she termed Zionist "massacres" of the hapless Palestinians in Gaza and the West Bank.

What's remarkable is that, having opined as much, she actually won the primary election as a Democrat in a district full of Jewish voters against her incumbent, ""establishment" opponent. The win over Rep. Joe Crowly in the 14th Congressional District said quite a lot about her: that she appears smart, articulate and ever so refreshing to many people across the U.S. -- especially those Democrats tired of same old who may realize that in the upcoming mid-term elections and later for the Presidency, the Democrats don't have a good chance to take back control of the House nor to defeat Trump in 2020, who has already amassed and election war chest of $90 million to spend on his future reelection bid.

Ocasio-Cortez has frightened the U.S. political establishment like few other candidates in recent memory, and brought smiles to the faces of many voters, especially those depressed for decades about U.S. policies and actions in the Middle East. But already, interviewed extensively about her astounding win over Crowley, she is equivocating.

We don't know to what extent and how exactly she has been threatened, but during an interview on face the Nation on prime-time television the impact of threats has become apparent. She claimed, for one thing, that her comments had been the comments of an "activist" and that now, she is no longer an "activist" (whatever that is exactly unless it simply denotes a person willing to tell the unvarnished truth) and that she is henceforth willing to "learn and evolve" (read "revise") her former postures. While stating that she remains a supporter of the "two state" solution in Palestine, she clearly was a bit flustered when her interrogator, Margaret Hoover, asked her what she meant by the term "occupation" with respect to the illegal Zionist presence in the West Bank and the blockade of Gaza. She then said she "may not use the right words" to characterize the situation, and for her the entire matter is one of "human rights" and her own humanitarian concerns. She added that she firmly believes in Israel's "right to exist" except that, just maybe she may believe, which went unstated, not under the kind of policies promoted by the current Israeli government.

Ocasio-Cortez's "evolution" is sadly predictable since her recent success, however undesirable this is too many of those who remain "activists". She is no doubt surprised that she did win, and loves all the media attention, but going forward no one knows whether she will remain or become a steadfast advocate and voice for sanity with regard to Middle East matters. But she so far remains a person whose views are at least healthier and more honest than most all her future, potential colleagues in Washington. Still, many wonder: what if she were a candidate willing to hold firm to her views when she was an "activist" even at the potential cost of her losing the election in November? No other candidate I am aware of has yet been willing to threaten their chances of election success by literally continuing to tell the unvarnished truth about "Israel" (and other concerns) and its blatant apartheid in Palestine.

And make no mistake, telling the truth about Israel is literally the cornerstone of truth telling generally about so many issues affecting the U.S.: the widening gap between rich and poor in the U.S., the maddening and overwhelming influence of rich, selfish oligarchs on U.S. foreign and domestic policies, the precarious U.S. economy (where economic "growth" over the past decade has not been organic but merely the result of vast money printing by the Federal Reserve bank that has pumped up financial markets like never before), the lack of affordable healthcare for many Americans, the out of control spending for the benefit alone of the Military Industrial Complex and the enormous fiscal debts, and so much more that literally, some believe, threaten the future of a very divided U.S. population.

Still, young Ocasio-Cortez is worth watching, and so are a handful of other rare candidates for the U.S. Congress who are willing to tell more of the truth about the Mideast than ever before in recent decades. If, miraculously, enough pressure via truth telling is brought to bear to substantially change attitudes about the Zionist state in the U.S., and ultimately foment policy changes, however marginally, then this will, in turn, bring about changes even in attitudes about Iran and more revulsion against U.S. sanctions on Iran and the abrogation of the JCPOA in May.

But change remains highly contingent on Iran's leadership also addressing the desires of its own citizens for reform and avoiding gross instability inside Iran, which has been the primary aim of the Neocon infested Trump administration since inception. One cannot stress this enough, this requirement that Iran's leadership show wisdom and flexibility. Patience remains key as always, too.

A litmus test of sanity: the fate of Iran and Assange both

July 23, 2018

Americans are mostly a parochial, unsophisticated people. A clear majority have never traveled abroad. Almost 70 percent of Americans don't even have and never have had passports, and even for those that do their passports largely go unstamped by a foreign country.

O sure, some do travel abroad, but most of them go to Canada, or maybe they get on some cruise ship in Florida and see the Bahamas while others cross the southern Texas border for a holiday tequila in Mexico. Sadly, the young people that travel abroad are mostly military, and they are fools wreaking havoc in faraway lands at the behest of corporations and plutocrats who generally run things in the U.S., which was not always the case. Meanwhile, the U.S. government has been hijacked by the powerful, wealthy few. Perhaps this mostly began with the Vietnam War and the faked attack on an American naval vessel in the Gulf on Tonkin. Just before that, leaving office, President Eisenhower was absolutely correct when he warned of the dangers of what he called the Military Industrial Complex. The so-called Deep State in Washington, and the Neocons and Zionists are also fully implicated in the descent of the U.S. as a respected major country. These entities are screaming at Trump right now as some kind of "traitor" for his talks in Helsinki with Vladimir Putin. One may fear for Trump's life.

Trump makes sense regarding a warming of relations with Russia. He makes no sense at all with his Mideast policies, which seem set largely by the Zionists. Many who did vote for Trump in the 2016 Presidential election did so because he seemed to want better relations with Russia, the primary other country with enough nuclear weapons to end life on earth. Hilary Clinton was always corrupt and bloody. She led the destruction of Libya for one thing and set the stage for the near destruction of Assad's Syria, and she was never about to improve relations with Russia. She'd also have been a greater disaster than Trump has proven to be for peace in the Mideast, if Iranians can believe that. I know, it would be difficult to believe that for Iranians especially. It's enough to make a sensible, grown man weep.

As one who has never visited Iran, I am still sure of one thing: Iranians, even those who have never left Iran, know more about what is happening outside Iran than Americans do about what's really happening, and why, outside the U.S.. There are a number of good American and foreign journalists who tell the truth and inform well, but they are not a part of the mainstream media any longer, which is almost totally a corporate, corruption influenced media now. So most Americans, who don't read much anyway, are ill informed, and if they do read, it's a local paper somewhere with canned news, especially regarding other countries. What seems impressive about the Iranian media is that, at least, there is more truth and Iranian writers and leaders opine correctly about the dangers of U.S. foreign policies.

Trump and Pompeo and Bolton among others seem set on regime change in Iran, with or without war, as the Zionists demand. At the very same time "Israel" has gone full tilt, legitimizing full apartheid with actions this month in the Knesset. If anything ever becomes their downfall, this will be it eventually. Neither the U.S. nor "Israel" have friends any longer, or soon won't. It is simply horrendous that the U.S. and "Israel" might be brought down eventually by causing further destruction and carnage in the Middle East with an attack on Iran, or just won't go away quietly with the pursuit of rational, benevolent policies at home and abroad.

All this and more has become quite a personal matter for me, too.

My bright son, age 32, was recently mentioned as Julian Assange's physician. Well, in fact, he is not formally so, but over the last year he has drawn worldwide attention to Assange's medical woes and demanded treatment for him, after he and a team he assembled evaluated his medical condition at the Ecuador Embassy in London late last year. It appears that very soon the corrupted new President of Ecuador, Lenin Moreno, may turn Assange over to the British government, ending his six years of embassy asylum in London, and possibly agree to his extradition to the U.S.. In the U.S., Assange could well disappear forever. And he has done nothing wrong except be the primary reporter/journalist who has brought attention to U.S. military and internal political misdeeds since 2010, beginning with exposes of U.S. war crimes in Iraq.

Caitlin Johnstone, a very independent Australian journalist, has said it most succinctly this week regarding Julian Assange. She writes that those of good conscience should be prepared to "shake the earth" if Assange is further tortured, or is shipped off to the U.S.. And she adds: "If we allow them to imprison Julian Assange for practicing journalism, that's it. It's over. We might as well all stop caring what happens to the world and sit on our hands while the oligarchs drive us to ecological disaster, nuclear annihilation or Orwellian dystopia. If we, the many, don't have the spine to stand up against the few and say 'No, we get to find out facts about you bastards and use it to inform our worldview, you don't get to criminalize that,' then we certainly don't have the spine it will take to wrest control of this world away from the hands of sociopathic Western plutocrats and take our fate into our own hands. The arrest of Julian Assange would be the fork in the road. It would be where we collectively decide as a species whether we want to survive into the future, and if we deserve to.

I would say the same thing regarding any U.S./Zionist attack on Iran. And so would many others, including knowledgeable Americans.

The U.S. has become a threat to itself, too

July 29, 2018

I can't help but imagine what a glorious world we might have were there to be accord between the U.S. and Iran, and if not actual accord, at least a Middle East where the U.S. treats each country in the region individually and equally, determining policies and initiatives and even criticism in a two-way give and take, the critique based solely on whether any actor is pursuing their own foreign policies with an aim to rid the region of violence and focus on beneficial, mutual trade and better relations.

Islamic history did erect one polity in a corner of its vast medieval realms like no other before or since – in a small corner of the Islamic world where the concepts of Oneness and Fraternity among citizens prevailed for several centuries with a sublime kicker. I am referring to al-Andalus in Muslim Spain around 1000 years ago. The kicker was simply that it was extremely inclusive and tolerant of citizens who happened to be Jewish and Christian, too.

I had the pleasure of corresponding briefly with the expert on al-Andalus, Maria Rosa Menocal, a Cuban born Yale University professor, before she died in 2012. Her last book was titled what Andalusians actually called their realm: "The Ornament of the World," And it was just that – profoundly dazzling. This extraordinary and vigorous society with its capital at Cordoba in southern Spain, and a bit later at a nearby royal city called Medinat az-Zahra, was marked by three achievements: ethnic pluralism, religious tolerance and what she called cultural secularism.

And none of these aspects were in fact or considered to be anti or un-Islamic. Menocal asserted these three qualities were inherently mandated as ideals anyway by Islam's core message, the holy Qu'ran. But then along came intolerant Christians from the north who by 1492 had destroyed the last holdout Muslim Nasrid kingdom centered on Grenada and the famous al-Hamra (Alhambra). At any rate, everything seemed to flourish for a while in al-Andalus, particularly cultural syncretism with inputs and achievements from Jews, Christians and, of course the dominant Muslims then in Spain.

It's worth noting that anyone who has some familiarity with the U.S. government's primary "allies" in the Middle East especially, Saudi Arabia and "Israel", are nothing like al-Andalus was: the former is a medieval monstrosity of social and political dementia harboring a gross distortion of ideal Islamic values, the latter a modern fascist apartheid replication of intolerance of both Christians and Muslims, native Palestinians, as wrong headed and cruel as Nazi Germany was towards Jews.

Not having been able to visit Iran, it remains reasonably obvious that Iran, for all its internal problems, remains more "democratic" and inclusive than either Saudi Arabia or Zionist Israel. In other words, more willing to adhere to the core, idealistic tenets of all the monotheistic faiths, including Islam. And yet, at the same time, Iran is demonized by some Western countries and by U.S. Mideast allies for at least advocating the elimination of injustice in the Middle East. (This is not to say that Iran under its current leadership has become as enlightened and broad minded as anything like al-Andalus allegedly was, but Iran seems perhaps father along in this respect even if one might argue maybe not far enough along yet.)

And lately one can read in the U.S. media an occasional story suggesting that the U.S. will launch a military attack on Iran's assets before summer's end -- correct or not, a startling and frightening prospect if even remotely possible or true. Consider how vacuous, to cite just one example, the U.S. mainstream media has become: MSNBC has broadcast stories about a buxom prostitute, Stormy Daniels, hundreds of times this past year because she allegedly had an extramarital affair with Donald Trump, while NOT ONCE reported on the humanitarian disaster in Yemen because of the war on Yemen by the Saudis and the UAE with U.S. logistical support.

Iran must be commended for trying to draw attention to the suffering there, and Iran's posture is clearly not entirely a matter a jockeying for geopolitical power or advantage, as any country may attempt. The key to understanding Iran, one would imagine, is that Iran has not offensively attacked any other country in over 200 years and just apparently wants to be left alone, or not harassed or sanctioned, to develop more harmonious and mutually beneficial relations with others wherever it can.

Trump (and his administration), especially under Neocon and Zionist control or influence, is without question such a loose cannon that no one can predict whether the threats are real or just bluster. While Iran's President Hassan Rouhani has been offering "peace" between the U.S. and Iran, as well as with other regional neighbors, and rightly said that war would be a disaster for the entire Middle East, the crucial and primary problem or fault with the U.S. government, as it has been for decades, is the fact that Washington has literally defined "peace" with other countries as simply submission to whatever the U.S. wants. This is a longstanding insanity.

Trump allegedly tried to contact Rouhani several times when Rouhani was at the same time in New York at the UN. Rouhani refused the contact. Was Trump literally trying to create the kind of accord, albeit superficial, he managed to generate with Kim Jong Un of North Korea at their meeting in Singapore? One cannot know. There have been faint glimmers that Trump alone may have at least some decent intentions, even if his close advisors like John Bolton do not. Trump has lately met with Vladimir Putin in Helsinki, and is said to be planning to host Putin in Washington later this year.

But making matters much worse, whatever Trump believes or desires, is the absolute madness of the hatred of Russia and Putin by the vast majority of politicians in the U.S. Perhaps it's the case that the U.S. literally needs an "enemy" like Russia to keep the Military Industrial complex humming along and profiting the few. And in the background is the fact that Trump won the election in 2016 in part because many voters liked his stated promises to seek détente with Russia! Now, Trump is being called a "traitor" by powerful interests in the U.S. aiming to destroy him politically.

With regard to Iran, Trump, having rejected the JCPOA in May (and Netanyahu has been bragging that he was behind the rejection), has this month claimed he wants to renegotiate a "better" nuclear agreement with Iran. But again, if Trump believes a "better" deal with Iran must involve Iran's complete subservience and submission to U.S. demands, he is way off base and in fact no wiser than the morons in Washington who have been leading the U.S. towards economic and moral bankruptcy for decades, starting spectacularly with the Vietnam War and leading onwards to the wars this century in the Middle East.

One good bit of news amid the gloom is that a recent poll in the U.S. suggested that almost three quarters of Americans do not want any kind of war with Iran. And most do not want a cold (or hot) war with Russia. That stands to reason as the latter could end human life on the planet. War on Iran, to satisfy the Zionist deplorables, unbeknownst to them in their wicked hubris, could easily spell their own end and wreck the Middle East further. It could also wreck the U.S., too.

Whatever anyone inside or outside thinks of Iran's leaders, they do in any case seem relatively rational and benign, and not deserving of attacks, sanctions or whatever, and I believe many ordinary Americans believe the same. But inasmuch as real "democracy" has fallen by the wayside in the U.S., it's not just Iranians who are at risk.

Iran may need reforms but the U.S. is absurdly regressive

August 4, 2018

Reports are rampant in the Western media about protests in Iran against the plummeting value of the currency and other economic ills. The same is happening or has happened in many other countries: Venezuela, Turkey, Argentina, to name just three. The U.S. dollar has been strong of late. Even the

Chinese yuan has been weak, but this is partly intentional to offset the threat of U.S. tariffs on Chinese goods and services.

Most disturbing are reports of alleged chants by protesters in Iran claiming the U.S. government is not Iran's enemy, but that Iran's government is at fault for the economic distress. This is an absurd thought.

The U.S. has been Iran's enemy for many decades and not because Iran has done anything wrong per se, except oppose U.S. hostility. Or at least it's been the enemy of Iran's people, simply because it has been a big, relatively rich country ripe for exploitation by foreigners. I have no idea the depth or degree of corruption by Iran's "elites". I have no idea how distressed Iranians really are there about Iran's leadership.

Actually, from a few Iranian friends I am hearing they either want to leave Iran, because being well educated, they seek greater economic opportunities elsewhere during these difficult times. Or they are feeling pride in Iran, and perhaps having been away on a trip to Europe, they still are pleased to return home even though they are quite fearful about the future and remain dismayed at why Iran is treated as it has been.

You cannot destroy a deal like the JCPOA, considered by all as a keystone, threaten the country, humiliate its government and then call for further negotiations. Deals like the JCPOA are based on goodwill and trust, mutual accommodations and respect. Trump's declarations that he would meet with President Rouhani without preconditions is simply a lie.

The preconditions, sanctions and the abrogation of the JCPOA, are already hurting Iranians. So Iran is expected to do what the U.S. wants and only then will the sanctions be lifted? I don't think so. And meanwhile Rouhani has no desire to threaten international waterways in the Persian Gulf, but he insists, and rightly so, that Iran be able to export its resources.

The U.S. under Trump is going mad. Russia, already sanctioned, may be facing further sanctions if the GOP leadership in Congress has its way. Turkey, long a U.S. ally, is facing sanctions, too, because Erdogan wants to deploy the Russian S400 missile defense system and may buy Russian aircraft. And even Europe may be sanctioned because of the Nordstream II gas pipeline into Germany under the Baltic Sea. And this is just the short list of threats to other countries. China appears to be a target, too.

I have no idea where all this madness is leading, but IF it leads to greater cooperation among nations that will jointly try to find ways to continue business as usual and avoid the bite of U.S. belligerence, then good. Above all, try to find ways to de-fang the U.S. dollar as a weapon. Move to bilateral trade agreements in national currencies, or other assets like gold, and shun the very concept of the Petrodollar…if possible. Eventually, the U.S. will have no friends except the craven Saudis, the UAE and of course the Zionists, who went too far with its recent "Jewish state" legislation. Even some notable U.S. Jews are turning against Israel.

Iranians who are condemning Iran's current leaders for the economic problems inside Iran now, in any event, are off base. They are playing right in to the hands of the U.S., which seems primarily to want "regime change" and/or chaos. What kind of "regime" would the U.S. support in Iran – one which solely did the bidding of the U.S. Make no mistake about that?

A government comprised of MEK members, whom Rudy Giuliani was courting recently in Paris?

A new Iranian government composed of U.S. puppets, as the Shah was, and who was rejected by Iran in 1979? Such acceptance would mark regression for Iran. Yet one has to wonder that a new government that was secular, not Islamic, but still maintained rejection of U.S. imperialism and support for Iran's allies in the Mideast, and the Palestinian cause, would still not be acceptable to the U.S. Neocons and the Trump Administration. Again, make no mistake. The U.S. government wants nothing so much as subjugation to U.S. diktat by Iranians, and nothing else. I am convinced of this. I watch the moves in Washington closely. I have my ear to the ground.

This is a bad time for Iran during which, for however long it takes, Iranians must hang tough and try to avoid internal discord as much as possible and the leaders there must not crack down so hard as to foment further unrest. They must listen, above all, and empathize and show flexibility and change what needs to be changed for the good of all Iranians. The difficulties will pass. But no one knows when.

PERILS COULD ACTUALLY HERALD

POSITIVE CHANGE

AUGUST 9, 2018

Sometimes, more often than not, I write against the U.S. as it was and as it has been since. I was born right after Fat Man and Little Boy were thrown at Hiroshima and Nagasaki. The public was told these two crimes against Japanese civilians, when Japan was already prepared to surrender, saved lives and shortened World War 2. It did neither. The war was already won in the Pacific The U.S. in fact was sending a message to the USSR, which more than any country had defeated Nazi Germany: "Look what we can do to you if you don't behave." Hundreds of thousands of Japanese perished to deliver what amounted, at bottom, to a threat to the USSR. And since then?

No doubt the U.S. government has done at least some good in isolated locations around the world, but on balance the idea and fact of "Empire" has gotten insanely out of hand since the turn of the century, and on balance the U.S. has caused more carnage and humiliation to others trying to maintain power and dominance than any other country in world history in the past century. Iran has suffered, beginning with the CIA and British coup against Mossadegh. But maybe, maybe the chickens are coming home to roost as the U.S. government as it has been, may be becoming of late more isolated and reviled, and if you ever imagined you might live in "interesting times", they have arrived. And oddly enough, amid the dangers, there may be cause for some hope ahead. Consider that the geopolitical deck is getting reshuffled, at least slowly. Alliances and perceptions are changing. Currently, for examples, Turkey seems to be falling out with both the U.S. and the EU, the U.S. falling out with the EU, Canada and Mexico (and others), Saudi Arabia falling out with Canada, Turkey and Qatar, and tradition Western allies appearing incapable of getting along, among many other instances of discord.

While one cannot disagree with some moves Trump has made, including the appearance at least of Trump's suggestions to reduce tensions with Vladimir Putin and the Russians, a suggestion which may literally threaten his Presidency, his greatest failings are, of course, his Middle East policies where the Zionists have been setting the agenda, particularly with regard to Iran. He can tweet and tweet idiotically, endlessly send out messages that he often contradicts the next day, but as long as he protects the super-rich oligarchs and permits the Zionists' to control him, and allows the U.S. Military Industrial Complex to do its worldwide murder and to loot the U.S. Treasury, he will be allowed to carry on, and meanwhile the Democratic opposition, which claims to be more "sane", really is not yet and its intentions though cast differently are just as inimical – until something breaks. And something will break. Perhaps it will be the faux health of the U.S. economy and its perilous finances. Perhaps it will be an overwhelming preponderance of breaks with allies like the EU that make it impossible for the U.S. government to maintain its desired status quo. Perhaps even some kind of revolution in the U.S. is brewing. No one is happy with the stance of Washington against Iran except the warmongers, and Neocons, and that includes many Americans. Do not be deluded: those who are pulling Trump's strings with regard to the Middle East would like nothing more than for Iran to fall apart and be drowned in chaos of the sort that ensued in Assad's Syria until recently. If Iranians were fully aware of this, they would hang tough through the sanctions and threats until they abate, and if Iran can manage somehow, they will abate.

And Americans are wising up through all the propaganda, at least at the margin, because they see that Republican Party domination in Washington of late is dismantling, or wants to dismantle, not only protections of free speech and the free press, but also environmental protections and cherished social programs like Medicare and Social Security – at the behest of greedy corporations and other "elites".

Iranians must be aware that the American PEOPLE, by and large, have no ax to grind with Iran. In fact, even such media pundits as Geraldo Rivera of Fox news have lately questioned why Iran, and not Saudi Arabia, has been demonized by Washington. He went on to suggest that Iran ought to replace the Saudis as an "ally" of sorts in the Middle East…but of course that goes against the Zionists' grip on foreign policy. And one must note that Jeremy Corbyn, leader of the Labor Party in the UK, attacked so viciously of late by Zionist zealots even in his own party, is actually gaining support among Jews in the UK even though he has long been a champion of human rights, has supported relief for the long-suffering Palestinians and claimed he would endorse Palestinian statehood. Grand it would be if Corbyn becomes Britain's Prime Minister, which is a real possibility.

Just this week, another promising development. The state of Michigan is likely to send the very first Muslim woman to the U.S. House of Representatives in November. This is Democrat and atttorney Rashida Tlaib, 42, daughter of Palestinian immigrants who just won a primary election. Representing part of Detroit and Dearborn, she may be joined by a couple other Muslim candidates in Congress come November.

In any broad survey of the geopolitical landscape, which is being reshuffled like never before in decades, the one clear takeaway is the necessity for not just Iranians, but all people distressed by narrow and desperate U.S. imperialists, to maintain solidarity and cool heads whatever the pains as something better and new may be born not merely in the U.S., but worldwide.

Can the U.S. do without friends in the long run? No

August 19, 2018

Iran's neighbor, Turkey, with a population almost as large as Iran's is suffering some of the same economic problems that Iran is suffering: a currency that has fallen precipitously against the "almighty" U.S. dollar, much higher inflation, and in Turkey's case debt rating downgrades by the likes of the debt rating agencies (those with the most clout based in the U.S.), calls for the Turkish authorities to bend over to Western financial authorities and institutions, to borrow money from the IMF and well, you know, lose gobs of their sovereignty.

Indeed, it's quite obvious the U.S. expects Turkey to do only what the U.S. wants, and that includes no further mending of relations with Russia, not building a gas pipeline from Russia across Turkey, killing plans Turkey has to buy Russia's S400 missile defense systems (far superior to anything the U.S. can cough up, and far less expensive). In addition, Turkey was supposed to get a bunch of U.S.-made F-35 warplanes. Frankly, one must hope they have not been paid for yet, and if they have been paid for, that the U.S. returns the funds. If Erdogan has any sense, he would not want the F-35 anyway.

This overly complex aircraft is plagued with problems that some, even in the U.S. military, say are not fixable, and the machine is the most expensive warplane ever. Frankly, it is a POS (Piece of S***), if you understand the acronym, and I know a little about airplanes, having been a pilot, at least of small planes, for decades. The Russian inventory of warplanes is far more reliable, and far less costly, and even by some accounts more effective.

Moreover, there's the matter of a failed coup attempt against President Recip Erdogan not long ago, and the possibility that an alleged "pastor" named Andrew Brunson, an American who has been in prison in Turkey for a while under suspicion that he may have been working for the CIA and that the U.S. may have been behind the coup attempt, is not going to be released from prison and returned to the U.S.

The refusal so far by Erdogan to release this sketchy "pastor" (and a handful of other Americans in Turkish prisons), who reportedly preached (or something) to a congregation of less than 30 followers and Allah alone know who they were and why any of them were in Turkey, has gotten Donald Trump all in a hissy fit of some sort whereby he's pulling all the strings he can grab onto to drag Turkey down, as Iran has already been dragged down by Trump's abrogation of the JCPOA and the reinstitution of harsh sanctions against Iranians and Iran's economy. The JCPOA abrogation alone was entirely illegal, as is much the U.S. has been doing for decades outside the U.S., and lately, inside, too.

Iran may be the prime target of the Trump Administration currently along with his gaggle of insane Neocon advisers, but Iran is not alone under attack by the U.S. Trump has added to the various sanctions against Russia and Russians over the Skripal affair in the past month, infuriating Sergei Lavrov, Russia's Foreign Minister, and no doubt Putin himself. Other countries are under sanction attack, too, and Trump has been threatening to apply sanctions against ANY country that buys Iranian oil after November.

It's interesting that a former top editor of the Wall Street Journal, and a high up appointment in the U.S. Treasury Department when Ronald Reagan was President, Paul Craig Roberts, who is now an independent writer and pundit, has had some things to say about a host of stupid moves by the Trumpists.

For example, Roberts, who is extremely wise, wonders why Putin is so damn nice towards the U.S. when, he claims, both Russia and China hold all the cards in the sanction wars. For one thing, Roberts says neoliberal economics is a hoax, but neither the Chinese nor the Russians get this yet.

Roberts believes all the lies and provocations against Russia would come to a halt if Putin said the U.S. would be destroyed if they continue with the provocations, and in fact Russia could wipe out the U.S. physically. A milder response would have Russia, among other things, stop selling rocket engines to the U.S., stem the flow of energy to Europe, ban overflights of U.S. aircraft and stop altogether the use of the U.S. dollar for oil trade.

China could nationalize U.S. corporate operations inside China, such as Apple Computer, says Roberts, and dump its holdings of U.S. Treasury bonds. U.S. corporations would demand that the U.S. be subservient to China, not the other way around. Also, says Roberts, Turkey is a perfect opportunity for Russia and China to step forward and remove Turkey from NATO, and offer membership in the BRICs, trade deals and mutual security treaties.

But Iran is neither Russia nor China and has nothing of the military power, relatively, nor the economic power to challenge the U.S. as, for examples, Russia and China could, if only the two countries' leaders had the balls to do so. However, what Iran CAN do is deepen its ties with both Russia and China and its Caspian Sea neighbors (as it has of late), and even more importantly, maintain a cool demeanor and internal accord and resistance to any pressures for "regime change" by both the U.S. and the Zionists.

And perhaps Iran is trying this now, carefully. One can only hope. For, in fact, the U.S. is not making friends, it seems, anywhere outside Saudi Arabia and Israel, and increasingly is perceived as simply a bully. The road ahead to a truly multipolar world is long and hard, but that's the task for all the rivals of the U.S. and it can be achieved for the betterment of the planet as a whole.

And that includes Iranians of course. No country like the U.S. can maintain such vast power that the U.S. has enjoyed for decades, and for long misused with malice and cruelty, if it has few or no friends any longer. It's time for the major powers like Russia and China to come to the aid of lesser powers like Iran and to begin to think about ways the U.S. can be sanctioned, too.

Geopolitical and economic

transitions are painful

August 25, 2018

Who knows what the real numbers are, but it's been estimated that since the end of World War 2 the U.S. has been responsible, one way or another, for the demise of some 25 million souls across the planet – many of them innocent, who were victimized by the overweening insistence that the

U.S. grab or maintain military or economic hegemony by damaging potential rivals.

There is nothing at all novel about this, for if one looks at history over the past centuries, there have been numerous governments and powers that sought to dominate their era and even, on occasion, managed to do some good. There are some peoples, polities and governments that quite literally have deserved reduction because on balance they have proven to be more destructive than constructive for humanity as a whole. Nazi Germany may be the prime example during the past century of a country that deserved the world's enmity.

The U.S. has long tried to fit the Islamic Republic into this category of polities that allegedly don't deserve to survive for the SOLE REASON, in fact, that Iran refuses to ally itself with U.S. and Zionist and Saudi attempts to control the Middle East and reap the benefits of its vast wealth. And even if the Islamic Republic, like any other country, sports aspects that can legitimately be criticized, Iran stacks up as a far more benign country today than severely undemocratic Saudi Arabia and Israel, the U.S.'s chief "allies" in the region, despite all the Western and Zionist propaganda to the contrary.

I have, in any event, been depressed witnessing the U.S. and Western failures of judgement, particularly with regard to Iran, and I have read that the suffering and confusion is immense within Iran, but at the same time I have tried to point out along the way that more than half the world's population is moving within a painful transition, with leadership from Russia and China, to a new and much more promising paradigm than what the U.S. has been trying to bully impose on the Mideast and Asia and even Europe. The U.S., in effect, may have been setting a trap for itself in recent decades that will eventually limit its impositions on other countries and force more cooperation.

Consider, for example, that a new bloc may be forming. It includes Russia, China, Iran and Turkey for starters, and may include India and Pakistan, too. Pakistan's new leader, Imran Khan, has lately expressed disgust with his country's allowing the U.S. to have its way. The BRICS may be turning into the BRICS plus. This is good reason for Iranians to look ahead and try to understand that they, too, face a brighter future than they have known for decades.

Turkey has been offered membership in the "BRICS plus" and the Shanghai Cooperation Organization for starters, and Erdogan has allegedly shown interest in both. Thus, Turkey may leave NATO and cast its fate not with the West, but with Asian partners. Trade deals are on the table, too, and trade will increasingly be settled in local currencies, not the U.S. dollar.

It's all about the integration of Eurasia. Iran is already reportedly preparing to engage, by the start of 2020, into a comprehensive free trade agreement with the Eurasian Economic Union, and neighbor Turkey could well follow. Turkey, like Iran, is in the U.S. doghouse because it plans to deploy Russian missile defense systems, has claimed it will continue to buy Iranian oil despite the sanctions, has apparently given up Western obsession with the deposition of Assad in Syria and will likely complete a gas pipeline across Turkey from Russia. (Why would Europe bother with far more costly LNG exports from the U.S.?) And meanwhile, even one of the Persian Gulf states, Qatar, has offered a $15 billion loan to Turkey and restored better relations with Iran that includes energy collaboration in the shared South Pars gas field in the gulf, the largest on the planet.

All this can only benefit Iran eventually provided the U.S. and Saudis and Zionists realize that further military aggressions in the Mideast will only deepen their worldwide isolation. In the U.S. there is, for example, growing horror about the Saudi and UAE war on Yemen and the humanitarian crisis there with calls for the U.S. by some in the U.S. Congress to halt whatever support related to the war that the U.S. military has been rendering to the Saudis.

I know for a fact that many "average" Americans are beginning to get a honest picture of just how relatively backward and corrupted and undemocratic the Saudis are. The possible beheading this month of a lovely Shia woman and human rights activist who lived in the Qatif oasis, a Shia enclave within largely Sunni Arabia, who simply expressed some opposition to the Saudi regime, has had an impact on transforming perceptions and I can say with certainty that in reading comments by many Americans attached to news articles about the Middle East that there is a strong revulsion against the Saudis, the Zionists, the Neocons in Washington and, in general, U.S. foreign policy in the Middle East.

Iranians ought not to think most Americans with any knowledge of the Mideast do not rail against the Trump Administration. Some new war in the region sparked by the U.S. or the Zionists will mark the end of the Trump presidency and the credibility of those who have supported its foreign policies, not to mention that the U.S. would sink further into unsustainable financial debt.

Saadi's words from the 13th century are worth remembering right now

August 29, 2018

History is not going to forget the JCPOA no matter what happens to the agreement itself. Ideally, it ought to stand with continued backing by the other signatories, which means the other signatories make it worthwhile for Iran to continue faithfully respecting its terms.

Whether these other signatories can with determination continue upholding the agreement with an effective quid pro quo with Iran remains to be seen. The jury is still out on this, but there are a few positive signs popping up, particularly in Europe.

What is most riveting is that now the U.S., and I believe it is a sign of desperation and not strength, is waging some kind of economic warfare of varying kinds and degrees with almost 15 percent of the world's countries with a total population of some 2 billion people, or over 25 percent of all of the world's citizens. This is, in a word, amazing.

That the U.S. government can imagine even for a minute that this economic warfare constitutes a sound strategy to maintain its power for very long is the height of arrogance and delusional thinking. Iran seems to be at the epicenter of this economic warfare.

Also, thousands of people from scores of nations have been included in the U.S. Treasury Department list of prominent designated nationals who have been more or less blocked from the U.S. dominated global financial system, where the U.S. dollar has for decades been the reserve currency of the world, particularly since the end of World War 2.

Donald Trump has been called a narcissist, but narcissism seems evident in spades throughout the U.S. governmental and the elitist establishment, and this is quite evident in the scope of the current economic sanctions against countries and individuals. One could argue that a critical mass may have been achieved, because push back is beginning to blossom.

The U.S. has always used the "extraordinary privilege" of having the preeminent reserve currency as a weapon against geopolitical rivals, but never before has the dollar been weaponized so much against so many.

According to Mike Krieger, an American blogger and economic commentator, the apogee of the so-called American empire is already toast, aside from the continued role of the dollar in the global financial system. Krieger believes that Trump's decision to scuttle the JCPOA is the primary catalyst that is causing the rest of the world to look for alternative methods with which to conduct global business.

Germany's foreign minister, Heiko Maas, for example, has said this August that the EU would be wise to set up its own payment system that would give the EU independence from Washington's diktat. French leaders have also subscribed to the same notion of a Europe shaking off its economic vassalage to the U.S.

And some Asian leaders are expressing some of the same sentiments of less obeisance to the U.S., including South Koreans and Pakistan's new Prime Minister Imran Khan. We know what Russia is doing: dedollarizing – selling U.S. securities and buying tons of gold every month.

I am anyway drawn back to recall some distant Asian and the Middle East history in the 13th century, a horrific period in which the Mongols swept westwards from the Far East and conquered widely, destroying many Iranian cities and in particular ending the Abbasid Caliphate, established in 750 AD, and wrecking its capital at Baghdad.

One anecdote of the fall of Baghdad is that the last Abbasid Caliph, al-Mu'tasim, was rolled up inside a Persian carpet and literally kicked to death by the Mongol invaders under orders from their leader, Hulagu.

One cannot help but remark that the U.S. these days is literally trying to kick the life out of the sovereignty of other nations, including Iran's. But there is another greater personage of the 13th century, the Iranian-Persian poet from Shiraz, Saadi. For one thing, Saadi, widely traveled during his lifetime, allegedly claimed that the prime virtue was simply patience.

Of all things now, patience (and courage and perseverance) are required, as it was in the 13th century during difficult times because of the Mongols, and now because of the U.S. Or, as Winston Churchill remarked: "If you are going through Hell, keep going...."

Former Secretary General of the United Nations Ban Ki-moon visited Tehran during his career at the UN and noted that at the entrance of the UN in New York hangs a huge Persian carpet, a gift from the people of Iran. He also noted that alongside this carpet are some words of the poet Saadi that translate roughly:

> All human beings are members of one frame,
> Since all, at first, from the same essence came.
> When time afflicts a limb with pain
> The others limbs at rest cannot remain.
> If thou feel not for other's misery
> A human being is no name for thee.

No, it's not the strongly cruel who survive in the longer run

Sept 2, 2018

"The weak crumble, are slaughtered and are erased from history while the strong, for good or for ill, survive. The strong are respected, and alliances are made with the strong, and in the end peace is made with the strong."

This is a direct quote of a Twitter submission by Benjamin Netanyahu this past week. It's been copied (and condemned) by a variety of people on the Internet, and if anything has ever been written that shows the true face of the Zionist regime, this has to be it. It is fascist, and could have been written by a Nazi in Germany at the start of World War 2. "Might makes right" is apparently Netanyahu's only thought. And, it seems, the only thought of the Trump Administration Neocons, too, who are directing U.S. foreign policies and sanction activity worldwide.

One hardly knows how to respond, practically, to such an assertion, except to wonder what this dangerous man has been smoking, but it is entirely in line with Revisionist Zionism promulgated by Vladimir Jabotinsky as early as the 1920's in Palestine. It was Natanyahu's father who was for a time secretary to Jabotinsky, and thus Israel's current Prime Minister was even as a child infused with an ideology that was anything but peaceful.

You can't teach a bad man new tricks. It's awfully clear what Iran has been up against in the Mideast since the 1979 revolution, and given the U.S. refusal to balance its policies in the Mideast, matters have only gotten worse, especially under Trump.

One can read every day of new atrocities in Gaza and the West Bank such that it appears the Zionists want to literally wipe out any Palestinian identity. This is genocide. And Trump has withheld funds from UNWRA and also wants to reclassify the number of Palestinian refugees from about six million in the Mideast to 500,000, forcing millions to give up any notion of equity and justice. The hard-right Zionists are going for complete domination of the region along with the U.S., despite the fact that quite a few better thinking Jews in Israel are protesting the Likud government under Netanyahu.

The statement above is fraught with error. For one thing, few anywhere in the world, except other Zionists, respect Netanyahu. He and his country are almost universally despised. He has no real alliances to speak of except with the U.S. government and some among the Saudis and perhaps others in the UAE. Any kind of real "peace" is not made with the "strong" since there is no real strength in militarism and cruelty.

It was the humble and meek and long persecuted Christians, for example, who in the three centuries after Jesus felled the mighty Roman Empire as it had been. It was humble but determined Prophet Mohammad who eventually overcame his naysayers, the recalcitrant and initially disbelieving tribes in Arabia in the early 7th century, which led to the ascent of Islam, a religion of brotherhood and peace in concept at least like no other.

The one thing that might be said about the U.S. government and the Pentagon and the all the various groups that comprise the so-called "Deep State", even if is not much solace to emerging market countries like Iran and Turkey, or to Russia and China, and to those others in the Islamic world and Mideast who are suffering because of U.S. and Zionist actions and postures, is that they reek of complete desperation -- by doubling down on previous failures by doubling or tripling up on aggression and militancy. Perhaps these operators know they are not holding a winning hand? It's like a person in a boxing match with an adversary, but the adversary looks like the eventual winner and in desperation the loser changes the game entirely – by drawing a gun on the unarmed opponent.

It may be that Trump is the culmination of America and Netanyahu is the culmination of the Zionist state. It hardly looks that way right now, but stranger things have happened. It really does depend on countries like Iran, Russia, China and Turkey, and even Germany, finding effective ways to carry on business despite U.S. sanctions and threats from both the U.S and the Zionists. Otherwise, there will be Hell to pay for a refusal to try to stand strong in spirit and at the same time, exactly what the U.S and Israel are not in desperation – cool headed.

Overreach and arrogance are the curses of every empire
Sept 5, 2018

I have an acquaintance and occasional correspondent who was a famed U.S. Marine Corps pilot during the Vietnam War. At age 20 he began two years in Nam and logged over 800 combat missions in F-4B Phantoms and other aircraft. He won Distinguished Flying Crosses.

A few years later he got back, after a lapse working elsewhere, into aviation and began ferrying aircraft of all kinds across oceans to countries all over the world. He holds a number of aviation records and a little over three decades ago he was the second (and last) pilot to fly an aircraft under and through the legs of the Eiffel Tower in Paris.

He wrote me not long ago: "I delivered the last F-227 aircraft in November 1979 to Tehran. I was there for a week and while the natives were restless, they were really nice people. The aircraft was going to the Shah's sister. She paid for each plane in her fleet every month. But Iranians were wonderful. They just did not like what the CIA did to them in 1953.

By not responding now, the Iranians are winning. The world is not blind. The U.S. Empire is going to crumble far faster than anyone realizes. If Iran keeps standing, they will win. Iran is doing the right thing and Europe is waking up to the realization that they have a choice. They can honor their agreements like the JCPOA for mutual benefit, or they can let the neighborhood bully push them around. One day they will realize who their friend is and who is not."

This man has called wars the U.S. has gotten involved in, including Vietnam, "stupid". He is correct, of course. And even if many Iranians don't think right now that they are "winning" anything under harsh U.S. sanctions, I agree with this former Marine pilot's views.

He has a firm grasp of geopolitics, and he is a real American patriot condemning many U.S. actions in recent decades. He would advise Iran to "cool it", or stay cool. He is everything as a pilot and a real patriot dead Senator John McCain was not.

It is, in any case, hard for anyone not in Iran to know what's happening there now. Some Iranian leaders are suggesting that the current economic problems are not so much the result of U.S. sanctions, but rather in part at least the result of internal problems (that can eventually be addressed) inside Iran with economic adjustments of some sort.

This may be the case. One would hope so. But what about my pilot friend's outright assertion that the U.S. empire will "crumble" sooner rather than later? We know of no "empire" in all of human history that has not eventually "crumbled", including even Persia's vast Achaemenid Empire more than 2000 years ago. And what caused that? Over reach. The

Persians, for one thing, were defeated by the Greek city states, particularly Athens.

Currently, we are witnessing the Zionist state going hog wild against the Palestinians, apparently greenlighted by the subservient Trump Administration. Part of this aggression is Israel cheering on Trump's evisceration of funding for UNWRA, which has been supporting Palestinians with basic human necessities since 1950.

But guess what? Even some Zionist commentators in the Israeli press are now saying this is a huge mistake, because SOMEONE is going to have to continue provide millions of Palestinians with the means to survive, and the burden may well fall more on Israel going forward.

Sure, the Zionists would like to see the Palestinians disappear and have been trying to make them disappear since 1948, but if the Zionists literally make conditions even worse in the West Bank, Gaza and beyond, and the world knows now how bad conditions are, they will be fast tracked to the ICC in The Hague for crimes against humanity. And BDS is working. Just this week a music festival in Israel lost almost all its foreign performers, to cite just one example of BDS success. The Zionists are now overreaching on steroids, to their eventual downfall.

And the same might be said about the U.S., which has been in overreach mode since the Vietnam War. And quite much more since the Iraq invasion in 2003, to the point where about $7 trillion in debt back then has grown to $22 trillion since, not to mention an estimated $200 trillion by one economist's estimates in unfunded liabilities. Never before in history has any country amassed so much debt.

The ONLY reason the U.S. dollar has not become mostly worthless is because it remains the world "reserve" currency and to date most all petroleum has been priced in dollars, the so-called "Petrodollar". President Richard Nixon in the early 1970s suspended all spending discipline when he cut the U.S. dollar's ties to any gold standard. And now the world is moving away from the dollar, led by Russia, and this trend is irreversible.

But monetary issues are not necessarily the primary problem facing the U.S. Negative world public opinion is, particularly since Trump abandoned the JCPOA. Over reach is what has and will cause the "crumbling" of the U.S. "empire", and good riddance the sooner the better, even for a majority of U.S. citizens if not for the entrenched, blind denizens of Washington.

Faint stars in a blackened heaven exist

Sept 10, 2018

Trump, in fighting parlance, may be on the ropes, may be impeached sometime in the coming months, and it does appear that the Democrats may achieve a majority in the U.S. House of Representatives in the midterm elections in November. The so-called "Deep State" and the MIC (Military Industrial Complex) are now going full tilt to bring Trump down, and Trump, given the loose cannon he has been, may prove his stupidity once again and try to deflect attention from his woes by starting another war.

Iran and the U.S. 2017 - 2023

It's important to note that George Bush won the Presidency in part because he promised a "humbler" foreign policy and U.S. extraction from overseas wars, that Obama became President because he campaigned on the same note, and that Trump himself won his votes by suggesting détente with Russia and winding down U.S. aggressions overseas. All three candidates basically lied to the American people.

I still believe that Trump would LIKE to reorient the U.S. away from all the carnage, but then his hands have been tied and he has, in many respects, gone the other way by surrounding himself with Neocon advisors. About all that can be said about the latter is that maybe he made such appointments under the concept that one might best keep one friends close, but also one's enemies even closer? This, however, is probably desperate, wishful thinking. And even if it were true, that Trump was and is smarter than anyone can think right now, it is not evident yet.

The other thing, if Trump might have been thinking (wishful thinking on anyone's part) about keeping an eye on his enemies, assuming he had any "peaceful" intentions, is that he threw the Neocons, many of them Zionist Jews, the ultimate bone: absolute allegiance to the Zionist agenda, what with the withdrawal from the JCPOA, the move of the U.S. embassy from Tel Aviv to Jerusalem, the cut in funds for UNWRA, the refusal to condemn in any way the extraordinary ramp up of Zionist aggressions – slow motion genocide really – against the natives of Palestine.

This truly has been Trump's cardinal sin to date, and unfortunately, it does not look like he's going to back off in other arenas. For example, just this week, he allegedly did an about face, 180 degrees, and claimed that U.S. troops would remain in Syria until, it seems, there is some kind of regime change involving Assad's eventual ouster. Also, this past week, if anything can be more telling, he cut millions of dollars in funding for Palestinian hospitals in East Jerusalem – meaning that critical cancer drugs, for one thing, for patients there may be unavailable in future.

It has lately been argued that the slide in Trump's political fortunes might be temporarily reversed by attacking Iran, if only by deflection, since Iran's leaders, and rightly so, have not responded to Trump's appeals for "talks" with Iran's leaders. Both James Mattis and even Mike Pompeo see risks in this gambit, but this does not lessen the risk than an attack could occur and then get out of hand, particularly before the midterm elections in November.

No question Iran seems never to have been in such a bind since before the 1979 revolution, and so unnecessarily and absurdly. However, it may be that that one positive note is that things may not get worse than they are now. The entire world in groaning under the lash of U.S. aggressions: wars, trade wars, sanction, threats and more such that backlash is growing: any notion that the U.S. can avoid becoming a pariah state, as the Zionist state already is, is hogwash. And there are other positives worth noting.

For one thing, a majority of the American PEOPLE are fed up with Washington, even if effective democracy has been severely weakened in the past three decades and voices of dissent are not heard enough, much less acted upon.

Also Dr. Lawrence Kolticoff, a respected economist and professor at Boston University, has lately reiterated strongly his belief that the U.S. is financially bankrupt and that financial catastrophe is dead ahead. And the why is obvious: U.S. foreign policy and spending since the breakup of the USSR.

It was back then that the "End of History" was proclaimed by some arrogant U.S. intellectuals with the end of the USSR, as if forever ahead U.S. world dominance would always prevail. Kolticoff believes the only politician who ever brought to light the U.S. fiscal situation was Ross Perot long ago, and since then it's been more or less buried by every aspirant to and holder of public office in the U.S.

O yeah, and one more bit of positiveness, and one wishes to cite more of same, but that's coming: Paraguay, initially moving its own embassy in Israel from Tel Aviv to Jerusalem on the heels of the U.S. move, just announced it's moving back to Tel Aviv. The Netanyahu government responded as expected: it closed its embassy in Paraguay. And I really can't imagine Paraguay cares one bit.

Not an easy time at all and no thanks to the U.S.
Sept 16 2018

The world waits to see what the Syrian Arab Army and allies are going to do now that the "West" has warned it will attack Syria if there's a full scale assault on the terrorists in Idlib. I would humbly suggest surrounding Idlib with a single exit corridor for civilians and starve al Qaeda and the rest of the terrorists into submission. Syria can appeal for support on the civilian question in Idlib.

Are the terrorists going to make hostages of the civilians there? And then what do you do with the terrorists? Where do they go if they ever are crushed and leave Syria? I suggest the U.S., which has coddled the morons, invite them to DC. I can‹t imagine Erdogan or Europe wants them, even though they were literally created and funded by both the U.S. and Turkey, and the Saudis especially. Best would be they lay down their arms and if any are actually Syrians, they submit and re-integrate into Syrian society as civilians. The rest must go.

At this point the real danger is whether the "West" can admit defeat in Syria and get out and let Syria recover. I for one cannot understand why Syria is a problem for the U.S., or Iran for that matter. Is ANY independent state in the Mideast that isn't comfortable with U.S. or Zionist imperialism at risk? It seems so. The Syrians are NOT going to attack the Zionists directly except with language and have not done so since 1973 during the Yom Kippur war.

The war almost toppled the Zionists, except that the U.S. stepped in and gave Israel massive backup and refreshed military equipment. It seems the U.S. and its allies and the Zionists never had any plan for the Mideast but chaos – aimed at making "Israel" indomitable. Not Iraq or Libya or Yemen or Syria or Iran have ever really presented any danger to the U.S. or Israel, except ideologically.

There are so many threads to U.S. hostility, perhaps including a fear that the integration of Eurasia based on Chinese initiatives will dethrone the hegemony of the U.S. economically if and when Eurasia prospers, and that includes

Iran prospering, too. The U.S. refusal to accept and even integrate itself to a multipolar world does indeed risk sparking World War 3 where the primary actors would likely be Russia and China allied with its allies against the U.S.

The entire world is grappling with a situation in which the Neocon conned Washington is so determined to overthrow Assad and leave Syria in the same chaos as Iraq and Libya, for examples, that the Trump administration seems willing to risk war with arguably the best equipped nuclear armed power, Russia. Never before in recent times have irrationality and even immorality had such a grip on any government.

And it's about the maintenance of the dollar, too, at a time when in the U.S. a $1 trillion fiscal deficit has already arrived a year in advance of 2020 predictions. Indeed, the fate of the U.S. dollar is key and it has strengthened and laid waste to national currencies in Iran, Argentina, Venezuela, Turkey and in many other countries. The U.S. is burning down the world to defend the dollar, which is the source of its economic clout aside from military power.

But what kind of world, in all fairness, is it where the U.S. can buy real goods from other countries with fiat dollars and expect those dollars to be recycled in to U.S. Treasuries to support U.S. spending profligacy and debts that are so enormous the world has never seen such sums before?

Indeed, it has been argued that one of the most important events of the last century was the decoupling of the dollar from gold by Richard Nixon in 1971. Since then, the world has seen the emergence of a financial empire that has largely brought the world to its financial system. America has grabbed (or stolen) physical wealth from almost everywhere by simply printing green paper, and by creating economic colonies subservient the U.S. empire.

And any country that refuses to go along with this scheme entirely becomes an enemy of the U.S. We are seeing this clearly now in the extreme weaponization of the dollar via sanctions and other nefarious moves that are crippling the economies of other countries, including Iran's economy. This economic empire is nonetheless unsustainable.

It is unsustainable because the primary rivals of the U.S., China and Russia, are slowly working towards a multipolar paradigm which in time will dethrone the U.S. dollar as the world's reserve currency. They are, for one thing, resurrecting gold as a currency of sorts and are not of late anyway buying U.S. paper, but rather many tons of gold.

IF the U.S. does not spark a World War, which could well devastate the entire world and send it back to the Stone Age, the new paradigm of multipolarity both economically and monetarily and militarily will emerge and end, once and for all, the sickening aggressions of the U.S., especially since 9/11. It is a shift requiring extreme delicacy on the part of every nation disgusted with what the U.S. has done to harm others. So, we wait and hope for good outcomes not only in Syria, but in every other country suffering the lash of U.S. aggressions.

Change is coming, but when is the question

Sept 24, 2018

It has been claimed that when Neocon warmonger John Bolton won his appointment as Trump's National Security Advisor and showed up at the White House that Trump, in jest or not, told him he was not going to permit him to start another war. Trump was signaling his alleged refusal to allow Bolton to start a war with Iran in particular.

But the question remains: why would Trump, who arguably won election in 2016 because he seemed far less hawkish than Hillary Clinton, appoint such a person as Bolton, as well as Pompeo (the "pompous") and others such as Nikki Haley who presides at the UN as ambassador? This question is, I think, not answerable, unless Trump was determined to keep these monsters close so he could check their hawkish impulses.

But, in fact, Trump, just like Obama and even George Bush, all of whom at least claimed to desire less destructive foreign policies, betrayed many of the voters who put them in office. And the U.S. electorate is taking note of this: the upcoming midterm elections are, quite possibly, going to be a disaster for the Republicans.

Even if Trump does not attack Iran militarily, in many respects he may as well have with his application of sanctions and extreme financial leverage to try to produce Iran's submission to U.S. demands. And along with the Saudis,

Trump may have supported the terrorist attack in Ahvaz that left scores of people there dead or injured.

Washington anyway is choking on talk of American "exceptionalism" which has been trumpeted as a foundation of U.S. foreign policy and sanctions. But sanctions remain an ineffective tool because most governments subject to sanctions resist making concessions to the U.S., and this resistance has moved Washington to apply even more sanctions in the vain hope they will somehow "work". Almost no country has been immune to sanctions or threat.

This past week even China was scored and sanctioned for buying Russian military equipment, as if no country can be sovereign enough to decide for itself who its business partners will be. For the U.S. it's a losing game, if not immediately, then eventually. Countries are beginning to pull away from the U.S. financial "system" and the weaponized dollar like never before. Trade will be increasingly conducted in national currencies, not dollars in coming years.

Countries under attack with sanctions by the U.S., including Iran, can have no better example than Vladimir Putin, who has enshrined a degree of patience and forbearance like few other leaders ever have in perilous circumstances. The callous and cynical ploy by the Zionists to set up a Russian aircraft for destruction off the coast of Syria is an example of this. After the aircraft went down and took the lives of 15 Russians, the Internet was abuzz with a desire to see Putin neutralize Israel and, at the least, establish a no-fly zone over Syria to preclude further Zionist aggression on Syria.

But Putin merely concluded the incident was some sort of "accident", a glitch in the chains of command. It is debatable but had Putin retaliated by shooting down an Israeli aircraft or two, he might have started World War 3? On the other hand, his reaction was measured and sensible: but he won't forget what happened, and if there happens to be a next time, he probably will respond militarily with the full support of most countries.

One day the entire world will understand that there is not a single "war" in the Mideast that the Israelis did not start themselves directly or by pushing its poodles, the U.S. and even Saudis, to aggressive actions. The Zionist regime bears, I think, the ultimate responsibility for millions of deaths in the Middle East over the past 30 years, and wrecked U.S. standing worldwide even if, for the time being, the threat of further U.S. and Israeli aggressions at the margin more or less maintains U.S. dominance, albeit a waning one, across the Mideast and elsewhere.

The U.S. needs a political and policy housecleaning like no other country ever has in my memory, and the sooner the better, for the sake of humanity at large. But if were to occur, perhaps fomented initially by crashing financial markets, it would be difficult for an economy so dependent on the Military Industrial Complex and for "average" Americans, who must somehow discover and grasp the wisdom of radical internal change. As an observer within the U.S., more and more Americans oppose Washington and Trump.

Banality and crudeness on display in Washington

Oct 3, 2018

The latest turn in attention in the U.S. in recent days has been somewhat away from imperial pretensions and overreach, sanctions on other countries, threats of attacks on Syria (and Iran) and any other country, including even Venezuela, that fails to bow to U.S. demands, whatever they may be. Long gone are the days (as when George W. Bush launched the so-called "War on Terror" to believing citizens), when the U.S. government could claim to be spreading (militarily, which is an oxymoron) some sort of enlightened "democracy" across various flashpoints and countries, particularly in Asia.

No one, not even most Americans, believe that any longer, believing instead that what the government has been about is the maintenance of the privileges and power of an entrenched oligarchy of politicians and Wall Street elites and military brass who for too long have been catering to themselves at the expense of most everyone else in the U.S. and a crumbling U.S infrastructure.

The attention for the moment is on the excruciating wrangling in Washington and across the country over the nomination by Donald Trump of one Brett Kavanaugh, 53, a conservative judge, to the U.S Supreme Court. Several women have charged him with crude, traumatic sexual advances when he was a younger man, actions not befitting anyone who is entitled to gain a lifetime appointment to what was at least formerly considered the most august deliberative court anywhere.

And if the U.S. Senate does vote later this week, after some albeit restricted FBI probing of the charges, to install Kavanaugh to the Supreme Court, the primary concern is what this entirely banal character might do to the future autonomy of women, over half the U.S. population, to control (to use the words of one widely respected scholar and law professor of the U.S. Constitution, Garrett Epps, who happens to be the former husband of a sister of mine, "their own reproduction, their healthcare, their contraception, their legal protection at work against discrimination and harassment".

The question is, Epps writes, whether the U.S. "shall move backwards to the chimera of past American greatness… when the role of women was -- supposedly for biological reasons -- subordinate to that of men". Moreover, Professor Epps has written, this theme became obvious when Trump before the 2016 election said he would pick judges who would overturn landmark legislation that obviated punishment for women who sought abortions for an unwanted pregnancy. It is possible that this platform propelled Trump to victory in 2016 because many "Christian" evangelicals chose to ignore Trump's own perennial immorality, believing he would end any women's control over reproduction.

Indeed, Trump's "base" of evangelicals has surely informed and amplified his dangerous and obtuse foreign policies in the Middle East, especially when evangelicals claim that "Israel" will usher in the return of Jesus Christ and some sort of Apocalypse -- which would, if it ever occurred and it won't at least as they imagine, be the ruination and extinction of all of humanity, including those of Jewish faith, too. Trump and his supporters in the Republican Party, in any event, really don't care what evangelicals or anyone else literally believe regarding religion as long as this bloc of voters continue to support the current status quo of power and privilege in Washington and elsewhere.

You'd think that anyone of sincere faith, whatever their religious faith, would have long ago rejected Trump since he is a man with no morals whatsoever, and has proven it time and again since he became an adult. As for entirely banal Brett Kavanaugh, who once advised and cheered on George W. Bush during the disastrous war on Iraq, he may well become a Supreme Court justice in a few days, but for Trump and the GOP this could become a welcome disaster for them with female voters and liberals in the midterm elections on November 6th, and GOP legislators seem unconcerned about that possibility or just blind to it.

In the broadest terms, as a "empire" of sorts that is faltering and pretends otherwise, and has few real friends overseas, any extant presumption in the U.S. that rationality and wisdom prevail, and that the U.S. is a beacon of it AND an exemplary "democracy", has to be the sad joke of the century, and most Americans tremble at the growing divisions inside the U.S. that may make the country virtually ungovernable before too long. Iran, meanwhile, a storied country with thousands of years of fascinating history, whatever its current make up and government, whatever its merits and demerits (and governmental and cultural perfection has always and everywhere been a complete chimera) suffers again because the U.S. just won't let it and other nations alone to work out any internal social or political issues they may have.

However, despite the urgings of Trump's Neocon advisors and the Zionists, it remains hard to believe that as long as Iran and Iranians manage to remain intact and forbearing during this difficult period, that the U.S. will literally attack Iran militarily. That would surely be the undoing of any credibility the U.S. government still has. It was anyway refreshing to hear President Rouhani speak at the U.N.: his words were thoughtful and measured, and he wasn't even close to being laughed at by the General Assembly as Trump clearly was.

Those who are temporariily losing badly often do win

Oct 7, 2018

By the time this column is printed it's more than likely Brett Kavanaugh will have won a seat on the U.S. Supreme Court, voted in by the slight majority of GOP senators in the U.S Congress… to the dismay and consternation of most all thoughtful Americans, including (notably) many hundreds of professors at law schools across the country.

Kavanaugh will have won despite the fact that he is a proven liar, that he treated at least a few young women badly as a young man, and in interrogation before Congress he did not display the kind of temperament that one ought to expect from a future Supreme Court justice. Moreover, as a judge and government advisor in years past, his record is shabby if one considers civil rights important, if one considers checks and balances against overweening power by the President and the executive as well as business interests important.

Kavanaugh appears to be anathema to the concerns of the common man, the least powerful among the citizenry. His appointment has been so divisive that it's hard to imagine the split in the U.S. between the haves and the have nots has ever been so caustic and disappointing, suggesting that "democracy" is nearly a thing of the past.

Kavanaugh is part and parcel of Trump's "maximalist" strategy not only to enhance his own power and that of Republicans in government, but also his foreign policy strategy aimed at crushing any country, including Iran, by sanctions or war, whose policies don't cater to every imperial and fascist whim of the U.S. oligarchy. And according to Tehran-born Vali Nasr, dean of the Johns Hopkins School of Advanced International Studies in Baltimore, Trump's maximalist pressure strategies are destined to failure. Consider:

According to Dr. Nasr, the Trump administration, advised by John Bolton, appears to be pursuing a 2003 deal wherein Muammar Qaddafi gave up Libya's nuclear program entirely. We saw what happened to Libya a few years later, thanks to Obama and Clinton. Perhaps both N. Korea and Iran will consider the costs of not talking to Trump too high, but both countries will resist surrender, perhaps attempting to outlast Trump.

In the case of Iran, and this is Nasr's critical point, talking to Trump would kill the JCPOA, an agreement fully in force, faithfully adhered to by Iran and so far faithfully underscored by the other signatories to it. The only serious question is whether the other signatories can effectively devise countermeasures against U.S. economic sanctions, such as the so-called "Special Purposes Vehicle" that would permit Iran to continue to do business and reap at least enough of the benefits inherent in the JCPOA as originally conceived. In other words, more or less defanging U.S. sanctions.

Iran is not currently benefitting, except morally in the world's estimation, by staying in the JCPOA, but if the deal should be obviated entirely, it is most definitely not going to benefit Iran outside the deal and Iran would give up, or be forced to give up, its rights to any nuclear program (for peaceful purposes) which is a part of the deal. It is correct that Iran's leaders have called on the U.S. to re-join the JCPOA as a baseline before any further negotiations occur to try to modify it.

But will Trump and minions re-join the JCPOA? That's about as likely as Iran becoming the first country to colonize Mars. So, stuck as it is between a rock and the proverbial hard place for the moment, what's Iran to do?

I say nothing, or not much.

Because I believe the Trump Administration and the U.S. government, in something akin to a drug induced high on hubris and bullying almost everywhere, is losing ground (allies and respect) at exactly the same time it seems to be at the apex of its power.

It is extremely ironic, too. But this is the way the world often works, with Karma, with vengeance and with retribution against not merely individuals who far overstep the boundaries of fairness and good sense, but entire countries, too. Look at what has happened in Syria, to cite just one example. The Zionists' aircraft hid behind an unarmed Russian surveillance plane to bomb northwestern Syria last month and the Russian aircraft went down with 15 Russian lives.

Those who are temporariily losing badly …

And as a result, the Russians finally delivered what may be an effective defense against Zionist and even U.S. aggression on Syria – the S300 missile defense array. So far, there has been no further bombing of Syria by the Zionists, and the U.S. has been squealing and screaming about the Russian reaction ever since, to no avail. Putin has played his cards well, it seems.

He was long patient, some said too patient, with the attacks on Syria. Putin looks like a good model for Iran: be patient, build out alliances and good will, keep up pressure on the other signatories to the JCPOA to come up with effective countermeasures to U.S. sanctions. And meanwhile, watch the U.S. lose eventually. It will.

The GOP, in the likelihood of winning its bid to install unsuitable Brett Kavanaugh in the U.S. Supreme Court, ramming this character with no character in to the court, I predict, is going to lose bigtime, too. It may be just a matter of time, because GOP candidates up for reelection on November 6th and beyond could very well lose and hand over Congress to a Democratic Party majority. Decent Americans can deal with nearly as corrupt Democrats later, but first priority is to stuff the GOP. One step at a time, I say, to real change and reform.

The beginning of Trump's unraveling may be at hand

Oct 15, 2018

You have to wonder about the Saudis who, aside from the Zionists, are considered the number one U.S. ally in the Middle East. And the latest incarnation of Saudi Arabia's "leadership" is Muhammad bin Salman, the designated crown prince of the Kingdom, who for stupidity may know no equal at the moment.

There are many ways to assassinate anyone. Heaven knows long beleaguered Iranians know about this, who have seen a few of its nuclear energy scientists, for example, murdered in recent years, most likely by the Zionists or their paid shills. But to directly lure journalist and Saudi critic Jamal Khashoggi into a Saudi consulate in Istanbul from whence he apparently never left, except perhaps literally in pieces, has to be about the dumbest move "MBS" may have ordered to date. And we know a number of Saudi henchmen were in all likelihood dispatched from Riyadh on a Gulfstream jet to do the dirty deed. Maybe the world will never know for sure what happened to Khashoggi, that he or dismembered parts of him may never turn up, but connecting the dots could hardly be much easier to reach a plausible explanation.

Khashoggi, in any event, is widely admired as an Arab journalist, and a fearless one, who was a writer committed to finding and reporting the truth, regardless of any threat to himself in doing so. But what's most interesting now is that one might be able to conjecture the beginning of some serious changes in Western attitudes towards leading Middle East countries, namely Saudi Arabia and Iran. The Saudis have in recent years been the Mideast darlings of the Western establishment and the Trump gang. To the extent Saudi Arabia falls from favor, Iran may benefit – not that Iran literally NEEDS favor with the U.S. except to the extent that the U.S. stop meddling in Iranian affairs and trying to wreck its economy.

Trump is currently under pressure by many in the U.S. Congress to completely condemn Khashoggi's disappearance and probable murder by MBS, and even to stop selling arms to the Saudis and to disavow support for the Saudi and U.A.E. war on Yemen.

Trump's first reaction to the story coming out of Istanbul was to downplay Khashoggi and point to the lucrative arms sales to the Saudis. (You can't get more venal than that, but it's entirely within character for Trump`, who loves nothing so much as money.) And even his ignorant son, Donald Jr., who likes shooting African wildlife on "safari", has gotten into the act. He's been trying to say Khashoggi supported Islamic terrorism, pointing to a 1988 photo of Khashoggi holding a RPG with some al-Qaeda fighters in Afghanistan. Do you think young Donald realizes that in 1988 the U.S. was in full support of the mujahideen in Afghanistan and at the time al-Qaeda was not deemed a "terrorist" group but rather a group of freedom fighters trying to liberate Afghanistan from the grip of the Soviet Union? One conservative website in the U.S. has even gone so far as to claim that Khashoggi's defenders and supporters are being duped by Iranian "interests" looking to damage relations between the U.S. and Saudi Arabia. This, of course, implies that damage to relations with the Saudis does benefit Iran.

Iran and the U.S. 2017 - 2023

In any case, as sad as Khashoggi's disappearance and probable murder is, for he is or was a respected and brave journalist, there are other factors at work that may also mark the beginning of the unraveling of Trump's credibility and his Presidency, as at least with the upcoming midterm elections in early November, a shift to a Democratic Party majority at least in the U.S. House of Representatives. Consider:

The forced installation of Brett Kavanaugh by the GOP and Trump onto the U.S. Supreme Court, according to many leading law experts in the U.S., has virtually destroyed what used to be the most venerable and respected court anywhere, because now it is an unreliable, partisan court.

This month the U.S. markets for both bonds and stocks came tumbling down some. Not much, but enough to scare investors who for almost a decade have seen nothing but rising stock and bond values. Trump of late has been crowing that his economic policies gave rise to the rising market values. But he got a lot of egg on his face this past week, and tried to deflect blame onto the Federal Reserve Bank for raising interest rates And before he was elected and campaigning in 2016, Trump was claiming the U.S. markets were in a "bubble"!

There are, in fact, a number of other issues coming to the fore suggesting that Trump's glory days may end sooner or later, and that with a current "approval" rating of only about 38 percent of Americans, that number could fall dramatically in the months ahead.

As an observer, I have written time and again of the necessity for patience and forbearance, not merely by Americans disgusted with Trump, but by Iranians disgusted with the U.S., too. No question Iran looks more and more like the state Saudi Arabia may wish it could be, and don't forget Trump himself dissed the Saudis this month saying that they would not last more than two weeks without U.S. support. The Islamic Republic of Iran has lasted for decades with nothing but venom and cruelty from the U.S. That is saying quite much.

Human pigs find pleasure in fights so avoid them when possible

Oct 21, 2018

Oddly enough, but not surprisingly, I had a bit of an altercation this past week with one Josh Block on Twitter. I hurled a condemnation at a post of his, and he hurled one back at me and called me an "anti-Semite" and a bit more. To his invective, I did not respond, recalling British play writer George Bernard Shaw who wrote decades ago that tangling with pigs was bound to be unproductive and that pigs actually LIKE a fight, that fighting with them gives them pleasure.

Who is Block, or should I say "Blockhead"? Well, he is CEO and president of an organization called The Israel Project, based in Washington and Jerusalem, that is a lobbying organization providing pro-Zionist talking points to the public and to journalists aimed at giving people a "more positive public face" to Israel. Block formerly worked for several hawkish, pro-Zionist lobby groups in the U.S. including AIPAC.

Iran and the U.S. 2017 - 2023

Given headlines around the world claiming that Saudi Arabia under Muhammad bin Salman had carried out the grisly murder of journalist Jamal Khashoggi, a Saudi citizen who was writing for the Washington Post, Block was going whole hog, literally, to try to exonerate the theocratic dictatorship over the apparent murder of Khashoggi.

Block tweeted that Khashoggi was "a radical Islamic terrorist who was close to Osama bin Laden, ISIS, and Hamas who wanted to overthrow the Saudi ruling royals who oppose both Sunni terrorists, sponsored by Turkey and Qatar, as well as Iran's Shia terrorist armies and allies."

Block is about as twisted as anyone can be, so let's just make a few honest, valid points.

First of all, Khashoggi was by all accounts a Saudi patriot and as far as Arab journalists go, which could be debatable as a general matter anyway, a good one for decades. He was quite liked by colleagues at the very "establishment" and largely pro-Israel Washington Post, for one thing. His last column for the paper, printed I think after his disappearance, focused almost exclusively on his insistence that the Arab world, and especially Saudi Arabia, promote a free press, or at least a much freer one than has been witnessed in many years.

Another point must be that, even if it has not been trumpeted in the Western media, Saudi Arabia has funded "terrorists", Sunni terrorists, like no other Arab country, particularly of late in Syria, and Israel (and the U.S.) has also funded and supported terrorists with arms and money, including al-Qaeda (however it may have been renamed) as well as ISIS – all with the aim to topple Assad in Syria and other alleged "enemies" of chaos in the Mideast.

Israel has frequently sheltered ISIS and other terrorists with other organizations near the Golan, and given medical attention to those in need of it. As for the U.S., Trump and even Obama aided ISIS repeatedly in Syria – all the while falsely claiming that the U.S. was IN Syria to destroy ISIS. In fact, were it not for Iran and Russia and of course the Syrian army, ISIS would still be rampaging, and what remnants of ISIS that still remain in Syria, well, they are sheltered to some extent near U.S. troops in the east of that country.

In any event, it's a positive that some in the U.S. Congress are condemning MBS and Saudi Arabia for Khashoggi's murder, and also at least hinting about a need to cut at least some ties to the Saudis and even, possibly, withdrawing support for the Saudi-led war on Yemen.

One big obstacle is that the Saudis could threaten the so-called "Petrodollar" in retaliation and also dump further arms purchases from the U.S. But don't expect much from the Trump Administration in this respect unless pressure is augmented by world opinion. Trump has been careening back and forth between condemnation of the current Saudi leadership and trying to cast blame for the murder on some alleged "rogue" Saudi elements or individuals in an effort to exonerate MBS.

As for aggressive Jewish/Zionists lobbyists like Josh Block, their primary concern in trashing Khashoggi and lying about him and virtually suggesting that he deserved to be murdered, is all tied up with the Zionist desire for the U.S. to lead a war on Iran – which could not be started or executed without the full support and participation of Saudi Arabia.

Because, simply, it would hardly look at all good for the Israelis and the U.S. alone to launch a military attack on Iran. World condemnation would be off the charts and could well end U.S. and Zionist aggressions in future. The Khashoggi matter, if it does result in real condemnation of the Saudis and MBS by the U.S., severely disrupts those in Israel and the U.S. Neocons who have been pushing for a war on Iran.

As for MBS himself, he is not and never has been a serious social (or any other kind of) reformer. Anyone who spends a billion dollars on a yacht and a palace or something in Europe is frankly not worthy of respect on that alone. It was almost funny this week to hear New York Times columnist Tom Friedman, who was charmed by MBS and wrote glowingly about alleged "reforms" MBS was going to institute, struggling to defend himself in light of the apparent fact of the murder of a well-known Arab journalist who worked at the primary rival of the New York Times. People like Friedman and others of his ilk, apologists for Israeli criminality, should live in infamy.

SO MANY QUESTIONS, SO FEW

ANSWERS SO FAR

OCT 23, 2018

It's a bit of an imaginative stretch, if not a preposterous one, but there may be some reason to think that the murder of Jamal Khashoggi might set the stage for positive changes.

No question, for example, that there have been significant decisions made by some power brokers not to attend the so-called "Davos in the Desert" conclave in Saudi Arabia, and some of Washington's warmongers seem to be turning against Muhammad bin Salman somewhat.

Whether the outrage against the current "leader" in Arabia is fake remains to be seen, because the Saudis do have the capacity to make life difficult for the West, if not the entire world, even by cutting down marginal oil sales to fill the presumed gap that may be coming if the U.S is successful in halting the sales of Iranian oil into the markets after sanctions against Iran are ratcheted up on November 4th.

Much higher prices for oil could threaten an economic recession, particularly in the U.S., which is the sole economy at the moment that's at least claimed to be performing quite well. If the U.S were to fall in to recession, and if the equity market were to tank, Trump and the GOP would be in huge trouble politically since he's owned the markets, claiming they have performed well since he became POTU.S. because of his tax cuts (primarily benefitting the already wealthy) and deregulation moves.

The U.S. middle class continues to be eviscerated by high debt levels, stagnant wages and GOP threats to cut cherished and long-established social programs like Social Security and Medicare to staunch the coming budget deficits which are headed well over a trillion dollars annually over the next decade at least.

In fact, cutting the budget for the U.S. military, a budget which is extremely wasteful, would be by far the best course of action ahead. Consider, for example, that Russia alone, with a defense budget less than a tenth of that of the U.S. has the military capacity and armaments to lay waste to the U.S.

if, as Putin recently said at Valdai, Russia were ever directly attacked by the U.S.

At any rate, the perception is growing that MBS has gone too far too many times, that he is little but a thug, and some of his moves before the Khashoggi murder did not have U.S. approval. The blockade of Qatar was a case in point. Trump and son in law Jared Kushner and the Neocons around Trump have been trying to enhance the alliances with the Saudis and the Israelis, which allegedly languished under Obama.

Trump has enjoyed some victories. Brett Kavanaugh was confirmed for the U.S. Supreme Court. The Mueller investigations over Russian political collusion appears to have turned up almost nothing of substance. And Trump could well come out of the mid-term Congressional elections smelling like a stinking, hybrid rose whose odor is so strong, even as a rose, that it's repellent.

If the Democrats don't win a majority in the House of Representatives come November 6th, it is possible Trump on his crew of GOP aligned gangsters will have little to no opposition to do whatever they want. I reckon the question is whether Trump will be forced turn his back on MBS. It's likely, because Trump's supporters don't seem to have much affection for MBS, and anything that staunches Saudi influence in the U.S. media and over U.S. foreign policies is not a bad development.

MBS does not fact have many friends now, not even within the Saud family, since he imprisoned a number of them in the Ritz Carlton in Riyadh for a time and also stripped some of them of a portion of their assets as he consolidated his power. It's possible the Saudi regime cannot survive, but who can

So many questions, so few answers ...

replace them one has to also wonder. But here methinks are the real questions:

Might Trump at least moderate his attempts to take down Iran's Islamic Republic if he moves away from the Saudis and MBS? Was the resignation of toxic and ignorant Nikki Haley from the U.N. post somehow pushed by Trump himself, or was it because Haley realized she had compromised herself by taking liberties with her expense account and enjoying some excessive personal advantages given her position?

And what about Defense Secretary James Mattis being called by Trump a "Democrat" of sorts recently? Mattis has been supporting the U.S. presence in countries like Syria and Afghanistan. Might Trump be thinking of changing his Cabinet and augmenting his control of foreign policy away from Zionist influence and the Neocons like John Bolton? Who knows, but it's possible that when Trump catered to Neocons and Zionists he did so with some reluctance, realizing that he needed their support at a time when many GOP members in Congress did not offer him much support and considered him unfit for high office.

Consider that if the House of Representatives manages to retain a GOP majority next month, Trump's power and control of the GOP and future policies will be mightily strengthened. He may feel freer to chart an independent course, especially with respect to foreign policy. It's important to remember that when he was campaigning in 2016 he was talking about reducing U.S. military adventurism overseas, and I know for a fact that many who voted for him in opposition to bellicose Hillary Clinton did so because they were sick and tired of the U.S. bullying its way around the planet and all the insane spending on the military rather than on domestic needs.

Of course, all this may be wishful thinking on steroids by those in and outside the U.S. who strongly lament what's become of the U.S. since the invasion of Iraq in 2003, if not well before. Like the Israelis and the Saudis, the U.S. really has few friends now, even in Europe, and what country or individual can long manage, or even want to, without friends? Islam, in any event, has been sullied by the Saudis and their control of Makkah and Medina, and one heartening suggestion recently was that that both these Muslim holy cities be reconstituted as something like the Vatican for Muslims worldwide.

A General Overview of this Era of Discord
Oct 27, 2018

Yes, it is obvious. Iran and a number of other countries would be far better off today, economically and thus socially, if the U.S. was not militarily attacking or threatening to attack someone, somewhere, and especially in the Middle East. It's vital to know some facts about all this and try to analyze it and prognosticate what may or may not happen geopolitically, and the Tehran Times does as good a job of this as any newspaper I know.

As an American journo, one can say things in the Tehran Times, for example, that are not readily going to find a mainstream publisher in the U.S. One case in point was when, several years ago, I was writing paid opinion pieces in what used to be one of the top 10 newspapers in the U.S. where I worked fulltime for a while in the 1970s – the Providence

(Rhode Island) Journal. But like so many newspapers in the U.S. today, the staff at the Journal is a third of what it used to be, and the paper has shrunk in terms of pages by two thirds, too. I had written a column there about the 19th century roots of Apartheid in South Africa after a visit to that country. Apartheid was in full force until Nelson Mandela was finally released from prison on Robbins Island and became President. In that prospective column I ended with some ideas about what soon became the JCPOA, and suggested that the U.S. would do well to balance its treatment of Iran with that of Israel. This meant, of course, that uncritical support of the Zionists would have to fall by the wayside. However, the editor at the Journal refused to publish the column as if the comment about a more rational and fair Mideast foreign policy was "anti-Semitic". This editor had never been to the Mideast and knew next to nothing about it. He was also allied with the Neocons like Bill Kristol and John Bolton and many others, presuming that whatever they thought was good enough. They did not support the JCPOA. I roundly criticized this editor and cut my ties to the Providence Journal, a mainstream regional paper in New England.

Iran is not the only country threatened by the U.S. at least by sanctions and other measures aimed at preserving U.S. hegemony of some sort. Look at China, for example, also threatened. Where the U.S. has prioritized military interventions for decades, whether overt or covert, China, whose economy by some measures is now the largest in the world, has not. Trump as a campaigner in 2016 promised a very different foreign policy, one that would halt efforts to topple foreign governments, and the Chinese may have even worried about this potential change. Because if the U.S. shifted its focus to its internal problems and pursued a benign foreign policy, it might prove to be a challenge to China's rise to global power. Trump, however, did not change U.S. foreign policies. In fact, he has made them much worse. Even if this lack of change has proven to be an irritant to China and worse for smaller countries like Iran, circumstances are bound to improve. Countries like China that focus their efforts on building and not bombing, or not on wars it cannot win, and not on economic sanctions, stand to win in the longer term. The U.S has been sowing the seeds of its own destruction but China has not and nor has Iran. (China in fact has not engaged in a foreign war since 1979 when it invaded Vietnam, and Vietnam fended off the Chinese and the Chinese soon withdrew from northern Vietnam.)

There may be a lesson in the Chinese example of waiting things out for smaller but equally important nations like Iran. But waiting for what? Well, for the U.S. to fall apart eventually, and it will unless it changes course.

For one thing, a U.S economic crisis, another one that's bound to be worse than the 2008-09 experience, is probably ahead. The U.S. financial markets are beginning to telegraph that right now, and the country has rarely been so divided politically and socially. And the U.S. increasingly has fewer allies, and none of moral standing in the Middle East. "Allies" Saudi Arabia and Israel are reviled around the world. Even the U.S. dollar is at risk like never before. At some point China is going to insist, for one thing, that it won't buy Saudi oil unless payment can be made in yuan. A farewell to the Petrodollar seems inevitable, however long it takes, and China is now the largest oil user and importer.

But patiently waiting for the U.S. to implode in some substantive way must not be a merely passive exercise, but rather one where, despite the suffering and economic dislocations brought about by the U.S., Iran and other beleaguered countries seize difficult situations as opportunities to address internal issues, to promote further democratic representation and question policies that fail to address the needs and aspirations of all citizens, not just the current ruling elites. In the U.S. the elites are making a mess of things and consequences are ahead.

When in time the current burdens of outside interferences fall away, that will have happened in part because leaders have been open minded and generous. This prescription may seem trite and too general even to mention, but to the extent that Iran, to cite just one example, gathers new friends and allies relatively while sloppy, repressive dictatorships like Saudi Arabia further lose influence and clout, as with the recent murders of journalist Jamal Khashoggi and many Yemenis, the payoffs will someday be enormous. As Sun Tzu, an ancient Chinese political and military strategist and philosopher was alleged to have said: If one waits patiently by the riverside, one's enemies will eventually float by.

Ignorance is the bane of humanity

Oct 31, 2018

U.S. citizens will likely not anytime soon hear the end of the horrible tale of the gunman who last week went into a Pittsburgh, Pa., synagogue and killed 11 Jews who were worshipping there.

The gunman was a crazed white nationalist terrorist who no doubt had been listening to Trump for too long, but they don't call what he did "terror", which it is. Trump hardly appears as an anti-Semite given his overweening love affair with the Zionists, but his views generally are bound to stir up ignorant, racist whites, even neo-Nazis. It's important to note that officially nothing is labeled "terror" unless some incident happens to be done by an "Islamist", according to directives (since Trump took office) by the U.S. Department of Homeland Security.

The very name of this governmental "department" established after 9/11 reeks of pretensions of "empire": the notion that the U.S. physically is the "homeland" and everywhere else the U.S. has a presence, especially a military presence, are mere satellites – not truly sovereign nations. The concept is quite "Nazi" as with Germany under Hitler. And it is abhorrent, as is the U.S. under Trump.

I anyway posted a note to "Facebook" bewailing the fact that what the Zionists/Israelis have been doing is "terror", too, and the same for what the Saudis have been doing to Yemen. "Friends" agreed, but then I don't literally have "friends' who are ignorant about the truth. Later, I posted a response to a Twitter conversation by a bunch of Zionist American Jews where I questioned whether what happened in Pittsburgh might be related to Zionist actions in the Mideast? The response was furious and immediate: I was labeled "anti-Semitic scum."

My first response to this was: "I was working and living in a kibbutz in Israel before you were even born." (Actually, during summer 1969.) That shut them up temporarily. But then someone noted that I had been writing columns for the

Tehran Times, as stated on my Twitter page. And I got this response:

"Iran just directly funds Hizballah, takes American citizens captive, attacks its neighbors, threatens Saudi and tries to get nuclear weapons. They aren't called the Mad Mullahs for nothing. And you are on their payroll. Shame on you."

This comment revealed more abysmal ignorance and I continued responding:

"Iran is not perfect. No country is. Hizballah has protected Lebanon from repeated Israeli offensives and even occupations. It has no direct nuclear weapons program. Such a program has been a myth for many years. And Israel even takes dissident Jewish American captives sometimes. And NO, I take no salary as a writer."

"We know why Iran has been sanctioned. But Iran has not on offense attacked another country in over 200 years. It also has the second largest Jewish population in the Middle East. Jews are treated far better in Iran as a minority than Arabs of whatever religion are treated west of the Jordan River, and they are not even a minority there. Duhhh."

"It's not Iran that is the pariah nation now. The pariah nations are Israel and Saudi Arabia and even the U.S."

One response I received amid the verbal flurry was: "I don't see Israel sanctioned by the U.S. for terrorism. I see Iran…." This response to my comments above demonstrated extreme ignorance with the implication that any country the U.S. sanctions has to be doing wrong. I further followed up with a comment that American Jews ought to visit the

West Bank and Gaza and see first-hand for themselves the human rights abuses and war crimes perpetrated by the IDF. And I also stated that the Saudis were corrupt and cruel, that the Khashoggi murder was just one instance of such. And Khashoggi was a beloved Washington Post writer, etc. I added that I had been an editor for a bit for Aramco Magazine and learned to despise the Saudis, and that their variant of Islam was a "bloody joke".

At any rate, it was clear what I was dealing with: Some American Jews (and others, but not all) who had bought hook, line and sinker the Zionist and Neocon propaganda about Israel and other Mideast countries. It was interesting that after I had posted my responses to their personal attacks, they went quiet, realizing that they were dealing with someone who knew far more than they about the Mideast, and had actually spent significant time in the region, including Israel. But the key point is that the attitudes expressed by these virulent people are so deeply entrenched that it is difficult to imagine how they can ever be relieved of their ignorance, and not just about Iran. Still, one must try when given the opportunity.

For beleaguered Iranians under U.S. economic sanctions, and for people of many other nations under sanction, it remains important to realize that many, many better-informed Americans do NOT agree with U.S. government postures even if they cannot really do much about them except vote, as during the upcoming mid-term elections to Congress on November 6th. The world will see how that goes soon enough.

Meanwhile, imagine the U.S. government under Trump as the Titanic headed inexorably and generally towards an iceberg, a reckoning, and perhaps incapable of turning away before disaster strikes. No country has probably ever been so badly advised by ignorant counsel and propaganda as the U.S. this century.

Some Arabs increasingly look like abject pansies
Nov 4. 2018

An older brother, who has spent his life traveling with his wife (they are childless) and photographing and writing light travel articles, has been in Oman these past two weeks and writes me an enthused e-mail about how Sultan Qaboos is such a "leader", having recently hosted Netanyahu and even Mahmoud Abbas on visits to Oman to promote "peace" between the Palestinians and Israelis. Little does this brother really know: the Zionists have never wanted peace, just submission.

Oman is claiming that Israel should be fully "accepted" in the Mideast by other countries while the Zionist state "also bears the same obligations." (I presume this latter involves the Israelis making "peace" not solely on their own terms but on terms cognizant of the aspirations of others, too.) Bahrain's foreign minister as well as the Saudi foreign minister at the same time expressed the view that "peace talks" would help normalize diplomatic ties between Israel and the Arabs.

Why the lovefest of late between Israel and various states on the western side of the Persian Gulf? I don't understand it unless:

1. The Arabs are simply exhausted by decades of discord and enmity with Israel.

2. They see some gain, probably economic, from what amounts to almost total abandonment of the human and political rights, enshrined in international law, of millions of Palestinians at the precise time they, the Palestinians, have never been under such duress and attack in the West Bank and Gaza.

3. Arab alignment with Israel puts more pressure on Iran to conform to U.S. and Arab demands, given that Iran is feared by the Arabs. 4. They don't have guts.

One cannot anyway assume that "Israel" is not going to be around, at least not in any foreseeable future. One cannot say that "Israel" has absolutely no right to exist even if Palestine was literally stolen from the natives last century. But what "Israel"?

Who could legitimately argue with Israel if it fully democratized and gave up the "Jewish state" insistence, or alternatively gave the Palestinians an East Jerusalem capital and a viable state with the "Green Line" its border?

And also gave the Golan back to Syria. If Israel did all this, would it have to, as it claims, be so worried about Arab or Iranian hostility? No, because the hostility would vanish.

But what is most distressing right now is that these various Arab states are making friendly overtures to the Zionists at the precise moment that Israel has become a full-fledged pariah to 95 percent of humanity, and while its sole big benefactor, the U.S., is at risk of losing its monetary control of much of the world as well as it's "empire", because it is slowly bankrupting itself fiscally and morally and making enemies with its sanctions almost everywhere.

Now, for example, John Bolton and Trump are even trying to sanction Venezuela for attempting to sell some of its own gold reserves. It seems as if the concept of national sovereignty has been abolished by the U.S., including national/private property.

Sanctions don't appear to work, at least with Iran. In fact, if recent history is any guide, they have only worked when concessions have been made TO Iran, which is another way of demonstrating that some real "fairness" has been applied. (And in any case, Mike Pompeo's 12 demands of Iran are insulting and concede nothing.)

Further, Trump is going to fail to push Iran's oil exports to zero, and some waivers have already been granted to some Iranian oil importers such as India. But attempting to escalate sanctions now, even if Iran remains in the JCPOA and thus will not expand its nuclear program, is likely to witness an escalation of Iranian interests in Syria and Iraq.

Also, inasmuch as there is a crisis underway, this is a crisis the U.S. fomented unilaterally. The JCPOA was working just fine and the Trump Administration could have leveraged off that and addressed Iran with more, serious diplomacy to try to manage other issues. Guess who scuttled that approach -- the Zionists, whose idea of "peace" reflects the musings of the Roman historian Tacitus when he wrote about the Roman conquest of Britain – "making a desert and calling it peace."

This latter is something the weak-kneed Arabs seem to be forgetting as they kiss up to the Zionists and Natanyahu like a bunch of abject pansies.

The world prays for the wisdom and cool of Iranians
Nov 10, 2018

An Iranian friend, a photographer known internationally for fine documentary work, asked plaintively last week when the U.S. might stop trying to sink Iran and Iranians. I had no ready answer, but the question was painful to hear because I could also hear concern, grief and empathy for others.

No question the re-imposition of extreme sanctions is damaging, particularly for average Iranians. The Trump Administration would have the Iranian people believe it is on their side (it's not) as the administration also tries to claim Iran's government is the cause of all the troubles. (Clearly, Trump and gangsters wants chaos in Iran and the fall of the current leadership.) But claiming that the government is largely at fault is simply a lie.

Iran is historically and resource rich and has a talented population, but one currently and primarily beleaguered by U.S. sanctions and hostility from the Saudis, Israelis and Emiratis, the sole serious U.S. allies in the Middle East. Sure, things look grim currently to most Iranians like my famous Iranian photographer friend, but one might argue that the situation for the U.S. is potentially even grimmer.

THE WORLD PRAYS FOR THE WISDOM ...

There are Middle Eastern natives right here in my hometown in North Carolina who understand the situation far better than most Americans. One happens to be the elderly manager of a BP gasoline station who arrived in the U.S. from Jordan long ago. Whenever I stop by we talk and he said this week: "The U.S. is not that far away from becoming a 'Third World' country." And in some ways, he is correct even if such a judgement seems implausible.

Consider what a box the U.S. has put itself in to since the early 1970s. It's a box long in the making. Richard Nixon's decision in the early 1970s to cancel the gold standard and Washington's arrangement with the Saudis to have oil priced in dollars, which in part allowed the U.S. to finance its economy through the simple action of printing fiat currency, supported by the Petrodollar, required other countries to buy U.S. Treasury bonds.

The pricing of oil in dollars has been crucial, but the U.S. has in effect been printing waste paper (fiat dollars) and obtaining consumer goods and resources in return, a situation that has permitted the U.S. to squander many trillions of dollars on wars without suffering economic consequences so far. Yet those economic consequences are looming like never before because in many respects the U.S. is so heavily in debt now it is virtually broke – unless the fiat money printing can continue in exchange for valuable resources.

This explains why the U.S. cannot easily scale down its relationship with Riyadh, and why the Saudis have been allowed to erect such a now widely recognized corrupt, undemocratic and repressive regime and also promote jihadism, even as the murder of Jamal Khashoggi last month has provoked many, even in the U.S., to condemn the Saudis.

Iran and the U.S. 2017 - 2023

And remember, many of the 9/11 operators were Saudis, and Saudi Arabia was not sanctioned as a result of 9/11 and its longstanding statecraft of using jihadist terrorism as its primary geopolitical methodology.

It's a "box" alright that the U.S. cannot extricate itself from given the risk that extrication would likely crash the lynchpin of U.S. imperialism and economic power – the dollar. And in the background the Zionists have been wielding enormous influence in Washington as the sole other serious "ally" of the U.S. in the Mideast, and that country, too, is certainly one of the most reviled on earth for its aggressions and war crimes and human rights violations. No country has ever had such horrible "allies" in the Mideast as the U.S. now has, and it can't easily let go of either. And it's sad the U.S. did not use the JCPOA towards additional accords with Tehran.

Meanwhile, Iran has long been the prime target of U.S., Saudi and Zionist ire, especially since the revolution in 1979. The propaganda has been intense against the Islamic Republic for decades mostly because Iran has refused to cave to U.S. demands and has remained independent and has not jumped in to the toxic "box" of craven users and abusers in league with U.S. efforts to maintain its destructive Empire of Chaos.

From the U.S. and its "allies" point of view, nothing Iran has done has been met with favor, including the widely respected signing and negotiation of the JCPOA, which the U.S. rejected last May. But most of the rest of the world community has and remains in favor of Iran and is trying to maintain the JCPOA, and respects Iran for its adherence to it. Iran, in fact, has been looking far better to the world community and the U.S. propaganda against it has been looking to many increasingly like, well, bullshit.

The world prays for the wisdom …

It's a world that is growing mighty tired of U.S., Saudi and Zionist military aggressions. This is above all a delicate, slow PROCESS wherein the U.S. and its allies in the Mideast are losing their credibility, friends and respect, and above all, this process must be allowed to continue. (Foreign minister Javad Zarif has suggested Iran is willing to negotiate with the U.S. but only on a basis of U.S. respect for Iran.)

And this process could be interrupted, even reversed, by hardliners in Iran who, feeling defensive and set upon and fearful of losing their power, use threats to try to fend off the U.S. and its two Mideast allies.

Iran quite possibly will "win" this current challenge eventually provided it maintains a cool posture and continues to reach out to sympathetic countries, Muslim or not, great powers like China and Russia or not, for ways to circumvent the sanctions and maintain some balance even while Iranians suffer unfairly for a while.

And even while Iran's leaders feel threatened, and rightly so under current circumstances, they can further their cause, one must imagine, if they are also willing to address and reduce internal discord and repressions that have been so wildly announced and grossly amplified by the U.S. and allies as false "proof", relatively, of a "bad" Iranian government.

The fact remains that the Saudis and Israelis have horrific governments, far most troubled and undemocratic than Iran's. As for the U.S., it now has a relatively shallow patina of real democracy and its warmongering in recent decades will be seen for what's it has been – utterly criminal – in time.

The recent liberalized scene at Azadi is purely good, smart anodyne
Nov 17, 2018

Just to demonstrate how inaccurate and craven the U.S. mainstream media can be, one must note a late-night news broadcast this week about the further carnage in the Gaza arena. The talking head commented that the Zionists responded with massive bombing runs on Gaza because Hamas sent flying 300 or so (ineffective) "firecracker" rockets in to Israel, and now Israel may be preparing another invasion of what amounts to the largest open-air prison on earth – an amplified and defenseless Warsaw Ghetto redux.

However, the broadcaster failed to mention that exactly at the moment where some sort of ceasefire between the Israelis and the Gazans was at hand, it was the Israelis who invaded Gaza, breaking any ceasefire, with a few handpicked guerrillas (gorillas?), some dressed as women, riding in a civilian vehicle to murder a targeted group of Hamas commanders. The Zionists expected Hamas to respond, and they did, creating a pretext for a massive assault on Gaza that may be forming.

There seems no end to Israeli cruelty and subterfuge and no end to dishonest reporting about Israel in the mainstream U.S. media. But note also that probably the greatest living intellectual in the U.S., Noam Chomsky, formerly for decades at MIT and now semi-retired in Arizona, has just recently penned an article spelling out what most of the world already knows, and he is Jewish, too.

Echoing a prominent but now deceased Israeli scholar, Chomsky pulls no punches in describing what he terms "Judeo-Nazi" tendencies in the Holy Land. In short, those oppressed by the Nazis have become Nazi-like oppressors, but this really is no secret to astute observers. What's interesting is that a Jew in the U.S. of Chomsky's stature is saying it loud and clear.

Perhaps some in the U.S. Congress may eventually get around to saying something similar, but holding one's breath for that is not advised. However, it is heartening that with the midterm elections this month the Congress now has two Muslim women, for the first time ever, seated in the House of Representatives as well as a native American Indian.

In any event, with the full-on economic assault against Iran underway with sanctions, one would be a fool to misunderstand Iran's efforts to contain the damage by clamping down on any dissidents inside Iran. Iran's leaders have every right to be a bit paranoid.

(We Americans where I live especially, in the U.S. South, must imagine what it would be like to be members of an ethnic minority living in a house with one's family that has been surrounded, say, by white-robed Ku Klux Klan fanatics waving torches and burning crosses. Iran can hardly feel less set upon by the current fanatics in Washington and Tel Aviv and Riyadh.

It's just incredible, too, that many in the Trump Administration have been favoring the MEK, a known cult-like terrorist organization that formerly was designated as such by the U.S., to dominate Iran politically. This terrorist organization once tried to counter the Shah's pro-Western policies of modernization and opposition to Communism! The inanities and insanities just continue to pile up in Washington.

Consider, for example, that the New York Times just reported this month that unnamed sources have detailed how top Saudi intelligence officials allegedly conspired with the U.S. a couple of years ago to assassinate Iranian leaders, including Qassem Suleimani, in a vague plot that might have cost $2 billion with the use of private contractors like Erik Prince, the former head of Blackwater and at the time an advisor to the Trump transition team.

Whether the plot was ever actualized to any degree remains unclear, but the fact that it was ever discussed gives absolute credence to the horrific pressures Iran has faced which, one must state again, arise ultimately from Trump's slavish attention to Zionist demands.

The only good part of the New York Times' revelations is that they were reported and that they fully demonstrate two things: one, the nefarious nature of the Trump Administration and most importantly, two, the ongoing restraint and cool of Iran's leaders so far which one must presume ought to be maintained no matter what lies ahead.

Iran's Ayatollah Larijani has been correct in stating that Iran has become or is becoming a "symbol of resistance" in the entire Mideast and beyond, and that Iran's "power" has been underestimated by its foes. It is the power that resides not in the military, but rather in smart thinking and restraint that demonstrates Iran is not some bloody and stupid regime like the one the Saudis maintain.

Those in the U.S. and Arabia who hope to see Iran's economy literally collapse and usher in the fall of the Islamic Republic are going to be disappointed.

Economies don't collapse really, it has been noted, but they do shrink sometimes and Iran is facing that prospect right now with the sanctions. Iran's prospects for resisting and somehow managing economic contraction without tremendous internal upheaval (given the current round of sanctions) may be relatively good compared to previous periods of sanction stress because Iran enjoys what has been termed a "superior moral position" that is being recognized. Why?

Because Iran truly is facing an unpopular U.S. administration this time around and the European Union allegedly is attempting to set up a payment system that could permit Iran to continue at least some normative business as usual.

The latter can't come soon enough. And kudos to Iran's leaders for permitting hundreds of women to attend a football match in Azadi Stadium last week and enjoy a splendid and even musical halftime respite from the justified gloom in Tehran. More of that social liberation is definitely in Iran's longer-term interests.

U.S. POLICY ERRORS MOUNT WITH TRUMP'S BANALITIES AND DELUSIONS

Nov 25, 2018

It is aggravating to see Donald Trump and minions squirm and contort themselves about the misdeeds of Muhammad bin Salman, otherwise known as MBS. Might I suggest the real meaning of "MBS", and apply it to Trump and minions, too? Is not M-ighty B-ull S-hitter better? Yes, I think it is much better.

It has been nearly two months since Washington Post columnist Jamal Khashoggi was suffocated and chopped and sawed in to pieces and then possibly dissolved in acid in or near the Saudi consulate building in Istanbul. Nobody or parts of one have so far been discovered. All along the way, the Saudis came up with one story, then another, then another. Finally, the Saudis admitted to the murder and MBS shrugged it off as the action of a rogue group of actors comprising a "hit" team close to him or whatever you want to call the current Saudi government. (The entire enterprise called "Saudi Arabia" looks rogue to me, a monster with far too much in the way of oil and gas, sold for the wrong things and the wrong reasons and making the wrong people wealthy.) But almost as bad has been Trump's response so far.

Trump and gang have paid the usual knee-jerk lip service to the crime itself. Yes, it was "horrific or ugly or stupid" or whatever negative adjective that comes to mind, even to the puny mind of Donald Trump. But it's all okay, Trump and gang seem to be saying, too, there's no DIRECT proof tying the murder to MBS (even though it's a virtual certainty to anyone with a gram of brains that MBS gave the order to kill Khashoggi and was even informed when it was underway.) So Trump is apparently of the belief that given a few more weeks, Khashoggi and the murder will have been forgotten because, well, the Middle East is a "difficult" region anyway you cut it (forgive the pun), and any disruption of Saudi-U.S. relations is a no-no, and underneath festers billions of dollars and potential profits that would be at risk if, say, the Saudis and MBS were "sanctioned" or diplomatic relations were diminished to any degree.

The whitewash and MBS (and Trump himself) stink like rats. The thing is, if you do smell a rat, there's one close by. In fact, it's likely you will find an entire pack of them and they are called "Neocons" and "Zionists". The abrogation of the JCPOA and the re-imposition of draconian sanctions on Iran is precisely what rats do if readers can forgive vitriol here. And as an American, my olfactory senses are also shared by many others inside the U.S. There are a couple dimension to all this mess that must be noted:

First, there is definitely something quite sociopathic about many who are in positions of "leadership" in the U.S., and in Israel, too, which has more or less dictated U.S. Mideast policies for decades. The great American Catholic monk and writer Thomas Merton, who died during the Vietnam War on a trip round Asia, once said about the Nazi war criminal Adolf Eichmann who was captured in South America and brought to trial and execution in Israel for his role in the so-called "Holocaust" after the war, that psychiatrists who examined Eichmann pronounced him perfectly sane. In many respects he was because if Eichmann had also been a psychotic as well as a sociopath, his cruelty might have been easier to understand.

Merton wrote that the alleged banality and sanity of Eichmann was "disturbing" because normal people equate sanity "with a sense of justice, with humaneness, with prudence, with the capacity to understand and love other people. We rely on the sane people of the world to preserve it from barbarism, madness, destruction. And now it begins to dawn on us that it is precisely the sane ones who are the most dangerous…. The whole concept of sanity in a society where spiritual values have lost their meaning is itself meaningless."

Secondly, one can readily posit that ANY country that puts itself and profits and power and the enhancements of a narrow leadership at the top of its priorities is, in fact, a "meaningless" society and one that has already descended into chaos to one degree or another. The random shootings and murders by disaffected people of innocents in the U.S., which seems to occur almost weekly now, is just one example of social and political decline. The longstanding inattention to the health, education system and even the U.S infrastructure is obvious, while trillions are poured into the military and into senseless wars. There is now a thinness and desperation in U.S. society and America is NOT or no longer in fact the "richest" country in the world.

The real wealth, actually the social wealth of any society, is measured by the quality of its commonly lived environment. There is a reason why the U.S, for all its supposed "wealth", now looks and feels brittle. And even abject poverty, individual and social, which exists inside the U.S. today, is not an accident. It's all about the allocation, or misallocation, of resources. And that's exactly what the U.S. is dealing with now, and it's not a pretty sight as the country careens towards market dislocations and a possible economic recession of such proportions that it may well be a game changer.

Mention of such facts and ideas may seem to many extreme, even wrongheaded, but actually such mentions comprise warnings of a sort to any country or society where power, as in the U.S. currently, is exalted and where narrow-minded "leaders" like Trump and many others in Washington cling selfishly to their privileges to the detriment of the majority of citizens. The true "wealth" of any country, including Iran's, is not found in its natural resources, for example, but in the wisdom of its governance to serve others, even in hard times, no matter what.

One must fear for any country or society that has drifted, like the U.S., towards what is dangerously meaningless, to cite Thomas Merton. This is something that has completely eluded Trump, who has been claiming the U.S. has never been better off and that he has been the best of all possible Presidents in recent decades. His lies are enormous, his postures ridiculous, and ought to stand as a general warning to governments anywhere, including Islamic governments, to continue expressing and stressing spiritual values above all others.

Bold counter moves even if naïve are worth examination at least
Nov 28, 2018

President Rouhani and other leaders in Iran have lately been appealing for unity among all Muslims to counter the threats posed by the Israelis and the U.S. and the Saudis to sow yet more chaos in the Middle East. No one can argue against the idea of such unity, but aside from a few discrete periods in Islamic history the effective unity of the "ummah" has been and seems to remain a chimera, a least when viewed from any purely political angle.

In the lands where Islam as a religion has expanded and dominated since the Ummayad and later the Abbasid caliphates, even in periods when the "West" was not meddling and forcing its imperialistic pretensions, as especially in the past century when the last serious Muslim "empire", the Ottoman one, dissolved, Islamic polity has rarely been unified as an entire, powerful bloc.

The Middle East and beyond to the Far East has been too ethnically and politically diverse to realize the grand ideal of true Islamic unity at least as regards the kind of unity that could not be disrupted and split politically by internal factions and frictions and the impositions of Western imperialism.

Rouhani has recently claimed that the U.S. is "more isolated than ever" over its multitude of sanctions and not just on Iran and that the sole answer to it all must be Muslim solidarity, and that includes solidarity with the Saudis who he says are perceived by Iranians as "brothers" whom Iran is ready to help defend against "terrorism, aggressors, and superpowers".

It certainly has not escaped President Rouhani, and should not escape anyone, that the Trump Administration looks primarily like an extortion racket. For example, the price tag for Trump not punishing the Saudis and specifically

Muhammad bin Salman, the idiot "prince", for what appears to be a direct order to murder Jamal Khashoggi back in early October, is an expenditure eventually by the Saudis of $450 billion in additional purchases of U.S. goods, particularly arms, to enrich the coffers of the U.S. Military Industrial Complex (and Trump's domestic standing) which has become a big but bad part of the entire U.S economy – exactly what President Eisenhower warned against in 1961.

President Rouhani apparently, and rightly so, considers this extortionist demand by Trump little more than a "humiliation" and not just of the Saudis, but of Muslims generally. He cited a cynical statement by Trump a couple years ago that Saudi Arabia was a "milk cow" for U.S. interests. Rouhani is exactly correct in his attempt to point out to the ignorant Saudis that they have also been played by the U.S. as well as by the Israelis, who seem to be directing U.S. foreign policy like never before in the Middle East.

But this is all destined to eventual failure, because just as the U.S. grows more isolated worldwide, so also does Arabia under the Saudis. The utter absence of a moral compass in the U.S. under Trump, in Israel under the Likud maniacs, and in Saudi Arabia under MBS, reminds one of the words of Martin Luther King during the Civil Rights struggle in the U.S. who said that while the arc of history is long, it bends (ultimately) towards "justice". Maybe the arc of history does not bend towards complete and full "justice", but justice does present itself to some extent at least in time as history has proven.

But so much remains unclear. Dealing with this is tortuous. Will Iran be able to suffer through this sanction period and maintain some level of acceptable internal unity and stability? Will Europe and China and Russia manage to erect alternative economic mechanisms to dilute the effect of sanctions and not just those burdening Iran? Will the U.S. economy enter another recession soon and expose Trump's wild claims of "success" as President as falsehoods, which they are?

Will even the expanding Boycott, Divestment and Sanctions movement against the Zionists eventually force Israel towards real democracy and the dismantling of "apartheid" in somewhat the same manner that abhorrence of South Africa's apartheid led to its dissolution there? These and many other questions remain to be answered and answers are eagerly awaited.

In any event, Trump and those who are advising him on Mideast policy, are certainly insane. If, for example, the aims of the Trumpists are in fact a change of government in Iran and submission to U.S. demands, why in the Hell are they championing a known terrorist cult, the MEK? Do they really believe, or can they believe, that the MEK would ever be an acceptable alternative to Iranians? This alone spells out what Trump and his Zionist pals really seem to want: disorder and chaos, not eventual harmony among nations.

And one must wonder what Iran might do going forward to best counter and further expose the U.S. IF U.S actions and postures are as claimed based on concerns about international or just national "security", what if, say, Iran's leaders came right out and stated, backing up President Rouhani's gestures of goodwill to Muslim "brothers", that its policies have been and will remain entirely defensive in character. Additionally, with acceptable quid pro quos (such as lifting sanctions and that just for starters), Iran might reduce its presence in Syria and Iraq and even its support of Hizballah and as well reduce its defensive efforts with rocketry (as it did with the JCPOA with regard to nuclear technology).

No question any such bold suggestions or moves would be starkly courageous and perhaps even dangerous to Iran, but it seems a certainty that the U.S., Zionists and Saudis and others would have to respond positively – or else become so further "isolated" as to lose ALL credibility and respect worldwide. Yes, obviously, ideas such as these may be quite naïve and preposterous, but at the margin, they may be worth study.

The loss of the American empire

is baked in the cake

Dec 5, 2019

So much going on round the world of note, and too few remarking at attempts to torture or waterboard free speech in the U.S., except this time if the subject literally drowns or dies, which journalist Jamal Khashoggi did in his own blood, no problem – that may be the intent anyway, to eliminate all dissenting voices that are, to one degree or another and maybe too loud about it, appalled by various rampant, overextended "isms": Zionism, Neo-liberalism, run amok Capitalism, Communism, Nationalism, Nazism, Wahhabism, Americanism, and others.

But clearly the most egregious of them all, as perhaps has been the case since the beginning of recorded time, is "stupidism", the fatal ailment of too much of homo sapiens particularly when now we read about climate change, which may be the most dangerous development of all, which allegedly has gone past the point where it might be reversed. It's all rather frightening and in the case of Iran, too, when one considers limited water resources and a population which has soared in the past century. The remarkable "Qanats" worked well for centuries, but going forward? But that's another subject.

One must wonder that if everyone arose each morning, sat on their edge of whatever space comprised their bed, and asked themselves one question, it does seem anyway that the human world might be immediately improved. That question would be: Can I be aware enough today to evaluate and react properly and wisely and honestly to whatever I must face?" But regarding press freedom, or simply the telling of truths by a few enlightened reporters, it remains remarkable that some reporters in Israel get to tell dissenting truths more than American observers without gross punishment. Gideon Levy, who writes for Ha-eretz, is a case in point.

Levy has done two things for years: he has slammed a cowardly American mainstream media in which the natives of the Holy Land can only be villainized, and he has pointed to the gross misuse of the charge of "anti-Semitism". The recent firing by CNN of Marc Lamont Hill, a Black American writer and university academic who has called for the freedom of Palestinians in a speech at a U.N. conference, Levy has also condemned. An Israeli newspaper gets to publish this condemnation by Levy, but not American media outlets. And Iran, too, had long been vilified for supporting justice in Palestine, or at least some kind of equality for half the beleaguered population west of the Jordan River.

The utter corruption over the issue of not merely relief for Palestinians but over a host of other issues is telling. For example, a recent bill circulating in the U.S Congress to halt U.S. military and other support for the Saudi and Emirates war on Yemen was condemned by a couple score of U.S. senators who happened to rake in many thousands of dollars paid by lobbyists for Saudi Arabia. And all the lies, too!

One whopper of late is that Iran's alleged testing of its latest defensive missile technology was claimed to be a direct violation of the original terms of the still alive but nearly moribund JCPOA deal, but it was not such. Yes, U.N. Security Council Resolution 2231 does "call upon" Iran not to conduct missile tests, and for all U.N. member states to try to refrain from actions that harm JCPOA commitments, but if Iran is in direct violation of anything, as Mike Pompeo claimed, so is the U.S. under Trump who completely canned U.S. participation in the JCPOA.

Iran has anyway long maintained that its missiles have never been designed to carry nuclear weapons, and given Iran's reliable and strict adherence to the JCPOA to date, only a fool would not believe Iran. Is not Iran, or ANY country for that matter, not allowed to develop defensive deterrents in such a hostile environment? The Trump Administration and the Zionists and Saudis have been all about a desperate search for any pretext to attack Iran further, boasting recently of an extant "military option". Iran must not provide a pretext because the U.S., despite its economic and military clout, is losing the battle for hearts and minds worldwide.

Perhaps the key to understanding what is likely to happen in future is a recognition of the fact that the U.S. "empire" of hegemonic pretensions cannot be maintained given its dependence on the strength of the U.S economy. Even Neocon John Bolton is aware of this given a recent statement of concern about "national security" – which would not really be threatened by a debt crisis, but an eviscerated dollar and any loss as the primary "reserve currency" would likely limit what the U.S. could do globally. This is what Neocon Bolton apparently fears the most. Real "national security" is NOT a valid concern for the U.S. because it is, quite simply, defense of the geographical U.S and its borders.

But make no mistake. A U.S. debt crisis is a certainty in coming years. Maybe not in the next two or so years, but eventually, because the U.S. government is literally addicted to profligacy and the careers and livelihoods of too many of the political oligarchy are dependent on it. The vast majority of the population would be in open revolt, say, if the causes of rampant debt creation, aside from overseas military activity and empire sustenance, such as Medicare and Social Security entitlements, were diminished substantially. And if they were, there would be immediate demands for the elimination of a huge chunk of misnamed military "defense" outlays.

It has been suggested, for one thing, that the reason Vladimir Putin has seemed wary about taking action against the lies and provocations by the U.S. against Russia is because he probably sees an implosion of U.S. financial markets ahead, which would of course curtail America's capacity to start additional wars and sow more mayhem internationally. The inevitability of a collapse under more debt than has ever been accumulated by any country in all of human history is precisely what leaders in Iran must await patiently to finally witness relief from U.S sanctions and hubris.

What dooms nations can be surprising, and it resides internally

Dec 14, 2018

One can believe without fear of realistic opposition that people in general are much the same everywhere. Sure, cultures vary, religions and social systems vary, but the fundamental aspects and challenges and even joys of human life remain constant. This is no great epiphany, just simply the result of exposure. That said, feel-good narratives are all over the U.S. media, but most all of it is propaganda to give the largely unexposed public the impression that all is well. It isn't.

Of late one feel-good narrative has focused on George H.W. Bush, who died. You would think this former one-term President was some kind of Christian saint, or maybe a man of al-Ghazzali's wisdom and stature in the Muslim world. No way. Bush was in fact the epitome of a White Anglo-Saxon Protestant butcher masquerading as some sort of "man of peace" when he was President, and before in other governmental positions.

He actually was responsible for the butchering of hundreds of thousands of human beings. One notable incident occurred when he butchered many thousands of Iraqi soldiers who were in hasty retreat from Kuwait during the first Gulf War. This was unnecessary carnage. The war had already been won, and anyway it had originally gathered steam because of a false report that Iraqi soldiers were murdering babies in incubators in Kuwaiti hospitals.

Anyway, George H.W. Bush had a fancy funeral in Washington. At the official funeral ceremony his eldest son, George W, Bush spoke. You know, the President who ginned up the so-called "War on Terror" and invaded several countries, most notably Iraq. He is reported to have butchered maybe a couple million Middle Eastern people, most of them Muslims. Like father, you might say, like son.

Now, it has become accepted wisdom, even in the U.S., that the Iraq War was a "mistake" (for a number of obvious reasons only sub-cretins could miss.). Since Bush junior was responsible for this war, inasmuch as he was overwhelmed by bad Neocon and Zionist advice, he has not been particularly popular since he left office. In fact, he has often been ridiculed as a horrible President, and as well widely considered Not Very Bright (NVB).

But lo and behold, at his Dad's funeral service, he kind of redeemed himself according to reports as a man of substance and even as a President of substance, even though there was no evidence to support such a reassessment – except, allegedly, for the fact that when he was delivering his eulogy for his father at the funeral service, he choked and cried like a baby. Imagine! History gets revised in mainstream media reports because George W. Bush wept at his father's funeral, because he showed some emotion publicly.

The problems with and in the U.S. have become too deep and they've been around too long, and past errors continue to be compounded by further errors. For example, we just learned that oversight (or fraud) by the Pentagon has resulted in Saudi and U.A.E. warplanes waging war on Yemen while being refueled in midair by U.S. military tanker aircraft for free – or rather on the U.S. taxpayer's dime.

Who knows if this was intentional, but the Pentagon has also pooh-poohed a halt to funding for the war on Yemen because, and this is a quote, "it would send the wrong message". I wonder what that message might be that is "wrong"? That halting mass killings is "wrong"?

And this week we got to hear from General Joseph Dunford, the Chairman of the Joint Chiefs of Staff in the U.S., who said that the U.S. military will stay in Afghanistan because if it pulled out it would risk "another 9/11" in the U.S. Frankly, it's just the opposite: Usama bin Laden's primary complaint was the presence of the U.S. military in Arabia! But these errors of judgment or fraud and more by past and current U.S. "leaders", bad as they are, are minor compared to, arguably, the greatest error of all:

The ability to put one's self in the shoes of other humans and therefore understand why they may have a grievance, rather than assuming they are simply not human or somehow of a sub-species. Let's be clear: this incapacity is ultimately the death of nations or governments or regimes.

The two most prominent countries which are currently failing are the U.S. and Israel. In Israel, we hear from Gideon Levy, that country's finest journalist, who says that the far-right Zionists and even a majority of Israelis are completely "at peace" with the Occupation in Palestine. Why is that? Because, Levy says, most Israelis really believe that they are Allah's "chosen" people. That and the Holocaust have given

Jews to imagine they have the "right" to do ANYTHING they want anywhere they want.

They simply do not care at all about Palestinians and many others, who are considered sub-human, just as the Jews allegedly were by the Nazis. In somewhat the same vein, people like the Bushes and General Dunford and many other "leaders" don't give a damn about the suffering the U.S. military and U.S .policies have caused worldwide for decades. Why? Because people of different cultures and governments, especially if they don't succumb to U.S. imperialism or hegemonic demands, are considered lesser human beings, if not sub-humans.

General Dunford is worried about another 9/11 which dropped three tall buildings in New York with some peripheral damage and killed 3,000 plus people … when the U.S. has laid waste to vast portions of entire countries and killed millions since the end of World War 2? The attack on Fallujah alone in Iraq during the Iraq War leveled thousands of buildings and killed tens of thousands of civilian residents. Is it not clear what I am driving at? Here it is:

Countries with leaders that do what the U.S. and Israelis have been doing, to cite just two nations and there are several others, are literally doomed. They may not be doomed this year or even next or even in five years, but doom remains inevitable. They are doomed sub specie aeternitatis, to use a Latin phrase, "under the gaze of eternity". They are doomed from the standpoint of what is universally and eternally true.

For example, one truism is that people are much the same everywhere and share the same characteristics, good and bad. And the action by one group or nation against another, as if this is not true, as if one group obviously human is considered sub-human, this is deadly to the group or nation or leaders with such beliefs on offense. History shows this clearly. And one other truism is that it is very difficult, but definitely possible, to be a wise leader, and I hope Iran's leaders are. Bush junior would have been far better weeping in sorrow for his own and his father's miserable Presidencies, too.

At bottom, what ails the U.S.

looks like mental illness

Dec 21, 2018

Frequently, if a person in America has friends in Iran, one must address those friends with empathy when they write directly or on social media about their dismay and even fear of U.S. policies and actions in the Middle East. It hardly warrants repeating what the dismay consists of and why it exists because almost everyone knows already. It's been obvious for years, especially after Bush invaded Iraq.

One response that ought to provide some balm, if not real relief, for Iranians is the fact that while Iran has been the prime focus of U.S. hostility under Trump (so far in Iran's case the hostilities have been mostly economic) is that it seems NO country, not even European ones that want to continue trade with Iran and some other countries, and augment trade with Russia, have escaped threats of sanctions or some other kind of attack by the U.S. The U.S. is throwing "sanctions" around like confetti at a wedding. An estimated 30 percent of the world's population is operating under some kind of harmful U.S. sanction.

No country but a few exceptionally unpleasant exceptions such as Israel and Saudi Arabia have managed to evade the ire of the U.S. government as it is currently composed. This almost beggars belief, that this could be. But it also suggests that no Iranian or Russian or citizen of any other country disapproved of by the U.S. government should imagine that this ire necessarily rests upon any fault of theirs or of their own government. Anyone knows that there is no "perfect" government anywhere, but the primary U.S. complaint of sanctioned countries is simply, and incredibly, that they won't be U.S. subjects or pawns, as Iran was from 1953 to 1979 under the ridiculous, almost buffoonish Pahlavi "Shah".

The fact is that the U.S. is a sick country or the majority of its "leaders" are sick and have managed to influence too many Americans, or the government has not yet literally repelled or disgusted enough Americans to foment some kind of revolution. But this is interesting because if one reads social media and reactions to various news reports about any sort of conflict with countries outside the U.S., it is those countries like Iran and Russia, and leaders like Vladimir Putin, who often seem to be more respected and believed than American "leaders" despite media propaganda to the contrary.

Anyway, one can say that the U.S. is a "sick" country because either its "leaders" are especially obtuse and ignorant and know no better, or it is "sick" in the exact same manner that individuals can be "sick" with an intractable mental illness that makes them virtually impossible to deal with, frightful and possibly dangerous to others.

At bottom, what ails the U.S. ...

For example, a friend was once under attack by a family member of his, and this person could have gone to prison for the unwarranted charges. He consulted an attorney for help and was asked to describe the threatening relative. He so described and the attorney asked him to pull a nearby book from his office shelf. The book was titled "The Diagnostic and Statistical Manual of Mental Disorders", an internationally recognized and compiled tome of various mental ailments and their descriptions. The attorney opened the book immediately and found the page he wanted and showing it to his client, asking: "Is this the person and disorder you described?" It was, exactly. Thus, it was suddenly clear to client and attorney just what they were going to have to deal with – a severe mental illness.

Now it's debatable whether entire countries like individuals can be infected with some dominating mental illness, but one can imagine so leafing through history and reading about insane "leaders". So, what is the U.S. illness? It's hard to say exactly, but extreme, Grandiose Narcissism might be the best description. The next question: how does one deal with a Narcissistic aggressor who derives pleasure from the suffering of others? Perhaps by not acting ruffled, by remaining self-assured and confident. (Leaders like Zarif have shown these traits.) And perhaps one should suggest that not being threatening back may win the moral high ground.

Most would agree that Donald Trump is an immoral man and "leader". He is grotesquely immoral and without real substance as a human being. So are many of the people he has chosen for his administration, particularly people like John Bolton and Mike Pompeo. The supreme irony, or the ultimate absurdity, is that these people and the bulk of their fans amid the general U.S. public like to think of themselves as good "Christians" – "People of the Book" to Muslims – Ahl al_Kitaab -- when in fact they are irresponsible losers and imposters who have latched on to evangelism and magical thinking that absolves them from ever taking responsibility for the outcomes of U.S. policies. And to make matters worse, Trump and minions don't even care about these losers except to extract support from them. But they don't know this. They are deluded.

In any case, the U.S. financial markets are beginning to unravel. Trump claimed his policies in September had resulted in record equity market prices and a relatively strong economy. Now, he is looking like a fool and is literally pleading with the U.S. Federal Reserve Bank not to raise interest rates this week by 25 basis points. Also, U.S. debt and fiscal deficits continue to explode higher. It's just a matter of time before Trump and his mentally deranged minions are vanquished, and the only worrying question is what more damage to other countries they and the apartheid loving Israelis and corrupted, bloody, medieval Saudis will do before they are gone.

U.S. may be bumping up against the limit of its "empire" schemes
Dec 23, 2018

Ray Dalio, head of Bridgewater, the largest and one of the most most successful hedge funds in the U.S., and no fool when it comes to finance and economic matters, has warned that because of the expansion of debt both personal and governmental the country might be facing sooner or later an inflationary debt crisis that could see the value of the dollar decline by 30 percent or more.

This is an ominous warning, and from the standpoint of geopolitics, if a crisis ever occurs, it will have immense ramifications for geopolitics – especially on the U.S. capacity to project military power and even apply odious sanctions on other countries like Iran.

Triple-digit inflation has taken hold in countries across the globe by storm in 2018. Argentina, Iran, Turkey, Sudan, Zimbabwe and Venezuela and others have all suffered economic and financial blows this year, and in the U.S. virtually every market – real estate, stocks and bonds -- has declined except for the cash dollar.

On top of this, Donald Trump has done something this month no one predicted – announced a withdrawal of some 2000 troops from Syria, which marks a concession, if it happens, that the U.S. lost its war with its allied and various terrorist groups on Syria and the Assad government. It should be noted that Trump probably won the Presidential election in 2016 because he claimed to want to pull the U.S. out of military engagements in the Middle East, and seemed to recognize that the war in Afghanistan, the longest by far in U.S. history, was accomplishing nothing and could not be "won".

Trump has also announced plans to halve the number of U.S. soldiers in Afghanistan. In announcing the withdrawal from Syria, he also claimed the U.S. had defeated ISIS and therefore implying that the U.S. had no reason to linger in Syria – even though everyone knows that the U.S. (and Israel's) aim in Syria was to destroy the Assad government and leave Syria in chaos and ruin -- something that was almost accomplished were it not for the assistance Russia and Iran and even Hizballah rendered to the Syria people.

ISIS was actually served by the U.S. at critical moments in the conflict. Trump was never going to say the U.S. was defeated or even that it had not been aiding ISIS from time to time, but this is not important. Let him falsely claim the U.S. "won" something in Syria when in fact the U.S. squandered many billions and maybe more than a trillion dollars in Syria.

The only discouraging aspects of Trump's moves are that the Neocon and Neoliberal denizens of the U.S. Congress and government, especially the corrupt Democratic Party opposition, are angry about the withdrawal and will use it to make Trump look foolish.

Trump's "Defense" secretary, "Mad Dog" general James Mattis, also known as a "Chihauhua" if he were literally a "dog", resigned in a huff of opposition, too. Hilary Clinton is also screaming about the Trump decision as some sort of "victory" for Vladimir Putin, when it's really a victory for the entire world.

How these sudden moves play out, and who might replace Mattis, is anyone's guess. But the Trump-Zionist plan to topple Iran's government or go to war on Iran will be less viable or possible with the withdrawal of U.S. troops from Syria. Syria is, after all, an ally of Iran and owes it as much support as it can give, even if it's just moral.

Erdogan, meanwhile, has allegedly said Turkey will do whatever it can to reduce the effects of U.S. sanctions on Iran, and some of the Arab states are warming a bit to Syria and Assad and seem to be preparing to establish diplomatic relations once again. And as well, Muhammad Bin Salman remains in the U.S. Congressional "doghouse" by and large with even some of the most hawkish Congressional members like Sen. Lindsey Graham calling for action against MBS.

But here's the real question: at the far margin, given what Trump has stated this month regarding Syria and Afghanistan, and the message he successfully campaigned on in 2016, is it even slightly possible that he's having second thoughts about his Mideast policies to date so far? And with the stock market collapse and signs of weakening economic activity worldwide, is it possible that Trump sees, or is beginning to see, that the U.S. is way too far extended in every respect overseas and must address growing problems internally in the U.S., even if it may cost him popularity with the warhawks and imperialistic extremists in both parties, and also with Netanyahu, who has vowed to step up action against Iranian assets in Syria even though the Zionists risk facing a solidified and coordinated air defense system run by Syrians and the Russians? My bet, even though it is tentative, is that the U.S. may soon be bumping up hard against the limits of its "empire" schemes, which will be a relief for practically the entire world.

Trump may have begun a serious turn for the better in the Middle East
Dec 29, 2018

Iran and the U.S. 2017 - 2023

Rarely does a U.S. President show common sense and a recognition of what is obvious. Donald Trump is indeed having some second thoughts about U.S. foreign policy, as suggested in a recent column, and it is extremely welcome even if hopes for change prove erroneous. He told some top brass in the military that: "We are spread out all over the world. We are in countries most people have not even heard about. Frankly, it's ridiculous. You can't have any more time. You've had enough time," Trump stated.

One may ask, "enough time" for what? That's a good question that can't be easily answered. But the answer logically goes something like this: "Enough time" to have literally the entire world, or ALL the natives wherever the U.S. military is, quaking in their boots or shoes or sandals or bare feet or whatever in abject submission to the U.S. as if no one else exists except U.S. military personnel, or no one else with even a scintilla of an independent idea or an aversion to having U.S. soldiers on their soil.

This is the heart of the idea behind U.S. imperialism – that there can be NO opposition of substance at all in any particular country, which is an extreme absurdity. In fact, this absurdity has been used as a ploy or trick or device to ensure that U.S. soldiers never have to leave some foreign location or base or whatever or never can leave because, and this links to the second absurd fallacy: that as long as opposition to the U.S. remains, the U.S. cannot pull out because a pullout might expose the physical U.S. to another 9/11 sized "terrorist" event on U.S. soil.

It's obvious, too, that enough American voters have bought into this bullcrap such that the same Neocon-ish characters get sent back again and again to Congress or a White House staff to maintain the same old tired policies that have virtually bankrupted the U.S. And worse.

The sad part is simply that aside from all the sheer damage the U.S. has done overseas to make life difficult for millions of people, the U.S. is now considered the most bellicose country on the planet – in a line, no friend to humanity at large. Many travelers know this now, which is one reason why when someone overseas asks "where from", an answer can feel embarrassing. Many Americans simply say "Canada" provided they are not obliged to show their passports. It's almost as bad and unsettling as having an Israeli or Zionist stamp of any kind in one's travel documents.

No one can say, by claiming what he has recently, that Trump is some kind of genius. But he does show some common sense even while his Mideast policies have been and remain radically awry and dangerous. And make no mistake, Trump is beginning to bow to reality and that reality is simple enough: the U.S. with all the fiat dollars and all the debt it has churned out or created for decades is broke even if it gets away with pretending otherwise for a while longer. The U.S. as world policeman? It's about over, and the Muslim world may rejoice ultimately. And where "terrorists" do exist, they exist largely because of destructive U.S. policies that have created anger abroad.

Anyway, the nearly trillion of fiat funny money dollars all told that will be spent in fiscal 2019 is not required to protect U.S territory, which anyway is separated by two oceans from most of the rest of the world. The U.S. has been squandering resources overseas for decades, really beginning with the Vietnam War (which forced Nixon in 1971 to abandon the dollar's remaining link to real money, gold) and now, at last, this cannot continue without the ruination of the nation. It is probably this realization that has forced Trump, against many in Congress and all of his advisors including warmongers John Bolton and Mike Pompeo, to pull some troops out of Afghanistan and as well all U.S. soldiers out of Syria.

Trump's decision this December to abandon Syria, an Iranian ally, was the first time he ever took a stand against the Neocons and interventionists in Congress, in the military and in his administration that have dictated U.S. foreign policy.

Some have even claimed that this decision has finally, after two years of blundering around, made him "presidential" – whatever that means. Trump's focus may now be on preventing Turkey, Russia, and Iran from forging an alliance and on keeping Turkey in NATO. The idea of perpetual war in the Mideast to foment chaos and little more may be a thing of the past now and it appears the idea of creating a Kurdish state, which would likely be allied somehow with the Zionists, between Syria and Iran is dead. In many respects, if Trump holds firm, he has finally fulfilled the campaign promises that likely got him elected in the first place. More importantly, while hideous economic sanctions may remain against Iran, the likelihood of a military attack against Iran and thus a major war looks to be dead, too, because it is too fiscally difficult if not impossible. More surprising decisions by Trump may be ahead, too, that might relieve some of the pressures on Iran which has done good in sticking with the JCPOA.

Perhaps Trump and others in the U.S. government will also begin to see that carte blanche support for anything the Zionists want, as has been the case for decades, does not also make for policy beneficial to the U.S. in the Middle East going forward. What's interesting is that the entire ugly edifice and cruel plans of the Zionists, which Netanyahu has pushed hard for, may not be sustainable without that carte blanche support the U.S. has maintained for decades.

Israel is not going to dissolve. It's too strong militarily, but it may have to get real and become a friendlier neighbor to other countries in the Mideast, and kinder to its natives, the Palestinians, to survive at all in the longer term. You might say "Israel" could have within itself aspects of a Ponzi scheme that makes the entire colonial project unsustainable, as it has been, without a blank check given by the U.S. to do as it pleases.

For Iran as with Syria, a determined mass of unified and determined citizens will defeat aggressors

Jan 5, 2019

No one can say whether U.S. President Donald Trump is changing his stripes. But he is sure as the perfection of the Muslim "Jannah" or the beauty of an exquisite Iranian rose or a fine carpet from Shiraz shaking up his usual allies, and not those merely in the U.S., but overseas, too.

It's delightful to watch this happen, but one could be tempted to get too giddy with anticipations of real change when it's possible Trump, as some are claiming, may literally be losing his mind under the pressures inherent in his job and those foisted on him from those who despise him, or he's just being especially impulsive and his big mouth has gotten far too loose.

Some are claiming that before the end of this new year he will resign. Others can readily wonder that he has so angered the U.S. establishment, whether on the conservative or the faux liberal side of the political and social divide, that he may be, Allah forbid it, killed. Many have posited in the past that former President John F. Kennedy died because he wanted to utterly forbid the Zionists from getting hold of nuclear technology from any source and as well did not believe expansion of the nascent war in Vietnam in 1963 was a good idea.

The big-ticket item of controversy currently seems to be Trump's decision to pull U.S. troops out of Syria. He seems to be pushing the honest recognition (finally) that the semi proxy war on Syria and the legitimate and even popular Assad government, despite all the destruction and carnage worse than anything the Mongols (non-Muslim "barbarians" at the time) meted out to the Muslim heartlands in 1258, has been an utter failure.

The goal was, of course, exactly what the Zionists have long wanted: just chaos and little or no organized government east and north of the Jordan River, and lots of dead people. Trump was also quoted as saying that "Iran can do what it wants" in Syria.

That goal has clearly backfired: Syria, though still in shock from all the destruction and death of its people and others, may be militarily stronger and more of a challenge to the

Zionists than it has ever been since 1973 and the so-called "Yom Kippur" war which, had it not been for the lack of drive at a critical moment on the Golan, might have recovered the heights. Syria is said to be in possession of GPS guided missiles that can hit any target in "Israel", and its air defense systems, augmented by Russia, are improving all the time.

Furthermore, Syria and Iraq are getting much closer, and that, in turn, means that Iraq and Iran are getting much closer, and meanwhile, Iran and Afghanistan have been involved in creative and constructive talks for some time. Think of it: the U.S. is not only obliged to leave Syria, but also to take its troops out of Iraq, and Trump has already ordered half the American soldiers in Afghanistan to leave, or some 7000 soldiers.

And the Zionists are having a hissy fit, especially over Syria and Iran. But again, imagine: Iran, Iraq, Syria and Afghanistan drawing together as friends and allies and not just to destroy the remaining terrorists in the region, but to enhance mutual trade, too, including China's vast "Belt and Road" project.

Trump is of the opinion that U.S. sanctions and the abrogation of the JCPOA last May have materially weakened Iran to the point where he, as President, can't be bothered by what Iran is doing in Syria, that Iranians and the government are SIMPLY or only struggling to survive now. I seriously doubt this is the case, but I hardly want to minimize the challenges U.S. sanctions and other threats represent. For example, porcine Defense Secretary Mike Pompeo, fatter than ever, recently demanded that Iran halt all missile development and no more testing.

Javad Zarif said "No!" to those demands, pointing out how the U.S. had unilaterally pulled out of the JCPOA to the horror of the entire world, except for the Zionists. One can imagine that had the U.S stayed true to the JCPOA and otherwise reached out a bit farther for normalization of relations with the Islamic Republic (and in turn stopped being a slave to the very insatiable demands of "Israel"), Iranian leaders like Zarif might well have been more open to Iran spending less of its precious resources on "defense" and more on its citizens.

Here's the thing: Syria and Syrians managed to survive years of attack by Western powers and some Arabs, including hordes of Arab and even some European terrorists paid and equipped mostly by the U.S. and the British and Saudis.

It seems almost a miracle that the Assad government exists, so how is this possible? Ibn Khaldun's Arabic concept of "assabiyya" seems the reason, or the solidarity and unity of enough Syrians ready to STAY unified to ward off their enemies. Syria, by the way, is a multi-religious and multi ethnic country. Iran is by the terms of the 1979 revolution "Islamic" but many Iranian citizens are of other faiths, too.

Iran can defeat whomever it wants, just like Syria has, with the same kind of determination and unity. Questions about more social liberalization in Iran and more democracy, while important, can wait until after Iran has been liberated from the burdens imposed on it by the U.S., Zionists and Saudis.

A RANDOM LITANY OF POTENTIALLY BETTER NEWS FOR IRAN SEEN FOR 8000 MILES
JAN 8, 2019

Iran is allegedly planning joint naval exercises with Russia in the Caspian Sea. The government in Kabul is said to be open to stronger ties and cooperation with Tehran. More countries are allegedly intending to keep open trade channels with Tehran, especially India and Pakistan, even if there's no clear evidence yet of a European "Special Purposes Vehicle" to bypass U.S. economic sanctions on Iran for trade purposes.

There is evidence of more bilateral contact between Tehran and its neighbors. Reports exist suggesting that Iran is weathering the harsh sanctions to some positive degree at least. Some of Iraq's leaders have come out and stated they wanted the U.S. military out of Iraq. The Syrian government definitely wants the U.S. military out of Syria, and currently there is supposed to be a four-month timetable to withdraw American troops from Syria.

The Kurds allegedly are inviting Syrian soldiers in to areas of eastern Syria, perhaps in the realization that the Assad government will prevail in regaining all Syrian territory, and they fear the Turks more than they do Assad. Russia has allegedly warned the Zionists that further attacks on Syria will not be easily tolerated. There's almost universal sentiment against the war on Yemen and the humanitarian disaster it has been, even in the U.S. Congress.

The alleged trial and possible execution of those Saudis involved in Jamal Khashoggi's gruesome murder may be ahead, with the unfortunate whitewashing of Muhammad bin Salman's obvious role in the crime. On the other hand, one must wonder that IF the perps are slated for execution, might there be a backlash in Saudi Arabia with the perps pointing the finger at MBS, saying they were only following orders from him?

(At any rate, the Saudis are none too popular, even in the U.S., where most people understand now that Saudi "liberalization" schemes are a joke.) Lastly, a U.S. Grand Jury will be created for the first time to look into 9/11 and try to uncover the truth of what really happened and who was behind the attack. The official narrative is full of holes.

Furthermore, the very first bill circulating in the U.S. Senate this year aims to make criticism of Israel and support for the BDS movement a crime. This bill is so hubristic and preposterous, and so unconstitutional that it's almost unbelievable. It's the crowning outrage of the "Israel firsters" in the U.S. government, and it is entirely against the most cherished keystone of "democracy" in the U.S.: free speech.

BUT even if this legislation manages to squeak through the Senate, it probably won't survive for long with a rejection from the House of Representatives possible, and will thoroughly expose, and especially to "average" Americans, just how deeply corrupted the Congress and Trump Administration has been, and for many years before, kowtowing to Netanyahu and aiding the Zionists with yet more billions of dollars. It could even, in time, put the political careers of bill proponents at risk, especially in a Congress that for the first time has a couple notably progressive females who are Muslim, including a Palestinian American, and they sure are not shy about speaking out.

There will come a time when those who champion equal rights and simple justice for Palestinians, and who despise "apartheid", can no longer be branded as "anti-Semites" by Zionists and their supporters and will be accepted as honest heroes of a sort. And Iran, which has opposed the mistreatment of Palestine's natives for decades will be honored for having done so early on.

Perhaps such notations as these constitute a clutching at straws for positive news in a very unsettled geopolitical climate. Mentioning these items is not intended to be either pro or anti Iran. But every one of these items at the margin at least has the potential to be a part of a very broad matrix that nudges forward the evolution of a safer, more balanced, more peaceful world order.

Meanwhile, it seems the vocabulary used by the U.S. is insane. "War on Terror" goes without necessary mention: it is senseless. But we see Mike Pompeo and other U.S. State Department officials talking about the "threat" from Iran, and how the U.S. has turned some Arab countries to consider Israel an ally against Iran. But no one can explain what the Iran "threat" really is, since Iran has no intention of fighting anyone except in defense.

Worse, the U.S. increasingly considers China the biggest "threat" of all, claiming it's a threat to all the world's people. But this makes no sense since a big chunk of people in the world is in China, and anyway, China's neighbors aside from perhaps Taiwan are doing a brisk business with China, and don't consider China a "threat". What in fact the U.S. oligarchy fears is having to share power with the rest of the world and work for cooperation and conciliation, not conflict.

But there is one important caveat to a peaceful world order, which the U.S has not promoted: No country or bloc of countries or alliances can or should overreact to provocations, which are legion. Overreaction can be deadly and macho behavior is a sign of weakness. A descent from here in to a far deeper geopolitical hellhole, sparked by some retaliatory action -- the proverbial grain of sand that destabilizes a mountain of sand and causes it to come crashing down in an avalanche of unintended consequences -- is entirely possible.

The U.S. wants to incite Iranians
and this must be rejected
Jan 12, 2019

After a while a rational person begins to think Arabs, or at least Arab "leaders", bar a handful of reasonably sane souls that includes Syria's Assad and some others probably in Iraq and Lebanon, maybe in Kuwait and Qatar and even Yemen (it's difficult to say, much less name names) are just flat stupid – especially when compared with most Iranians whatever their posture is towards the rule of Shia Muslim authorities in the Islamic Republic.

Outstanding among the stupid (and corrupt) has to be Mahmoud Abbas as self- appointed spokesperson and leader of Palestinians. He has done NOTHING for his people west of the Jordan, it appears, for decades. Arafat at least tried.

The U.S. wants to incite Iranians …

The Israelis make life ever more difficult for Holy Land natives, ethnic cleansing continues unabated, colonial Zionist "settlements" continue to sprout like weeds on stolen land, etcetera, in an area now where Arabs outnumber Jews if one includes Gazans. But this is an old story.

The U.S. has lately been trying to cobble together what's been termed an "Arab NATO" to confront and weaken Iran. This idea is somewhat analogous to NATO itself where a host of various countries within NATO at U.S. urgings portray a larger country by land mass, Russia, as some kind of aggressive demon aiming to expand and attack Europe when in fact Russia has no such aims but its own defense. Any "Arab NATO" collection of countries would confront a much larger country by geographic size, Iran, similarly and for the same false reasons, one must suppose. And Iran clearly has no aggressive aims but it does intend to defend itself. What to make of the Arab NATO concept?

Well, one thing seems indisputable. That there is nothing benign about U.S. intentions, and it's all about dividing the Muslim world (as usual) on the back of a selfish imperialistic desire to augment U.S. presence and control in the Middle East. John Bolton, who has influenced Trump to delay any pull out of U.S. troops from Syria, talks about creating "a more vibrant and secure" Middle East (with the downfall of the Islamic Republic).

It's a wonder that ANY Arabs believe this nonsense, and maybe some are beginning not to. For example, Jordan has lately called for the end of the Israeli occupation of the Golan, and some Iraqis are demanding the end that the U.S. military presence in Iraq. Also, pompous U.S. Secretary of State Mike Pompeo has had the gall to claim that the U.S. only wants a "better life" for the Iranian people with some sort of new governance, and at the same time has made life hard for most all Iranians with economic sanctions and other threats. Does that make sense? Of course not.

This is not a claim that ought to be in any way "bought" by Iranians generally – that the U.S has ANY intentions but to create discord, division and chaos in the Middle East for the alleged benefit of any country EXCEPT itself and Israel, which has so fully captured many in Washington that some "leaders" are willing to throw away the most cherished amendment to the Constitution – free speech -- by making criticism of Israel a crime. In fact, if the U.S. wants any coherent Iran at all, it wants a government in Iran that, like the Shah's, was simply a repressive one eager to do the bidding of the U.S. and open up Iran to the exploitation of U.S. corporations.

However, it's also fair to say that what the U.S. is dangling before the Iranian people is some kind of appeal to further upset by the downsizing if not the eradication of Iran's current rule of (Islamic) law. To be clear, there are social and political controls in Iran that have limited "free speech" and what may be termed full "democracy".

But this is no more evident, and perhaps far less so in Iran, than in the harsh kinds of social and political controls so apparent in Saudi Arabia and even in Sisi's Egypt, to name just two countries. And it's interesting to note that Assad's Syria, an Iranian ally, is in fact far more if not entirely "secular" in orientation than most all other Arab countries today. It's a huge positive that some Arab countries are now beginning to reestablish diplomatic relations with Assad and Syria.

The U.S. wants to incite Iranians ...

This apparent "dangling" by the U.S. of some sort of "freedom" of social license from Islamic rules for Iranians, really constitutes little more than incitements directed towards Iranians generally to create division and discord inside the Islamic Republic for – ultimately -- the benefit of the U.S. and Israeli imperialism and its further consolidation.

Even if there is merit in the idea of more "democracy" for Iranians, it's far more important to realize that the Trump Administration does not in fact give a hoot about real "democracy" in the Middle East. If it did, let's be quite clear, it would NOT be supporting or allied with the Saudis, the Zionists or even Sisi in Egypt about whom it can easily be said are not sincerely "democracy" minded.

The real tragedy of the Middle East is that the predominate Muslim populations, tolerant of other faiths and minorities, and whether Sunni or Shia, have failed to recognize the power and benefits inherent in hanging together as a first priority and advocating for each other to create more unity and peace regionally.

Perhaps this may begin to dawn on the Arab and Muslim masses, because one thing is certain: over the last 100 years since the end of the Ottomans the "West" and particularly the U.S., the British, the Zionists and the French, too, have made life miserable for too many in the Middle East.

It behooves largely Muslim lands to avoid becoming like Saudi Arabia
Jan 19, 2019

A fire broke out in a school building in Makkah back in 2002 from which young female students tried to escape. The Saudi "religious police" allegedly forced some if not all the teen school girls back inside the burning school because they were, in their hasty attempts to escape the fire, not wearing their headscarves and black robes.

Fights reportedly broke out between fire fighters and members of the "Commission for the Promotion of Virtue and the Prevention of Vice" to keep the girls inside the school because they were not wearing the hijab or maybe black robes -- or whatever the Saudis deem appropriate garb for young females -- and 15 of the girls allegedly died in the Muslim holy city as a result. There also was, as would be expected, criticism of the "police" even in the Saudi media.

The English-language Saudi Gazette was one media outlet which criticized the "police". The newspaper reported that the "police" even stopped people who tried to assist the girls escape from the blaze, claiming that it was "sinful" to approach them.

If any incident better speaks of the cruelty of Saudi mentality, not to mention the murder of Khashoggi and lies about that crime and many other scandalous incidents, it is hard to know what it might be. This was clearly an extreme example of Islamic "rules" gone awry in practice.

But it's entirely correct to insist on modesty in dress. This is a Qu'ranic mandate and it makes a lot of good sense, but in general terms it is a call for the prevalence of modesty is all walks of life and frankly it ought to apply in ANY society, whether Muslim or not. Modesty is a great virtue, and the problem, as usual, arises in what amounts to the application of the mandate.

Far be it for a Westerner, including any American Muslim, to criticize opprobrium towards anyone engaging in truly immodest and scandalous behavior, but the situation in Saudi Arabia, where there are NO churches or synagogues (as there are and supported in Iran), and where the application of what are called "Islamic" laws are so extreme that one has to question whether the Saudis have any claim whatsoever to consider themselves true advocates and champions of Islam. Frankly, the Saudis have no such valid claim and frankly Makkah and Medina ought to be "independent" of the Saudis, perhaps in the same way the Vatican for Catholics has been essentially independent of the country, Italy, where it is located.

In fact, the Saudis have done little but give the last and most complete monotheistic religion a bad name in the opinion of many across the world, whether Muslim or not, and it is utterly shameful that the U.S. has anything to do with that country.

If the U.S. were itself a solidly virtuous society with a virtuous international polity, it would demand the end of a "Saudi" Arabia. It is difficult, anyway to call American society and its warmongering and hostility to others of different cultures "moral" even while most American citizens are good people, at least in their private lives.

What is really scandalous is Mike Pompeo speaking in Cairo this month and claiming that America is a "force for good" in the Middle East. How can a force that has been responsible for millions of deaths and tremendous destruction be a "force for good"? Washington has become a sump of licentiousness, corruption, greed and overreach even while many there in government, and the American people in general, are no worse than any other people where ignorance, not necessarily bad intentions, often prevails.

Meanwhile, some in the Trump Administration, including figures like John Bolton and the "evangelicals" Pompeo and Vice President Pence, and some members of Congress, seem to have latched on to some kind of sick mania to attack, one way or another, Iran, at the ultimate behest of the most corrupt and literally most immoral society on the planet -- the one dominated by far-right wing Zionists, or Israel, where real Judaism has been largely forgotten.

The question is whether Trump himself has the wisdom and courage to avoid further attacks on Iran, and especially any kind of military attack. Last September, for example. Bolton allegedly asked the Pentagon to draw military plans to bomb Iran, still claiming that Iran intends to build nuclear weapons. This request by Bolton was apparently looked upon with horror by Pentagon brass, which is obviously a good and welcome reaction, suggesting that there are at least some sane minds in Washington.

It behooves largely Muslim lands to ...

It would appear, anyway, that there exists some kind of horrific horserace underway between people like Bolton and Pompeo (and maybe Trump), and potential developments in the U.S. that would definitively forestall further U.S. aggressions against the Islamic Republic. One potential "development" in this race is some kind of economic or monetary collapse that forces the U.S. to rearrange its priorities both domestic and foreign. Many Americans are literally praying something like this will happen to obviate the likelihood of the U.S. further damaging its standing and reputation globally.

There are so many huge shifts in global geopolitics underway now that the U.S., so far, has failed to get ahead of them, and the deployment of brute force, or threats of it, is no answer to the shifts. The growing understanding of Central Asian nations, including Iran, that they exist increasingly in a more interconnected and integrated region is one thing that illuminates U.S. failures so far to adjust to new realities by dropping bizarre and preposterous demands, and not just on Iran, but also on the biggest U.S. rivals, Russia and China.

It's possible that the U.S. has set itself up for more failure, especially in the Middle East, even if there is no dominating internal "development" like economic or monetary collapse, and especially if the U.S. resorts to more militancy. Meanwhile, it behooves Iran's leaders to permit Iran's people a louder voice in Iranian affairs of state and in the formulation of domestic mandates. Above all, Iran ought not to be or become like Saudi Arabia is as a Muslim country.

In U.S. one NYT columnist just made a serious impact

Jan 26 2019

The Power of the Press, provided it's the right particular medium, packs at least an incipient punch. Take for example the so-called "newspaper of record" in the United States, the New York Times, which despite decades of obfuscations and bias in certain arenas such as the Middle East remains the one newspaper which, if the mainstream media were to be absolutely shunned, would probably be the last to meet that fate.

Too many smart readers who more or less try to keep up with politics and international affairs and have some grasp of things at least have continued to "trust" the NYT, and when it is clearly pointed out or revealed that the paper has erred time after time and misled readers in the past, it's like dropping a stink bomb on the morning commute train into the Big Apple with potential reverberations all across the country and particularly in Washington.

One column last Sunday in the paper by one Michelle Alexander, a recently hired writer, has heartened seekers of truth like few others in years. Alexander, a respected professor now at Union Theological Seminary in Manhattan and a longstanding and respected civil rights advocate, wrote such a lucid piece about Palestine that it has flummoxed the entrenched "Israel can do no wrong" masses and left them in the dust, gasping unsuccessfully to counter her arguments (especially on Martin Luther King Day) that it is high time the

In U.S. one NYT columnist just ...

wrongs against the Palestinians are addressed and Likud Israel is at last challenged for its various and obvious crimes. Iran, of all countries, well knows what those crimes have been for seven decades or more against the natives of the Holy Land.

Ayatollah Khomeini, who led the revolution in Iran, was speaking out against the Zionist program way back in the 1960s, if not earlier, even when he was exiled from Iran by the Shah for over a decade, and it's one of several big reason the Israelis and the U.S. have long sought the end of the Islamic Republic since 1979.

What Alexander, a Baha'I by the way, especially did in her column was write – eloquently -- what few have dared utter: that there are many "progressives" in the U.S. who, knowing right from wrong, have not dared challenge Israel because they feared they would be smeared so harshly that they would be unable to carry on their work in other worthy causes, having been declared "anti-Semitic" if not worse.

There are so many cases in the U.S. of smart people being marginalized and slandered for decades by Zionists and their supporters, people often losing their jobs, that it is almost unbelievable how deeply and powerfully this has played out – maybe, just maybe, until now when other thinkers like Alexander may be emboldened finally to speak truth to power about Israel, as Iran's leaders have long done and as Alexander has now just done. Yes, she is being smeared by the usual culprits, but it appears to no affect. Maybe the NYT will fire her as a columnist, but one must doubt it: it would be so transparent if they did. At any rate, her column has been deemed a "strategic threat" by Zionists.

It seems a corner has been turned in the push for justice at last, and justice in Palestine is the key to winding down the awful terror of the so-called War on Terror instituted by George W. Bush and the Neocons, many of whom remain in powerful roles in Washington under Trump. And one reason the NYT allowed the publication of her column, it has been suggested, is that last year the newspaper elevated a new, young publisher of the same Jewish family that has long been at the helm of the paper -- a young Jew and no doubt Zionist who sees the future better than his predecessors did.

Presuming a new page is beginning to open up in the U.S. whereby those who have been hurt for challenging Israel's cruelty find some vindication. I happen to be one minor victim of real hostility for trying to write as a journalist about Palestine on several occasions in the past, going all the way back to the mid-1970s after I spent a month at Jabalia Refugee Camp in Gaza.

We few Americans who have at least attempted to shine a light on Israel's misdeeds and human rights abuses must now also wonder what this possible change of atmosphere might mean for the campaign long underway by Israel, the U.S and some Arabs against the Islamic Republic. Might this odious campaign against a sovereign Iran be somehow abbreviated and neutered to some extent, if not absolutely halted? It is difficult to know, but one thing is certain: the dialogue in the U.S about the depredations of Zionism seems about to expand, and there may be some spillover with regard to dampening Washington's warmongering in the Middle East.

(The criticisms and demands for a reckoning with Muhammad bin Salman over the Jamal Khashoggi murder last October, for example, continue with one of the most fervent Zionist supporters, GOP Senator Lindsay Graham. If Graham manages to push moves to throttle and punish MBS, might his next realization be, at the margin, a change of heart regarding his carte blanche support for the far right-wing Zionists?)

Some Iranians, anyway, are saying just the right things, and one must quote one unnamed Iranian: "The U.S. and its allies can sanction Iran, threaten her, demonize her, raise false flags to spread lies, BUT they will never break her. Why, because she stands on the right side of history, on the side of the oppressed. As an Iranian, I have the right to question my government, to hold it to account and even change it. Iran is not a perfect country and we need a lot of work to make it better for everyone, BUT no other country has the right to tell us what is best for us. Anyone looking to the U.S. as an ally or a country that brings "democracy" or "human rights" to anywhere be deluded or a traitor. The notion that we in Iran need help from outsiders is a false and dangerous idea that will only lead to harm and destruction. Never again."

Trump may get his personal donnybrook, but in Venezuela Jan 29, 2019

It appears that Trump (and now especially with his appointments of some of the worst of the Zionist Neocons who planned decades ago the march to destroy polities that did not exactly kowtow to U.S. demands and submit to the "Empire of Chaos") has been searching for a signature interference and possibly a war to assert U.S. hegemony.

Perhaps Trump and minions have found their primary target now, which is the lowest hanging and geographically nearest fruit – resource rich Venezuela – given the political and economic problems faced by Nicolas Maduro, which in fact are largely the result of U.S. economic and other sanctions on the proponents of the so-called "Bolivarian Revolution".

What would be Trump's signature war many have asked? All his predecessors in the White House had at least one, the most damaging of which to date was the Iraq War, with Libya and Syria not far behind. Might it be North Korea? Nah, probably because the Norks had developed a nuclear deterrence and the means to deliver nuclear bombs, at least in East Asia if not farther out to Hawaii and California, and anyway Kim Jong Un has an arresting and even jovial personality that Trump seemed to like, and Kim has proven to be rather smart in seeking détente or better relations with the other half of the Korean peninsula in the south.

Might it be a ramp-up of U.S. hostilities towards Syria? Nah, because with the help of the Russians and Iran and also Hezbollah, and the bravery of the Syrian army, popular Assad managed to drive out or kill most of the mercenary terrorists funded by the U.S. and the Saudis.

But what about Iran? The jury is still out on a U.S. or Israeli military strike on Iran outside of Syria. The U.S. has, however, attacked Iran with the cancellation of U.S. participation in the JCPOA and harsh economic sanctions aiming to turn Iranians against the Islamic Republic and its leaders.

One huge mistake by the Trumpists has been its promotion of the despised MEK as an alternative for Iran, or even the restoration of the son of the former shah. From a distance, this appears to have shored up at least nominal support inside Iran for the current government despite the lambent hardships suffered by Iranians generally.

Iran may simply too hard a nut to crack for the craven warmongers in Washington and Tel Aviv given the heavy investments in Iran and the alliances Iran has more or less maintained that seem to have turned Iran into a "red line" for countries like Russia and China. Iran may constitute a bridge too far, and anyway, if Iran were attacked, there would be Hell to pay throughout the Middle East and particularly in the Persian Gulf.

How does a barrel of oil costing over $200 sound to the warmongers? You'd see an economic collapse in the West and the U.S. like none before, and the fortunes of both political parties in the U.S. would go up in smoke. Not to mention the fact that Trump was, allegedly, primarily elected to dampen U.S. military adventurism overseas and focus on domestic problems, which are rampant and growing by the day.

So, for now at least, with Venezuela and Maduro in the crosshairs of U.S. regime change efforts, horrible as that is potentially for the people of Venezuela, it seems possible that Iran, even if sanctions are not lifted, might witness some reduction of pressure upon it and allow the Islamic Republic to consolidate what bulwark it has developed against further attack.

Imagine, for example, if the situation inside Venezuela goes "Mad Max" with civil war atop the economic disasters already present, and with the potential that the U.S. might invade. Venezuela has a population of about 32 million as well as the largest (heavy) oil reserves on the planet. While it is not nearly as big a country like Iran, it is far bigger than Iraq or Libya or Syria, for examples, and you can bet that if the U.S. did move in to attack Maduro militarily, the opposition there would be or become extreme. The Venezuelan armed forces have already said they support Maduro and not the lightweight fool who unilaterally and illegally declared himself "president".

For now, too, Maduro is trying to buy some time and has just declared that U.S. diplomats will not be kicked out of Caracas immediately. The U.S. could, if it makes the wrong moves, find itself MORE bogged down in Venezuela than ever it was in Iraq and as it has been in Afghanistan. And this, if it were to occur, would certainly take the spotlight off of Iran and quite possibly result in rejection of Washington and Trump and not just outside the U.S., but also inside the U.S. (It's important to realize, as has been proven in so many countries faced with upheaval since World War 2, that a mere 10 percent of so of any population absolutely determined to radical change and willing to sacrifice for it can make it happen.)

Indeed, if Trump wants his personal donnybrook, he can have it with Venezuela, a far softer and closer target but also one that could prove to be equally as disruptive, it seems, as any further attack on Iran. At any rate, one ought not to be surprised if Trump, now having fully embraced the Neocons, is not elected for a second term in the White House. This latter would be glorious for all the world.

You cannot put lipstick on a pig and make it pretty

Feb 2, 2019

It is obvious. Piggish American imperialistic foreign policy under Trump aims to overthrow uncooperative foreign governments and install subservient regimes, often to make way for the plundering of natural resources and to open markets for U.S. corporations, particularly arms makers.

John Bolton declared clearly why the U.S. is going for regime change in Venezuela: OIL. The Trump regime uses every means at its disposal, particularly economic ones, and even if in outrage a country has halted diplomatic relations with the U.S., as Iran has fairly done for decades, that in itself is cause for some kind of attack. The Trump regime is also now threatening European countries over the erection of the SPV for trade with Iran, a move that one would hope thoroughly alienates European governments.

What is happening right now in Venezuela has been in the works, carefully coordinated and planned, for a long time. It's quite remarkable that while the U.S. has been trying to choke and destroy Nicolas Maduro, as it tried to choke Chavez, stealing billions in dollars and gold and impoverishing many, it has the gall, via a blustering Secretary of State Mike Pompeo, to offer $20 million this month in "humanitarian assistance" to Venezuela at the same time. That current offer is exactly equivalent in a hospital to taking away every painkiller, every medicine, perhaps even bed linens And food, from an ill patient, and handing that patient a single band aid. What's a mere $20 million in chump change to a country that can conger fiat dollars at no cost whatsoever?

And those countries, including European ones, that aver from kowtowing to the Trump administration become alleged threats to U.S. "national security", a phrase that has lost specific definition aside from implying that some government elsewhere merely sees things differently than Washington does and is thus deemed a "threat".

Many countries, many European ones, many in Latin America, even Canada now and some in East Asia like Australia, have become mere slaves to the "empire", slaves to U.S. hegemonic pretensions, and all the while the U.S. government has the gall to designate itself the leader of the "free world" which in fact is a world that in many lands has mostly relinquished sovereignty because of U.S. threats real or implied.

It is not just foreigners, including Iran and its people, who have been under some kind of onerous attack. So have many Americans, too, by their own government.

Trump, for example, shut down segments of the U.S. government, depriving almost a million federal workers of salaries for over a month, while demanding billions of dollars for a wall (like Israel's wall snaking through the West Bank) along the border with Mexico to keep out Latinos looking for a better life and this largely because the U.S. literally has made life difficult for them in their home countries, which has including propping up right wing governments that also have become slaves to U.S. imperium while the U.S. offers personal benefits to their narrow claques of "leaders".

No doubt it would seem to the U.S.-designated "president" of Venezuela Juan Guaido (who was never elected in a country that former U.S President Jimmy Carter says has the fairest electoral system anywhere) that he has "benefitted", because otherwise he is of such little merit that this political wanker would otherwise be a perennial non-entity.

And internally, Trump has minimal relative popularity now along with the U.S. Congress where the very first piece of legislation under consideration in the U.S. Senate in this new session post midterm elections has nada to do with aiding the American people, but rather with breaching the U.S. Constitutional amendment guaranteeing the long cherished right to free speech by making it a crime, with punishments, to support efforts, even with speech, championing the basic human rights of Palestinians -- all at the behest of arguably the most criminal country on earth, Likud Israel. If this weren't happening, it would be unbelievable that it ever could happen.

Simply put, the U.S. government has drifted towards becoming a bare-faced fascist enterprise, one not much better than what Nazi Germany was if one can be so bold to speak the truth.

But also consider that the U.S. government has become a virtual slave itself, and to whom is important. With regard to foreign policy in the Middle East, it has become a slave to the Zionists and oligarchic Zionist American billionaires who have literally purchased influence in Washington from politicians whose primary concern is staying in office and having the financial wherewithal to do so. Israel is preparing in time to annex the West Bank, all of it, and moreover, it is demanding -- and has support among some members of the

U.S. Congress for the full and permanent annexation of the Syrian Golan.

This alone breaches many covenants of international law, the very "rules-based order" the U.S. claims to have tried to maintain. But the extant alleged "rules" apparently are not "rules" at all, because rules imply something fixed and well honored. The "rules" seem now to have no meaning because they can be modified whimsically to suit the illegal, in this case Israeli, demands of the moment.

What is interesting, and maybe particularly for Iranians, is that some of the very bravest U.S. politicians now happen to be female Muslims elected in November to the U.S. Congress for the first time. Democrats Ilhan Omar and Rashida Tlaib, who along with non-Muslim Alexandra Ocasio-Cortez, are not shy about speaking truth, as they see it, to power. And despite the fact that they are under some attack themselves for doing so on both sides of the aisle in Congress, they are opening up heretofore unrealized domains of discourse on many important issues in Washington and beyond, and not just on the matter of destructive U.S. foreign policies.

But even more importantly, among the American people, if not among the long-entrenched politicians, they are gaining some traction and admiration from Americans generally for their bravery. On that note there is reason for some optimism, however faint, in an ambience that would shock even British writer George Orwell, who long ago imagined a future totalitarian world bereft of individual freedoms.

Rarely has the world been so challenged by U.S. hubris
Feb 4, 2019

Who knows, but it may be that the people of Venezuela, beset with upheaval and possible civil war if not an invasion by the U.S. or proxies, will become the sacrificial lambs who finally sink the U.S. thoroughly in world opinion and the U.S. could get bogged down there to some extent the way they did in Vietnam and Iraq, not to mention the real costs in money and lives.

Maduro may well fight, it›s just hard to say how MUCH support he has in his country, but a recent poll suggests that he has a majority of the country behind him, at least to the extent that Venezuela›s people despise the U.S coup attempt. And it does appear that many Americans are not, and would not be, keen on seeing Trump ignite another war.

Trump, under the thumb of the troika of Pence, Bolton and Pompeo (and other Neocons like Eliot Abrams, who has been tasked with directing the coup in Venezuela), lurches from one dramatic, hysterical move to the next, including yet another treaty abrogation, the INF, which regulated some missile defense balances between the U.S. and Russia.

National security advisor to Trump, John Bolton, has proven his complete insanity (as if further proof were needed) by threatening to send Nicolas Maduro to the U.S. prison base at Guantanamo Bay, Cuba if Maduro does not quietly retire and leave Venezuela. It would make sense for Maduro's Cuban allies to shut down the Guantanamo base and reclaim the far east of Cuba, whatever the reaction. Imagine, if you will, the war on Cuba, too, and never forget the Bay of Pigs debacle decades ago, a losing bid to topple Fidel Castro.

Caracas has anyway committed the ultimate "sin" – really by attempting to bypass the U.S. dollar and trade its resources for other assets or currencies, perhaps even the "Petro". But the attack on Maduro at the bottom also constitutes an attack on Eurasian integration between key countries: Russia, China, Iran, and Turkey, all of whom are, to one degree or another, trading or beginning to trade without the fiat dollar.

China, in particular, may eventually buy all its oil imports with the "Petroyuan". China is Saudi Arabia's number one oil customer, and if Saudi Arabia were ever to do anything positive, it would accept other currencies for its oil, too. (There must be some kind of curse on countries that have oil, given the U.S., nonetheless.)

Key is what China and Russia might do going forward. China is apparently Venezuela's largest creditor. Last year Maduro visited China and received an extra $5 billion in loans and signed a score of bilateral agreements. And Russia is also invested in Venezuela, having recently been given access to mine that country's gold resources, for one thing, and last December Putin infuriated the U.S. when it flew a couple Russian bombers to Caracas for a friendly visit.

Putin has given full support to Maduro, citing that interference in Venezuela by the U.S. "violates the basic norms of international law". No question about that. The U.S. has been violating international law for decades, thinking it IS "international law". Interesting to note that the best expert on

Russia in the U.S., Dr. Stephen Cohen, claims that the current situation between the U.S. and Russia is more dangerous than the post-World War 2 Cold War ever was.

The U.S. has made its move against Maduro, but it has not been a kill shot (as imagined it might be) and the situation may well stabilize. It did when the Saudis, for example, tried to overthrow Qatar's government with a financial and military blockade. Every day that Maduro manages to hang on in Caracas raises the odds of a failed coup as the panic diminishes and Venezuela may eventually get on with selling oil for the so-called "Petro", not the buck, and relying on China and Russia to help renovate infrastructure.

As for Iran, it's hard to know whether the attack on Venezuela and apparent efforts to ignite a civil war there involves a capitulation of sorts whereby the U.S. is going after control of Venezuelan resources because of the realization that it may not be able to grab dominance over and control of Middle East and Eurasian resources as it desires.

If, for example, Trump is aiming for U.S. withdrawal from Afghanistan and Syria – despite huge efforts by U.S. politicians demanding the Trump not withdraw – then the move on Venezuela and its resources makes some sense to the Neocons, and perhaps to the eventual benefit of Iran, which so far has not made stupid moves especially with its adherence to the JCPOA and with its measured appeals to Europe to erect the SVP and make it work.

And also, IF the U.S. gets bogged down in South America, it's quite likely that the mere concept of war with Iran or war with yet another country will look increasingly insane and so stretch a virtually bankrupt U.S. as to make it impossible.

Overreach and hubris have always finally proven to be the bane of every historical "empire" that has fallen, and the U.S. "won" none of its major military engagements in decades, especially the Vietnam War despite all the horrific carnage and destruction it has wrought in so many places.

Respect warranted for at least two bright Americans
Feb 13, 2019

One does not normally equate a person (who is retired now from decades in the CIA) as one with sound views and good instincts about the challenges to the world of a government that has been making – to put it simply – stupid moves and continues its errant ways under Donald Trump. But one such person is Philip Giraldi who writes articles outside the mainstream media about what he sees that is slowly destroying U.S. credibility worldwide.

In one article penned this month by Giraldi, he points out that the most disturbing aspect of the Trump gangsters is their presumption that decisions made by the government are binding on the rest of the world, as if the U.S. literally rules the world. For example, no other country has ever demanded that nations halt trading with each other outside of actual war, and sought to penalize them if they did trade.

Various rulings against Iran in the context of legislation have been particularly damaging, but any group or country that has been deemed a "state sponsor of terrorism", and that includes Syria of late, have been vilified. The notion that the U.S. ought to respect the sovereignty of other nations even when their internal policies disagree with the U.S., Giraldi says, has been abandoned. Nothing new here, sadly.

Giraldi is an American patriot in the very best sense of the word because he is not merely knowledgeable, but also quite simply an honest person at a time when, given the fact that most of the world's oil business is transacted in fiat dollars, the U.S. uses dollars, or their withdrawal, to interfere overseas and quite literally impoverish other countries that don't do the bidding of the U.S.

Iran is a case in point, but there are many others such as Maduro's Venezuela. But at the same time the U.S. is also, inadvertently, slowly destroying U.S. dollar hegemony, having weaponized it, to the point where across the world governments are trying desperately to figure out ways to do business without it. Someday, and no one knows when, the Petrodollar itself will in all likelihood be a relic of the past.

Will, for example, Saudi Arabia begin to sell oil for other currencies, and what would be the ramifications of that? A U.S. takeover in some fashion of Saudi resources, as the U.S. blatantly has said it wants to more or less take over Venezuela's vast oil reserves? That won't fly. The U.S. would fast lose its only firm ally, besides Israel, in the Middle East.

But besides right-thinking commentators like Giraldi, and he is just one of several worth noting, there are others who are emerging and one definitely worth attention is U.S. Congressional Democrat representative from Hawaii, Tulsi Gabbard. She recently announced her 2020 candidacy (in what is going to be a very crowded field) for President.

Gabbard, 37, a Hindu, a still serving major in the U.S. Army National Guard had two regular Army tours of duty in Iraq and independently went to Syria a couple years ago and met with Assad to try to figure out on her own initiative what the Syrian war has been about given the misinformation spewed by the mainstream U.S. media. She has been under attack because of her views by the "establishment".

Gabbard's primary campaign initiative has so far been to condemn U.S. interference, sanctions and wars of choice by the U.S. on other countries for "regime change", and not because she "sides", say, with Assad's Syria, but because countries like Syria or Iran or Venezuela do not, she claims, literally threaten the U.S. In fact, she points out correctly that U.S. warmongering actually damages the U.S. widely and deflects attention from pressing and growing problems inside the U.S.

In one recent interview on national television on a morning talk show where the interviewers tried desperately – and embarrassingly – to corner Gabbard and force her into a misstep and destroy her candidacy, she acquitted herself brilliantly, soundly deflecting the attacks to the point where she has likely made herself, if any female could be, the most viable female candidate for President ever.

This is because, to cite just one reason, a majority of Americans – outside Trump's base of ignorant faux "Christian" evangelicals and Zionists and Neocons, seem to be realizing that U.S. militancy and regime change wars are quite simply wrong, unhealthy and counterproductive.

Meanwhile, Trump just this week delivered a delayed annual "State of the Union" address to Congress to the usual obligatory and absurd applause. It was delivered by the Prince of Lies, Trump, and was full of lies about the real state of the "union" under his Presidency. And on top of that the Senate passed legislation that effectively would undercut the cherished 1st Amendment to the U.S. Constitution (that in part guarantees "free speech") by making it a crime to support the BDS movement to halt Israel's war crimes and crimes against humanity.

Hard to know whether the rest of Congress will agree with the Senate vote, but if it does make it in to law, it's bound to reach the U.S. Supreme Court for review. If the court did not strike it down, you can kiss U.S. democracy goodbye forever and the U.S. government will be further reviled and damaged in world opinion by its obsession with supporting Zionist apartheid.

And for sheer lunacy, Secretary of State Mike Pompeo, grubbing for any reason to send U.S. soldiers on a rampage in Venezuela, is claiming that Hebzbollah has installed active "cells" in Caracas and throughout South America. Hmmm. One wonders where that assertion originated. Can you spell Zionistaland?

Coexistence between Sunnis and Shias must be a primary goal

Feb 17, 2019

It may seem improbable but the very key to whether the world enjoys real (and somewhat relative, if not absolute) "peace" going forward, as well as the fate of the U.S. as any kind of somewhat respected but former imperial (and absurdly imperious) power, depends on two things: the end of U.S. disrespect for international laws, most evident in the "regime change" wars, and on the fate of the Palestinians and whether they are given civil rights and released from bondage in their own country.

Listening to honest voices, for a change, anywhere in the U.S. will be the country›s salvation and turn the U.S. in the right direction after three decades at least of what the wisest Americans could call a treasonous misdirection.

One such honest voice of late is Ilhan Omar, the first Muslim Somali-American woman of color ever in the U.S. House of Representatives. Twice in the past week, she fearlessly brought condemnation upon herself by the usual culprits (most of the corrupted U.S. Congress and Trump himself) by calling out the undue and obvious influence of the lobby group known as AIPAC on matters pertaining to the Zionists and Israel. Her comments were deemed "anti-Semitic" and in fact, they were not.

And then a couple days later she, as a member of the House Foreign Affairs Committee, grilled Eliot Abrams, appointed to oversee the attempt at "regime change" in Venezuela. Omar publicly exposed Abrams for the responsibility he bears for actions in Central America in the 1980s that resulted in the deaths of many thousands of innocent people -- something that could easily happen in Venezuela if the U.S in some way invades directly or by proxy to install unelected Juan Guaido. (It is vaguely similar to the final installation of the Shah in Iran in the 1950s as a U.S. puppet until the Revolution, which marked a release of years of pent up anger and frustration in Iran which may have been too extreme in the years immediately following 1979, because some innocents suffered, however natural it was given the circumstances. The U.S. certainly latched on to this, and the hostage crisis, to turn Iran into an "enemy".

In any case, this diminutive young woman, Omar, while apologizing for suggesting a so-called anti-Semitic "trope" prevalent during the Nazi era, has not substantially backed down in any respect in calling out AIPAC and other lobby influence on U.S. lawmakers. And she has gotten quite a lot of respect for doing so, at least among the best journalists and commentators. As one AIPAC staffer once said: "The lobby thrives in the dark." But it is no longer so much in the dark.

But perhaps even more striking is the failure of the conclave in Warsaw, originally aimed at drumming up hostility to Iran and even war. Many European leaders did not attend, for one thing, and U.S. VP Mike Pence made a fool of himself there, as did Netanyahu. Regarding Pence, he sanctimoniously reprimanded major European countries for the creation of INSTEX, and made other comments which firmly suggest that Pence has nothing so much on his mind, if he has one, as the concept of Armageddon and the absurd return of "Jesus" and the "end of days". Now it's one thing for the Shia faithful to believe that someday the Mahdi may someday appear from occultation to institute a reign of justice and peace, but quite another to invoke an Armageddon scenario based on evangelism and the reappearance of Jesus.

But Pence went further in exhorting European signatories to the JCPOA to abandon the deal, as Trump and minions did. Pence, incredibly, accused Iran of plotting a "new Holocaust" which, if this were true, the many thousands of minority Jews in Iran would have already been extinguished. And Iran's leaders have explained what the chants of "death to America" (or Israel) means: not the "death" of the citizens of the two countries but the end of the imperialist warmongers presence in high positions in both countries. However, the Warsaw conclave failed to keep the spotlight on Iran specifically and dissolved into an appeal for "stability" in the Middle East.

Well, who of sane mind does NOT want stability anywhere, but the word itself has just one meaning to Pence and the Trump Administration and related Neocons: Mideast countries that do nothing but the bidding of the U.S. and the Israelis. And this same faux "stability" is sought in South America: if, for example, Guaido is fully installed and Maduro goes into exile from Venezuela, no question that Cuba will be the next target, and then maybe Bolivia, and so on. But Venezuela is the key target for now because, like Iran, it has vast petroleum and other resources.

Meanwhile, the U.S. has been trying to foment a war between the Shias (namely Iran) and the Sunnis (namely Saudi Arabia) if for no other reason but that a divided Islamic world suits the predatory and hegemonic designs of the U.S. Efforts simply to divide Muslims have been prevalent for the past century at least. But people like Eliot Abrams, Trump's point man for Venezuela, a convicted (but Bush pardoned) felon, and a Jewish Neocon (are there any of note who are not Jewish?), like many others, fail to understand the fervor and courage Iranians displayed in pushing back Saddam Hussein for six years in the 1980s. Pence has the idea that sanctions and other threats will lead to the dissolution of the Islamic Republic. This is highly unlikely.

Iran, as far as one can tell, has not been as claimed by ignoramuses like Pence and Trump a "state sponsor of terrorism" but rather a state eager to achieve co-existence with other Muslims, if only it could. THAT, in essence, implies a more or less united (if that's not too strong a word) Islamic world. And THAT is what terrifies the Western imperialists. A reasonable coexistence between Sunnis and Shias has existed before, and the tragedy is that it apparently does not exist today, largely because of the U.S. and the Zionists.

Maybe it is always darkest, like now, before any dawn
Feb 23 2019

The best possible slap in the face of the GOP and Trump and his gaggle of warmongering advisors and appointees arrived recently when the National Iranian American Council as well as the Democratic National Committee apparently adopted a resolution to return the U.S. to compliance with the JCPOA and suggests it is possible…should the Democrats manage win back the White House in late 2020. But don't count on a Democratic victory in 2020 yet, whoever the nominee turns out to be. Why?

Because the field of candidates is already possibly too large with Democratic Party competitors, for one thing, and for the average voter, given the fact that each one of the candidates have staked out different positions (and they are not set in concrete among any of them.) It's all too darn confusing for the average confused American voter, and Trump may just have to remain Trump and he is already in the White House.

Tulsi Gabbard, a Congressional rep from Hawaii, is just one case in point. She began her campaign last month demanding that the U.S. end its regime change war, leave the Mideast including Afghanistan and Syria and focus on internal problems in the U.S. This posture has frightened the so-called Deep State, which presumably includes the "national security" complex of organizations like the military and the CIA, and also the Zionists represented by secretive and not so secret Think Tanks and lobbies such as AIPAC …all of whom are on the gravy train for money and perks of all kinds from the overspent Treasury.

In addition, already, Gabbard is weakening her position by claiming this week that Assad in Syria without a doubt used chemical weapons in Syria to defeat the opposition – throwing a bone to the dogs of war. She formerly seemed to deny that Assad deployed chemical weapons.

And one does not even have to mention candidates like Bernie Sanders who, despite raking in a record amount of money upon announcing his bid for the Presidency a few days ago, may well have a platform that, ironically, is far too radically sane and sensible to beat Trump.

You can bet that the GOP and the Trump Administration will lie like crazy and even create false flags to scare the voters into thinking there's an imminent attack on the U.S. by some other country, including Iran. (Bush did it in 2003.) Sanders it seems had just one chance to beat Trump back in 2016, and may have had he not folded and supported Hillary Clinton after the rigged, corrupt primary. He ought to have created an independent campaign in summer 2016.

Moreover, Sanders must be suspect because he supported every war the U.S. initiated as a senator from Vermont. At any rate, entrenched, extant Presidents are hard to bring down, and it's also highly likely that some Democrats will not line up firmly behind a Sanders, for they, too, are almost equally as corrupted as the GOP.

It remains to be seen, regarding the regime change efforts, whether Maduro can manage to hold on in Venezuela. He has the backing of a majority of Venezuelans at least to the extent that most don't want U.S. meddling, much less any kind of military attack or a civil war. But the Trump gang and the Deep State seems hell bent on finding the next country to eff up, and whether the next is Venezuela is beside the point.

Even though some Democratic Party members see the validity of and virtue in the U.S. returning to the JCPOA, we can already witness the various warmongers casting about for a casus bello, just as they did in the lead up to the war on Iraq and Saddam Hussein in 2003 with claims of Iraqi WMD as well as claims he was allied with al-Qaeda.

Of particular note this past week is an article published in the Washington Times newspaper, a rag of a paper if ever there was one, stating that Iran has been providing high-level al-Qaeda operatives with secret sanctuary in Iran and funneling money and weapons to al-Qaeda across the Mideast.

The aim is to provide a legal justification for military attacks against Iran or its proxies by the U.S. and Israel given the fact that economic sanctions have not, as anyone with half a brain can understand, resulted in the breakdown of the Islamic Republic.

But of all Mideast countries besides Assad's Syria, Iran has been vehemently opposed to terrorism, and the deadly attack blamed on an al-Qaeda linked group in Iran's southeast which resulted in the death of 27 Iranian Revolutionary Guard soldiers, is clearly not indicative of Iran's change of posture against terrorists of any stripe. And neither Hezbollah nor Hamas are "terrorist" organizations, it must be said, even though the U.S. and Israel claim they are.

As for the JCPOA, saving the deal finally will not be easy because Trump's drive to destabilize Iran and foment military actions seems to be accelerating. And the Trumpists have been appealing to the deal's other signatories to abandon it. One could argue that all this merely smacks of extreme desperation because so far neither Venezuela nor Iran has crumbled like cheap houses of cards despite all the Trump expectations that they would.

However, amid all the Trump Administration BS, there are growing factures between the U.S. and its allies, especially in Europe, who do NOT want the U.S. to attack Iran, who want the JCPOA to thrive, and who are beginning to see that the U.S. has not been a partner for peace anywhere. (China and Russia have known this for a long time, by the way.) When and at what point do countries like Merkel's Germany stand up for themselves and definitely break with Washington's destructive, hegemonic schemes?

And if they do, will that be enough to deter the Neocons and other warmongers and force them to back down? The recent conclave in Warsaw was an abject failure for both Trump and Netanyahu with respect to demonizing Iran further. As dark as these times are, it is always darkest before the dawn, presuming that dawn will appear somehow, someday, and World War 3 does not descend on humanity and wreck the planet.

The U.S. may have created a pool of quicksand...and jumped in

Feb 26, 2019

It has been suggested that the various hostile moves initiated by the Trump administration against Venezuela and Iran, to cite just two countries under economic siege, is that the U.S. literally has no alternative. No alternative but to try to counter every single development anywhere that might diminish the concept (at the least) of America as the sole superpower and hegemon, as it has been especially since the fall of the Soviet Union. This, it has been argued, is because the U.S. is fundamentally tapped out financially (with over $22 trillion in debt and at least $100 trillion in unfunded liabilities) and must resort literally to stealing resources and power and demanding obeisance wherever it can be had wherever it may be waning.

A simple case in point is U.S. hostility to Germany and Russia over the Nord Stream 2 gas pipeline that may go on line later this year and augment Germany's and Europe's access to relatively cheap energy and, as well, shore up if not expand Europe's relationships both diplomatic and economic with

Europe's natural partner to the east, Russia. But just about anywhere you look, challenges to U.S. hegemony and a multi-polar world are cropping up.

It appears that the U.S. game plan involves threats of war and destruction unless the various challenges to "empire" can be obviated by other means. But it is definitely a double-edged sword, for as much as the U.S. over extends itself overseas, it also risks internal implosion in the so-called "homeland" and above all, further rejection of the prime lynchpin of U.S. power which is the dollar.

And the U.S. seems clearly to be overplaying its hand. Regarding Venezuela, where the regime-change efforts have so far not gone to plan and "progressed" appears to have stalled out, the only further option seems to be an outright invasion or the stoking of a civil war – both of which even many U.S. elites consider foolish and counter- productive. And regarding Iran, it is absolutely heartening that Iranian leadership has been faithful to the JCPOA, because it does appear that Iran's steady cool is gaining the Islamic Republic increasing respect and viability.

Meanwhile, desperation in the Trump administration is mounting, just as it seems to be in Israel. In the U.S., for example, there is worldwide disgust at twit Senator Marco Rubio's tweet this week threatening Nicolas Maduro of Venezuela with Ghaddaffi's cruel fate in Libya. And in Israel, Netanyahu, desperate to remain in power with the upcoming April 9th election there, has admitted in to his prospective Likud coalition people who even in Israel are considered by some the absolute worst kind of racists, even terrorists -- lingering advocates of those who long ago championed

Meir Kahane and the Kach organization, now essentially reconstituted into Otzma Yehudit ("Jewish Power").

This move by Netanyahu, shifting Israel even farther to the fascist right, is even being condemned by many Jews in the U.S, and by the primary Zionist lobby, AIPAC, which is beginning to realize it is losing its grip on the Palestine narrative and its ability to advocate successfully for the Zionists in the U.S. But real danger exists.

Will Trump, if somehow regime change fails in Venezuela, as its been envisioned by the likes of Pompeo, Pence, Abrams and Bolton, then go for broke with the Zionists and the Saudis in a Hail Mary pass of sorts involving a military attack on Iran, where economic pressures and sanctions have so far failed to create the kind of chaos inside Iran that might destroy the Islamic Republic?

Will the search for and demands for some kind of insane "victory" in the face of repeated failures by the Trump administration occur? It is possible, but even with that there would be no victory but rather further condemnation of U.S. foreign policy and further erosion of U.S. clout with countries increasingly eager to break with obeisance to U.S. diktat and the dollar, the source of U.S. economic power.

It should, at any rate, be obvious to anyone in the West that Iran does not intend to pursue nuclear weapons, unlike, perhaps Saudi Arabia, which reports suggest has allegedly been receiving or is going to receive critical nuclear technology from the U.S. The hypocrisy is almost unbearable given the fact that of all Middle East regimes, the least "democratic" and the most rogue, aside from Israel, happens to be the Saudis.

Thus, it appears – as with Venezuela – the real aim of the U.S. is to prevent countries from pursuing independent energy and economic policies. Mounting efforts to conduct business by Venezuela, Iran, Russia and China, among other countries, without the use of the dollar, if successful, would likely crater some major Western banks and financial markets.

In some ways one might conclude that Iran so far has, despite the pain and the U.S. withdrawal from the JCPOA, outwitted Trump and the Neocons by maintaining steadiness and cool – and this is increasingly appreciated and working towards the erosion of harsh views of the Islamic Republic globally.

Anyone who was a child as I was during the 1950s when the U.S. was largely seen as a force for some good in the world has been thoroughly corrected in the past three decades: the U.S. is all out for itself and no one else, and more and more Americans are, in fact, realizing that if ever there was a rogue superpower, the U.S. is it. At the least citizens in the U.S. are incredibly tired of the various wars initiated by Washington and supported by small-minded psychopaths like Sen. Marco Rubio and his Neocon ilk.

Muslims can be proud of Omar and Tlaib in U.S. Congress
March 6, 2019

Muslims worldwide can be proud that the most courageous and quite possibly, with tremendous luck and time, the most effective U.S. Congressional representative in years may turn out to be Ilhan Omar who won election from a district in Minnesota last November. And it is all about remarkable courage, something that even her detractors must eventually recognize -- as it is human nature to recognize real courage when it is so evident.

Omar has touched, and is still touching, the so-called "third rail" of political discourse in the U.S. by calling out the absurdities and dangers of U.S. foreign policies that for decades have awarded overweening support for criminal Zionism and which has resulted, directly and indirectly, in more carnage and human suffering and financial waste than any other aspect of U.S. foreign policies and actions in the Middle East. And this is because for years the most basic posture of various U.S. administrations and the U.S. Congress has revolved around giving Israel anything it has wanted well before doing much else.

Speaking last week at a forum at a Washington bookstore along with freshman Rep, Rashida Tlaib of Michigan, Omar says she fears any and everything she and Tlaib might say about Israel is or would be construed as "anti-Semitic" because both women are Muslims, and that such insidious charges prevent a broader debate about Israel's 70 year plus mistreatment of Holy Land natives, the Palestinians. She is not at all incorrect about this.

Earlier, Omar used Twitter to express her dismay over the powerful influence the AIPAC lobby has had. And last week she made this statement: "I want to talk about the political influence in this country that says it's okay to push for allegiance to a foreign country." And added: "Why is it okay for me to talk about the influence of the National Rifle

Association, or fossil fuel industries or Big Pharma and not talk about another powerful lobbying group that is influencing policy?"

With that, some Jewish leaders said they were appalled by Omar's suggestion that Jewish-Americans have divided loyalties, reviving an old allegedly anti-Semitic trope. However, and this is important, some notable progressive Jews came to Omar's defense saying that it is not inherently anti-Semitic to criticize Israeli government policies or AIPAC. Meanwhile, AIPAC slammed Omar's suggestion of dual loyalties, as expected, as did long entrenched members of Congress on both sides of the aisle. Where is all this sound and fury going?

For one thing, you can bet that come the next election cycle for Ilhan Omar, some Jews and most all devout Zionists will be mounting a huge effort to have her, and Rashida Tlaib, ejected from Congress by voters if only because of bias against Muslims, at bottom a reaction against 9/11 because the perps were, by the official account, Muslim. (In one view, if it's the case that the U.S. government always has to have an "enemy" to justify its prodigal military spending, it may be that "Muslims" replaced "Communists" in the dark corners of the unofficial American psyche as the designated "enemy" – given the fall of the Soviet Union. And regarding Iran, the hostage crisis at the beginning of the Islamic Republic no doubt gave the U.S. government ammunition to vilify Iran for the past 40 years, pushed by the Zionists, since Iran has advocated for the oppressed at least in Palestine.)

It's a given that Omar and Tlaib will be targeted for defeat in the next election cycle, but at the same time, it's quite possible that by then the debate about undue Zionist influence in the U.S. will have finally achieved some sort of critical mass and more and more Americans, heretofore totally ignorant about the realities of faux Israeli "democracy" and Zionist cruelties – since they, the Zionists, always want to play the victims – will have different ideas about right and wrong and re-elect both Omar and Tlaib. And make no mistake, when Americans are fully apprised of the true facts of any particular situation, their generally fair-minded and fundamentally decent nature comes to the fore. And what in fact has held it back for decades with regard to Middle East matters has been such a volume of disinformation and propaganda, and money spent to create it, that even Josef Goebbels, Adolf Hitler's Minister of Propaganda, would be thoroughly surprised. It was, after all, Goebbels who once stated that if a lie is big enough and if it is stated often enough, people come to believe it – including the liar.

One argument the Zionists and lovers of modern Israel incessantly trot out is their loud complaint that detractors single out Israel especially for criticism when there are so many OTHER governments around the world that are allegedly less "democratic" and cruel than Israel's. They point, to cite just one example, to the Islamic Republic as a country where human rights have not – allegedly – been championed strongly enough. Whether that's true or not only visitors to Iran can rightfully decide for themselves. But the deep reason Israel is ever singled out for derision, if it has been, is because IF the mighty dam of misguided public opinion regarding the Zionists begins to crack and reveal truths to the masses, particularly in the U.S., it will mark the beginning of the end of some serious governmental corruption in the U.S. (and in other Western countries like the U.K) and of policies and actions damaging to the perceptions of Islam and to some

Muslim countries. It may well mark the beginning of the end of U.S. warmongering, foolish "regime change" wars of choice, and a variety of other ills that have plagued the Middle East.

One can only, for now, blissfully imagine a Holy Land where Palestinians, Muslim or Christian, and Jews are treated as equal citizens, and what that would mean for the flowering of the Middle East as a whole and for Islam. But in preparation for this, if it should ever come, it would be hastened if countries like Iran where there has long been more "democracy" than in Israel or Saudi Arabia, make sure that there is continued movement towards good government that literally works for the betterment of the lives of all citizens and not just for some powerful, relatively wealthy elite.

A wild theory about Trump is a sign of natural despair and desperation
March 13, 2019

Donald Trump is more than halfway through his first term and (insha'a Allah) last term as U.S. President and by most sane accounts he's been a looming disaster so far -- a disaster that remains mostly prospective because of things already done and decided and which await some kind of unpleasant denouement.

The U.S. economy is doing well, relative to most others, and unemployment is low even if most jobs are menial and

A WILD THEORY ABOUT TRUMP IS ...

most Americans are eyeballs deep in debt. But this is almost certainly because of a dump of $trillions in printed money in to the economy and nearly zero interest rates by the Federal Reserve Bank. This was supposed to be "temporary" and the Fed was supposed to "normalize" policy…but found last autumn it cannot when asset prices plummeted. This Fed's latest action is akin to keeping a sick patient alive with daily injections of high-grade heroin. Somewhere down the road the entire monetary system will likely crash and have to be replaced with something new. The entire world will be suffering a depression in the transition.

Trump has warped U.S. foreign policy more than any recent President, trashing agreements and treaties right and left (such as the JCPOA and the INF and the Paris Accords on climate). The Trump administration has given green lights to apartheid Israel to do as it pleases, and also to the Saudis. It has sanctioned and threatened allies and alleged foes alike over a host of issues. It is going for overt regime change and resource theft in Venezuela and has largely supported right-wing dictators, not proponents of democracy, everywhere.

The accounts of malfeasance and ill-advised moves could run for pages, and to boot, Trump is a proven liar, a con artist, a tax cheat, a womanizer of the worst kind, a poor businessman, a real estate grifter and a slob (all by his own admission intended or not) and he probably ought to be in prison, but oddly enough his "base" of support in the U.S. happens to be evangelical Christians (and far right wing lunatics and white supremacists) who, in truth, are anything but "Christian" and give the entire "faith" a bad name. As horrified as many Democrats are by Trump, they lack credibility but for a few brave, outstanding voices in Congress that include Rep. Ilhan

Omar and 2020 Presidential candidate Rep. Tulsi Gabbard of Hawaii.

The Democratic Party leaders may be just as corrupted as the Republicans under Trump, and Nancy Pelosi, House Majority Speaker, claims any attempt to impeach Trump is misguided because Trump is "not worth the effort". This of course makes no sense at all, for if Trump is worthless, then he surely ought to be impeached as fast as possible.

Never before in the history of the United States has the country been in such potentially dire straits longer term, been governed so badly, and had such senseless and destructive and baldly desperate foreign policies – ones based on greed, hubris, insecurity, paranoia, xenophobia and, worst of all, abysmal ignorance. Countries seem to get the governments and leaders they deserve. The U.S. is a glaring example of this, it seems.

But is there something else afoot with Trump?

One indication of how desperate some relatively thoughtful Americans are for good news and positive directions (who are outside of government) is that they think Trump is far more of a master tactician – which is unlikely although the presumption is based on some reasonable policy postures he had during his campaign for the While House in 2016.

It has been anyway put forth that Trump has figured out that the sole way to "Make America Great Again", assuming it ever was, is to disentangle from perpetual wars that have done nothing for U.S. security, have virtually bankrupted the country, bolstered a useless system of costly alliances and demonized Russia, which is not an enemy of the U.S.

However, Trump, the theory goes, realized he could do little to change any of this because the notion that the U.S. is "indispensable" and "exceptional" has been so deeply embedded in government and has prevailed against all rational odds particularly overseas. Thus, he has, the theory advances, had to adopt a back-door approach to force change by OFFENDING just about everyone on the planet to force them to unilaterally disengage from the U.S. (One example of Trump offense among others is his recent demand that allies pay for the maintenance of U.S. troops and "protection" on their own soil.)

But still, nothing has really happened yet.

America's European allies have not yet quit the U.S., but are charting some mildly independent courses including a clear aversion to Trump's and the Zionists' and Saudis' dreams of attacking Iran. And the JCPOA remains alive and the signatories (aside from the U.S.) seem to be honoring it if not doing everything they can to ensure their trade with Iran is not eliminated by U.S. sanctions. (This despite Mike Pence's exhortation to U.S. allies to quit the JCPOA in Warsaw, which fell flat.) And no one has so far pulled out of useless NATO, too. Thus, what has occurred so far is only that some obvious cracks are growing between U.S. and allies and according to some theorists, this is a SUCCESS for Trump's alleged schemes to reorder and reorient U.S. priorities more to domestic problems and concerns.

At any rate, desperation even for those who want to believe in positive change (and that Trump is not insane) has become as thick as polar ice, and this is natural, too. But anyone who thinks Donald Trump really understands what he is doing, and has some wildly complicated master plan to impose or transform some decent campaign promises he made in 2016 into real policy, is sadly mistaken. Any President who chooses Mike Pompeo or John Bolton or Elliott Abrams for top positions, all three of them despicable sadists, can't possibly be thinking of anything but their own survival and the deployment of brute force.

Pity any nation that has veered from the moral messages of Christianity and Islam
Apr 6, 2019

Donald Trump is more than halfway through his first term and (insha'a Allah) last term as U.S. President and by most sane accounts he's been a looming disaster so far -- a disaster that remains mostly prospective because of things already done and decided and which await some kind of unpleasant denouement.

The U.S. economy is doing well, relative to most others, and unemployment is low even if most jobs are menial and most Americans are eyeballs deep in debt. But this is almost certainly because of a dump of $trillions in printed money in to the economy and nearly zero interest rates by the Federal Reserve Bank. This was supposed to be "temporary" and the Fed was supposed to "normalize" policy…but found last autumn it cannot when asset prices plummeted. This Fed's latest action is akin to keeping a sick patient alive with daily injections of high-grade heroin. Somewhere down the road the entire monetary system will likely crash and have to be replaced with something new. The entire world will be suffering a depression in the transition.

Trump has warped U.S. foreign policy more than any recent President, trashing agreements and treaties right and left (such as the JCPOA and the INF and the Paris Accords on climate). The Trump administration has given green lights to apartheid Israel to do as it pleases, and also to the Saudis. It has sanctioned and threatened allies and alleged foes alike over a host of issues. It is going for overt regime change and resource theft in Venezuela and has largely supported right-wing dictators, not proponents of democracy, everywhere.

The accounts of malfeasance and ill-advised moves could run for pages, and to boot, Trump is a proven liar, a con artist, a tax cheat, a womanizer of the worst kind, a poor businessman, a real estate grifter and a slob (all by his own admission intended or not) and he probably ought to be in prison, but oddly enough his "base" of support in the U.S. happens to be evangelical Christians (and far right wing lunatics and white supremacists) who, in truth, are anything but "Christian" and give the entire "faith" a bad name. As horrified as many Democrats are by Trump, they lack credibility but for a few brave, outstanding voices in Congress that include Rep. Ilhan Omar and 2020 Presidential candidate Rep. Tulsi Gabbard of Hawaii.

The Democratic Party leaders may be just as corrupted as the Republicans under Trump, and Nancy Pelosi, House Majority Speaker, claims any attempt to impeach Trump is misguided because Trump is "not worth the effort". This of course makes no sense at all, for if Trump is worthless, then he surely ought to be impeached as fast as possible.

Never before in the history of the United States has the country been in such potentially dire straits longer term, been governed so badly, and had such senseless and destructive and baldly desperate foreign policies – ones based on greed, hubris, insecurity, paranoia, xenophobia and, worst of all, abysmal ignorance. Countries seem to get the governments and leaders they deserve. The U.S. is a glaring example of this, it seems.

But is there something else afoot with Trump?

One indication of how desperate some relatively thoughtful Americans are for good news and positive directions (who are outside of government) is that they think Trump is far more of a master tactician – which is unlikely although the presumption is based on some reasonable policy postures he had during his campaign for the While House in 2016.

It has been anyway put forth that Trump has figured out that the sole way to "Make America Great Again", assuming it ever was, is to disentangle from perpetual wars that have done nothing for U.S. security, have virtually bankrupted the country, bolstered a useless system of costly alliances and demonized Russia, which is not an enemy of the U.S.

However, Trump, the theory goes, realized he could do little to change any of this because the notion that the U.S. is "indispensable" and "exceptional" has been so deeply embedded in government and has prevailed against all rational odds particularly overseas. Thus, he has, the theory advances, had to adopt a back-door approach to force change by OFFENDING just about everyone on the planet to force them to unilaterally disengage from the U.S. (One example of Trump offense among others is his recent demand that allies pay for the maintenance of U.S. troops and "protection" on their own soil.)

But still, nothing has really happened yet.

America's European allies have not yet quit the U.S., but are charting some mildly independent courses including a clear aversion to Trump's and the Zionists' and Saudis' dreams of attacking Iran. And the JCPOA remains alive and the signatories (aside from the U.S.) seem to be honoring it if not doing everything they can to ensure their trade with Iran is not eliminated by U.S. sanctions. (This despite Mike Pence's exhortation to U.S. allies to quit the JCPOA in Warsaw, which fell flat.) And no one has so far pulled out of useless NATO, too. Thus, what has occurred so far is only that some obvious cracks are growing between U.S. and allies and according to some theorists, this is a SUCCESS for Trump's alleged schemes to reorder and reorient U.S. priorities more to domestic problems and concerns.

At any rate, desperation even for those who want to believe in positive change (and that Trump is not insane) has become as thick as polar ice, and this is natural, too. But anyone who thinks Donald Trump really understands what he is doing, and has some wildly complicated master plan to impose or transform some decent campaign promises he made in 2016 into real policy, is sadly mistaken. Any President who chooses Mike Pompeo or John Bolton or Elliott Abrams for top positions, all three of them despicable sadists, can't possibly be thinking of anything but their own survival and the deployment of brute force.

The aggravation of Trump's lack of vision is the world's burden

Apr 8, 2019

Now that Americans have been informed that the Mueller report conclusions investigating alleged collusion between Trump and minions and the Russians was little more than conspiracy pornography concocted by Obama and Clinton and by those who were appalled that Trump won the election in 2016, the Republicans and Trump may breathe a sigh of relief for a short while, but no one else can.

To any extent that Trump and the Neocons are emboldened further by the alleged conclusions of the Mueller investigation, it's not just Americans who are at risk, but the entire world. A world which is groaning under the lash of a President doing all the wrong things to "make America great again". Trump is mostly making America despised.

As odd as the analogy may be, I had the distinct displeasure of having to spend an entire night last week at a newish terminal at Newark airport outside New York City, and felt that the actual fixed layout of the place served to describe the country today. By all appearances the terminal appeared nice enough, but every single chair for those in transit, including those at food kiosks, was firmly bolted to the floor, and not a single one induced relaxation or provided much comfort.

The entire terminal was all a matter of appearances that delivered little for weary travelers. So it is for people yearning for relief from the efforts of the Trump administration to attack with sanctions or threats of war just about every country on earth: with policies that seem bolted down, like the chairs at Newark airport, and averse to any qualitative change, designed to resist even the slightest challenge to U.S. imperium and unilateralism.

Amid a welter of bad news, including the floods in Iran (but which may revitalize in some respects a very arid country overall) one must note in random order: Turkey is not bowing to U.S. pressure to cancel the S400 deal with Russia, Europe is responding positively to China's Belt and Road initiative and showing some independence for the first time in decades from U.S. dominance, North Korea notes how John Bolton shot down any agreement with Trump in Hanoi this winter and is not bending to absurd demands, Trump is not looking particularly good for reelection in 2020 but the Democrats are still looking foolish generally by not embracing progressives and progressive policies.

The U.S. mainstream media has become untrustworthy and sentiment among many U.S citizens, noted last week in France, too, is sour and dour and frightened by Trump who has dismantled environmental safeguards in favor of the corporate oligarchy. The financial markets have been rigged by the Federal Reserve bank and Trump, and this is becoming clearer by the day.

Maduro, for all his faults (and there are many) is hanging tough in Venezuela and Trump hasn't a clue what to do next to try to install the hapless puppet Guaido short of invading the country. Trump is thoroughly opposed worldwide and at the U.N. by his unilateral declaration that the Golan is Israeli territory in an attempt to insure Netanyahu wins reelection given that his "base" are the illegal settlers in the West Bank and Golan. The Saudis have at least threatened to sell oil in some other currency such as the Yuan or the Euro. And this is just the short list.

What all this and more actually demonstrates is that the harder Trump tries to shore up U.S. "empire" as it has been this century at least, the more he incites opposition and disgust everywhere, like an abusive husband whose wife (or wives) still cower in too much fear of a bully and a tyrant.

But no one ever said the fall from grace of the U.S. in world opinion and the fraying of the Empire of Chaos would ever be easy, however necessary for the future health of humanity in general it seems to be. And more than ever, it is incumbent upon countries like Iran that are distressed and hurt by U.S. moves to try to do the exact opposite of Trump and keep an eye on the big picture as it unfolds now and in future.

The lie of the U.S as a current champion of democracy and peace is increasingly apparent even inside the U.S although countering moves remain difficult. This means that those who oppose Trump become especially big champions of democracy at home and multilateralism and peace elsewhere.

Trump has been so malleable because he is a know nothing. He has been made a servant to the Zionists and the Neocons. But one must wonder that if someone of sound mind got his ear, he might change course? He is such a narcissist that one must wonder that if he actually heard a good argument pointing out how to make himself a world hero, he might change.

Wishful thinking it is, but if he were to declare a balanced policy in the Mideast, resurrection of the U.S. adherence to the JCPOA, vast relief funds that are not bribes for any country struck by natural disasters as Iran has been of late, the end of overweening support for the Zionist agenda, the end of smothering sanctions, détente with Russia, an end to the arms race and a vast cut in wasteful U.S. military expenditures, the freeing of Julian Assange, restored safeguards against environmental decay, and much more, Trump would no doubt find himself the most popular President ever everywhere.

And this is precisely what is most aggravating, that he and his administration and many in the U.S. Congress don't see and understand this. Why not, is the question? The answer is that Trump and many others are hostage to special interests and their own utter stupidity, and the risks are enormous.

The U.S. under Trump and his crazed Neocons aim to tyrannize the entire world.
Apr 25, 2019

In the broadest sense, without all the nuances and other information, this is how things stand very basically regarding the United States:

At least $6 trillion (If not $20 trillion which the Pentagon cannot account for) has gone down the drain over the past 20 years or so with the U.S. efforts to gut or destabilize seven countries as per the "Project for a New American Century", a dangerous scheme concocted by Zionists both inside the

U.S and in Israel. It all, and by that I mean all the aggression economic or military, has had little to do with any perceived benefit for the U.S. because there is none unless one counts an economy that has become too dependent on the Military Industrial Complex that former President Eisenhower warned against when he left office in 1960. The sole beneficiary, and even this is questionable long term, has been the racist, apartheid entity that calls itself Israel. Meanwhile the U.S. economy has over the decades been completely financialized, with the top five percent or less of citizens having benefitted while and the middle class and labor have been eviscerated by neoliberal policies. Yes, the U.S. economy has been "growing" since 2009 and the last recession, but this growth has been anemic at best and it also has been dependent on the growth of debt and "money" creation in the trillions that has never in all of history been previously witnessed.

The U.S. political system and the two-party status quo, which remains intact but teetering, is slowly proving unworkable. The system has turned rotten from the appearance of mindless political wannabes and the entrenched hangers on in Congress, many of whom resemble termites, and the partisan U.S. mainstream media can no longer be trusted to report the truth. Not a single foreign policy pursued by the U.S. has been born from goodwill towards other countries, but it is increasingly in fact the result of fear and panic that the Empire of Chaos will fall and its oligarchs and the MIC will face at last their well-deserved day of reckoning. That day has not arrived yet. But it will. Goodwill in the long run cannot be denied. The world is too intertwined.

Trump, as many know, has reneged on virtually all his campaign promises with regard to foreign policies. He has been thoroughly captured by appointed Neocons like

Bolton and Pompeo, which is to say he has been captured almost solely by Netanyahu and the oligarch Jewish/Zionist billionaires in the U.S. How else can one explain the moves Trump has made beginning almost a year ago when he cancelled U.S. participation in the JCPOA?

No question Trump and his administrative lackeys want above all for Iran to buckle and leave the JCPOA. Trump wants Iran to provoke a U.S./Saudi/Israeli military attack, and not just on Iran, but on Iran's allies, in particular Hezbollah in Lebanon and on the Assad government in Syria. Trump also seems to be pushing, with its demands to kill Iranian oil sales, to provoke Iran to try to block commercial traffic through the Straits of Hormuz, providing yet another reason for war in the Middle East. At the moment, in this almost delirious swarm of bad actions, China reportedly may not obey Trump and may actually be planning to boost oil purchases from Iran. Russia and Turkey, India and Japan and other countries, would be advised to follow suit or at least not cut their purchases of Iranian crude oil. This may be the moment, if ever there was one, to break the stranglehold the U.S. has enjoyed for decades as the world's number one bully. The sheer arrogance of the U.S. government under Trump acting like the world's dictator is almost beyond belief. It reeks of desperation, too. As Philip Giraldi, a former CIA employee who visited Iran last year with other notable U.S. citizens writes: the U.S. has "heightening tension with major powers Russia and China while also threatening Iran and Venezuela on an almost daily basis. Now Cuba is in the crosshairs because it is allegedly assisting Venezuela. One might reasonably ask if America in its seemingly enduring role as the world's most feared bully will ever cease and desist, but the more practical question might be "When will the psychopathic trio of John Bolton,

Mike Pompeo and Elliott Abrams be fired (and replaced) so the United States can begin to behave like a normal nation?"

No question, anyway, that a faltering U.S. "empire" like many previous empires has become more strident, demanding and dangerous exactly at the time when its credibility and popularity are dying. And whoever gave Trump the "right" to hand over (and more) the Syrian Golan to Netanyahu and Israel, breaking international laws and norms as if they simply never existed? Make no mistake, most if not all the world outside of Saudi Arabia and Israel are against this raw power play. But this in not news to Iran nor to anyone else. It's time Europe stepped up, too, and condemned the Trump regime. South Africa, for one, has already broken off most of its diplomatic relations with the outlaw Zionist state. Others may follow.

What the U.S. has at bottom decreed to the entire world is that the U.S. alone gets to decide who trades with whom. In effect, national sovereignty according to Trump does not exist anywhere. As one commentator has remarked, this goes well beyond a merely aggressive foreign policy. It suggests a global dictatorship enacted by the U.S. Countries like China and Russia and Iran must now and forevermore decide to resist, or else become slaves to U.S. tyranny.

Trump's one opportunity to survive with any positive legacy: dumping his Neocon, Zionist advisors
Apr 27, 2019

Well, for sure, the designation by Trump of the IRGC as a "terrorist" organization is a foolish move, but not Iran's tit for tat response to it – designating the same for the U.S. central military command, or CENTCOM. This all can mostly present a warning for the remaining 5000 U.S. soldiers and diplomats in Iraq and the 2000 or so still lingering in Syria.

The Trump move is clearly because John Bolton and Mike Pompeo and some other de facto Zionist Neocons in his administration seek some kind of clear provocation for a military attack on Iran and not merely an attack on Iranian forces outside Iran. But Trump, intellectual and strategic weakling that he truly has become, wants nothing but fuel for his narcissism and popularity, which he is not going to get from the American voters by sparking another Middle Eastern war. None has gone as planned by the U.S. and Trump's tenure and any kind of positive legacy may be dependent on NOT starting any more wars in the Middle East and not in Venezuela, too. Will Trump understand this? Hard to know.

And does Trump fully realize that Syria, Iraq, Iran and even Lebanon are beginning to bind themselves closer together in a mutual allegiance of some sort? And Egypt has just refused inclusion into the Arab "NATO" that the U.S. wants to create. Of course Trump knows all this, and it could be fuel for further U.S. aggression in the region, but to use it as such is a mistake of the first order.

At any rate, these countries along or near the northern edge of the Arab Mideast, and Iran, are talking about connecting and rebuilding their railways, providing Iraq and Iran, with Chinese assistance related to the Belt and Road initiative, a means to access ports on the Mediterranean. This project could take several years given that much railway infrastructure, which was in fair condition until 2011, has been destroyed in the wars.

If one stands back a bit and takes a look at the overall picture of U.S foreign policy currently, and not just in the Middle East, it is failing. Even while many, Iranians especially, suffer from it.

The Neocons have been stalled in Venezuela and a few hundred Russian and Chinese troops are there to help the stall stick. The Syrian government continues to consolidate its grip despite Israeli missile attacks and further attacks by terrorists in the Idlib area on Syrian civilians. Iraqis may be close to demanding the exit of U.S. troops. Most in the U.S. Congress want to deny the U.S. further support for the Saudi war on Yemen, but Trump just foolishly vetoed the legislation while the best of the Democratic challengers for the 2020 election for POTU.S. are pushing harder for a full stop end to the foreign wars.

The most notable among them is the eloquent and attractive Rep. Tulsi Gabbard of Hawaii whose consistency and vision is attracting more and more fans. She has the makings of the best possible female candidate ever to campaign to occupy the White House. But no question Trump has gotten a boost in the popularity polls by his apparent exoneration from conspiring with the Russians in the 2016 election where he did not even win a plurality of the popular vote.

The long running and absurd "War on Terror" since the turn of the century, it is clear, is in effect a war on Muslim countries that have foreign policies independent of Washington and especially the Zionists, with other targets like Venezuela under Maduro. The world knows, at least, who the real "terrorists" are. Iranians need to know this latter fact whether anything can be done about it immediately. There are some scattered positives appearing:

Executives at the IMF, for example, have allegedly voted NOT to recognize puppet Juan Guaido as president of Venezuela, realizing it may not be wise to condemn themselves to dealing with a bloc that lacks any sovereign authority. Jimmy Carter, the last U.S. President who could possibly claim to be attempting to adhere to moral principles was preaching in his hometown church in Georgia last Sunday pointing out that the U.S. in its 240 plus years has only been at peace for 16 years, making the U.S. "the most warlike nation in world history".

He went on to point out that China has been at war with no one for decades and enjoyed enormous economic benefits, including a growing infrastructure second to none, while the U.S. has spent itself towards moral and financial bankruptcy. Trump's MAGA plan: a very sick joke.

Perhaps best of all, some observers have noted that Trump's foreign policy advisors, notably John Bolton, whose prescriptions for decades have been disastrous for the U.S., ought to be fired immediately. Most of these advisors like Bolton have been shills for the Zionists and pushed Trump to make his number one foreign priority support for the Zionists, who by the day are more reviled than ever worldwide. But just as some Democrat presidential hopefuls have vowed, if elected, to push the U.S. to rejoin the JCPOA, the Zionists are pushing for attacks on Iran's nuclear facilities claiming that such would not lead to a wider war in the Mideast.

This latter is a complete lie, as Iranians well and rightfully know. Israel has been and remains the most self-serving, and corrupted country for over seven decades, and their traitorous U.S. servants, like Bolton and other Neocons, MU.S.T be derailed somehow.

U.S. undermines itself clinging to hegemonic notions.

May 4, 2019

Anyone looking at Iran from afar could presume conditions have not been worse in the past 30 plus years, or since the end of the Iraq-Iran war, a war which never would have occurred if the U.S. had not urged Saddam Hussain on and given him chemical weapons. Little did Saddam know that in a few more years he would be hung by the Americans after the U.S. military had killed hundreds of thousands of his countrymen and destroyed much of Iraq's infrastructure.

Any good student of history knows that the U.S. has been the most destructive, murderous country in world history. The numbers simply bear it out, and Hiroshima and Nagasaki are examples. It's indisputable. One might have said the same about the Mongols in the mid 13th century CE. The Mongols wrecked much of Baghdad (and other Muslim cities east and west) and ended the Abbasid Caliphate, but it was not much later that the Mongols assimilated and were spiritually seduced by Islam and the glories of Islamic culture and civilization. Americans, if truth be known, are neither sophisticated nor knowledgeable enough to realize their culture is primarily shallow and crude and without particular merit, at least in recent decades, compared to the Muslim world in its best iterations over the centuries. Rampant materialism does not a sublime culture make.

One is reminded of Mahatma Gandhi, who once was asked by an American reporter in India not long before he was assassinated: "What do you think of Western civilization?" (Gandhi as a young man had trained and worked as an attorney in both South Africa and England and knew both East and West.) Gandhi looked squarely at the reporter and answered: "I THINK IT WOULD BE A GOOD IDEA."

Indeed, if the U.S. has in the past tried to don some veneer of respectability with propaganda about respect for "democracy" or "human rights" or whatever, those days are over. There was never much under the veneer anyway in recent decades, but now even the veneer is gone.

Look what has been witnessed in the past month! Mike Pompeo, probably the absolute worst U.S. Secretary of State ever, was caught bragging about how when he was chief of the CIA he helped establish training classes in theft, lying and murderous subterfuge. He thought this was amusing, too. Worse is John Bolton, who was literally telling the truth when he said forthrightly that the U.S. was not sanctioning Venezuela and hurting its people or trying to install Juan Guido because the U.S. wanted to see more "democracy" there, but because the U.S. coveted Venezuela's oil. An active coup attempt is allegedly underway now in Caracas.

And for all the world knows, Julian Assange, who has done nothing wrong, may never emerge from some odious prison in Britain or the U.S. Not to mention the U.S. government's primary allies, both condemned by most of the world: A Saudi hellhole that this past month beheaded 37 people, some of them juveniles and most of them Shi'a, and an Israeli racist apartheid machine that can't stop destroying the lives of the native Palestinians. The Trump Administration uttered not a single word about the Saudi executions and has been Zio-nized all along by money, political brobery and flattery. Yes, some of Trump minions have actually said U.S. Mideast policy is in fact directed by Netanyahu.

On the other hand, U.S. sanctions and other measures against Iran are said to be exerting maximum effectiveness right now, but Iran has not gone begging to the U.S. to desist, but Javad Zarif in the U.S. has appealed to reason.

From now on the damage of sanctions could wane. They will lose efficacy, but this will take time and patience. Iran can use its diplomacy and its excellent diplomats to continue to line up support from Russia and China, for one thing. A significant part of and reason for any U.S. attack on Iran is the aim to disrupt or block the Chinese "Belt and Road" initiative across Asia, where Iran is a key country in this grand economic scheme. The U.S. should be joining the program, but it's jealous and will eventually be left out in the cold. Moreover, the ace up Iran's sleeve is its last resort option to close the Straits of Hormuz and drive oil prices into the stratosphere…and set off a worldwide economic Depression. Iran's many and growing sympathizers certainly don't want that, and interestingly, Russia is setting up joint naval maneuvers with Iran in the Persian Gulf and Iran's Navy has recently conducted joint naval maneuvers with Oman. Technocratic advice and exchange between Iran, Russia and China and neighbors is likely to expand powerfully in the months and years ahead. Many countries are desperately figuring out ways to carry on creatively despite the U.S.

Meanwhile, the U.S. use of the world reserve status of the dollar as a sanctions and trade weapon means that countries will fast seek alternative ways to conduct bilateral business and when they do, they will never return to the dollar. Trump has done little but accelerate the U.S. decline because he hired Pompeo and Bolton, who from the beginning may have been promoted to check Trump, do Israel's bidding completely, scuttle the reunification of North and South Korea, and make stupid demands on Lebanon and Syria and many other countries, too.

It is a shame that Washington cannot so far accept any other role in the world except as a punishing dictatorial hegemon. A shame because the role is eroding U.S. influence just as bankruptcy does for individuals: slowly at first, then all of a sudden.

Trump's "threat" administration is a one trick pony so far

May 11, 2019

The Trump Administration ought to be renamed "The Threat Administration". Even the so-called "special relationship" between the U.S. and the U.K. has been threatened simply because the Brits seem to want to buy top of the line Chinese 5G Huawei broadband technology. In fact, it's not hard to get the impression that Trump and his foreign policy team, Bolton and Pompeo especially, are now bouncing off the bloody walls of the White House of late frustrated by their own failures so far and beginning to bump in to each other.

First, the apparent biggest failure of late: The planned coup d'etat and the failed installation of the hapless Juan Guaido, who now may be more useful dead than alive to the coup plotters in Washington. They have found no firm pretext to militarily invade Venezuela even though invasion may be the last card they have, and they have been looking for one, but not even the people of Venezuela and its army, who have rallied behind Maduro on balance, want to deal with American military gringos rampaging in Venezuela.

But the result of stalemate in Venezuela has evidently shifted the focus rather decidedly towards Iran, based apparently on some bogus "intelligence" coughed up by the Zionists suggesting that American troops may have been specifically targeted by Iran should military hostilities commence. Thus, Trump has sent a flock of four B-52 bombers to the big

American airbase in Qatar, and as well sent the aircraft carrier Abraham Lincoln through the Suez Canal towards the Persian Gulf. What to make of this? Well, it's no secret that Trump or at least Mike Pompeo and John Bolton want to provoke Iran in to some action that might serve as a pretext for an attack. But the qualifier "at least" is important here. Because Trump, if he has any sense at all, must be aware that a new war anywhere will sink his Presidency and his reelection chances IF he caves to the belligerency of his advisors towards Iran. One not privy to Iranian forward contingency planning cannot know what Iran's leadership is exactly thinking, but to say any action by Iran might be dicey must be the understatement of the century so far.

One thing is known, however. Trump has expressed alarm at the idea of a war on Venezuela, which Bolton and Pompeo have threatened, and he has lately expressed some dissatisfaction with Bolton. Whether he has the intelligence to fire Bolton remains to be seen, but it must have at the margin occurred to him that Bolton has been leading him towards actions that will ultimately spell his personal doom as President and make him a one termer.

Observers note that a number of notable Americans have ensconced themselves in the Venezuelan embassy in Washington to obviate any of Guaido's comrades setting themselves up in the embassy as de facto representatives of Venezuela, but Guaido supporters have gathered on the streets outside the embassy in Washington and tried to break in, and meanwhile the police and Secret Service members have permitted power cuts to the embassy and refused to allow well-wishers to deliver food to the brave people inside. How long the peace activists can hold out under pressure inside the embassy is anyone's guess at this point, but the key point is that Trump had or may still be having misgivings about his advisors that could, with some luck, spill over to the delicate situation with Iran and the bad advice he has received from them.

Spokespersons for Trump claim Trump does not want a war with Iran, but at the same time the administration maintains "maximum pressure" on the Islamic Republic. What does this "maximum pressure", which has just included sanctions against Iran's metals industries (in addition to Iranian oil) aim to achieve? One obvious bet is that Trump or at least Bolton want to provoke Iran to precipitous actions that would be used as a pretext for what Bolton has called "unrelenting" military action. The pressure is on Iran to change its foreign policies, but no one has cited specifics about exactly what changes are desirable a year after Trump scuttled American participation in the JCPOA. Iran, in any event, is unlikely to roll over and suddenly become a whimpering puppet for the U.S. and abrogate its independent postures which, in fact, do NOT constitute anything but ideological differences with the U.S. and its imperialism and never have. One might easily wonder if the U.S. government has lost its mind, so easily does it think, on both sides of the aisle, that militancy is okay… except for people like Rep. Tulsi Gabbard and Senator Sanders, both of them the best candidates for the 2020 election.

But Iran's leaders have announced that it would halt compliance with marginal, self-imposed elements of the JCPOA commitments without throwing the deal overboard unless the situation improves and the remaining signatories to the nuclear deal get off their backsides and fulfill their trade promises with Iran. And meanwhile, Mike Pompeo paid a surprise, four-hour visit to Iraq this past week trying to "trump" up a panic about Iran's alleged plans to attack U.S. troops in the Middle East should the U.S. commence war.

The Iraqi Prime Minister Abdul Mahdi insisted nonetheless that Iraq would not participate in any economic boycott of any country, apparently declining to cooperate with U.S. efforts to squeeze Iran. President Rouhani's threats to restart some modest enrichment of uranium stock may or may not be foolish given that this could provide ammunition to the warmongers in Washington, even while this does not constitute steps towards a bomb. It must be noted, as ever, that Iran has never ever intended to create nuclear weapons on sincere religious grounds.

Pompeo in any case must be bonkers, because if a war does break out, how can he possibly expect Iranian forces, in defense, NOT to try to fend off the American troops, ships or bombers, putting American troops at risk? How gullible is the American public not to see through this dangerous game? We shall see, but one minor positive is that the B-52 bombers now on the tarmac in the Mideast are in Qatar, a country that has maintained relatively good relations with Iran, which came to Qatar's aid in 2017 when the Saudis imposed a blockade on Qatar while Trump tweeted falsehoods about the Qataris siding with the Saudis.

Given that members of the Trump gang are proven dissemblers, they don't deserve credibility. And Iraq's Shi'ites, including Muqtada al-Sadr, whatever else they think, remain anti-imperialists at bottom and have claimed that U.S. pressure to stop doing business with Iran may result eventually in the closure of the U.S. embassy in Baghdad, the world's largest, and the expulsion of some 5000 remaining U.S. troops in Iraq.

It's a wonder the embassy has not been shut down already, like years ago.

The utter truth is that Trump and gang know very little about the Middle East, and have no serious interest in the general welfare of the people of the region. This fact alone is ultimately going to haunt the U.S., and not merely in the Middle East. As well, the closer ties the U.S. has developed with the fascists in Israel, who have for decades pushed for war on the Islamic Republic, will also ultimately haunt the U.S. If Trump wants to sink himself, and he's already doing that to some extent domestically even by withholding his tax returns, he's well on his way to perfidy by listening to the warmongers surrounding him. His Presidency has been a nightmare for many thoughtful Americans.

Whether more U.S. sparked chaos or real accord is the question that haunts the world
May 18, 2019

Iran's leaders, Iran's many friends and the people of Iran well know what is afoot right now with the Trump Administration, with John Bolton and Mike Pompeo, and with at least some members of the U.S. Congress and with other Neocons in D.C. "think tanks" and their various institutions.

Iran also knows the Israeli role in drumming up potential war in the Mideast, just as the Zionists did in the lead up to

Whether more U.S. sparked chaos or ...

the invasion of Iraq in 2003. It is quite obvious that Trump and colleagues are searching for a pretext to attack Iran, saying that virtually anything Iran does or might do to defend itself or to ward off an attack may constitute a pretext for war.

Mike Pompeo on May 13 landed in Brussels to discuss Iran with EU leaders, skipping a day when he earlier intended to visit Russia and Putin and Lavrov. Pompeo did not talk to the media. European leaders urged "restraint" on the U.S. But as imminent journalist Pepe Escobar reported, it is "naïve" to think the Europeans "will grow a backbone" and definitely condemn Pompeo and Trump.

At the same time some prominent European military brass countered the U.S. and said there had been no particular "threat" from Iranian-backed forces in Syria and Iraq, but they were rebuked by the U.S. It may be a futile hope that wiser people in the Pentagon and military will decline to take orders from Pompeo now and from National Security Advisor John Bolton. But what about Russia and China in particular?

Neocon Paul Wolfowitz, one of the primary pushers of the war on Iraq, said back in 2003 that the Russians would not stop the U.S. He was correct then, but now? It was Putin who stood up before the U.N in New York several years ago and posed the rhetorical question to the General Assembly in reference to the U.S.: "Do you realize what (the U.S.) has done?" in Iraq, Libya and so many other places in the Middle East.

One must wonder that Putin has to be further appalled by what the U.S. has been doing since, in particular supporting the Saudis in their genocidal war on Yemen, in the support of terrorists in the war on Syria, and with the U.S. abrogation of the JCPOA a year ago and draconian sanctions on Iran and sanctions on other countries around the world. But does Putin have enough of a backbone to come to Iran's defense should it be attacked militarily?

Does China and do other countries? This must be a major question should the U.S. err so grievously again. Some bright observers like Britain's former MP George Galloway have said that an attack on Iran by the U.S. could prove to be the greatest mistake in all of history. And he's not wrong when one considers that World War 3 could result from U.S. missteps. China and Russia have both said at least they will not permit Iran to be destroyed.

Perhaps the biggest obstacle to sanity in any final analysis is that, as many know, neither Trump, Pompeo nor Bolton are rational humans, each irrational in their different ways, and neither is the Israeli government nor "Bibi" Netanyahu. All are dangers to humanity, with perhaps the worst being Pompeo who has given indications that he believes in the so-called "Rapture" promoted by like-minded Christian evangelicals, who constitute Trump's primary political base in the U.S. Pompeo (and Bolton) marks the ultimate degenerative evolution of creators of U.S foreign policies that began decades ago with the Vietnam War when the U.S. went to war based on the fake, false flag pretext of the Gulf of Tonkin incident.

One potential positive is that Trump campaigned for the Presidency with talk of reducing if not eliminating U.S. military engagements overseas, although he has done and threatened anything but this, particularly over the past year when he seems to have been captured fully by the Zionists. And Trump has also later said he wants to talk with Iran's leaders, but at the same time, he absurdly expects Iran to pick up the phone and call him. Such a move by Iran might well have been possible if Trump had not canned the JCPOA and backed himself into a corner.

And apparently from Iran's point of view – a justifiable one – it behooves the U.S. to resurrect its participation in the nuclear accord and reduce economic sanctions as first steps before negotiations towards any modification of the deal and other potentially positive de-escalation moves. Iran seems to be open to this, contingent on the JCPOA re-endorsement.

The most worrying factor is the possibility that Trump and others in the U.S. government have never had any intention towards anything but full-spectrum dominance worldwide and the submission of other countries, not caring at all about the chaos it has unleashed in the past and would further unleash in the future, particularly in West Asia. This chaos may well be what, at the bottom, the Israelis most fervently desire without saying so as a means to maintain its cruel, expansionary apartheid state, and what the U.S. won't admit it also most desires in the erroneous presumption such chaos will in the long run do anything but destroy the U.S.

Iran, whatever it further suffers, is going to win in the longer term
May 23, 2019

To whom is Donald Trump answering? Ignorance at bottom. There is almost nothing he has not upset. He is like the proverbial bull in the world shop of china. But first, imagine. Imagine for example that Barack Obama had gotten a third term in the White House and carried on as President as he had during his second term.

First, it must be noted, Trump won the 2016 election arguably in significant part because he campaigned with a message of withdrawing the U.S. from overseas military engagements. Hillary Clinton, on the other hand, had largely fomented the attacks on Libya and the destruction of that country – and bragged about it -- and also strongly supported and aided the infusion of arms and terrorists in to Syria and as well she helped devise the coup in Ukraine. She appeared relative to Trump in 2016 like some crazed crone hell-bent on revenge against the world for perceived, personal slights. (But still, had she won the election in 2016, it remains possible that she would have moderated her positions somewhat with respect to belligerent foreign policies.)

But back to Obama and the impossible third term. Had it materialized, he would have likely begun the withdrawal of the U.S. from Afghanistan. He would have maintained U.S. participation the JCPOA and, who knows, may have developed further accords with Iran. And he still did most all of what the craven and thoroughly unappreciative Zionists demanded of him (he's Black, after all, and the Zionists and Trump supporters. many of them anyway, are racists). He gave billions of dollars and arms to Israel, but he likely would have also been making noises about the necessity that Israel eventually come to a fair agreement with the Palestinians, perhaps offering them equal rights west of the Jordan if not a viable state of their own on the West Bank. He would not have moved the U.S. embassy to Jerusalem nor cut humanitarian relief for the Palestinians.

The real question here is IF the U.S. were in difficult straits with respect to its maintenance "empire" in 2016, and it did not appear to be, it certainly seems to be now, and Trump and his advisors are the reason why. From economic sanctions, especially on Iran, to trade tariffs on China and sanctions on other countries, to the attempted but so far failed coup in Venezuela, and recent threats of war on the Mideast, there has never been a President so apparently determined to make the U.S. a rogue, out-of-control and hated menace to world peace. And opposition to the Zionists is mounting across the world like never before and also inside the U.S. So far, Iran seems to be making the best moves it possibly can under the circumstances.

President Rouhani has said he welcomes U.S. diplomatic overtures but has refused new diplomacy under the fact of economic sanctions and threats of military actions. He has chosen "resistance". How does any head of state make deals with Trump who has destroyed previous deals like the JCPOA? How could the U.S. be trusted in the absence of anything but threats? How can Iran walk away entirely from the JCPOA without bringing down the wrath of the U.N. and other countries, including the other signatories to the JCPOA? It makes no sense for Trump to insist that Iran, displaying weakness and submission, call HIM for further negotiations.

From a tactical and logical standpoint, Iran's leaders like President Rouhani have said they don't want a war with the U.S. This goes without saying for any country, and as much as Bolton and Pompeo and Netanyahu and Muhammad Bin Salman and others may push for a U.S. attack on Iran, it's hard to imagine that they don't realize that even if Iran suffers mightily as a result of U.S. bombing, Israel and Saudi Arabia would also suffer mightily from any Iranian defensive retaliations, and so would the economies of every country on earth.

It seems apparent that the "maximum pressure" the U.S and its "allies" have inflicted on Iran cannot (logically anyway) have any other aim but to bring Iran to its knees with abject demands for relief from sanctions and threats. Trump and minions have made a truly absurd bet: that suffering Iranians would rise up against their government. If anything, Iranians are tighter with the extant government than they might otherwise be. Any desired internal reform on the part of Iran's people will wait for expression on the absence of military threats and sanctions by outsiders.

In some odd respects, it may be fair to say that Iran comes out a winner no matter what the U.S. and allies do, although the "victory" should military attacks commence would in the end be largely pyrrhic. But still a victory. Trump simply does not understand Iran's and the Iranian people's capacity for sacrifice to maintain its sovereignty and independent political and social culture, whatever it may be. And Trump also seems to be ignorant that the U.S. has nothing but a handful of "allies" who are primarily posturing selfishly for themselves, not the U.S., unless they all have been rendered utterly daft by hubris.

At the least, it seems accurate to say that the U.S. has become desperate to shore up its flagging influence and its "empire", and desperation or desperate moves are exactly the things that will prove to be counterproductive in the longer run. Iran has been around for almost 3000 years and is not ever going away even if it suffers, as if has often in the past, outrageous challenges.

There are good reasons why Iran won't fold to U.S. extremism
May 28, 2019

President Donald Trump claims the vast Military Industrial Complex, otherwise known as the MIC, which has become everything Eisenhower in 1960 warned against, is somehow "pressuring" him in to war on Iran.

One would imagine, however, that it's not so much the MIC (or the Pentagon per se), but rather malign if not psychopathic individuals in the administration like Mike Pompeo and John Bolton who have had the President's ear for the past year who began with urging Trump to can the JCPOA and reimpose economic sanctions on the Islamic Republic, along with the

Zionists who have been trying to drum up a U.S.-led war on Iran for decades.

Additionally, there are figures like Patrick Shanahan, the acting "defense" secretary, who knows next to nothing about the military but quite a bit about corporations like Boeing which are part of the corporate gravy train standing to profit from military action anywhere. And even Bolton is apparently working out of the Pentagon mostly, not the White House, as National Security Advisor to Trump.

The provocations against Iran have become increasingly intense, and already there have been alleged attacks on an Aramco facility in Arabia and some damage to three ships in the Persian Gulf – attacks blamed on Iran. But even a moron knows, given history since the Vietnam War, that these are false flag ventures. The mere thought Iran, at this point, would be inviting U.S. military action has to be entirely unbelievable.

Iran is postulating some kind of non-aggression pact between countries on the Persian Gulf, and Iran's leadership has stated clearly that it does not want further hostilities with the U.S. And more importantly, on national television in the U.S., Trump has also stated he does not want to fight Iran, at least militarily. He seems largely opposed to stupid wars, including the war on Iraq in 2003 – perhaps the greatest single mistake since the Vietnam War in the 1960s.

But Trump is not all that attentive as any kind of chief executive and he has Bolton and others around who seems to exist for nothing but war, and to them it may not even matter where war may be – just that the U.S. is throwing its military power around and trying to prove forevermore that the U.S. is THE hegemon and intends to remain so.

There are good reasons why Iran ...

It really is a terrible situation for Trump, because if he wants to avoid igniting another war in the Mideast, he almost MU.S.T fire both Pompeo and Bolton and this just for starters. And this was or is a real estate tycoon, and not a very good one with a trail of bankruptcies, who was alleged to be completely surprised that he won the 2016 election and may have not wanted the Presidency all that much given his lifelong primary interests around the accumulation of lucre and female "conquests" in or outside of marriage.

The fact is that if the U.S. bombs Iran, it won't "work" if the expectation is that Iran is suddenly going to do whatever the warmongers want. Iran, it appears, is going to be well prepared and focused in retaliation, and will prove it if necessary. What then? A U.S. invasion of Iran? The U.S. public, one can be certain, won't have it, nor will most of the rest of the world.

The U.S. will NOT be able to muster, as it did almost 20 years ago with Iraq, any kind of remotely credible coalition, although its likely that the Saudis and the Zionists will be involved. An invasion of Iran, smart observers have noted, will end the U.S. role in future in the Middle East, and may even finish off the U.S. globally and destroy the so-called "empire" the U.S. has stitched together since World War 2. And one must not downplay Russian and Chinese pledges NOT to permit Iran to be destroyed.

On this latter possibility, that the U.S. could wreck itself, and on this alone, one has to wonder that some of Iran's hardliners may not be entirely averse to a military tangle with the U.S., although they won't likely do anything to provoke it directly, unless one imagines that defensive preparation is provocation. Indeed, it's not difficult to put forward the notion that after almost 70 years of U.S. meddling or hostility to Iran, some Iranians might be willing to serve a sacrificial role to get the U.S. off Iran's back once and for all time.

During the revolution in Iran 40 years ago, angry Iranians erected a poster in Tehran directed at the U.S. that read in English: "Vietnam wounded you; Iran will bury you!" Of course the warning was hyperbolic. Justifiably angry people anywhere tend to hyperbole. But consider:

A wise mother once told her several children: "If you catch a bird in your hands and grip it too hard to keep it (as the U.S. is trying to hold on to its worldwide hegemony), you will kill it. But if you let it fly free, it will probably fly back to your hands." So now we see the U.S. doing everything possible (desperately) to maintain the economic and military disparities between itself and other nations.

This is the primary objective behind American-instigated trade wars, economic sanctions and military threats wherever they have occurred. But screwing other nations is not a productive game longer term, and most of the world understands this. The best hope is that the people who make decisions in Washington wise up. Meanwhile, let's also hope Iran's proposed non-aggression pact with its neighbors bears fruit.

Iran's potentials despite economic sanctions must be realized eventually

May 29, 2019

NORTH CAROLINA - From afar one can't help thinking about how lucky Iran really is in many respects. I mean this sincerely.

Sure, the economy over the past year has dropped nearly 10 percent, according to some economists, and Iran's people are hurting as they watch whatever standard of living they had decline while inflation has taken a toll and put out of reach many of the goods, especially luxury goods, average people want, even if – probably – the economic problems have not much impacted Iran's elite. And the reasons for the declines over the past year have mostly but not exclusively been attributed, and rightly so, to the harsh economic sanctions imposed by the U.S. in the wake of the abnegation of the JCPOA for no good reason.

But there is a different way Iranians might think about all this, taking a longer-term view.

First, consider how utterly rich Iran really is compared to maybe four or five other countries in the world, even if Iran can't currently sell nearly as much of its riches – mostly petroleum – as was possible a year ago. Also consider what it was mostly selling its riches for what will ultimately be worthless paper.

And further consider these factors: even with a population of some 83 million people, it will be generations, if Iran could never sell much if any of its oil any longer before Iranian citizens would ever be without more than enough subsidized energy resources for transportation and heating and the myriad other uses for oil. You can't say this about more than a handful of other countries. Moreover, Iran has a relatively educated population, and the gene pool might be labeled "SMART". No one else likely could have invented chess!

One might imagine that the U.S., with five percent of the world's population (but burning up nearly 30 percent of the world's energy resources annually) and living relatively "high on the hog", is eventually going to suffer worse than Iran ever has or will. Yes, the U.S. is allegedly generating over 10 million barrels of oil a day where a few years ago the figure was maybe 6 million BPD. This is because of the recent discoveries of shale oil in the Dakotas and in the Southwest of the U.S.

Shale oil, however, has not proven to be an economic bonanza. For one thing, it's not a cash flow positive enterprise, and also the wells pumping shale oil rapidly deplete. The various companies doing it are deeply in precarious debt. It has been estimated that 75 or more percent is gone from shale wells within two or three years. (No one can say that about Iran's oil or gas fields, or for that matter, Arabia's, such as the granddaddy of them all onshore, Ghawar, or the offshore Safaniya field to name just two.)

Part of the reason (when energy resources really begin to taper worldwide) the U.S is hit harder is because it has been such a profligate user of oil, and wasted so more of it by subsidizing the oil industry and not using those funds to turn strongly to alternative energy such as wind and solar, or even geothermal and oceanic tidal or current sources. (And of all countries, Iran has an abundance, too, of sunshine and wind to make energy, if it ever wants to exploit that route.) Iran can be energy independent virtually forever, but the U.S.? No way at anywhere near today's levels of greedy usage.

Indeed, according to economist and writer James Howard Kunstler, one must look at both China and the U.S., the world's two largest economies. He compares the two countries to passengers on a sinking ship drifting beyond the reach of salvation on a powerful historical current. "That current," he writes, "is the one telling nations quite literally to mind their own business, to prepare to go their own ways, to strive to somehow become self-sufficient, TO FINALLY FACE THE LIMITS OF GROWTH, TO SIMPLIFY AND DOWNSCALE THEIR OPERATIONS."

In fact, Iran already has a head start in these directions, thanks or no thanks to the imperial U.S. And not having an especially strong economy for now, despite the petroleum riches, Iranians are accustomed to hardships and the necessity for simplification, and probably can survive and deal with hardships in future far better than, for examples, either China, with its huge population just recently enjoying a "middle class" existence or the U.S. with its insatiable greed.

And look at Russia. Russia has also been under the lash of U.S. sanctions and even though it supplies Europe with at least 35 or more percent and growing of its energy needs, and outside of Venezuela may have the largest oil reserves of any country, Russia has begun to prosper increasingly by attempting to develop industry and agriculture that makes it possible to reduce dependency on energy sales. Russia has just begun to supply China with soybeans, for one example, to the horror of American farmers, given the extant and growing trade war between the U.S. and China.

Iran's leaders, whoever they are or may become, can over time chart Iran's own way with the same general course Russia is on today: less dependency on a natural resource economy and more on diverse ways to meet the needs of all Iranians and overseas customers in a world that is being forced to do what James Howard Kunstler knows makes sense.

Iran deserved credit and attention for trying

June 3, 2019

Credit to Iranian foreign minister Javad Zarif and deputy minister Abbas Araghchi for their efforts to visit other countries and put forth ideas to ease Arab-Iranian tensions and develop proposals to eliminate differences between Iran and other Persian Gulf countries.

The most interesting of these proposals is one that suggests a non-aggression treaty between Iran and its most immediate neighbors such as Kuwait, Oman and Qatar, which would be those states the most willing, at least, to listen to Iranian diplomats.

The Saudis, on the other hand, seem the most intransigent by far and the least willing partners to any de-escalations regionally, largely because the Saudis are either Trump Administration puppets, or vice versa, and because the Saudis perhaps have (erroneously) the most to "lose" by reducing hospitality towards Iran.

The concept of "loss" with regard to the Saudis is a curious one, and that it exists at all is telling. But of what? Loss with respect to its "alliance" with the U.S.? Loss with respect to its almost genocidal war on Yemen "rebels", who are claimed to be allied with Iran in some fashion?

Loss with respect to their vaguely covert but still obvious (awkward) bedfellows, the Zionists, who are desperately attempting to neuter longstanding Arab hostility to an apartheid state that has treated millions of Palestinians, including millions of fellow Muslims, abysmally during and since the Nakba in 1948?

The Saud family dynasty has to be one of the most bizarre political creations ever, one that was originally underwritten by western powers and that largely because of a desire to control oil resources, the Petrodollar becoming the keystone to that control. It is anything but a democracy.

It is a dynasty of paranoid freaks who are worse than poor representatives of Islam and who have created a Hell on earth of repression and barbarity against its own citizens who at the slightest signs of criticism, not to mention dissent, are literally subject to losing their heads. And no one can forget the dismemberment of Jamal Khashoggi, a writer for the Washington Post, last October, who was lured into the Saudi consulate in Istanbul.

One has to wonder what the Saudis are so fearful of and why they feel obliged to spend untold billions on U.S weapons. It must be because the Saud family is despised even within its own borders and feels obliged to sustain itself solely on the backs of U.S. and even Israeli approvals and arms. But the so-called "Arab street" across the Arab world does not approve, however quiescent it has been in recent years.

The mere fact that the Saudis have sort of signed on to the virtually stillborn "Deal of the Century" developed almost solely by Zionists like Jared Kushner and others in the Trump orbit, and which will NEVER be acceptable to Palestinians no matter how much they suffer, suggests that in time most all repressive Arab regimes will likely face a second major surge of revolt from the Arab street as was first witnessed in 2011, particularly in Egypt.

Whether Arab or not, all countries, rich or poor, that rely solely on the projection or threat of military power are ultimately brought down, because they have no real friends or allies, just alleged mutual "interests" to maintain themselves. The U.S is no exception to this rule in the longer run, too. All such countries tend to bankrupt themselves both morally and financially.

For an observer from afar, the absolute greatest tragedy suffered by Muslims over the course of decades now of Western domination of the Mideast has been the failure of Muslims, whether Sunni or Shi'a, to unite as a single cultural bloc of mostly unified people to ward off predatory Western imperialism, which has done little but sow discord across the Middle East.

The U.S. continuously blasts propaganda about Iran or any other largely Muslim country that refuses to buckle to Western control as "terrorist" states whose primary aims are to create an absence of "peace" in the Middle East. So, if that's

Iran deserved credit and attention for ...

the case, what is one to make of the fact that Iran, for example, has not gone on a military offensive for over 200 years and is calling, again, for mutual non-aggression pacts with its neighbors? Is this something countries do when they want to dominate or harm others, one must ask. No, of course not.

In any case, non-aggression pacts historically have not been that effective in warding off conflicts between nations, mostly because they have often been violated by one side or another, but that hardly speaks for not attempting to create them, as Iran is trying. This failure, it has been claimed, is because there has not existed an international system to enforce treaties or pacts.

A fair example of the absence of enforcement is that the U.S., ought to have been sanctioned (just as Iran has been sanctioned) by the other signatories to the JCPOA when Trump, just over a year ago, canned U.S. participation in the accord. Why has the U.S. and Trump have not been sanctioned in some creative way? The only answer seems to be cowardice and fear of reprisals from the U.S., and meanwhile Iran has faithfully abided by the term of the accord all long.

While individual Arab states on the Persian Gulf see Iran somewhat differently, there has long been the problematic fact that Iran is a much larger country in terms of land mass and population. This alone has created some unease with neighbors but there is nothing Iran can do about this. Then there is the divide between Sunnis and Shi'as, which goes way back initially to the seventh century.

The Iranian revolution in 1979 augmented sectarian differences and distrust between sects. But perhaps the biggest problem are the Israelis and Americans, who virtually depend on maintenance of what influence they have in the Mideast on Muslim division highlighted as division between Iran and neighbors. No question Arab Gulf states would probably not talk with the Israelis at all if ties with Tehran were improved. And as well, relations with the U.S. among Muslims generally would suffer as well…unless the U.S. got off its high horse of imperial domination.

With U.S. President Trump, money Trumps all
June 8, 2019

Donald Trump during his career as a real estate mogul cheated any number of contractors over several decades who helped build his real estate holdings. He did not pay them what they were due, just as he cheated the world of continued U.S. participation in the JCPOA, and with that cheated or robbed the Iranian people of relative prosperity by applying draconian economic sanctions. (Not to mention the threats of war.)

But anyway in recent months there's been something of a big-league and dangerous standoff between the U.S. (such that the Trump gang allegedly represents the U.S., whatever the latter is or has become in these late stages of American "empire") and a variety of other countries. But most notably there's been the standoff between the U.S. and Iran, and between the U.S. and Venezuela.

With U.S. President Trump, money trumps ...

In both cases the U.S. wants a U.S.-friendly government installed in Caracas and Tehran so U.S. business interests, at bottom, can get a grip on the oil resources of both countries. In other words, both countries are expected more or less to give up their sovereignty. Good luck with that: Trump and his completely vapid, clueless, shallow cipher of a son in law, Jared Kushner, cannot even get the desperate, long-abused Palestinians to sign on to the so-called "Deal of the Century" despite the prospect of billions of bucks in bribe money.

One actually has a hard time trying to figure out just what, exactly, has been successful about the Trump Presidency so far.

Iran, meanwhile, has been quite successful as a severe underdog over the past year. It has not disintegrated despite the harshest attacks short of U.S. B-52 saturation bombing runs over Iran; it has maintained its allegiance to the JCPOA; it has correctly chastised the other signatories to the JCPOA that they have not done enough, or much of anything, to ensure that the benefits of the deal for Iran are intact, or just materialize; it has made a huge effort to try to shore up solid (or at least improved) diplomatic relations with a variety of countries across Asia, and particularly with a few of its Persian Gulf neighbors; it has not panicked.

Iran's leaders have even, marginally, one hears anyway, relaxed some social controls on Iranians, allowing them to express themselves a bit more freely as individuals than before. What's not to like? This latter is very hard to discover.

And one might marginally conclude, also, that maybe Trump and Mike Pompeo are modifying their postures towards Iran. (One cannot expect such from John Bolton, the Saudis and above all, the nitwit Zionists.)

Consider that it was just a few weeks ago that Pompeo, swelled up with hubris and a sense of invincibility and even perhaps Christian evangelical zealotry, announced 12 demands on Iran during a speech at the Heritage Foundation in Washington. The 12 demands were so extreme that, if met, Iran would have literally castrated itself in every possible way -- far beyond what has been expected of any other country by the U.S., including North Korea. But then…

But then, just this past week, Trump and Pompeo apparently did an astounding about face: they decided they wanted to talk to Iran without pre-conditions. (Those 12 pompous demands of a few weeks ago seem to have vanished, although no doubt they will, in part anyway, resurface if Iran does ever talk to the U.S. again.) This sudden change was allegedly THE question at the secretive, annual Bilderberg Conference of Western "elites" in Switzerland.

The question apparently has to do with the Straits of Hormuz, which, if ever blocked in a war on Iran, would immediately cut off or delay 20 percent of world petroleum supplies reaching markets, and this in turn would result in oil prices spiking at least to $200 a barrel, and that in turn would crush the world economy and destroy the notably corrupted financial and monetary systems of the world under U.S. tutelage primarily and bring on a worldwide economic Depression.

Is Trump now suddenly saying essentially that Iran has little strategic value to the U.S., recognizing that Bolton and Pompeo over the past 14 months or so created a huge heretofore unrecognized problem for Trump who seems to be looking for a way out. Iran, after all, is not asking for meetings with the U.S. It's the U.S. doing the asking – given the apparent fears of Western "elites".

And given these new circumstances, if one can believe them, what's Iran to do? Exactly what it has been doing over a very rough year past. Demand politely that the U.S. rejoin the JCPOA before there are ANY discussions about possible modifications to it. Demand politely that the U.S. lift the onerous sanctions on Iran, too. But perhaps at the same time express an openness to renegotiation in an environment of mutual respect. This does not constitute "pre-conditions" for Iran to consider changes. It is merely a return to what was fairly and deliberately and carefully negotiated by the world's leading countries before Trump became POTU.S..

Nothing is so dangerous as a wounded beast backed into a corner by itself

July 14, 2019

Trump's foreign policy slant in the past year has gone so far off the rails touting the demands of right-wing Zionists and their supporters both in Israel and the U.S. that the U.S. is rarely seen as anything but a dangerous, rogue element across the world stirring up enmity and harm.

Iran and the U.S. 2017 - 2023

I am not alone in suggesting that this perverse obsession to warp U.S. policy around the demands of a single country could, in time, wreck what remaining influence – aside from the threats of military violence – that the U.S. has in world affairs. (Trump, for example, just successfully shoe-horned in yet another dual loyalty Zionist to a high-level position, this time one David Schenker to the long vacant post in the State Department as the assistant secretary for Near Eastern affairs.)

And just this past week, Mike Pompeo has been threatening to interfere in upcoming British elections to ensure that Jeremy Corbyn, who has been wrongfully slandered as an "anti-Semite" time and again, does not ever inhabit No. 10 Downing Street. Why? Because Corbyn has been an advocate for Palestinian statehood and long descried the cruelties meted out to the natives of Palestine. You can hardly find a bigger instance of hypocrisy as that exhibited by Pompeo.

Across the board, dual loyalty Zionists are in charge, influencing a President who, if he were asked, would probably be unable to cite what the Balfour Declaration of 1918 was, which, it can be claimed, kicked off this burgeoning mess in the Middle East 100 years ago. This is, after all, a President who knows next to nothing about history, and it's likely if he were asked who Mohammad Mossadegh was, he would not have an answer!

And worse is the fact that Zionist enablers like Mike Pompeo and V.P. Mike Pence are "Christian Zionists" who literally, as former CIA officer and now retired commentator Philip Giraldi has noted, believe that "Israel" today is a part of biblical prophecy that will lead to a war and "the end of the world as we know it and the second coming of Christ". They all, including John Bolton, seem to advocate a war beginning chiefly on Iran, which if it were ever to occur, would be a lambent calamity like no other and one "justified" in the warped minds of Trump's minions by the alleged reappearance of Christ which any SANE person knows is a cruel joke.

Never before have alleged "leaders" in the U.S. been so arguably demented, and never before has the U.S. had such a poor President. As one notable writer, Australian Caitlin Johnstone, has said, the U.S. has become like bad drunk wielding a broken beer bottle in a pub and menacing everyone there who are hoping the fool has a few more drinks and passes out before more damage is done.

But none of this is news to Iranians. The apparent ignorance of the American people is at bottom the primary problem. What can wake them up to the dangers of their own government? The only thing that comes to mind immediately is an economic implosion that shatters the sense of entitlement and wellbeing in the U.S. But at the same time of late, geopolitical changes ARE occurring that ought to give Trump and so many others in the U.S. government pause. In effect, the Trump Administration has sparked a frantic scramble among countries to extricate themselves from the effects, economic and political, of U.S. "empire's" pretensions and paranoia currently running amok.

Europe, for example, is allegedly scrambling to make good on its promises to continue trade with Iran by erecting mechanisms to bypass the weaponized dollar, but more telling are the rapidly increasing efforts to erect a true, multipolar bulwark against U.S. predations.

Of particular note is the establishment this month of a firm strategic partnership between China and Russia in negotiations in Russia between Xi and Putin. Many bilateral deals were signed in Moscow, but the most important one was allegedly a commitment to trade with mutual payments using the ruble and the yuan, not the dollar.

What has been put forth is a plan to integrate Eurasia further, including of course Iran, and the creation of the multipolar world, and it is this precisely which has been brewing for several years and has, or will, isolate and perhaps limit U.S. foreign policies and economic chaos that at bottom have been caused by the overweening support of the Zionist agenda by the Trump gang. Aside from military strength, the primary keystone of the edifice of U.S. control and "empire" has been the U.S. currency, which is increasingly under attack because the U.S. has used the weaponized dollar to try to hold the entire world hostage.

The G20 will meet later this month in Japan and it's bound to be a doozy of a conclave. If, for example, the U.S. goes further off the rails in trying to dictate to the world, it has been noted by experts that Russia could strengthen its links with China even further, and Russian oil could even be redirected from the European Union to China, making Europe entirely dependent on supplies coming through the Straits of Hormuz. According to one source, Beijing may have realized that the various Trump Administration offensives (of all kinds) are not so much mere trade wars, but serious attacks on China's (and Russia's) economic advances over the past two or three decades. Indeed, claims exist that poverty in China is now LESS than that perceived inside the U.S., which has wasted its treasure in military activities this century and seen its own infrastructure erode towards "third world" conditions. The U.S. went from being the largest creditor nation in the world to the largest debtor nation ever, and this in just the past two or three decades. It behooves all countries, particularly Iran and its sympathizers, to remain careful, to avoid overreacting to the slings and arrows of outrageous current fortune and to disallow the U.S. any pretexts to ignite another war anywhere. Patience, as ever, remains key. Positive changes are coming, inshallah.

Iran is wisest not to damage burgeoning favorable public opinion

June 19, 2019

Has the current American government become so sanguine as to assume the American people believe dubious charges that Iran attacked ships near the Straits of Hormuz? Well, maybe it has, and the American people have become or remain that blind or ignorant to believe what the Trump gang tells them.

But at least many Americans are pushing back against one major medium of ill reputation for beating war drums, the New York Times. And this comes at a time where, if the U.S. were to launch a military attack on Iran, it seems that aside from the Saudis, and the UAE and Israelis, and maybe the Brits, it would be alone and therefore condemned widely for doing so.

Iran and the U.S. 2017 - 2023

Last week the NYT editorial board published a weak and unsupported piece (with many omissions) about Iran to which almost 500 readers wrote comments before the comments section at the newspaper was closed. There was not a single response supportive of war on Iran and even of U.S. efforts to continue pressuring Iran with sanctions.

Granted that the readership of the NYT does not comprise "average" people but rather the far better educated, and these readers seem to have dropped any illusions that the U.S. is a force for good in the world and they readers harbor accurate notions of conspiracies, false flags and alliances with arguably bad actors such as Israel and Saudi Arabia.

This is important because in the lead up to the Iraq War in 2002-03, this was not the overwhelming reaction, or at least not so evident. Cited among the comments were references to the Gulf of Tonkin false flag that sparked the war on Vietnam and especially the false data about Iraqi WMD.

One reader from my home state, North Carolina, wrote for example: "Trump declared war on Iran and flaunted the rest of the world when it withdrew from the Iran nuclear agreement under pressure from Israel and Saudi Arabia."

There is anyway not a shred of hard evidence Iran attacked any tankers in or near the Persian Gulf. Maybe the time has finally arrived where the U.S. and its "allies" can't fool anyone any longer with falsehoods, as it did with the Gulf of Tonkin decades ago, with claims of Iraqi WMD, with false claims against Libya and Serbia, and as it has done on numerous occasions with Syria. The mere fact that Iranians literally rescued the sailors on one of the tankers hit in the Gulf of

Oman ought to be proof enough that Iran almost certainly did not attack the ships.

No one in the mainstream U.S. media has made the connection that the escalation against Iran has been pushed primarily by Israel supporters, but even Trump has admitted that casino magnate Sheldon Adelson, Trump's top Zionist donor (and we know Trump loves "money" above all else) advised him to hire hawk John Bolton. No question the tanker attacks are getting milked by the Zionists and the Saudis, who have stood between the U.S. and better relations with Iran that eventually would have evolved and been based U.S. maintenance of the JCPOA.

As for Secretary of State Mike Pompeo, it appears he's playing some kind of game and he even thinks it is funny. He admitted with a laugh back in April that as chief of the CIA the organization lied, cheated and stole, but this has been par for the course in U.S. foreign policy for decades, just as it has been for Israel and the Saudis, too. Pompeo does not seem to care whether a new war in the Middle East occurs, given his Christian "evangelical" beliefs about some supernatural outcomes regarding some absurd return of Jesus.

But of course the good news, if there is any at this time, is that the American public is not nearly as complacent and lazy as it has been, and more alert to what's been going on now and for decades. In any event, Trump's tenure in the White House has been marked by one crisis after another, and almost all the crises have been sparked by aggression of various forms against other countries, whether economic or military.

But as one observer who at least tries to be informed about the current dangers, it does seem possibly wise to suggest that's Iran's leaders not threaten or in fact chip away at components of the still standing JCPOA agreement by warning it is going to ramp up uranium enrichment unless Europeans, in particular, abide by their alleged commitments under the nuclear agreement. Doesn't this only or primarily fuel further false justifications for the war postures of the Trump Administration precisely at a time when world opinion in general, and even the opinions of many Americans, seem to be decidedly on Iran's side and against further conflicts in the Middle East?

Even if enhanced uranium enrichment were adopted by Iran, it's not likely such would prove to be a deterrence to Iran's enemies in the same way that North Korea, ALREADY HAVING the capacity to produce and launch nuclear weapons, is actually a deterrence to U.S. aggression. If Iran, say, were to push too far towards weapons grade uranium, even so far as 20 or 50 percent, it's not hard to imagine the U.S. and its "allies" would argue that Iran is headed towards making its own nuclear deterrence, and use that as a pretext to try to destroy ALL of Iran's achievements in nuclear technology for energy generation well before there was any chance Iran could (in theory anyway) produce nuclear weapons

To date over the past year, Iran has managed correctly to negotiate a horrific minefield of economic oppression which anyway is not permanent. Even if for a while Iran cannot sell its resources, it remains a rich country in so many respects. What is far less permanent worldwide is positive U.S. standing and "empire". And the same can be said for the barbaric Saudis and the apartheid loving Zionists.

Trump has a moment of sanity that begs for continuance

June 24, 2019

"Cocked and loaded" Donald Trump claimed the U.S. military was, just before, as he alleges, he decided not to attack Iran last week because the lives of an estimated "150 Iranians" were too heavy a cost for the downing of an unmanned drone that was brought down in Iran's territorial waters while on a spy mission. What is one supposed to think? That Trump suddenly has a heart? That he has a brain? Well, maybe a bit of the latter for a moment. It is, in any case, not hard to speculate about what happened:

The two tankers incident off Oman was probably an Israeli false flag, and when that did not "work" then the drone incident was staged. It is likely the drone was just over Iranian territorial waters, or else the Iranian navy would not have retrieved parts of the drone in its own waters. The drone pilots could not have been sure what Iran would do, but Iran did switch on its radars and brought it down, in effect telling the pilots something about Iran's defenses.

But Trump did the right thing, which was nothing. Not launching an attack was probably the high point of his Presidency to date. He deserves credit for that, likely realizing that the only way to destroy Iranian defenses would have to be a prolonged, like in at least a couple weeks, attacks on the entirety of Iran's southwest coast which would, as Iran has warned correctly, turn the Persian Gulf into an inferno and wreck oil production facilities along the entire coast of Saudi

Arabia and the U.A.E. That, in turn, might have sparked a revolution in Saudi Arabia, especially by the Shi'a component of the Saudi population, and serious trouble for the UAE. And farther to the west, who knows what?

It is likely the Zionists might have attacked Hezbollah, no pushover, and parts of Israel would also have been severely damaged. One could also speculate wildly about a recurrence of the "Arab Spring" in countries like Egypt, where sullen Egyptians are angry about Morsi's untimely death and where Sisi is hardly popular. Morsi was, it should be noted, the first truly ELECTED Egyptian president!

The Neocons warmongers and their supporters in the U.S. are upset Trump did not pull the trigger last week. War alone gives them purpose amid their manifold inadequacies, as journalist Glen Greenwald has opined. And what is even more incredible is that they have chosen to support what is probably the most unpopular (terrorist) organization to Iranians, the MEK, to supplant Iran's current leaders. This alone should tell the world that the U.S. isn't looking for better leadership for Iran's nearly 90 million people, but merely for Iran to be overwhelmed by internal chaos.

Trump may in time do something precipitous because he is under tremendous pressure. As said, it's either the firing of Neocons like John Bolton and Mike Pompeo…or Trump succumbs to their pressure … and ultimately and foolishly loses any chance he has to win a second term in the White House, too, which is his primary aim. And one must not forget Trump's original, possibly fatal mistake: groveling to the demands of Jewish billionaires in the U.S. who coughed up millions of dollars to support Trump and the GOP, provided he would tear up the JCPOA.

In fact, if Trump had not scuttled U.S. participation in Obama's signature foreign policy achievement on Zionist demand, none of what's happening now would ever have occurred. At bottom, Trump insofar as he attacks Iran militarily, could set off a chain of events that could destroy the U.S. economy and even collapse the world's banking system, leading to an economic depression like no other. And then atop all this is the threat of a war that becomes a world war.

And meanwhile, Israeli military analysts are apparently afraid that a WEAK U.S. attack on Iran could precipitate an Iranian attack on Israeli interests. What could they possibly be hinting at? The necessity of a nuclear attack on Iran? This, of course, is worrisome, but you cannot discount some ultimate Zionist or Israeli depravity. Zionist Sheldon Adelson has already said not long ago that the U.S. ought to nuke some under populated part of Iran as a warning.

The great tragedy is that for 60 years the U.S. has been hostile to Iran and its people, a hostility which at the beginning of it in the 1950s was largely due to the fact that Iran had and still retains an abundance of natural resources. The creation of an independent-minded Islamic Republic 40 years ago, in part the result of previous U.S hostility, only added to the blind refusal of the U.S. to recognize Iran for what it has been for millennia.

A unique land and culture and people which though many political iterations have stood the test of time that few other countries have ever achieved. It is impossible to imagine the U.S. will ever achieve nearly as much, or give the world so much as Iran has over the millennia. The U.S. "empire" looks to be but a brief, dull flash in the pan given its greed and hubris and militancy this century.

Iran and the U.S. 2017 - 2023

Cry not for hapless Trump: he created the current mess
June 30, 2019

No one can legitimately feel sorry for Donald Trump. For 14 months he's been in way over his head in geopolitics, and that primarily about Iran, but with the various sanctions and threats cast upon every continent like confetti at a wedding everyone knows eventually is going fail and wind up in divorce court, Trump looks the clown to most all the world.

And he also looks awfully ignorant: since when does the head of state of allegedly the most "powerful" country the world has ever known sanction the former leader of the revolution that created the Islamic Republic who has been dead for 30 years? I mean, admittedly, the names Khomeini and Khamenei are rather similar, but NO Administration or POTU.S. in its right mind would be so careless to commit such a faux pas. This is equivalent to a bride's groom farting very loudly and redolently at the exact moment, he slips a ring on the finger of his beloved at the wedding ceremony. You can't forget such mindless errors. They are just too glaring or grotesque and occasionally very funny.

Anyway, pundits are chiming in about the close call where the U.S. had already more or less launched a military attack on Iran (ostensibly because Iran shot down a quarter billion-dollar piece of U.S. drone technology flying four miles inside Iran's territorial waters!), and then for some reason or other Trump as U.S. "commander in chief" pulled back. That was a smart move, pulling back, but it seems credit must go to Iran's leaders for their decisive response to the spy drone.

Indeed, if Iran ever looked like some buffoonish military pushover, one might argue correctly that Trump and his merry coven of Neocon gangsters might already have attacked Iran. John Bolton, who last week was accurately called a "tapeworm" that (despite failures) apparently cannot be dislodged from the bowels of Washington, has been trying to wreck Iran for decades. (It was Fox News commentator Tucker Carlson who had the balls to so designate Bolton, albeit a tapeworm with a hideous mustache.)

Does anyone ever question why Trump and his mob have not attacked North Korea? For the same reason probably Iran has not been bombed yet – it has shown smarts and strength and some capability, and everyone knows bullies like the U.S. or the Zionists don't usually pick on anyone who can fight back. Look at it this way:

If Iran does not have any nuclear weapons, and it does not and has not been attempting to make even one, it has something invaluable to ward off military aggression, just as the Norks have their extant nukes. Iran lies immediately on the Straits of Hormuz, which is just as effective as having nukes. Iran can and will close down Hormuz to sea traffic and oil dispersal IF it is attacked…and send the world economy plummeting into the sea just as fast as that U.S. drone. Maybe this is why Trump wised up suddenly: he damn well knows his reelection chances are nil if he starts a new war in the Middle East.

And this latter point about Trump becoming a one-term President if he launches an attack seems to have been born out. Last Wednesday night the Democrats had their first of many debates among candidates for the nomination next year. First, there are far too many candidates already, and the debate was, to be frank, quite boring with most everyone promising economic freebies to the American public if they are elected. In other words, the usual BS, bribery, pie in the sky, whatever you want to call it. But one candidate stood out: Hawaiian U.S. House Representative and military veteran Tulsi Gabbard, 38, who stuck to her original message: end the U.S. foreign wars. Period. And lo and behold, she was allegedly the debate winner by a country mile Wednesday night. That tells you the U.S. public is sick and tired of U.S. imperialism and warmongering.

The public also recently heard from long-silent (on Iran) and long-established columnist Thomas Friedman of the New York Times. This rotund oracle of frequent nonsense and an alleged Mideast "expert" makes several hundred thousand dollars a year in salary at the newspaper and is allegedly paid $40,000 for a mere speech. We should all be so lucky. But as usual, Friedman, a Zionist Jew, was implying lies: suggesting that Iran literally has a nuclear weapons program, for one thing. His entire column was in fact dreck except, just maybe, for one suggestion he made: that IF the JCPOA could ever be renegotiated, its provisions extend for 30 years, not merely for a decade or so.

On the one hand, if Iran is sincere about nukes, this is not necessarily a bad suggestion to mollify the anxious. But on the other hand, the JCPOA must first be restored as it was and all sanctions against Iran must be dropped. Iran is correct to refuse to consider negotiating anything until this occurs. But this points to another problem, a conundrum of sorts:

The U.S. and the Zionists have long been squealing about an Iranian nuclear weapons program that does not exist. If they were honest, and they are not, they'd say what their primary objection is: that Iran has the knowledge and in time the capability, if not the desire, to produce a nuclear weapon. That is precisely why, if reports are accurate, Mossad and maybe even the MEK have directly or by proxies assassinated some Iranian scientists. This, however, is useless madness: because no one can make a country unlearn something it has already basically learned and written down and even taught in multiple places, even if a few notable, senior scientists are murdered.

And this is why Iran must be on guard: because it suggests that Zionists and their barbarous co-conspirators in the U.S. want to destroy Iran entirely.

Iran will have the world's respect, and prevail

July 9, 2019

An outsider with just some knowledge about Iran can be easily whipsawed by the horrible dilemma the U.S. has dumped on the country over the past 14 months. Yes, Iran must do all it can to defend itself, if it is attacked military, and meanwhile must do all it can to circumvent, with assistance, the draconian U.S. economic sanctions.

The most remarkable aspect of the current impasse is the posture of Mike Pompeo, U.S. Secretary of State. Pompeo maintains that Iran's pending decision to enrich uranium to a higher level of toxicity, and yet still far from anything constituting weapons grade, is "proof" that Iran aims to or has already broken the terms of the JCPOA. But everyone in the world knows that it was the U.S. that broke or is breaking the JCPOA (and also imposed economic sanctions).

Pompeo's is such a bald face lie that it boggles the mind, and yet the demonization of Iran continues unabated by the U.S. and Pompeo reminds one of the Nazi propagandists who well knew that if one tells a lie often enough, too many people sometimes believe it. Moreover, Pompeo tells other lies repeatedly: the whopper lie is that Iran is the world's biggest state sponsor of terrorism, and getting one's head around that is impossible. Let's break it down and dispel it:

Iran objects to Israeli warmongering and apartheid. Iran may to some degree have assisted the Houthis in Yemen to try to fend off the Saudi-led attacks on that country. Iran has some troops or proxies in Iraq, a country ostensibly allied with Iran in the fight against ISIS and other terrorists. Iran, on invitation by the Syrian government, has bolstered the fight against terrorists in Syria aiming to destroy the Assad government, another Iranian ally of sorts. Iran has supported the Lebanese government, insofar as Hezbollah is a big part of that government, where the primary effort has been to force the Israelis to think twice (at least) about attacking or occupying parts of Lebanon (and Syria) as it has done on several occasions since the 1980s.

Iran verbally has supported Hamas in Gaza which does maintain some token resistance to Israeli cruelty against the Palestinians there and elsewhere, such as the West Bank. Iran, even while attempting to suggest ways to cool mutual hostility between the Saudis (and the UAE) and Iran, has still criticized the Saudis (and the UAE) for their paranoia about Iran and their manifold political and human rights abuses, which included last year the murder of Jamal Khashoggi, a writer for the Washington Post.

Meanwhile, Iran has spurned suggestions of bilateral talks with the Trump gang, and rightly so, given the facts of the sanctions and other threats, including so far at least a couple apparent false flag attacks on some shipping in the Persian Gulf. Who in their right mind would sit down with the Americans to negotiate or renegotiate ANYTHING with a veritable axe poised above their head. And particularly so when Mike Pompeo has been claiming that Iran must give up entirely its efforts to have any kind of nuclear technology or program when the U.S. may be sharing nuclear technology and know-how with the Saudis, not to mention the fact that the Israelis have scores of nuclear weapons and has long refused completely to abide by any of the conventions related to the ownership of nuclear weapons.

One must think that NO country has ever been so pressured and unfairly treated as Iran has in decades. This is precisely what it looks like, anyway, to someone who, however imperfect their information as this writer's is, is apprised generally of what's been going on in the Middle East of late.

But still, the big lies perpetrated by the Trump gang keep coming, and it seems obvious the U.S. and its Mideast "allies" want to bring Iran to its knees one way or another. Just as it has brought other countries to grave suffering, hurting above all the general populations of those countries. The assumption in Iran's case is that the pain will become so great that internal discord will bring down the Islamic Republic.

But this latter has already proven to be a chimera and Iran, one would have to say, has quite heroically not buckled – and must not, under any circumstances, however increasingly vile the circumstances could still become short of actual military conflict.

Someday, when the U.S. and the Zionists and the Saudis have been chastened and disempowered by their arrogance, Iran's heroism will be remembered by most of the world, and Iran will once again prosper. It will happen and the sole thing in dispute is the timing, because the U.S. and its allies have literally forgotten how to make friends. Even if China and Russia, for examples, can't quite do enough for Iran as this juncture (but are trying) to alleviate the suffering, and even if Europe, including the European signatories to the JCPOA, have proven to be too cowardly so far to stand up to the destructive actions of the U.S. and its allies, Iran is going to manage to maintain its sovereignty and "win" (if not every battle) the world's respect.

China, for one, does not appear to be giving in to U.S. demands. And other countries may well, in time, follow China's lead and try harder to circumvent trade restrictions.

Trump, interestingly, sent John Bolton off to Mongolia and brought along newsman Tucker Carlson to Korea's DMZ. Carlson has clearly been against war on Iran. This is a positive, and maybe Bolton will be fired eventually. As said before, Trump well knows he won't be reelected if he starts a war with Iran.

A bold and fascinating prognostication also recently emerged with excellent journalist Sharmine Narwani, who was trained at Columbia University in New York and is now based in Beirut. Narwani believes that after the first response of Iran to any military attack, the Arabs will suddenly turn and become Iran's allies. Can one imagine the overthrow of the Saudis in Arabia and worldwide revulsion against the Zionists, and in the U.S., too? Stranger things have happened historically and Narwani may well have made a reasonable prediction, but let's hope no war occurs.

The Jeffrey Epstein case could sink U.S. elites and induce real change

July 14, 2019

If anything can get worse, like the corruption among the powerful and wealthy in the U.S. in recent decades, it just has.

Of late there's been reams attention paid to the arrest last week at Teterboro Airport in New Jersey of Jeffrey Epstein, 66, a super well-connected Jewish billionaire who is a known sexual pervert and convicted sex offender with an obsession for underage females and lots of notable friends formerly or currently in high places. People like Bill Clinton, Donald Trump and Alan Dershowitz, among scores of others, and even codgers like Henry Kissinger. Epstein was returning from Paris on his private jet when the FBI nabbed him and charged him with various grave offenses that could land him in jail for the rest of his sordid life.

The list, in fact, of "friends" of Epstein includes so many politicians and celebrities and wealthy individuals it is stunning. What did this bag of sleaze have to offer? Well, allegedly, young, underage hapless, needy teen girls for one thing for trysts at Epstein properties, but it remains unclear just exactly who, aside from Epstein, also committed sex crimes although it's a pretty good guess that Bill Clinton and perhaps even Trump may have participated back in the 1990s and into this century. Epstein, currently in prison and not yet out on bail, if he ever gets bail which seems unlikely, has offered to name names of those who PAID for his pimping services in exchange for a reduced prison term of no more than five years. But this is a joke of an offer because you can bet the very rich people who know Epstein would not have literally paid for such services as Epstein's "friends" and associates. At any rate, Epstein's re-arrest after over a decade when he was earlier convicted and received basically a slap on the wrist and the potential revelations ahead and further convictions could be the biggest scandal in the history of the U.S. And as well reveal the utter depth of the corruption of the "elite" and monied in the U.S.

But there is another angle to this worth exploring, and that may eventually be explored. The possibility that Epstein was working for a foreign "intelligence" agency and may have filmed or recorded various people in compromising situations for the purpose of blackmail by some non-U.S. government entity. In fact, the federal attorney who managed to get Epstein off with minor punishment a decade ago is Trump's current Secretary of Labor, one Alex Acosta, who claimed he had been notified that Epstein was part of the "intelligence" community and thus went easy on him just over a decade ago. To make matters even more bizarre, Epstein's former lover, friend and co-conspirator was one Ghislaine Maxwell whose father, Robert Maxwell, a former newspaper tycoon in the U.K., was once linked to Mossad.

Another fact is that Epstein, a man who never even earned a college degree but who worked on Wall Street for a while and then went on his own with some kind of alleged hedge fund, lived like a billionaire, but no one as yet has accounted for HOW exactly he became so wealthy, and no one has apparently come forth to claim they invested money with Epstein's firm or even worked for the organization. Was Epstein connected with Mossad in some nefarious way? Did Mossad make him rich? That's the biggest speculation flying around right now.

It's hard to say but this is a case that remains murky indeed and the public may never know exactly who and what Epstein was all about and who he answered to ultimately. Some other pundits have also opined that Epstein had (to have had) a "state" sponsor and was running a blackmail operation targeting the most powerful people in the U.S. The evolution of this story at the moment has the most public attention of any.

One observation when one spies the breadth and scope of this story, and the many powerful people involved and who may be caught up in this scandal and who could wind up in prison, too, suggests that Epstein could NOT have managed this alone, nor his rather vast holdings of multiple homes on both sides of the Atlantic and in the Caribbean. Where was all the lucre coming from? How could he have managed to operate such a scheme for so long? These and many other questions may or may not be answered fully as Epstein eventually goes to trial once again. Bill Clinton for one is alleged, based on flight logs, to have gone on 24 trips aboard Epstein's jet, aptly named the "Lolita Express", but Clinton is claiming he only took four trips abroad courtesy of Epstein. People who have reason to condemn Epstein's operations are coming forth to spill the beans like never before, and it's anyone's guess how this tale is going to play out and whom it's going to finger for criminality. But the potential here is that the full scope of the corruption in the U.S. may for once be exposed.

Obviously, the question here is what this bizarre and lambent mess of crime has to do with Iran?

It may not be very probable, but it is still remotely possible, that at least part of this tale involves the grip the Zionists have had on U.S. foreign policy because many of the people who have MADE U.S. policies in the past two decades at least have been involved with or at least knowledgeable about Epstein. And if bribery has been a factor in warping U.S. policies in the Mideast, which admittedly is not a sure thing with respect to Jeffrey Epstein, it may well impact, at last, the public's perception of the role of the Zionists in their control of U.S. "elites" and thus policy. It's the sort of tale that could mark a sea change in the U.S. and abroad, because the public's eyes may at last be opened. One really can't speculate further about this now because so much more needs to be exposed and proven, but the case of Jeffrey Epstein is worth watching from afar. Nothing like it has ever surfaced before.

Demand that the Mideast become a nuclear free zone!
July 20, 2019

Petty and small-minded is the sole way to describe the restrictions on Iran's Foreign Minister Javad Zarif's movements to a six-block area around the United Nations complex while he is in New York to address a UN group. This kind of action and mentality is the stuff of petty tyrants, not befitting the alleged leader or government of an "empire" that has any serious, responsible sense of itself or of others overseas or internally who don't happen to be "Caucasian". Or "Western" or whatever.

Trump stepped into a hornet's nest when he blathered on both in front of the press and on Twitter about four ladies of color in Congress, all young Democrats, and then even while the House of Representatives in the U.S. Congress condemned what were clearly racist comments, only four members of the House on the Republican side of the aisle joined in the condemnation. The series of Tweets aimed at the Congresswomen who hold policy positions antithetical to his own on multiple issues could only be characterized as racist.

Trump's primary exhortation involved telling the four women -- Alexandria Ocasio-Cortez, Ilhan Omar, Rashida Tlaib and Ayanna Pressley – that if they did not like Trumps views or the actions of his administration they ought to return to the countries they came from and leave the U.S. But three of the ladies were born in the U.S. It seems that only pure Caucasians are valid "Americans" to Trump, and one of the women is an American-born Palestinian who certainly is not welcome in the Zionist entity, Israel. Some commentators seized on the comment and claimed, jokingly, that Trump had also called for the return of millions of Palestinian refugees to Israel to their former homes, too, when he suggested that Rashida Tlaib leave the U.S.

Anyone alive during the Vietnam War, and back then opposition to it was relatively extreme, remembers the oft stated command: "Love it (America) or leave it." The "it" referred to Washington's war policies under both Lyndon Johnson and Richard Nixon with respect to Vietnam. The reference had nothing to do with the country as a whole and with its alleged tenets of democratic inclusiveness and American "ideals" of fair play and rational policies, such that these beliefs or policies existed to any degree back then.

It also has come to light that Trump likely trashed the JCPOA as well as other U.S. endorsements such as the Paris climate accord simply because they were accords upheld and promoted by Barack Obama, a Black man, and the same goes for internal policies involving healthcare and other matters. It's rather hard to comprehend that a fair number of Americans claim that Obama was the "best President" in their lifetimes when even Obama's actions when he was in the White House compared to Trump's were to date more extreme in terms of actually attacking other countries (like Libya) and supporting or sparking revolutions, as in Ukraine. No question that Obama, even if he did not live up to his alleged views, was one relatively smooth talker and a President of charming disposition compared to Trump's abrasive and divisive postures.

One might credit Trump that he has not started yet another war in the Mideast despite the urgings of people Like Bolton and Pompeo. Perhaps the overriding factor that has held Trump back has been Iran's clarity and consistency as well as Iran's threats to strike back overwhelmingly around the Persian Gulf if it were attacked militarily.

But make no mistake. a Jewish female commentator in New York has written: "What has taken place over time is that a relatively small group of extremists have received moral support from right wing media outlets in recent years and those with racist proclivities have been nurtured among Trump's "base" of voters to form a movement that is anti-democratic and pro-fascist." What also seems to be occurring is that there is a convergence between treatment of alleged "enemies" overseas and the treatment of Americans who don't support Trump's policies whether internal or overseas.

Iran spokesman President Rouhani, in any event, has stated it is ready to attend negotiations with the U.S. to defuse war tensions provided Trump returns to the JCPOA and lifts sanctions that have barred Iran from exporting its oil resources. Although Trump's administration has also announced it is open to negotiations with Iran on a more far-reaching agreement on nuclear and security issues, the U.S. president declared on Wednesday that sanctions on Iran might soon be increased "substantially." This latter comment is hardly encouraging, but just more of the same arrogance.

According to diplomatic leaks from the United Kingdom mission in Washington, a former U.K. ambassador warned London that the U.S. administration had committed an act of "diplomatic vandalism" by withdrawing from the nuclear pact, considering that behind the move last year there were ideological and personality motivations.

Here is what could possibly be a posture for Iran (that would appeal to the world) if and when negotiations ever occur again. Yes, it's vaguely possible that if the JCPOA were resurrected it might be, after serious talks, modified somewhat without Iran being obliged to dismantle its entire nuclear program and expertise, or dismantle its defensive missile capacities.

What if, for example, Iran were to suggest again what it has suggested before and do it decisively and fully: That Iran is open to change IF or on condition that the U.S. also pledges to work honestly towards making the entire Middle East a nuclear weapons free zone. This means, of course, that the sole country in the Mideast that actually has nuclear weapons, Israel, gives up their own weapons in the interests of regional peace. Nothing else could be more constructive for the region, but inasmuch as Trump has maintained a myopic foreign policy that has catered almost exclusively to the right-wing Zionists and Netanyahu, this may be and probably is impossible. Israel has been determined to kill any good deal with Iran, and even an Israeli NGO is suing the European Union over INSTEX, and trying to assert that Iranian assets in it, if any, ought to belong to Israel. Stealing Iranian assets in Europe based on U.S. court rulings, as part of an effort to undermine EU attempts to save the nuclear deal with Iran, is clearly a huge problem. But the EU may well object to an attempt to impose U.S. policy on them.

As it has been for decades, the U.S. willingness to give the Zionists whatever they want, including the destruction of several countries in the Mideast, has been the primary fly in the ointment that could in time lead to relative peace in the region. The only thing positive here is that more and more Americans are becoming sick and tired of the Zionist control over U.S. foreign policies and insane charges of "anti-Semitism", despite all the mainstream media propaganda.

Is Biden up to the challenge of wise governance…?
Jan 9, 2021

Donald Trump has probably done more damage to the U.S. than any president ever has, and inciting the violent raid on the Capitol in Washington in which five people died and much physical damage was done is his last destructive act and the end of his political career.

He also, along with many of those who wreaked havoc on January 6 around and inside the Capitol as the final Electoral Vote certification was underway, could quite possibly be prosecuted himself. The fear of a military attack on Iran, a fear which has been in play ever since Trump lost the election to Joe Biden on November 3, seems to be waning the closer Biden gets to his inauguration on January 20. So, this latter – that Iran may be "safe" for now - is one positive outcome of Trump's overreach and his petulant refusal to go quietly.

Trump virtually handed the two run-off elections in Georgia for the U.S. Senate to his Democratic foes, Warnock and Ossof, which means the Senate is now evenly split between the two political parties but also in the Democrats' control given the extra vote on legislation in the hands of Biden's Vice-Presidential pick Kamala Harris.

And as well, some of the most prominent Republican Trump supporters in the Senate have virtually destroyed their longer-term political prospects and dreams going forward, especially Senators Josh Hawley of Missouri and Ted Cruz of Texas. Both these men, and other Republicans, helped egg on the violence at the Capitol. What were they thinking? One must ask rhetorically. As for members of the mob on January 6, the new Department of Justice is likely to put many of them in jail for insurrection. And to boot, General James Mattis, who for a time was a part of the Trump Administration, has called for Trump to lose his citizenship and be exiled to another country for his alleged traitorous perfidy. And Trump has announced he will not attend Biden's inauguration, breaking with tradition. Yes, it's true: Trump managed to create a cult following of voters with his lies and bombast over four years, and now he has gone too far and they, too, will be in disrepute going forward assuming the country is literally not split apart in coming months.

Few Americans can legitimately pity Trump's fall from any grace. He has been the worst President in U.S. history. He had no legislative victories but his huge tax cuts for the wealthy and corporations. He rescinded scores of environmental safeguards. He turned the Department of Justice into joke. His cabinet appointees like Mike Pompeo were a joke, and he turned the U.S. into what amounted to a burgeoning fascist state like Israel. And this not to mention how he sullied most all of any respect the U.S. had on the international scene with his sanctions against what sometimes seemed like the entire world, but especially Iran. He rescinded working deals like the JCPOA and so on. He threw millions of Americans out of reliable healthcare access, too. In sum, Trump has always been an ignorant rube whose prime focus has consistently been himself, not Americans. Far from MAGA, he has accelerated U.S. decline. But now the question must be with Biden, decline to what?

Well, for one thing, the long-established so-called "Deep State" which was horrified when Trump became President, is now going to be firmly back in the saddle of governance under Joe Biden. But Biden as Barack Obama's loyal Vice President was hardly a person to cheer about. He was instrumental in supporting the war on Iraq earlier and then Obama's wars on Libya and Syria. He supported the coup in Ukraine and later his family, or his son, profited from Ukraine's corruption.

But now, still, with Biden as President and Trump out of the way, at last, there is a chance at least that the listing monster ship that is the U.S. may right itself at least very marginally – but the government will be much larger along with financial debt and deficits and further erosion of the country, but at a more subdued pace. Bad actors who supported Trump will be deeply diminished and even supporters like his lawyer and former NYC mayor (during 9/11) Rudy Giuliani could be prosecuted. In a line, Biden is likely to take America back to some facsimile of the governance it had during the Bush and Obama periods, which were nothing to applaud except in comparison to Trump's four years in the White House.

Would this be progress? Not really, unless Biden eschews wars of choice, resurrects the JCPOA, cuts the Pentagon budget and eliminates overseas military bases, begins to consider honestly the extension Medicare to all Americans, re-creates environmental safeguards, and attacks the racism and racists so visible in Trump's tenure. In other words, Biden must fully become who he has mostly pretended to be in the past – a wise steward and leader of fresh policies that benefit ALL citizens and not just the wealthy.

Indeed, one can say that if Biden does not take bold, progressive steps to lead the U.S. out of its self-inflicted morass and division and repair the image the U.S. has abroad, he, too, will as Trump already has, accelerate the decline of the U.S. even more. But at least for now, there is a chance for improvements with Trump who finally this week admitted that a new Administration is directly ahead.

If any country has erred this century, it's the U.S.

Jan 6, 2021

"Though we (the U.S.) spends a trillion dollars a year between our military and our intelligence and our "national security" circles, that trillion dollars has built, you know, things that can stop all the planes and the missiles and all kinds of things from other countries. But we missed the one thing other countries like China have deployed, which is not to fight at all, not firing a bullet or missile at all, but taking the U.S. out from within. And that's what's going on."

So writes an American expert looking at China. And one must remark, imagine the U.S. now if the government had not wasted many trillions on war and "defense" and the military and piling up debt like never before anywhere in recorded history. Might Americans citizens have otherwise enjoyed

If any country has erred this ...

universal healthcare and free education at public universities and a modern (not horrible) infrastructure and sanity and so much more including a much smaller debt load like some other modern, "Western" countries? Yes, of course. But NOW Americans face a government and ruling class trying to cling to U.S. hegemony and empire by threats of war and potential nuclear war with countries Washington calls "enemies", which includes Iran.

So what's the real story here, particularly with regard to the hostility towards Iran and the recent changes in West Asia which have seen several Arab countries normalize their relations with Apartheid Israel?

The truth? The many trillions of dollars have been wasted in this century especially on the application, by sheer stupidity, of bad will to other countries, some of which have challenged U.S. economic power simply by their relative excellence and growth, and other countries (like Iran) which have never presented any kind of real challenge to the U.S. either economically or militarily.

The so-called Abraham Accords between the Zionist state and several Arab countries allegedly take this into account: the geopolitical position of Iran. Global measures are said to rank Iran's position well ahead of countries such as Saudi Arabia and even Israel, at 14th in the world. This index includes over 50 factors, including Iran's population, size, land mass, coasts, natural resources, infrastructure, and military discipline among other factors.

Thus it has been further remarked that Iran's nuclear program is NOT the primary concern of the U.S. and alleged allies, but rather Iran's huge potential as an economically powerful and thriving nation outstripping any of its rivals in West Asia. The Abraham Accords is simply a reaction of new alliances against Iran's potential to become the leading country in West Asia. And as well, the accord with the Zionists destroys the concept of making West Asia a nuclear weapon-free zone, something which the Arab states have rightfully said to have supported so far. Far from creating stability in the region, the accord is increasing instability.

Interestingly, the Zionists have already not proven themselves good allies to the various Arab states with whom they have recently "normalized" relations. For example, there are reports that Israeli tourists and visitors to the UAE have been caught literally stealing accessory items in hotel rooms they have inhabited, stuffing goods like coffee makers and ice buckets and towels into their baggage on departure. Some have been caught red-handed by various hotel managers. These Zionist tourists are so accustomed to theft of land and lives in Palestine and elsewhere for over seven decades that they apparently believe that petty theft is quite okay. They have no shame. Anything is game for theft unless goods are well defended or nailed down. One must wonder if the Abraham Accords are already souring and fraying at the margin. But this fraying is likely to be ongoing since the alleged benefits of the accords mostly accrue to the oft-despised Arab dictators in these countries, and not to their subject populations.

But in general the world is waking up to the U.S. and Israeli game in the Mideast. A former Iraqi PM, al-Maliki, recently stated that Iraq would have sent an army to save Bashir Assad in Syria if he had been about to fall. Because that would have meant al-Qaeda and ISIS and other terrorists would have flooded Syria. One must conclude that the U.S. and the Zionists wanted this to happen, and it beggars believe that this should ever have been the aim. Assad it seems is beloved by most Syrians, and an observer can only further conclude that the U.S. and its allies have had only one goal in mind all these years past: complete chaos in West Asia to benefit the squatters in Palestine.

But if it should ever come to war between Iran and its craven allies, one must never forget Qassem Soleimani's words that Iran is a nation of potential martyrs. This is why man for man Iran's soldiers are far superior to soft U.S. troops and why Iran would win, at great cost, a conventional war against the U.S. in somewhat the same fashion that Vietnamese peasants won their war against the U.S. under Ho Chi Minh's leadership. But with ever more fervor.

The world can only pray it never comes to a regional war in West Asia.

Cruelty and Stupidity are the hallmarks of U.S. moves this century
July 27, 2019

One huge lie zipping around the Internet of late is the depiction of a map showing the (alleged) extent of the Persian "empire" in 300 BC, as it is labeled. It shows that the Achaemenid dynasty as empire controlling lands stretching from a small part of Europe west of the Bosporus across

Iran and the U.S. 2017 - 2023

Anatolia to Bactria and what today is Pakistan and western India.

Captions seen with the map are suggesting this same extent of rule or control is exactly what Iran's leaders are eyeing today, as if Iran is on some grand offensive to re-create the Achaemenid territorial reach. This propaganda in support of Western and particularly American hostilities towards Iran is sheer madness because it is false. Iran merely wants to grow and develop as it is now territorially.

But the propaganda map is a joke, too, because in 300 BC the Achaemenid empire of antiquity had already been defeated by the Macedonian, Alexander (the Great), and by 300 BC Alexander had been dead for over a decade and various former generals and compatriots of his were squabbling over who was going to get what of the lands Alexander had conquered. A stupidity piled atop a stupidity is the map itself.

Indeed, the most glaring earmarks of this century so far are two: stupidity, which is bad enough, but also cruelty, which is much worse, especially when it is based on stupidity. And this foisted upon the world by leaders, and they can easily be named with Trump and Netanyahu in the top positions, who by any assessment of their mentalities by professional psychologists, must be declared deeply damaged if not insane. (One might suggest impairment also for outgoing Theresa May, Jair Bolsonaro of Brazil, Macron in France and a host of less visible "leaders" of U.S. puppet countries around the world.)

The cruelty factor seems to play out almost daily, which does a tag team routine with the stupidity factor. Take what happened in the past week in Wadi Hummus on the outskirts of East Jerusalem on land the Palestinians allegedly control and where they were building or already had mostly built up a handful of high-rise apartment buildings for several hundred Palestinian residents. So, one morning hundreds of Israeli troops and police show up suddenly with teams planting explosives and deploying various other implements of destruction like bulldozers, order the residents out of these buildings so fast they barely have time to take ANY of their belongings, and over the next few hours reduce the entire neighborhood to rubble. This was such "in your face" ethnic cleansing that it literally shocked the world.

Why, allegedly? Because these apartment building were supposedly too close to the illegal separation wall or barrier that the Zionists earlier placed like a long viper across parts of the West Bank. And then, when the U.N. Security Council attempted to condemn the destruction in Wadi Hummus, the U.S. (the stupidity factor) objection to the measure killed it.

Events of the same low-caliber sense but high-level cruelty are occurring almost daily under the aegis, distant or far, of the Trump Administration. Like for example with Brazil's refusal (no doubt on command of the Trump gang) to fuel two Iranian ships laden with Brazilian agricultural produce. Like for example at the behest of the U.S. the authorities in Gibraltar changing their laws immediately this month to accommodate the piracy against and capture of an Iranian oil tanker allegedly taking fuel to Syria. (Hamdu li-Allah that Iran responded by grabbing a British tanker in response.)

But perhaps the greatest stupidity and cruelty so far of late is Trump's declaration that he could end the war in Afghanistan in a few days, and murder 10 million people, if he wanted. This is megalomaniacal cruelty. This is not something anyone in their right mind would even consider, much less speak about. And do not doubt he was speaking less to Afghanistan than he was to Iran, where sanctions have hurt the working and middle classes especially hard. It was a threat, pure and simple. In addition, the U.S. and the Brits have been talking about some kind of naval armada to "escort" ships through the Persian Gulf and Hormuz, as if transit has been endangered by Iran. This ploy really amounts to nothing more than a military blockade of Iran in the Persian Gulf and the Sea of Oman.

Any analysis of these moves suggests that Trump, who claims he does not want a war, in fact really does because he ought to realize that he is not fomenting revolution in Iran, but shoring up the determination of Iranians to resist and support their government. In fact, one can imagine that Trump does not know what he wants exactly except submission -- as if he's playing some sort of crude hardball to get a business (rather than a necessary diplomatic) deal he likes. But he will never get his kind of deal, even while he believes he can have it with John Bolton nearby. Bolton's eagerness to kill Iranians, Trump thinks, is a bargaining chip. It's another "good cop, bad cop" routine…which is so shallow and lacking in smarts and sophistication and sensibility as any kind of pseudo "diplomatic" strategy, it has already failed.

So again, what's Iran to do? It seems straightforward. Respond in kind but no more than in kind to aggression on Iran's interests, make sure the craven Trumpists and allies realize Iran isn't kidding about shutting down resource shipments through the Persian Gulf and the destruction of the vast petroleum infrastructure in the Persian Gulf if Iran is attacked militarily, and above all remain cool headed and patient. The U.S. empire is beginning to implode.

Iran's strength lies in continued patience

Aug 6, 2019

It's said that Donald Trump is likely to win re-election in 2020 if he avoids war with Iran, keeps up the tariff and political pressure on China, and if the Democrats nominate a neoliberal like Joe Biden or even Kamala Harris.

Conversely, if the U.S. attacks Iran militarily (the U.S. and the world are going to regret it mightily), Trump won't win re-election. And it's also likely that there are only two candidates, both of them often scorned or ignored, one for his "socialist" policies and the other for an anti-war posture, who have any chance of beating Trump assuming Trump does not bomb Iran. They are Sen. Bernie Sanders of Vermont and Rep. Tulsi Gabbard of Hawaii. Both these Democrat candidates are consistent, recognize the failures of U.S. policies, and don't seem to have been bought off by anyone to any significant degree, it at all.

But there is a caveat, too.

Trump is absolutely desperate in the face of slowly souring economic data in the U.S. and also in Asia and Europe, to weaken the dollar (and improve U.S. exports) and to keep the U.S. equity market near or above its recent all-time high. Trump "owns" the markets now, because he has been crowing for two years about how "great" he is and that his policies have caused the markets in the U.S. to rocket to all-time highs, and he has also claimed he is responsible for low unemployment (almost exclusively in very low-wage jobs) in the U.S., too. But all his claims are a chimera. The only thing that has happened since the crises of 2008-09 is that the Federal Reserve Bank printed trillions of dollars to bail out businesses and banks that ought to have gone bust and all the extra money went largely to further "credit" (debt) creation and into the stock markets while many corporations were buying back their shares -- which was illegal until 1982 when Reagan was President -- to boost quarterly (and annual) per share profits. Really, there has been almost a decade-long orgy of misallocated fiat "capital" and the chickens are soon going to come home to roost with what may become the worst economic contraction since the Great Depression of the 1930s, which affected the entire world. Also, the world is being fed truckloads of propaganda by the Trump gang about China and the Federal Reserve as the scapegoats for systemic economic problems made worse by the policies Trump pushed like financial heroin since taking office, but which originated during Barack Obama's tenure in the While House.

Indeed, U.S. hostility towards Iran, aside from the ever-present, crude and greedy Zionist demands and the Saudi fear of competition in West Asia, is sparked by what appears to be a tide of growing solidarity between Asian countries, led by China, to create a world of secured and growing trade ties that, because of U.S. intransigence and paranoia, threatens to exclude the U.S. Iran has become one of the key countries in this tidal movement given its location and size and its wealth of resources both human and natural. Moreover, the UNDP has designated Iran far ahead of most other countries as "very high" on human development. Anyone with a scintilla of knowledge about Iran loves its cinema, its poetry and its deep culture -- one honed over thousands of years – and even its food. And there is no basis for the hostility except: solidarity with other countries battered by Western imperialism, Iran's support of Syria under attack by Western funded terrorists and mercenaries, and Iran's moral support of Palestinians living under a cruel apartheid system that makes South Africa's apartheid system before Nelson Mandela was freed and rocketed from jail to the Presidency look like something far milder but still reprehensible.

Iran has been threatened by the U.S. and its "allies" in the Middle East with something at least a destructive as what the Mongols meted out to West Asia in the 13th century, and it is stunningly bad as policy. But slowly and surely, counter moves are developing, and most recently one move involves deeper ties and potential military cooperation between Russia and Iran.

The Trump Administration witnesses this expansion of cooperation between Russia and Iran along with other developments across Asia and seems to be inadvertently pushing the U.S. into the terminal phase of its unsustainable "empire", and this would only be hastened by any military attack on Iran. Quite aside from the dangerous threats of climate change, for example, it has even been suggested humanity itself may not long survive if the U.S. and its "allies" start yet another war in the Middle East.

Iran, meanwhile, has been scaling back its commitments inherent in the more or less defunct and disrespected JCPOA, which makes sense. Making no sense at all is Trump's sanctioning of Foreign Minister Javad Zarif because, some have opined, he "intimidated" with his deftness and smarts the bully Mike Pompeo, who has become a laughing stock. If anything, this sanction tells you a lot about the fragility of the U.S. government under Trump and minions. This fragility will be increasingly apparent, too, when the U.S. economy and markets unravel in the next year or two.

Occam's razor may be useful in explaining Jeffrey Epstein

August 13, 2019

NORTH CAROLINA - Of all the news items hitting the Internet in the U.S. this summer by far the most commentary among general readers involves questions and speculations about the pedophile Jeffrey Epstein, who either committed suicide or was killed inside his prison cell in New York City this past weekend.

He had been denied bail awaiting a trial slated for next summer on various sordid charges that might have resulted in 45 years behind bars – in effect, a death sentence for the 67-year-old alleged financier who over recent decades had played fast and loose with the "elite" whose names are a virtual litany of many of the most visible, powerful politicians, businesspersons and professionals in this current era in American history.

Every speculation or theory or conspiracy notion almost anyone has offered up in the wake of Epstein's not so surprising demise well before he could or might have named specifically who among the "elite" (quite possibly Trump himself and certainly Bill Clinton) partook of his services of procuring underage females for sex at one or another of his

Occam's razor may be useful in ...

lavish properties or on his aircraft is and has been fair game since his arrest in early July.

Almost anything is possible, and especially in an America where there is not a single arbiter or trusted voice any longer who has a record of discovering and then telling the truth about virtually anything the U.S. has been about, especially since 9/11 -- which itself has never been adequately examined or explained.

Imagine a world where nothing and no one can be trusted by the average citizen, where people are left to flail around trying to get a valid grip on the truth when the mainstream media, as well as the government, has often either lied outright or failed to tell the whole truth and nothing but.

And worse, Epstein's death, however or by whom it was accomplished, has come at the same time the FBI has been trying to deem any "conspiracy" theories or notions suggested by the public a literal threat to "national security". In other words, some or any "official" story concocted by the mainstream media or the government powers, probably in cahoots with each other, must be "accepted" as the truth, period – even if few can believe it. This is an atmosphere of totalitarianism, or something quite close to it.

The stories appearing in the mainstream media about Epstein and associates, some of them quite long and detailed, do undoubtedly have a certain prurient interest to the public, as if to tell the public: so THIS is how wealthy and powerful Americans get to live (if they want), this is what they do in a world where anything goes, where gobs of money count more than anything else, and nothing seems ever to be condemned, and perps rarely face any kind of justice or accounting.

Indeed, the ONE thing a public wants in any society (including any largely Islamic oriented society like Iran's) or country is an authority or authorities who are not simply self-serving and whose primary aim is truth telling and the effective and fair implementation of fundamental justice when it is required and which gives people a sense that at least their "leaders" are trying hard to do the correct thing to abide by the lofty principles upon which the society or country was founded, whether the base concept is representative "democracy" and related, long enshrined laws, or long established religious principles and its laws or whatever.

But this is no longer what the American people have, this sense that no matter what happens, justice can and will eventually prevail based on proper discovery of the truth. And this, in effect, suggests the demise of the American experiment and maybe, ultimately, the demise of American influence and power.

But with the Epstein saga, however complicated it seems and however difficult it may be to get to the bottom of it all, one must apply the famous "Occam's Razor". William of Occam was an English scholastic philosopher who died in 1347. He was an important figure in Western medieval thought who has been known for a methodological principle that bears his name. He developed a principle of parsimony (Occam's Razor as it came to be called) in explaining things and in theory building.

This principle states that if one can explain something at all, one must always opt for an explanation in terms of the fewest possible factors, causes or variables. In other words, simplicity often leads to the best explanation for some phenomenon – in this case, the phenomenon of Jeffrey Epstein.

Thus, if one were to apply Occam's notion to Epstein and his activities (and some few notable non-mainstream observers and writers with past experience even in one case as a CIA employee have already done this) it seems probable that Epstein's ultimate handlers and in part a source of his wealth, were quite possibly Israelis, and more specifically, in operational terms, Mossad.

Epstein's nefarious game was, quite likely, to snare and blackmail American elites who befriended him and got involved, directly or indirectly, in his offerings of sex with underage females. And since early July when Epstein was arrested, it's been safe to assume he would not live long. And he did not.

The question now is whether, in a country where few even in the government are not under the sway of Zionist imperatives and propaganda or just their own ignorance, this stark angle on the possible base of Epstein's activities will be thoroughly explored and possibly brought to light.

Crises everywhere and Trump and supporters are vapid

Aug 20 2019

Follow the best minds one has ever read on media applications and the overwhelming impression one gets is a world that has lost whatever moorings it may have once had and seems to be careening towards one disaster or another, all more or less fomented by Western "leaders" who have become desperate to maintain various narratives of control and dominance. And this in particular in the case of the U.S. with Trump as President.

And it is exceedingly difficult to figure out which of numerous extant or budding crises around the world warrants the most attention on the presumption that if just one or two of them is somehow resolved positively and with an outcome that generally satisfies the basic interests of disputants, the rest of the various crises may find an adequate solution in turn and in time.

At the top of the list must be, ultimately, the environmental crisis in a world where, just in recent lifetimes, world population has burgeoned from some 2 billion people to almost 8 billion, and largely because of what may have become the biggest bane ever in the past 100 years, which sparked the population explosion and even relative prosperity – the discovery of abundant and cheap oil and gas (energy) in countries like the U.S., Saudi Arabia, Kuwait, Iran, Russia and a few others scattered across the Middle East and in other locations. As much as say Iran, for example is a relatively rich country with its natural resources, and basic prosperity has expanded, it has expanded in the face of ever more demands by a growing population on those natural resources both for internal use and as a means of earning "money" to feed and house multitudes of citizens.

This is the case across every country that, like Iran, is rich in petroleum and gas resources, and this includes the U.S. It is a scenario that is largely insoluble in the longer run, and dangerous. Dangerous because resources eventually run out or can be depleted to such an extent that they can no longer support societies to the extent they have come to rely on them, not to mention the environmental havoc. And worse, in Iran's case, the existence of resources has often created political nightmares where Westerners, in particular, have tried to get their hands on or a controlling interest in another country's natural abundance for their own selfish ends. Just look at what the U.S. has tried to do to Iran since Mossadegh's deposition decades ago, and what the U.S. has been trying to do of late: destroy Iran's sovereignty and current political system. (One has to wonder that curtailing Iran's petroleum output at least for now will in some ways push Iran to figure additional ways to grow or just maintain its economy even while any depletion of its resources may be delayed somewhat.) And just look at what the U.S. has been trying to do to Venezuela or Syria, and what it has done to Iraq and Afghanistan and even Yemen this century.

Perhaps there is no grand solution to the looming crises involving energy extraction and the environment unless across the world countries are literally forced to adopt solar energy solutions and unless, by some scientific breakthrough, nuclear fusion energy can be developed to replace fossil fuels. But this will require a degree of political and social and scientific cooperation and sharing across the planet that seems a complete chimera for now.

And the greatest obstacle (this seems undeniable) is and has been the United States insofar as dominance and hegemony remain the primary aims, and this thrust has gone berserk with Trump and the current leadership in Washington. It may be said that if things literally fall apart worldwide, and there is yet another "world war", the primary culprit will be the U.S. And if there is another vast war, humanity may not survive. Such considerations, as self-evident as they seem, are no secret and many leading thinkers have expressed the same, and as simplistically as they are expressed here they are still worth expressing, again and again, to alert all to the current and expanding dangers ahead.

Trump (and his administration), in any case, seems to be the worst possible leader of an alleged "superpower" who could ever have been elected. He (and his gang including people like Mike Pompeo and John Bolton) have a mania for the destruction of extant accords and any possible constructive accord with many other countries. Just this past week, for example, on what may appear to be a minor issue (it's not minor) Trump trashed protections for endangered species in the U.S. in the same way that Bolsonaro in Brazil seems to be aiming to destroy Amazonia, the "lungs" of the planet. It's a kind of willful immorality that has gripped not just Trump and minions, but whoever supports him – his ignorant political "base" in the U.S. The sole candidates for the 2020 election with any serious merit to displace Trump seem to be Bernie Sanders and Tulsi Gabbard and perhaps Elizabeth Warren, whom the corporate, mainstream media in the U.S. despise.

It was Sanders, a Jew, who came out strongly against Trump's demand that compliant Netanyahu disallow Congressional Reps. Rashida Tlaib and Ilhan Omar to visit Israel and also take a studied look at the horrors long inflicted on the Palestinians in the West Bank and Gaza. Trump and Netanyahu are both, quite simply, racists, and little more. If anything of late could alert U.S. voters to the crimes of U.S. and Zionist actions in the Middle East, Trump's and Netanyahu's strike against these two Muslim ladies of clear mind and courage is it. Justice for Palestinians and for those who have long been concerned about their plight is the sine qua non action that indisputably can lead to other changes of all kinds that will guarantee a better future. Nothing else has such potential for good.

And Iran's Islamic Republic, whatever its shortcomings and to its everlasting credit, has known this for decades.

Crises everywhere and Trump supporters are completely vapid

August 20, 2019

Follow the best minds one has ever read on media applications and the overwhelming impression one gets is a world that has lost whatever moorings it may have once had and seems to be careening towards one disaster or another, all more or less fomented by Western "leaders" who have become desperate to maintain various narratives of control and dominance. And this in particular in the case of the U.S. with Trump as President.

And it is exceedingly difficult to figure out which of numerous extant or budding crises around the world warrants the most attention on the presumption that if just one or two of them is somehow resolved positively and with an outcome that generally satisfies the basic interests of disputants, the rest of the various crises may find an adequate solution in turn and in time.

At the top of the list must be, ultimately, the environmental crisis in a world where, just in recent lifetimes, world population has burgeoned from some 2 billion people to almost 8 billion, and largely because of what may have become the biggest bane ever in the past 100 years, which sparked the population explosion and even relative prosperity – the discovery of abundant and cheap oil and gas (energy) in countries like the U.S., Saudi Arabia, Kuwait, Iran, Russia and a few others scattered across the Middle East and in other locations. As much as say Iran, for example is a relatively rich country with its natural resources, and basic prosperity has expanded, it has expanded in the face of ever more demands by a growing population on those natural resources both for internal use and as a means of earning "money" to feed and house multitudes of citizens.

This is the case across every country that, like Iran, is rich in petroleum and gas resources, and this includes the U.S. It is a scenario that is largely insoluble in the longer run, and dangerous. Dangerous because resources eventually run out or can be depleted to such an extent that they can no longer support societies to the extent they have come to rely on them, not to mention the environmental havoc. And worse, in Iran's case, the existence of resources has often created political nightmares where Westerners, in particular, have tried to get their hands on or a controlling interest in another country's natural abundance for their own selfish ends. Just look at what the U.S. has tried to do to Iran since Mossadegh's deposition decades ago, and what the U.S. has been trying to do of late: destroy Iran's sovereignty and current political system. (One has to wonder that curtailing Iran's petroleum output at least for now will in some ways push Iran to figure additional ways to grow or just maintain its economy even while any depletion of its resources may be delayed somewhat.) And just look at what the U.S. has been trying to do to Venezuela or Syria, and what it has done to Iraq and Afghanistan and even Yemen this century.

Perhaps there is no grand solution to the looming crises involving energy extraction and the environment unless across the world countries are literally forced to adopt solar energy solutions and unless, by some scientific breakthrough, nuclear fusion energy can be developed to replace fossil fuels. But this will require a degree of political and social and scientific cooperation and sharing across the planet that seems a complete chimera for now.

And the greatest obstacle (this seems undeniable) is and has been the United States insofar as dominance and hegemony remain the primary aims, and this thrust has gone berserk with Trump and the current leadership in Washington. It may be said that if things literally fall apart worldwide, and there is yet another "world war", the primary culprit will be the U.S. And if there is another vast war, humanity may not survive. Such considerations, as self-evident as they seem, are no secret and many leading thinkers have expressed the same, and as simplistically as they are expressed here they are still worth expressing, again and again, to alert all to the current and expanding dangers ahead.

Trump (and his administration), in any case, seems to be the worst possible leader of an alleged "superpower" who could ever have been elected. He (and his gang including people like Mike Pompeo and John Bolton) have a mania for the destruction of extant accords and any possible constructive accord with many other countries. Just this past week, for example, on what may appear to be a minor issue (it's not minor) Trump trashed protections for endangered species in the U.S. in the same way that Bolsonaro in Brazil seems to be aiming to destroy Amazonia, the "lungs" of the planet. It's a kind of willful immorality that has gripped not just Trump and minions, but whoever supports him – his ignorant political "base" in the U.S. The sole candidates for the 2020 election with any serious merit to displace Trump seem to be Bernie Sanders and Tulsi Gabbard and perhaps Elizabeth Warren, whom the corporate, mainstream media in the U.S. despise.

It was Sanders, a Jew, who came out strongly against Trump's demand that compliant Netanyahu disallow Congressional Reps. Rashida Tlaib and Ilhan Omar to visit Israel and also take a studied look at the horrors long inflicted on the Palestinians in the West Bank and Gaza. Trump and Netanyahu are both, quite simply, racists, and little more. If anything of late could alert U.S. voters to the crimes of U.S. and Zionist actions in the Middle East, Trump's and Netanyahu's strike against these two Muslim ladies of clear mind and courage is it. Justice for Palestinians and for those who have long been concerned about their plight is the sine qua non action that indisputably can lead to other changes of all kinds that will guarantee a better future. Nothing else has such potential for good.

And Iran's Islamic Republic, whatever its shortcomings and to its everlasting credit, has known this for decades.

Iran is wooing and winning sympathizers, the U.S. is not

Aug 25, 2019

France's Macron allegedly want to defuse tensions between Iran and hostile Westerners and maybe even Zionists at the upcoming G-7 meeting, but this Frank, Macron, cannot even effectively address protests on the streets of Paris and elsewhere in France except with police violence, so one cannot expect much, and anyway, it seems that many "leaders" cannot or won't say what the U.S. and its Military Industrial Complex are really all about, and neither can the Western mainstream media.

The U.S. has become a country that literally thrives, if it thrives at all, on war plans or a war ongoing, somewhere, anywhere. There is no particular idea or ideology or forward, productive vision behind any of this, and in fact what "thriving" the U.S. has enjoyed since the last recession in 2008-09, which has mostly been relative to other countries, looks to be reversed soon.

Because no amount of bullying can win the day when one is losing friends hand over fist, which is exactly what is happening because of the Trump Administration. And on top of this mess of bad policies is one overriding fact about the U.S. monetary and financial system: it is unsustainable and may be dying. (And never forget it was Trump who, campaigning for the Presidency, vowed he would put an end to deficit spending, but now trillion-dollar deficits this and every fiscal year ahead are baked in the cake.

For the first time in thousands of years interest rates across all the major economies are plunging to zero or going negative, and in the case of the U.S., there really is no good alternative. Why? Because a normalization of interest rates, which would mark a healthy system, would mean that paying interest to bond holders (given all the debt) would crowd out virtually most all other expenditures starting with sacred items to the U.S. public like Medicare and Social Security and ultimately moving on even to the roughly trillion-dollar budget for the Pentagon and "defense".

Yet some Western economists think they have an answer to this which, described simply, involves conjuring or printing fiat "money" out of thin air, otherwise known this past decade as "Quantitative Easing" or "QE", which has not resulted in a particularly robust U.S. economy.

Voodoo economists believe the U.S. and the E.U. can get away with money printing to solve fiscal problems and stimulate demand when historically it has never worked for long. Weimar Germany in the 1920s is one stark example where it did not work and where first there was some deflation and then runaway inflation and impoverishment. And the canary in the coal mine? Precious metals which have just begun a historic ascent. The wisest of minds have suggested that gold could be priced at $10,000 an ounce or more in coming years, which would mark the utter debasement and evisceration of fiat currencies against what has been real "money" for 4000 years.

Against the possible impossibility of further future U.S. overreach and imperialism bolstered by a financial system that appears to be disintegrating, Trump and minions continue to ratchet up threats and sanctions and tariffs against its major trading partners like China and against alleged enemies like Iran, perhaps imagining that at some point the world (China, Iran, etc.) is just going to cave to petulant U.S. demands and do its bidding.

This has to be the gravest mistake of a notion the U.S. has ever imagined. And amidst this madness is the further madness of Trump crowing about comments that he has become the "King of the Jews", the "best President for Israel in the history of the world", that he is the "Chosen One" – and all the while telling American Jews that vote Democratic (as a majority of American Jews have always done) they are "disloyal" Americans…and reaping scorn even from many powerful, established Jews/Zionists inside the U.S.

At bottom here? The Trump Administration seems to be going berserk and Trump himself seems to be almost insane. And it's no secret that aside from cutting corporate and other taxes, especially for the wealthy, and sanctioning other countries wildly, Trump has been primarily Zionist-centric such that his foreign policies are beginning to look like a massive train wreck.

The U.S. has been deploying military force or the threat of it to gain influence and wealth for decades, but longer term this merely creates effective opposition to the so-called "empire" and not merely in the Middle East but globally. Iranians at this point can probably rest easy that the U.S. will not (or cannot) attack Iran militarily, because the result would likely be a regional war (at least) that would spell the end of the American presence through much of the region and collapse the Emirates and Saudi Arabia, too. An attack would also likely result in a global economic disaster as oil and natural gas prices would soar. Thus, one must ask, what good has been all the bluster and sanctions of the Trump gang? What good for the U.S.? So far, no good at all.

And to boot we have the fine spectacle of Iran's Foreign Minister Javad Zarif carefully and studiously traveling the world and presenting Iran's case for more accord and wisdom. It is a complete shame Trump failed to appoint wise counselors to his team and cannot do the same. No doubt Iran's patience may be wearing thin, but it sure has been a quietly effective posture so far that is winning sympathizers steadily.

The dangerous Mideast logjam requires lubrication by the U.S. for its release
Sept 1, 2019

Claims are that some of Iran's leaders think Donald Trump could be reelected next year and therefore some kind of negotiation over a "deal" with the U.S. may be necessary in the next year to obviate six more years of odious sanctions, which have had a marked impact on Iran's economy.

The negative impact of the sanctions exist in part because the other signatories of the JCPOA, which the U.S. unilaterally withdrew from last year, have failed to underwrite and engage in continued trade with Iran to neutralize U.S. sanctions, and also because the supposed key to the maintenance of trade, the "INSTEX" mechanism set up by Europeans, looks like some kind of bad joke, like the proffer of a feast of fine food which merely masks a plate of offal fit only for a dog. It's no wonder long suffering but proud Iranians don't trust Westerners, and particularly Americans.

From afar, like from the U.S., it has been presumed that Iran would, at a minimum, not engage with the U.S. at all unless the U.S. eradicated the sanctions first as an act of good faith and would not at least be of a mind to start any further negotiations without the concept, if not the immediate fact, of a fully restored JCPOA. This makes sense, of course, because Iran did nothing but abide by the JCPOA as it was, unlike the U.S., which ought never be trusted (without serious guarantees) by any country regarding any deal whatsoever. Maybe a proper guarantee for Iran might be a $200 or more billion bond?) But it was President Rouhani who allegedly indicated that Iran might be willing to meet with American negotiators IF it would somehow clearly benefit Iran. But then President Rouhani fast reversed himself perhaps under pressure from Ayatollah Khamenei.

Nonetheless, it seems apparent that some of Iran's leaders are vaguely warming to fresh ideas, and that if it is true that Trump wants a more comprehensive "deal" than that of the JCPOA, Iran likewise would be able to demand and expect iron-clad guarantees from the U.S. that the sanctions would never again be brandished.

At any rate, the Trump Administration must by now be aware that the sanctions and other moves by the U.S. and its Middle East allies, primarily the Saudis, the Zionists, and the UAE, have not at all destroyed Iran's government, nor have they fomented a popular uprising. One could almost argue that the U.S. has lost, or is fast losing its capacity to foment regime change, since all the world now knows that "regime change" actions are not premised on some idealistic notion of spreading goodwill or "democracy" in foreign lands, but rather at bottom they are all about the destruction of political and military competition anywhere with the imposition or the ignition of plunder and chaos.

Trump, in fact, may actually imagine he wants a better "deal" than the JCPOA was, and he further may imagine that if he gets a better deal, he will be lauded and thus have a far better chance of winning reelection late next year. Even if Trump is far more intellectually challenged than his advisors and other Neocons, he is not without a relative degree of innocence and warmth, which the Neocons are completely bereft of. (Currently, U.S. voter polls suggest Trump will lose to the top four Democrats fighting for the nomination.) But let's not kid ourselves. Even Trump's former appointees like General James Mattis (and others) have more or less stated that Trump himself knows very little and has a mind more chaotic and unmoored than any that has ever previously presided at the White House.

Here's the problem in a nutshell:

Forget talk about new "deals" and potential agreements between the U.S. and its competitors or its alleged enemies. It seems (upon fair examination) that the U.S. government as constituted in recent decades is not sophisticated enough nor imbued with the wisdom necessary to have a plan or plans that distinguish between different countries and also, therefore, crafts ideas and mutually beneficial proposals tailored to those countries for negotiation. And would the U.S., for example, get off Iran's back finally if, for example, Iran agreed to limit the development of its ballistic missile program, or returned to the limits the JCPOA imposed on its enrichment of uranium (or even set deeper limits to enrichment) and to other facets of its nuclear program? Would the U.S. get off Iran's back if Iran marginally unfriended its Syrian and Iraqi and Lebanese neighbors in some nominal way, say simply by declaring that Iran is henceforth strictly adopting a comprehensive political or military "neutrality" in the Middle East, just as Switzerland, say, has long done in Europe? In other words, Iran saying, in effect, "We won't mess with anyone anywhere, nor try to influence anyone anywhere, as long as no one messes with us or threatens us specifically."

The correct answer here to these questions is probably "NO". And the reasons for this answer are inherent in continued carte blanche U.S. support for the Zionists and anything they want. (They have been in a panic over the mere whiff of future negotiations between the Trump and the Islamic Republic – they only appear to want the destruction of Iran. Moreover, one can easily presume John Bolton and Mike Pompeo and V.P. Pence among corrupted others think exactly like the Zionists.) The reason for "NO" is also inherent in what the U.S. did to Ukraine in 2014, even though Trump is now threatening to cancel $250 million in further military aid to Kiev, and it is also inherent in what the U.S. has stirred up in Hong Kong this summer, where the unrest looks a lot like the cheer-led support the U.S. gave to the Ukrainian color revolutionaries, which never has resulted in any sort of real gains for Ukraine.

No. The real U.S. government game with Trump and minions may simply be the attempt to preserve U.S. hegemony and diktat militarily and economically worldwide with no care at all what this might mean, internally, for other countries. There is no benevolence evident yet in the Deep State of the U.S. wants China to implode. It wants Russia to lose its grip in the Mideast and its friendship with China. It wants the peaceful Chinese-led Belt and Road initiative across Asia to fail. It wants, in a word, yet more chaos benefitting the so-called Empire of Chaos and its fascist makeup.

Still, fresh negotiations between the U.S and Iran could be a positive development but posited on a clear willingness of the U.S. to dampen the fervor of its long established kissing of

Israel's hindmost parts and some determination to balance its diplomacy towards fairness in the Middle East. Any tangible evidence of such a shift, which might include initially Trump's dismissal of Pompeo and Bolton, could well be the oil that lubricates welcome change, along with the flow of the sale of Iranian resources worldwide once again with the lifting of sanctions.

Trump and fellow gangsters look increasingly foolish
Sept 7, 2019

The maintenance of the notion that Iran's leadership must remain steadfast and patient, as it has been since Donald Trump dumped U.S. participation and support for the JCPOA and slammed Iran's people with draconian sanctions, has never been more imperative, because it is in fact, however tortuous, a winning strategy.

As said before, aside from the fact that the` Trump Administration appears desperate to chalk up some kind of "win" in the Mideast and farther east, it continues to embarrass itself in world opinion while Iran curries increased favor incrementally simply because it has remained steady enough and rational enough despite all the sanctions and bad mouthing by the U.S. There mere concept that Iran is or has been an "aggressor" in the Mideast, that it has itself promoted "terror" willy nilly simply by standing firm with the important allies it has such as Syria especially, must be the biggest falsehood of this century so far. But the U.S. desperation is quite palpable.

For example, this week the world learned that Trump through his vapid spokesperson Brian Hook offered the captain of the Iranian oil tanker Adrian Darya some $15 million and a life of perennial ease if he just sailed his tanker into U.S. hands. Apparently, when the captain, Akilesh Kumar, did nothing but sail closer to Syria (and turned off the ship's transponder) where its oil may eventually be offloaded to a smaller ship than can negotiate a Syrian port, he was also "sanctioned" by the U.S. Had this sailor, an Indian, done the bidding of the Trump gang, he'd likely never have lived long enough to enjoy his sudden wealth: such is the infamy of most anyone overseas who now supports U.S. diktat and bullying. The U.S. looks utterly childish resorting to blackmail with the attempted the bribing of ship captains to try to get its claws on the Adrian Darya (or any other vessel transporting Iranian goods).

Some observers have lately questioned whether John Bolton will keep his job and may have been sidelined some by Trump (given the failures of sanctions so far to upend Iran's patient government, or even Venezuela's). Also, pressures have been ramped up by the usual suspects (Netanyahu, for example, whose re-election as Israeli PM this month is not certain) to avoid any U.S. give and take with Iran while Trump has suggested that he meet with President Rouhani for some bilateral talks at an upcoming UN General Assembly meeting in New York later this month.

How crazy is that, given that the sanctions have lately been targeted against Iranian shipping networks with any ties to the IRGC? Does Trump really believe he can strike any kind of fresh deal with Iran without dropping the sanctions first? How delusional is he? The overture, at any rate, was made through French intermediaries, and meanwhile, Iran has not released the British tanker Stena Impero. The "maximum pressure" campaign against Iran looks increasingly like some kind of bad joke where, even if Iran suffers, the U.S. loses in the more important court of world opinion. Bullies are insufferable given a basic human nature against them.

The longer view may be important to grasp, and so far this appears to be a view that Iranians may have encompassed and adopted to get through these difficult times. It rests on the realization that despite various iterations of governance or even dominant religious fealty – whether Achaemenid, Parthian, Seleucid, Zoroastrian, Sassanid, Islamic, Abbasid, Ilkhanate, Safavid, Qajar, Timurid or even Pahlavi right up to the current Islamic Republic now just 40 years old – Iran survives on the bedrock of a splendid creativity fostered by a basic culture that has withstood the test of millennia and foreign imperialism throughout recorded history.

Currently, of course, not just Iran but many other countries are having to deal with the aggression of U.S. and Western and Zionist imperialism, which are as horrific as, say, anything the Romans tried to impose long ago. (Remember what happened to the greedy Roman Crassus at Carrhae in 53 BC!) Iran, however it manages to deal with American imperialism, will remain – despite ups and downs which it has managed for thousands of years – simply Iran, when the U.S. and its "allies" have finally exhausted themselves and been reduced to temporal blips because of greed and short-sighted governance.

This is a primary question: why can't a U.S. government come along that reorients itself to an international posture of "live and let live" or "let's all try to prosper together"? What good, really, has ever resulted from Western aggression, and especially towards a country like Iran that really does not pose any kind of existential threat to the U.S.? Maybe that's ahead as the U.S. falters in coming years without a change of posture and thus a possible reclamation of some real leadership. Maybe Bernie Sanders or Elizabeth Warren could become the President the U.S. needs, just as Jimmy Carter has long been a former U.S. President who has demonstrated courage and wisdom. But if there is not as wholesale change of mentality in the White House and in parts of Congress one can bet the U.S. is not going to be successful going forward because the world is fast reorienting itself to multi-polar expansions that include more cooperative efforts among great nations.

Bolton and Neocons responsible for billions in opportunity costs - does Trump realize it? Sept 14, 2019

It's obvious Donald Trump, who touts himself as a superb "dealmaker", has not made any important deals yet as President. In fact, he's done little but tear up extant deals, and the most notable one he destroyed was the JCPOA. But at the same time, Trump literally likes talking to other leaders, and some other leaders have responded to him saying they actually thought he was almost charming and reasonably well spoken. One would like to imagine this is the case, because Trump made a lot more sense when he was on the campaign trail back in 2016 than he has in the past two years. Why the change, because now, very few people like Trump, and his reelection is in doubt?

Well, Trump literally had no idea whom to appoint to help him once in office. He wound up appointing people (Bolton, Pompeo, even Pence) opposed to many aspects of his original, campaign agenda, and above all, he appointed some of the worst people imaginable to soothe U.S. relations and establish fundamentally peaceful relations with other countries like Russia, China, Iran and some others in the Middle East, except for Israel (which has been totally rewarded by the U.S. alone for nothing good). The Neocons have long been particularly aggressive. With Bolton fired this week, and some saner names being suggested as a replacement, one can only hope that Trump is beginning to realize that if he wants to MAGA, it will be impossible if he caters to Neocon madness. Under the spell of these American traitors, who are mostly Zionist in orientation, Trump hit Iran with the worst economic sanctions ever imposed on anyone short of outright military attack. And the thinking was that Iran would do the bidding of Pompeo and Bolton, which was way off the mark, and even farther off the mark succumb to the overthrow of the Islamic Republic in favor of the MEK, which is a whacko terrorist organization.

But more importantly, with the U.S. meddling in Hong Kong and with the tariff war underway between the U.S. and China, China's President Xi no longer trusts Trump and seems to have concluded that trying to make a deal with the U.S. is a fruitless undertaking and that China might be better off just going its own way and doing deals itself with better partners. Such as Iran.

China has said it will invest $400 billion in Iran's oil infrastructure and other industry. (Iran is, after all, the keystone country in China's Belt and Road initiative given its size and location between East and West Asia. This scheme by China for Iran gives Iran the option of even continuing its current foreign policies in the Middle East.

Could it be that Trump realizes the opportunity costs the U.S. has borne with the Mideast policies it has maintained over the past three years? This may be too much to ask of Trump, such realization, but it's not hard to imagine the benefits of a slowly warming relationship between the U.S. and Iran had the U.S. stuck to the JCPOA. (This writer argued with an editor at a major U.S. newspaper for the "normalization" of U.S. relations with BOTH Israel at one extreme and Iran at the other back in 2013, but the ideas were rejected and the editor refused to publish them. The editor had Neocon pals like Bill Kristol, a Zionist.) With normalization, the U.S. certainly would have gotten the lion's share of scores of commercial deals with Iran, and China would not likely be preparing to make Iran a strategic partner.

Iran, for example, would likely have bought hundreds of Western-made aircraft from Boeing and Airbus, for one thing. The facts are that Natanyahu and the Jewish lobbies in the U.S., aiming to dominate naïve Trump as they did other Presidents, are ultimately to blame for what may be one of the biggest, commercial economic errors the U.S. has made since World War 2: pushing most of Asia and Russia together into a virtually united bloc that ultimately will declare a big "sayonara" to the unreliable, untrustworthy U.S.-led West.

Now, with Bolton out, it is possible that President Rouhani may have second thoughts about rejecting any talks with

Trump at the UN General Assembly later this month. The question may be (in some jest) that if "Bibi" Natanyahu loses the election in Israel, whether Trump will do something even crazier than appointing Bolton in the first place in 2018 and appoint "Bibi" or someone like him to replace Bolton.

Absolution from crimes by deflection and deceit is never successful
Sept 20, 2019

Vladimir Putin appears far and away smarter than any major Western "leader", especially Donald Trump and Mike Pompeo. Ansarullah appears to have attacked the Abqaiq oil processing plant in the Eastern Province of Saudi Arabia with drones or something, or claims it did. Maybe they fired off missiles of some sort that had adopted Iranian technology. It's a mystery, but whatever and whoever hit the plant, and it wasn't the homemade firecracker rockets that fly out of the Gaza Strip to land in some farm field around Sederot inside "Israel", whatever this "country" without defined borders really is geographically (it's never been reliably determined).

What hit the Saudi oil installations was well aimed or it aimed itself well and proved powerful enough to shut down half of Saudi oil production for a couple weeks more at least. And Putin masterfully and even tongue-in-cheek trolled the Saudis, offering to sell them the S-300 or S-400 missile defense systems. Priceless!

The Saudi regime is hopeless and helpless. After spending many billions of dollars on military equipment over years, and with virtually no "defense" against whatever it was exactly that bombed Abqaiq and Khurais, and with alleged military cover by the U.S., the Saudis nonetheless may still as well be driving mangy camels and not Ferraris, Lamborghini's or F-16s in the Eastern Province. Same goes for the UAE.

So far, Trump's response has been vague and has allowed others at least to blame Iran for the attacks, claiming the drones or whatever originated from somewhere in Iran, or maybe it was Iraq. Hell, maybe they flew from an Iranian missile base on the moon?

The truth is Trump and Pompeo and all the rest don't have a clue, and it is even quite possible – as claimed Robert J. Moriarty, arguably the best U.S. Navy/Marine fighter pilot during the Vietnam War and since the war an aviation record maker and holder – that the Israelis attacked Abqaiq and Khurais in an effort to spur the U.S. to gallop to the side of the Saudis and as the Zionists equally desire, attack Iran. Neither the Saudis nor the Zionists can fight anybody without gobs of U.S. assistance, and never really have.

False flags are nothing to the Zionists and they are good at creating them: the most notable being the attack in June 1967 on the U.S. Navy frigate "Liberty" in the Mediterranean cruising west of Gaza and north of Sinai during the Six Day War To this day the Navy veterans who are still alive and who served on the Liberty are treated like lepers by the U.S. Veterans Administration – such is the unholy grip the Jews have about the public ever being properly informed that the bombing and strafing of the Liberty was a premeditated Israeli attack in which dozens of sailors died. Those fine veterans know too much, it seems, just like Julian Assange of Wikileaks fame who is now officially a Western political prisoner, not a criminal, at Belmarsh dungeon in London, and he may actually be dying.

Let's face it: the Saudis are inept and the Israelis, stripped of their high-tech war tech (and nukes as threats), are only good for, for example, shooting and killing elderly Palestinian women (or children in Gaza) as they did this week at Kalandia checkpoint north of Jerusalem: the hapless woman, 50, apparently entered the wrong "lane" in the incredible, cruel maze of the checkpoint and was summarily murdered. The Zionist soldiers and police said she was wielding a knife, which as usual was a fabrication. She was 10 meters from anyone when she was gunned down and certainly no threat to anyone.

And it's not as if any country is entirely free at least of some oppression of citizens, Iran included, just as no individual person is ever entirely cleansed of occasional bad actions. But the reiteration of assaults on Iran does not justify in any proportional way even a tiny fraction of the much more severe and horrific postures and deeds of the U.S. and Israel and the Saudis. We see, for example, a raft of what has been called "Whataboutism" by Western apologists in the media, as if this absolves perps of obvious crimes.

Among the worst of Zionist apologists happens to be columnists Bret Stephens and Bari Weiss, both Zionists, at the New York Times. Whenever anyone questions them about Israeli apartheid crimes, they are inclined to say: "But 'what about' (for example) the way the Chinese treat the minority Muslim Uighers, or the way Modi in India is currently treating Muslims in Indian controlled parts of Kashmir?" Now we have the spectacle that a desperate Netanyahu may well be "out" as Israeli Prime Minister, this cat's nine lives perhaps used up. No doubt he fears he's finally going to be indicted for corruption, and may go to prison.

Absolution by way of deflection and deceit is absurd and can never be finally won. And the most remarkable aspect of such hypocrisy, hubris and exceptionalism is that almost the entire world is seeing through this very tiresome game and neither Washington nor Tel Aviv nor Riyadh (and some others) realize it enough yet to change course. But the day is somewhere ahead eventually when they will have to realize it. At any rate, this is part the reason why Trump has been unsuccessful in virtually all his foreign policy initiatives to date.

Foreign Minister Javad Zarif seems of the same caliber, generally, as Putin, and has so far navigated the stresses that Iran has been subject to with class and even, like Putin, with some humor. Good thing he did not resign earlier this year, as he suggested he might.

The U.S. has evolved to "Inverted Totalitarianism"

Sept 29, 2019

Mike Pompeo continues to write and speak garbage about Iran. His obvious aim: turn the person in the U.S. street against Iran, or at least, spew enough propaganda over and over so that no one of weak mind, a majority, is going to object to the

Trump gang doing whatever it wants in and to West Asia, and that in subservience to the Saudis and the Zionists.

Without the assistance of the mainstream U.S. corporate-controlled media, except in isolated instances where some columnist manages to get some truth published in a major U.S. newspaper like the New York Times or the Washington Post, there is still far too little direct objection to all the lies. But at the same time, clarity and some truth at least ARE making advances in a two step forward, one step backwards fashion.

This process is dangerously slow, but it is happening, as it appears that Trump has scant hope of reelection in 2020 if he ignites, or allows other to ignite, a military attack on Iran. The "public" seems to be simply tired of wars in the Middle East, and the deflection of tax dollars for foreign policies that have not served average Americans nor resulted in ANY "victories" for the U.S. – unless chaos has always been the chief aim, and almost no one in the government will admit to that.

It is a marvel to realize that the U.S., if it did have other objectives (aside from bolstering the apartheid regime in Israel and others which create chaos), that the U.S. has not won a single "war" (given alleged objectives) in decades, the Vietnam debacle being the primary example of a huge loss.

And there is virtually no corner of the globe where there is not a desire now, at least, to reduce the economic and military clout the U.S. has wielded to harm other countries. At the margin, this is increasingly a realization, but one can sort of understand why the process has been so excruciatingly slow.

The U.S. has evolved to "Inverted ..."

Perhaps in more than in any other country, and especially one with a government boasting hegemonic pretensions, the "average" American has little time or motivation to figure out what's happening overseas in the absence of some direct attack on the so-called "homeland". Many are beset with economic troubles, for one thing: it has been estimated that over 50 percent of Americans could not come up with $400 in an emergency.

What wealth that exists lies almost exclusively at the very top of the food chain – among oligarchs and billionaires and those fortunate enough, like many of Wall Street, to enjoy high salaries. The skew mimics the skew seen in 1929, just before the Great Depression of the 1930s. Plus there is the fact of U.S. geographic isolation from other cultures and polities.

Americans are not "bad" people, although it may seem so to Iranians and many others in Asia. They are mostly just ignorant and have allowed successive administrations over recent decades to chip away at the separation of powers, at the Constitution, at the rule of law and much more, such that the U.S. no longer is a constitutional republic, but something the great but now deceased Princeton University thinker, Dr. Sheldon Wolin, called a state of "inverted totalitarianism".

Writer Chris Hedges, who was for years a Mideast correspondent for the New York Times, but who was forced out of the newspaper for his opposition to the war on Iraq in 2003, explains this kind of totalitarianism best: "It does not find its expression in a demagogue or a charismatic leader but in the faceless anonymity of the corporate state.

It pays outward fealty to the façade of electoral politics, the Constitution, civil liberties, freedom of the press, a fair judiciary, (etc)…but it has effectively seized all the mechanisms of power to render the citizen impotent." (Except that now, Donald Trump literally considers himself a leader, and charismatic, and acts like a demagogue…and could be impeached, but don't count on it. Trump is still likely to win reelection, provided he does not do something even more stupid than he has already done, like his withdrawal from the JCPOA.)

Meanwhile, it appears Netanyahu will be the one trying to form a new government in Israel. Many are disappointed about this, but Netanyahu is likely to accelerate Israel's decline in world opinion since unlike Benny Gantz he won't have any kind of grace period as the reelected PM.

And the Saudis are in steep decline post the attack on Kurais and Abqaiq. The war on Yemen has been a disaster for the Saudis, especially now. Interestingly, many in the Pentagon knew it would be disastrous well before it all began in March 2015, but the Saudis gave the U.S. no advance notice of their attack that Spring. The Houthis were actually considered a bulwark against al-Qaeda in Arabia and some senior officers in the Pentagon reportedly considered supporting them in some fashion until the Saudis began the war.

Reasons to be optimistic and steadfast in Iran

Oct 11, 2019

So, Donald Trump is abandoning the Kurds in northeastern Syria and allegedly pulling out U.S. troops, giving Turkey a green light to try to ensure that a Kurdish state will not threaten Turkey's eastern Anatolia. But the fear is that ISIS will be resurrected somehow, and on it goes in a kaleidoscope of sectarian and political confrontations in the Middle East where the sands beneath one's feet seem to shift on a weekly basis.

But in the U.S., Trump's move this week, which some Democrat and Republican "hegemonic" devotees are already squealing about, seems to underscore what he originally promised on the campaign trail in 2016 – to get the U.S. out of fruitless, unwinnable and costly wars, even if this is just the first instance of his doing what he promised and the move comes well into his first and maybe last term as President.

Trump indeed has made many errors, with the canning of the JCPOA being error number one, but he has not started a fresh big war in the Mideast and for that he must get some credit. He has, for one thing, stuffed John Bolton, and now Bolton in a revenge move may be attempting to get Trump in deeper straits over the matter of trying to deck Joe Biden with regard to his nepotistic games in Ukraine.

First, it's fair to say that no public has been so propagandized as Americans. Especially with regard to the Middle East and particularly with respect to Iran and Syria. The mainstream media in the U.S. has been derelict, and there is some truth to Trump's assertion that a lot of the news is "fake" except that when he declares it as such, he is primarily saying so because he's being criticized about issues that can affect whether he is going to survive as POTU.S.. He's a narcissist who becomes apoplectic over criticism, warranted or not. The U.S. has never had such a loose cannon as President, nor one as impulsive and therefore dangerous.

However, there are a few reporters and commentators, many of whom have often been ignored and denigrated, who DO understand what's been going on over the last decade and their narrative is quite different from that of the mainstream media whores.

One of them is Sharmine Narwani, based in Beirut now but a former graduate of Columbia University Journalism School in New York (like myself) and then for several years a scholar at St. Antony's College at Oxford, has been called rather cynically an "idealist", and yet she above anyone else seems to have a big grip on the facts and the overall trends.

For examples, she has reported very much about the conflict over Syria. She has reckoned that Syria constitutes the main battlefield to date in what may amount to World War 3, where Western and GCC and Zionist funded and supplied terrorists like al-Qaeda were involved from the beginning of hostilities in 2011. She has reported about the internal, liberal reforms that Assad instituted almost a decade ago which were ignored by the West.

She has said that the reforms were "unprecedented" but still ignored, and that all the carnage since could have been avoided, and that a majority of Syrians supported, and currently support Assad overwhelmingly. She has remarked that the "axis of resistance" to Western imperialism and Zionist greed and control – Iran, Iraq, Syria and Lebanon – is a very real construct targeted by Sunni extremism funded by the West and its "allies", where the main goal has been to cripple Iran.

None is this is news to Iran, but then Narwani's idealism comes to the fore because she also asserts, as have some others but not as well, in taking the long view, that what the world is witnessing is a huge, major, global balance of power shift from West to East. One could argue that what Napoleon began with his invasion of Egypt over 200 years ago, Western imperialism on the Middle East, is on its last legs, is being eradicated finally, and in part because the West, principally the U.S., is more or less broke financially and has not "won" anything of any value this century or even since Vietnam. This shift favors an outlook that is Eastern, not Western, and one that focuses on regional cooperation and projects like China's Belt and Road initiative.

It is also worth stating that the Pentagon has reportedly spent many millions waging "war games" against Iran, and in every instance they show the U.S., being roundly defeated in all the important strategic angles. And no doubt, the emergence of China, and the re-emergence of Russia, and Russia's and Iran's aide to Syria which effectively turned the tables on the terrorists in Syria, have been important factors in this global shift which has been underway for the past decade. It may be said in time that Iran, Russia and China will be key players in this coming, fresher world order where Western imperialism will be vanquished finally.

The risk of course is that the global hegemon and its allies (who have become flat footed behemoths with ossified thinking) will refuse to fade quietly and create yet more horrendous conflicts, but the TREND of major change is what's important and what must be grasped by Iran and its allies and give them heart and confidence to hold together patiently while the world becomes better balanced toward mutually beneficial relations and trade

And it's worth noting that even some Iranians have remarked that sanctions may be helping "save" the country by forcing Iranians to begin to become producers, exporters and manufacturers of goods beyond petroleum. Russia, also under sanctions, seems to be prospering in many respects with the internal shifts it has been forced to make. Something to keep in mind in the Islamic Republic where internal liberalization, however slow, is happening – the latest move allowing females to attend soccer matches at Azadi is smart, for one thing, because it suggests more confidence among Iran's leaders.

A speculation about the Trumpian core
Oct 14, 2019

Here is a wild and maybe baseless hunch the Zionists and Israel could start working hard but covertly to see Donald Trump impeached by the Democrats in Congress. One might say this sounds bizarre and implausible given all that "Israel" has extracted from Trump and his administrative cronies: more billions of American taxpayer bucks than ever before, the "gift" of the Syrian Golan as recognized Israeli territory as if such U.S. recognition legitimized the Israeli hold on the territory, the further gift of a free hand for the Zionists to build more illegal settlements in the West Bank, the refusal to speak out against the horrors of life in Gaza, the move of the U.S. embassy from Tel Aviv to West Jerusalem, and much more.

This reminds of what the world has long witnessed regarding the Jewish, racist fanatics. They really don't care who they kill or hurt to expand borders that have not even been defined over 70 plus years as long as their agenda is shoved forward. They have made huge extractions from every U.S. president, and more from naïve Trump than any other POTU.S., and the speculation is might they now be angling secretly to cast him aside, gutted, because he has nothing more to give these the Israeli parasites. One must wonder, and this begs the obvious question: Why?

First, it is important to mention, and one might almost believe it, that Trump in his weeny heart of hearts is not a bellicose person. He may be all sorts of negative things. He may be a jerk, a misogynist, an often not so sharp businessman, an environmental rapist, a liar and manipulator and much more, including a not particularly bright man despite the chutzpah. But one must imagine he may not be a cold-blooded killer – not like Hillary Clinton, say, or or even well disguised Barack Obama behind his fetching smile, or well, clueless George W. Bush. One must further imagine the Zionists know this about Trump, that he is not a killer who lusts after foreign blood, and they must recall Trump on the campaign trail talking about the utter waste of U.S. wars of choice in the Middle East. The Zionists have forever wanted the wars to continue. Period.

Trump's instincts seem to be telling him NOT to start a war even if he has so far kept going those he did not start. But one must also ask why he peppered his administration with some of the worst Neocons and Zionist lovers like John Bolton and Mike Pompeo and Nikki Haley and others? Why would he have chosen such sinister souls to sully his administration? Could it be at some gut level Trump realized the importance of keeping his alleged friends close, but his enemies even closer? And recall that Trump did dump Bolton when it became apparent Bolton was working at cross purposes while Trump was trying to get a "deal", for example one with North Korea.

Now, with the demise of the Russiagate scam erected by "Deep State" opponents and Democrats as the sorriest losers of the election in 2016, and of late the erection of yet another not too credible charge that Trump was literally and baldly conspiring to twist the arm of Ukraine's Zelensky to dig up dirt on the nepotistic Joe Biden (a weak man and opportunist if ever there was one), the Democrats are back in full-blown impeachment mode and Trump, awkwardly at best, is scrambling to defend himself although it does in fact seem unlikely he can be impeached.

The Democrats are rabid about impeachment because they may well be more entrenched with the so-called "Deep State" powers than even the Republicans, although this is admittedly a very close call. It is anyway terribly unfortunate that Trump's "base" among the electorate happens to center on mindless Christian evangelicals who seem to care not a whit about anything but bringing on a war to end all wars to bring on the "rapture" or some other insane and impossible fantasy. As for the Democrats, yes, they are entertaining a few candidates like Bernie Sanders, a true progressive, and weaker ones like

Elizabeth Warren, possibly a faux progressive, but they are, it seems, NOT pushing the better candidates, especially the clearest anti-war mentality of them all, Tulsi Gabbard. And Joe Biden has been, if the mainstream media is any reliable voice (and it is not), alleged to be the front runner until recently and this seems to be some kind of bad joke. Moreover, there are some Democrats who literally think Hillary Clinton ought to jump in to the fray and run against Trump again, and she has marginally threatened to do this.

Clinton by any measure may the most "Zionified" and corrupted Democrat of them all, and it was she whom the corrupt Democratic Party nominated in 2016 in very questionable circumstances over Bernie Sanders, who probably could have beaten Trump had he not acquiesced to Clinton's nomination. But that is history, and it is quite possible that the party will somehow bend the rules once again and nominate someone who is far more like Clinton than anyone else currently in the race for the nomination.

This bears careful watching over the next year, in part because any Democrat who is not like Clinton probably stands a better chance against Trump than anyone else, but too many of the power brokers don't seem to care. Yes, Trump won in 2016, but it seems foolish not to believe the Zionists were alarmed by Trump's campaign postures about ending fruitless wars that have solely benefitted the far rightwing Zionists and the U.S. military industrial complex. And this is why one must wonder whether Israel is ready to pull the plug on Trump and covertly go for most anyone who is NOT talking about ending the various extant wars. We know the Zionists are appalled by Trump's move to pull back American troops from northeast Syria and allow Turkey to go in and decimate the Kurds, who have constituted Israeli allies. And Erdogan has not been friendly towards the Zionists even though he, like the Zionists, may still prefer to see Syria broken in to conflicted pieces. But that posture may be changing, too.

Whether there is any validity to these speculations only events over the next year will confirm or nullify, but Trump, however he may be reviled, does not look of late with the sacking of Bolton and the refusal to bomb Iran and the rejection of the Kurds any worse than most of the Democrats who again have stirred up a hornet's nest of charges and those hornets may well turn to sting them rather than result in Trump's impeachment.

A short rant after a personal visit to Syria
Nov 1, 2019

So, is there some kind of looming military confrontation between Russia and the United States in eastern Syria around Syria's oil fields, which the U.S. in a pirate role has more or less claimed as its own and seems to be all about looting the oil there?

Which never did belong to the U.S. but nevermind, the U.S. has been raping, stealing and killing around the world for decades in the name of "empire", and more than ever since the dawn of this current bloody century. This confrontation may be ahead. What is galling most is that the outcry against the brazen U.S. theft ought to be universal.

The only good in any of this is that there ought to be absolutely no question any longer that what the U.S. has been about in recent decades has not been the seeding of "democracy" or "human rights" or anything of that sort anywhere with its 800 plus military bases scattered across the globe and its pretensions of "exceptionalism".

One thing you can say about Donald Trump: he seems to be more honest than the two Bush screwball warmongers, Clinton, and Obama. At least he is not trying to hide bald faced aggression, theft and rapine, mostly in the service to Zionists but also for the Military Industrial Complex, which so dominates the U.S. economy now that weeding it out, if it is ever accomplished, is going to cause economic pain never before experienced in the U.S., but that all to a good cause if it can ever occur. The smart people in the U.S. are hoping for an economic depression as soon as possible to throttle the rush towards more U.S. threats in the Middle East. Currently, this seems to be the only brake to the madness.

Trump has by one report applied more than 8000 "sanctions" against other countries and individuals since he trashed the JCPOA in 2018, affecting 39 countries representing a full third of humanity. Think about that. If Iran or any other country feels particularly set upon by the U.S., maybe it's time for all countries subject to sanctions to accept them as just more obstacles to overcome, like say a particular spell of horrible weather that cannot be controlled. Until, anyway, the further erosion and ultimately the rejection of U.S. influence globally. This latter may seem an impossible occurrence, but consider: has any country long maintained itself as a powerful entity when it has become universally reviled as a criminal hegemon interested almost exclusively in self-service though intimidation and militancy?

Iran and the U.S. 2017 - 2023

If this writer seems particularly "anti" American at this juncture, it's because from October 14 through the 27th I was in Syria. I was in Damascus, Homs, Hama, Tartous, Latakia and Aleppo and points between with a small delegation of Mideast savants who have long been disgusted by U.S. foreign policies in the Middle East. I saw, just for example, the destroyed and formerly lovely Armenian Quarter in Aleppo. I saw the 50 plus percent of Homs residential blocks that are destroyed. I saw the destruction at the finest old suq outside of Iran in Aleppo, a literal wonder of the world, and frankly, so much more that we wept at times not merely at the damage to Syria, but over the warmth and kindness of the Syrian people towards visiting Americans. And all this, while the U.S military was allegedly preparing to kill the leader of ISIS holed up somewhere, is still not fully liberated Idlib province. Does anyone believe the announced death of Baghdadi, and then that he was buried at sea like Usama ibn Laden? The U.S. government has been lying so much and for so long that anything it claims, under Trump, is met with profound skepticism. And Baghdadi, who may or may not be a Zionist plant, has now been killed multiple times! Obama managed to do it more than once.

Syria is amazing for all it has suffered and survived. So is the popular Assad government, which did nothing seriously wrong but maintain its independence for decades from U.S. and Zionist control…and prospered. Syria was, and has been, somewhat like Libya was before the U.S. and NATO bombed and murdered the most prosperous country in Africa. Syria was and remains independent and still offers its citizens benefits that far surpass what the U.S. offers its slaves. It was and may still remain a positive economic model for countries that refuse to succumb to the U.S. "Empire of Chaos". It may also be a good political model: a secular country which allows its citizens to worship as they like – totally unlike most other Arab countries. In sum: Hats off in deep respect to Syria and its people.

Iran actually is managing misfortune with aplomb
Nov 9, 2019

Recent reports claim the U.S. is constructing a couple military bases or outposts in or near Syrian oil fields around Deir ez-Zor in far eastern Syria. It's hard to imagine anything more absurd or arrogant or, for that matter, illegal. It's not only illegal but stealing Syria's oil is nothing but raw, in-your-face theft, and if anyone EVER thought the U.S. was in ANY foreign lands to bring good tidings, democracy, respect for human rights that includes alleged women's rights, then this crass move ought to once and for all time rip the cover off any assertions to the contrary about what the so-called "empire's" true intentions are.

It's not smart from a public relations standpoint, presuming the perception of the U.S. and its allies like Israel and Saudi Arabia could sink any lower than it already has. And also consider that it may have been Trump's son in law, Jared Kushner, who gave Muhammad ibn Salman the green light to murder journalist Jamal Khashoggi in the Saudi consulate in Istanbul last year. It's no stretch of the imagination to believe it and it is hard to fathom what they are thinking, if the Trump gangsters have ever honestly thought at all.

Earlier this autumn it appeared that Trump might be removing all U.S. troops from Syria, if not immediately then over a period of a few months. Many across the globe cheered. But after a short while Trump reversed himself, evidently too weak minded to stand up to the ridiculous criticisms about the U.S. abandoning its allies such as the Kurds and by distant extension the alliance between the Zionists and the Kurds. In fact, Syrian President Assad himself seemed to extend a hand to the Kurds, an ethnic group that never did anything positive for Syria and is despised by the Turks.

Some $30 million a month in stolen Syrian oil has two purposes, including the feeding of U.S. greed. First is the concept of a permanent U.S. presence and perhaps the establishment of some U.S. dependent political entity in eastern Syria that serves as a block to the smooth flow of commerce and contact between Iran and ally Syria, and may also be considered an intentional effort to thwart China's Belt and Road project. In other words, an impediment to the so-called "Shi'a Crescent" and more across northern parts of the Middle East. Will it last, this thieving occupation? Mostly likely not for very long. It smells too bad. And Syria's President Assad nailed it with his refreshing candor in an interview last month: that Trump is the "best" U.S. President in recent memory because he hides nothing, is so transparently and obviously a pawn of the Zionists and the Saudis. The Aramco IPO notwithstanding, BOTH the Saudis and the Zionists appear strong but they are not. Both are skating on the thin ice of near universal hatred.

Those Jews who became fervent Zionists last century and the illegitimate state of "Israel" have a day of reckoning ahead that will be like nothing heretofore seen. Yet even while one cannot imagine how or when it might materialize, if justice counts for anything in human history it will be visited upon these godless animals, as well as their colleagues like ISIS and al-Qaeda whom the Zionists have supported in various ways in various war theaters this century. Most Americans have no clue, but that is because of the billions spent to spread propaganda and literally buy silence if not directly threaten and stifle dissenting voices. It is the primary source of the wreckage of free speech and real democracy in the U.S. and it is happening now – "it" being the Zionist juggernaut. Thankfully, not all Jews ascribe to Zionism, for it beckons a severe retribution.

It was anyway just over a year ago that the Trump gang started what it called its "maximum pressure" campaign against Iran and its people. It was aimed at causing Iranians to spurn the government as the economy went in to a tailspin… as if it was not the U.S. causing the damage. That has been shallow thinking indeed. Tehran has neither collapsed not surrendered to the U.S. It has still suffered a lot, but there are apparently signs that the economy may be stabilizing some. The IMF and the World Bank have predicted that in 2020 Iran will rebound from a recession to near zero percent growth. Meanwhile, the Iranian currency will likely stabilize, too, and while its GDP will be about on a par with 2015, that will be sufficient for the country's leadership to think that Iran can manage U.S. economic attacks for another year at least. And unlike Saudi Arabia, Iran's more diversified economy is far less dependent on oil sales.

One might conclude that the Islamic Republic has so far navigated the slings and arrows of outrageous fortune with some success. Iran has neither cowered before the bully nor has it done anything particularly rash, but by its measured steps is managing well enough. Better days are ahead.

Iran and the U.S. 2017 - 2023

The coup in Bolivia shines yet more dark light on America
Nov 13, 2019

Just when one might have thought things geopolitical might be about to turn for the better, which means the worldwide geopolitical nightmare engineered by the U.S. and Trump and all the rest of the mob in Washington might fade a bit, it just gets worse.

Bolivia's recently re-elected and then self-resigned President Evo Morales because he is graciously trying to avoid more upset and possible carnage in Bolivia, was on the chopping block of the U.S., and chopped he was although he is not dead yet and apparently hiding out among his indigenous supporters somewhere in Bolivia but has accepted asylum in Mexico.

Yes, Morales may have tried to overstay his presidential term by extending the term limits and maybe, just maybe, there were some very minor "irregularities" in the voting process in his country, but that's immaterial. He still won a huge plurality of the votes against his challenger. The U.S.'s government changing machine has been out for his head for over a decade, and he had the guts at the U.N. not long ago with Trump and Pompeo nearby to point out to the world just what the U.S. has been about for far too long: criminal meddling all over the globe.

It's weird, though. Evo did a good job for over a decade. You cannot argue about his economic record in Bolivia. He created, surprisingly, what might be termed a "prosperous socialism" wherein ALL boats were lifted, and especially the prospects for the poor majority. One would think the oligarchs and the "rich" in Bolivia might see some benefit in a society where most everyone got at least something better than they had. But the "rich" and particularly the obscene rich, and imperialists, they can never get enough. Any diminution in their wealth, or more importantly any restrictions on how wealthy they might become because some sharing with the poor is mandated by good government, has now been forbidden. Do they not realize that social calm for all, relatively, is better than total societal discord? Apparently not. Whatever new government is formed in Bolivia, the country is going to regress violently and the poor set back forcefully, with extreme prejudice. People who are by nature cruel and lacking compassion, feeling themselves exceptional, like oligarchs, never learn...until they are strung up on lamp posts and finally destroyed, as has happening time and again in history in various locations.

It may be hard to believe, but the U.S., which is largely controlled by multi-billionaire oligarchs (and this is a phenomenon that has been building for 30 or 40 years) under an increasing "neoliberal" regime (and not just in the U.S.), may see a day when even they will see their fortunes vanish both materially and socially. Lamp posts likely await them, too, when things become unbearable for the 95 percent of the citizenry. For the privileged, greed really is bottomless for most of this class of people. They live in a fantasy world. But of course there are exceptions. Yet the U.S. aims for resources overseas that it does not control – like Venezuela's oil, like Bolivia's as yet mostly untapped lithium, like Afghanistan's riches, and much more.

Which begs the question whether it was a good idea that President Rouhani told the world this week that Iran has discovered an additional 53 billion barrels of oil. Even if only 25 percent of this can be eventually extracted, it's fabulous. Iran IS wealthy, fabulously so in every respect, especially in its people, except that for now it can't market its petroleum wealth. Maybe that is a good thing temporarily, for Iran appears to be growing other industry, including the growth and export of saffron to name just one item.

Meanwhile, as risky as it may be, Iran has allegedly "blown past" uranium enrichment levels mandated by the JCPOA. This is absurd. Iran is allegedly enriching uranium up to levels of 4.5 percent. That nowhere close to bomb material at over 90 percent. The JCPOA permits 3.6 percent, allegedly. The IAEA and the European signatories to the JCPOA are concerned and want Iran to go back to the limits of the deal. This includes limits on the size of the stockpile of enriched material, too, which is currently, according to reports, less than 100 kilos above that limit.

However, Iran is doing just what it said it would and no more -- inching away from the JCPOA because the signatories of the JCPOA, the Europeans, have done virtually nothing, cowards that they are, to stand up to the Trump mobsters and realize that their long-term interests reside east of the Bosporus. At least Nordstream 2 is soon going to be a delivering fact. Europe did not back down to U.S opposition to that, and should have stood by Iran when Trump, caving to Netanyahu, abandoned the JCPOA. As far as many observers are concerned, particularly after the U.S.- coup in Bolivia, Iran is doing just the right things and the world, literally, prays that pariah America falls on its own swords.

U.S. STUPIDITY, AS NOW, FOLLOWED BY WORSE STUPIDITY
Nov 22, 2019

It is enough to make a rational, sentient person ill to witness Mike Pompeo telling Iranians he is "with" them, as he did again recently. Excuse me but I hope Iranians are not so deluded to imagine for a second that the U.S. government under Trump gives a gnat's ass about their welfare. And yes, the U.S. is cheerleading the apparent outbreak of protests in Iran, allegedly over the price hikes in the cost of Iranian gas to consumers.

Come on, Iranians, one must insist from afar, all must realize that the entire thinking, feeling, free world, the world that abhors U.S. cruelty and economic sanctions, stands with Iran and yes, that includes standing with the leaders of the Islamic Republic provided they maintain their cool as they oppose U.S. and Zionist imperialism and sanctions?

Understand that, citing several examples among many, the U.S. is not "with" the people of Bolivia or Venezuela or Hong Kong or any other country UNLESS U.S. government and corporate bidding is done completely, even if it means the cancellation of any real "democracy". Realize that the U.S. was proclaiming after the coup d'état in Bolivia that "democracy" had been restored to that country, which is a miserable and sad joke since the new self- proclaimed, non-elected president is a blonde, non-native floozy. Seventy percent of Bolivians have been disenfranchised just like over half the people living west of the Jordan River, the Palestinians, have been long disenfranchised and attacked (for over 70 years).

Iranians, any smart outsider must think, need to hang together and remain tough. This is not the time to be fearful nor is it a time for disunity. I say the U.S. government under Trump is cutting its own throat. True, the cutting may be far too slow as too many worldwide from Hong Kong across the Middle East to Cuba to Bolivia to Chile and many other places suffer under U.S. or proxies' policies, but those policies are so draconian and wrongheaded that they cannot stand for long the world's scrutiny.

One glaring example was Trump's unilateral decision this week to declare that Zionist "settlements" on stolen land in the West Bank and the Golan are not "illegal", that henceforth because his Administration says so, they are perfectly legal. Of course the U.S. does not get to decide unilaterally what is legal or illegal internationally. Extant, long-established international law, established over decades by many countries and legal scholars, does. A pinheaded cretin knows this. Some have opined that there will never be peace in the Mideast with this latest outrageous Trump declaration.

From afar one reads of protests in Iran against the gas price hikes. But one also reads that there are protests against protests over the hikes in Iran, like in Zanjan.

The knee jerk, ignorant reaction of many in the West is to wonder why Iran with so much in petroleum resources can't continue to subsidize inside Iran? Well, first, one must note that Iran can't "print" fiat "money" willy nilly like the U.S. does with its Federal Reserve Bank, which is not "federal" at all. The alternative is the printing of extra money but without any increase in productivity. This merely would cause even greater inflation, which is currently running at over 30 percent in Iran. Inflation hurts the poor, students and others on fixed incomes the most, and especially affects goods imported in to Iran.

One explanation comes from an Iranian friend who is not currently living in Iran. He claims that the price hike was reasonable and was aimed and freeing some funds for redirection to the very poor in Iran who are suffering the most from U.S. sanctions, and also to try to stop corrupt individuals in Iran from taking advantage of formerly the almost free gas in Iran by smuggling. He adds, however, that such radical pricing moves might better be discussed months in advance and before implementation to obviate discord and shock, and the suddenness of the implementation this month was in error. (But of course it's impossible to foresee what specific issues will arise under sanctions well in advance. The government must be able to respond quickly, as necessary.)

One thing Iranians, despite the pain, can absolutely rely on: The Trump Administration and the U.S. generally look increasingly foolish and even stupid with recent moves. Such stupidity may be sustainable for a while, but not forever. The world is disengaging as fast as it can from U.S. diktat and imperialism. This ultimately bodes well for Iran.

Little to no intelligence at the top of U.S. media and government
Nov 28, 2019

The tippy top of the U.S. journalism food chain is arguably The New York Times, and the best known "journalists" at the Times are probably the names most readers have seen for decades such as columnist Thomas Friedman. Friedman, and some of his colleagues at this strongly Zionist oriented newspaper (allegedly the paper of record whatever that means exactly when it is supposed to mean the most accurate and honest, but it has never been so) are well paid writers (or maybe shills) who consider themselves "intellectuals" of a sort, except that they are not very bright and are propagandists for the most part.

Friedman recently came out and defended the U.S. invasion of Iraq in 2003 and said he would do it all again. He defended the invasion and subsequent battles that killed probably two million or maybe three million people (very low-ball estimates are about one million) and maimed millions more, and the suffering goes on in Iraq from depleted uranium, wrecked clean water sources, destroyed infrastructure, ruined lives… you can name ANY horror and Iraqis have seen it over the past 30 years.

One thing hard to fathom is WHY the U.S. has any credibility in Iraq (it has none in Syria or Iran and is losing it in Jordan and even Egypt) and WHY the U.S, has not been kicked out of Iraq and diplomatic relations severed. In fact, the problem in the Arab or the Muslim world is, as it has long been, disunity and pandering to the West, especially the U.S., for gratuities and faux "protection" of one sort or another. But what is especially galling in Friedman's attitude is his condescension to towards the Muslim world generally.

Friedman, and he's worth focusing on because his views reflect the views of many others in positions to influence policy in Western countries, has written that on 9/11 the U.S. got hit with all the "distilled pathologies" of the Arab/Muslim world and if this culture does not open itself to religious and gender pluralism, it is going to die and "Israel is going to be surrounded by complete and utter chaos". This is worth parsing:

It is not yet been established who was behind 9/11. The CIA and the Mossad probably did have a role and knew what was coming before 9/11 arrived, and the official U.S. 9/11 investigation report is a joke that explains none of the anomalies at the scene of the crime – lower Manhattan, particularly the collapse of the towers and Building 11. So whose "pathologies" is Friedman addressing? And it is fair to say that the Zionists have ALWAYS benefitted from chaos in surrounding countries. Zionists literally thrive on Arab and Muslim disunity, and are terrified of Muslims and Christians speaking with one voice.

The countries that WERE destroyed or nearly destroyed by the U.S and its allies, if they still exist as functioning polities, do not have the surfeit of the pathologies Friedman cites most often: a lack of gender pluralism and a lack of religious freedom. In fact, the U.S. has supported and funded and armed the MOST reactionary, illiberal, anti-social religious nutcases the world has ever witnessed: this includes ISIS, the Saudis, an-Nusra (al-Qaeda) and others. And it has underwritten exactly the kind of chaos (faudhaa) that Friedman falsely claims to abhor. The U.S. has also twisted the arms of OPCW to falsify reports that Basher Assad used chemical weapons on his own citizens, this to justify attacking Syria by the U.S. and allies. But let's carry this further.

Which countries are the least "democratic" and oppressed in the Middle East? Certainly not Iraq as it was even under Saddam Hussain – the Ba'athists were secular even if free elections were frowned upon to support Saddam. Same with Syria under the Assads, where women, aside from constraints that may be imposed by their families, are little different than women in the U.S. And same with the Libya that was (before Hillary Clinton directed the destruction of that country (once the most prosperous in Africa) with Obama, and bragged about Qaddafi's horrible murder by bayonet. Yeah, the countries WITH the "pathologies" that Friedman cites are precisely the most oppressive and least "democratic" in the Middle East and the closest U.S. allies: Israel and Saudi Arabia primarily, but also Egypt under Sisi.

Friedman supported the 2003 invasion of Iraq because he claimed the establishment of a democratic Arab state in the Mideast would force other countries to modernize and liberalize. Nope. This did not happen. U.S. allies, cited above, became LESS liberal and less ideologically "modern" even while Syria has struggled to avoid being destroyed by terrorists funded and armed by the U.S., the West and the Saudis. Friedman was and even today is either lying or incompetent and ought not be writing for any media or have any kind of public platform.

Iran has long been demonized for its alleged lack of religious and social freedom, but which largely Muslim country with Muslim religious leaders in power allows the same degree of religious and social freedom as the Islamic Republic? Not the Saudis for sure. And which country has the second largest Jewish community in the Middle East? Iran. Iran is certainly a unique country, and it does have some internal points of contention that eventually might be addressed by all of Iran's citizens in a climate where it is not being attacked by outsiders. But the Islamic Republic is not and should not fall apart because of the U.S. threat and hostility and sanctions. The mere fact that the Trump Administration has supported the MEK (a terrorist group labeled as such by the U.S. in the past) or even anyone related to the Pahlavi (puppets) tells one all that's needed to know about the idiocy of U.S. thinking.

Virtually all the world, aside from the U.S. warmongers and resource rapists and the backward Saudis and the Zionists, literally BEGS that Iran remain steadfast and get through this difficult time intact and strong of spirit. Iran is a country that is going to emerge as a world leader in some respects if only the world can become truly "multi-polar" and dispense with the destructive hegemonic pretensions of the U.S.

Iran and the U.S. 2017 - 2023

U.S. has no right to slam violence (it has helped promote or executed) anywhere
Dec. 6, 2019

The tippy top of the U.S. journalism food chain is arguably The New York Times, and the best known "journalists" at the Times are probably the names most readers have seen for decades such as columnist Thomas Friedman. Friedman, and some of his colleagues at this strongly Zionist oriented newspaper (allegedly the paper of record whatever that means exactly when it is supposed to mean the most accurate and honest, but it has never been so) are well paid writers (or maybe shills) who consider themselves "intellectuals" of a sort, except that they are not very bright and are propagandists for the most part.

Friedman recently came out and defended the U.S. invasion of Iraq in 2003 and said he would do it all again. He defended the invasion and subsequent battles that killed probably two million or maybe three million people (very low-ball estimates are about one million) and maimed millions more, and the suffering goes on in Iraq from depleted uranium, wrecked clean water sources, destroyed infrastructure, ruined lives… you can name ANY horror and Iraqis have seen it over the past 30 years.

One thing hard to fathom is WHY the U.S. has any credibility in Iraq (it has none in Syria or Iran and is losing it in Jordan and even Egypt) and WHY the U.S, has not been kicked out of Iraq and diplomatic relations severed. In fact, the problem in the Arab or the Muslim world is, as it has long been, disunity and pandering to the West, especially the U.S., for gratuities and faux "protection" of one sort or another. But what is especially galling in Friedman's attitude is his condescension to towards the Muslim world generally.

Friedman, and he's worth focusing on because his views reflect the views of many others in positions to influence policy in Western countries, has written that on 9/11 the U.S. got hit with all the "distilled pathologies" of the Arab/Muslim world and if this culture does not open itself to religious and gender pluralism, it is going to die and "Israel is going to be surrounded by complete and utter chaos". This is worth parsing:

It is not yet been established who was behind 9/11. The CIA and the Mossad probably did have a role and knew what was coming before 9/11 arrived, and the official U.S. 9/11 investigation report is a joke that explains none of the anomalies at the scene of the crime – lower Manhattan, particularly the collapse of the towers and Building 11. So whose "pathologies" is Friedman addressing? And it is fair to say that the Zionists have ALWAYS benefitted from chaos in surrounding countries. Zionists literally thrive on Arab and Muslim disunity, and are terrified of Muslims and Christians speaking with one voice.

The countries that WERE destroyed or nearly destroyed by the U.S and its allies, if they still exist as functioning polities, do not have the surfeit of the pathologies Friedman cites most often: a lack of gender pluralism and a lack of religious freedom. In fact, the U.S. has supported and funded and armed the MOST reactionary, illiberal, anti-social religious nutcases the world has ever witnessed: this includes ISIS, the Saudis, an-Nusra (al-Qaeda) and others. And it has underwritten exactly the kind of chaos (faudhaa) that Friedman falsely claims to abhor. The U.S. has also twisted the arms of OPCW to falsify reports that Basher Assad used chemical weapons on his own citizens, this to justify attacking Syria by the U.S. and allies. But let's carry this further.

Which countries are the least "democratic" and oppressed in the Middle East? Certainly not Iraq as it was even under Saddam Hussain – the Ba'athists were secular even if free elections were frowned upon to support Saddam. Same with Syria under the Assads, where women, aside from constraints that may be imposed by their families, are little different than women in the U.S. And same with the Libya that was (before Hillary Clinton directed the destruction of that country (once the most prosperous in Africa) with Obama, and bragged about Qaddafi's horrible murder by bayonet. Yeah, the countries WITH the "pathologies" that Friedman cites are precisely the most oppressive and least "democratic" in the Middle East and the closest U.S. allies: Israel and Saudi Arabia primarily, but also Egypt under Sisi.

Friedman supported the 2003 invasion of Iraq because he claimed the establishment of a democratic Arab state in the Mideast would force other countries to modernize and liberalize. Nope. This did not happen. U.S. allies, cited above, became LESS liberal and less ideologically "modern" even while Syria has struggled to avoid being destroyed by terrorists funded and armed by the U.S., the West and the Saudis. Friedman was and even today is either lying or incompetent and ought not be writing for any media or have any kind of public platform.

Iran has long been demonized for its alleged lack of religious and social freedom, but which largely Muslim country with Muslim religious leaders in power allows the same degree of religious and social freedom as the Islamic Republic? Not the Saudis for sure. And which country has the second largest Jewish community in the Middle East? Iran. Iran is certainly a unique country, and it does have some internal points of contention that eventually might be addressed by all of Iran's citizens in a climate where it is not being attacked by outsiders. But the Islamic Republic is not and should not fall apart because of the U.S. threat and hostility and sanctions. The mere fact that the Trump Administration has supported the MEK (a terrorist group labeled as such by the U.S. in the past) or even anyone related to the Pahlavi (puppets) tells one all that's needed to know about the idiocy of U.S. thinking.

Virtually all the world, aside from the U.S. warmongers and resource rapists and the backward Saudis and the Zionists, literally BEGS that Iran remain steadfast and get through this difficult time intact and strong of spirit. Iran is a country that is going to emerge as a world leader in some respects if only the world can become truly "multi-polar" and dispense with the destructive hegemonic pretensions of the U.S.

A SEARCH FOR COUNTERS TO U.S. IMPERIALISM IS NECESSARY AND HARD

DEC 9, 2019

Few often learn anything until it is too late, and even then they may not learn much that matters except in a context of a disaster that probably could have been avoided. The reference here is to the relatively comfortable and well off, say the mid to upper levels of a shrinking middle class in a society such as the U.S. has.

Walk around the campus of the university here in central North Carolina and there is a wealth of entertainments like sports teams and presentations and parties of all kinds aside from classes and study. Idyllic it can appear. Everyone seems to act, at least, just like their forebears on campus seemed to act say 50 years ago, at the height of the U.S. war on Vietnam. Except for one thing:

On campuses back then there existed student protests and occasional rage over the Vietnam War – not so much on campuses in the relatively conservative southern states, but for sure on campuses like Harvard and Columbia in the northeast of the U.S. where students are notably brighter and more often concerned about U.S. directions. Today? It is depressing. There has been very little protestive demand about anything but something fairly inane such as the removal of a

100-year-old life-sized bronze statue of a Confederate soldier during the Civil War of the mid 19th century.

Why were students demanding the removal of the statue? Because it implied a time when slavery was supported in the Southern states of the U.S. and some students lately did not want anything on campus that signified the past existence of "racism" and slavery 200 years ago. It apparently is "cool" to have SOME conscience about something appalling, at least about something that was long ago and is not really going to upset or diminish the criminality of current Washington warmongers. Students today are relatively boring compared to students half a century ago and part of the reason is that there is no forced "draft" into the military as there was for decades up until the early 1970s when it was suspended. Young Americans back then, if drafted and most young men were, could be sent to die in Vietnam or elsewhere. Over 55,000 Americans did die in the rice paddies of Southeast Asia – a sacrifice for absolutely nothing of any merit.

Then the warmongers and profiteers in Washington after the Vietnam debacle figured they could get away with advancing the imperialist and militarist agenda even more if soldiers, fodder really, were just volunteers. Recruits nowadays are often relatively poor, not especially smart, not often reliable college material, starved for money and reliable advancement potential and even sometimes healthcare. It's a huge scam. The suicide rate among U.S. soldiers has never been higher: they don't have a clue what they are fighting for overseas except for platitudes drilled into them in boot camp, even as they are in fact fighting for wealthy oligarchs and powerful U.S. corporations and banks and their owners and corrupted politicians and profits, profits they will rarely if ever themselves enjoy.

Iran and the U.S. 2017 - 2023

America's probably fatal disease, long centered in and emanating from Washington, seems to be primarily greed and a broad lack of understanding, appreciation, and magnanimity towards other cultures, like the Islamic world's, and other people in other nations. This altogether is surely reflected in rampant U.S. imperialism and the apparent desire to dominate and exploit others. And there are many thoughtful Americans who fervently want change but who lack the power to summon it except, possibly, through the vote and the election of better representation in Washington. But real democracy has been cancelled by an entrenched class of powerful people, Republicans or Democrats, whose hands are on the levers of power for their own benefit and maintenance. In sum, whether the U.S. government can change before it sets itself and the world on fire may be impossible. The real question is what can countries under sanction or attack by imperialism do not only to influence radical change in the West, but also to avoid further U.S. attacks whether by war or by sanctions. One obvious mandate is to try to erect effective defensive arrangements – alliances or military preparedness – that might obviate the progression of U.S. imperialism as it has existed particularly in this century.

One idea that may be useful in this regard for countries like Iran is to lower "defensiveness" (if not actual, latent and necessary defenses) and try to set examples of better ways to contend with and defuse foreign challenges and enmity. Ayatollah Khamenei recently hinted at this when he suggested or invoked the notion of "Islamic mercy" -- a powerful idea in its own right and expressed by Khamenei in the context of how to deal with the protesters and dissidents within Iran who expressed themselves during the recent disturbances over the gas price hikes. One must wonder to what extent it may be possible for Iran's leaders to extend the concept or practice of Islamic mercy and magnanimity towards the Islamic Republic's enemies, even if this should involve relatively straightforward measures such as unilaterally pardoning and releasing foreign prisoners, as has been done recently and from time to time, or by reducing the vocalization at least of (defensive) threats to countries like the U.S. or its allies, particularly the Zionists and the Saudis who are not respected most everywhere.

It may be worth further study to discern exactly what might be the most effective balance between the expression of Iran's defensive actualities and implied military counter measures against Iran's enemies, and an Iranian/Islamic posture of mercy and forgiveness that includes an expressed desire for building accord with hostiles like the Trump Administration. Iran under attack by sanctions, for example, has already proven, since the U.S. withdrew from the JCPOA and erected the sanctions, to be patient and counter-responses have been measured and thoughtful.

Some responses by Iran to date have involved steps to ramp up very marginally the country's efforts to develop further its extant nuclear expertise. But what, for example, if Iran's leaders halted the expansions, which are implied if not real threats to Iran's enemies, and declared unequivocally and unilaterally that it was going to maintain its nuclear activities solely within the broader confines of the JCPOA even if the other JCPOA signatories still remain dilatory about honoring their own promises to Iran under the original terms of the deal. Would this not help at least to obviate actual military aggressions against Iran, because any military attack on Iran – which the Trumpists have tried to justify at the behest of the Zionists mostly, would be a disaster for Iran and in fact the entire world. Most all of humanity is entirely against more war in the Middle East and especially war on Iran.

The question here is whether, with most of the world already cognizant of the unfairness and aggressive nature of America's and its allies' actions, whether even more mercy and magnanimity (which Khamenei has hinted at internally) might act as a way literally to further SHAME the U.S. in the world's opinion with the chance that this shaming may produce dividends by somehow forcing the U.S. eventually to reduce its bellicose posturing and begin to seek real accord and reduced tensions with Iran. In any event, Iran has correctly sought the elimination of sanctions and a U.S. recommitment to the JCPOA. What, exactly, can Iran do best to defuse and reduce U.S. imperialism pushed by literally craven "leaders" in Washington, which has to be the most tiresome and unproductive thing the alleged superpower pushes? Perhaps the search for answers is in vain, but maybe not.

The U.S. has spent (and wasted) an estimated seven trillion dollars in the so-called War(s) on Terror, a misnomer if ever there was one. It has been nothing but an expression of a destructive imperialism that has not benefitted humanity at all, and that includes no benefits whatsoever for most Americans, too, including college kids in North Carolina, at a time when humanity MU.S.T begin to tackle together threats, environmental and otherwise, to the species as a whole.

Boris Johnson, an unhealthy choice anywhere

Dec 16, 2019

British voters know not what they did in elevating the Tories to their biggest victory in decades, and in defeating the Labor party and eliminating a humble, good man – Jeremy Corbyn – from a further role in politics. The voters know not what they did focusing far too much on demands that the country leave the EU, which the winner, Boris Johnson, has pledged to execute early in 2020 while at the same time Labor waffled amid suggestions of holding another referendum on Brexit.

This waffling and lukewarm if not cold stance towards the Brexit question was a major factor in Corbyn's defeat, as there are indications those who would have voted Labor foolishly switched their vote to Boris Johnson over this issue alone, disregarding other concerns about Johnson's nefarious plans. But there were other factors, too, just as onerous and disastrous, and anyway, no one expected such a lopsided vote.

Disastrous one can say because there are many Brits and many others in the West and across the globe who literally ached for the kinds of potential changes that might have begun had Corbyn become Prime Minister. This election was the one chance the British and much of the world had to begin the establishment of policies of Hope for relief for those under the thumb of Western imperialism and the power of oligarchs like Rupert Murdoch and Sheldon Adelson, to name just two, and their obscene wealth and privileges. The next chance for real change may be in the U.S. election coming next November. And that chance may be the last for many years ahead. The defeat of Trump is for now not assured unless between now and next November the U.S. economy and markets crater. Ejection from office before then is a very bad bet.

One can strongly blame the interference of Zionists and their co-conspirators in British politics. Alleged Russian meddling anywhere is nothing compared to what the Zionists have been doing. No candidate, perhaps ever, has suffered such outrageous attacks as Corbyn did given year all false claims he was in bed with "anti-Semites" simply because he has long insisted on an equitable solution to the plight of Palestinians and the end of the apartheid system in Israel, as well an end to U.S. and NATO warmongering in the Middle East. Heck, Corbyn probably would have even released the world's Number One journalist and chronicler of U.S. war crimes and other abuses, Julian Assange, from his torture in Belmarsh dungeon in London and thus obviated extradition to further torture and imprisonment in the U.S.

Corbyn's advocacy for the many, for the People, versus the oligarchs and plutocrats, the very few, was nullified by the imperialists including especially the Israel lobby. But the election is done now and the question is whether the few (not the many) have gained an even stronger mandate with their allies in the corrupted and bought media, and not just in Britain, to continue wrecking the world for selfish ends. One would have to conclude "yes" for now, but perhaps, perhaps, not forever. The victory in Britain by Power and the powerful, even as they may be strengthened by the possible reelection of Trump next year, who is reaching out to bolster his base of Christian evangelicals and fundamentalists, the utterly ignorant in the U.S., may, with some luck, prove to be their undoing in time even as the Zionists and warmongers, for now, are gloating over the election results.

Corbyn made errors, aside from not coming out strongly for Brexit, as that has been apparently desired by a majority of Brits. He has not been one not to rage against even his opponents such as the Zionists and against the smears he has suffered. One might say that being relatively "nice" does not work against such vile detractors. So will Senator Bernie Sanders, who could be nominated by the Democrats with some luck, take a lesson from the Johnson victory in Britain? He, a Jew, is already being set up for the same kind of abuse Corbyn failed to counter effectively from the Zionist lobby, and such smears would only be amplified if somehow he wins the nomination to run against Trump. But perhaps, for now, it's better to examine the incitements of Johnson's victory.

At the top of the list is whether Britain overall will benefit from Johnson's Brexit? This is unlikely, especially from an economic standpoint, but the jury may remain out on this for a long time. Also, Scotland's nationalist party, the SNP, looks likely to fight to remain in the EU and for independence, for one thing, and the Irish seem to be studying unification with Northern Ireland and their own independence from London. Both the Irish and the Scots appear to be appalled with the election results. Moreover, Boris Johnson, an uncouth champion of the rich, has positioned Britain to become more of a poodle, if more poodle behavior is possible, to U.S. control and the Trump Administration's malignant designs. Britain may be severed from the EU, but this merely establishes what amounts to slavery to the demands of the Republicans and Wall Street in the U.S.

Privatizing Britain's beloved National Health Service at the behest of U.S. corporate plunderers may now be inevitable, and once that begins, even partially, and British citizens could be forced to buy health insurance, there may be a huge backlash against Johnson's government. In sum, what happens when the public, whether in Britain or the U.S., finally wakes up to the evils of full-blown Facism (which both Trump and Johnson are essentially implementing)? And what happens when the remains of benevolent public institutions and programs in both countries are further eviscerated along with the shredding of the vital social safety nets? Is this not a recipe for revolution in some fashion in the future, especially by those who have sought peace and justice in foreign affairs and domestic relief from plutocratic predators on both sides of the Atlantic? One can only hope, but for now the British elections casts a darker pall everywhere, including over Iran.

If it had a soul, America may have lost it

Dec 21, 2019

So, Donald Trump has been impeached. So what, one must say, aside from the fact that he is only the third President to have ever been so stained by the U.S. House of Representatives (exactly along party lines), which will no doubt drive him to even more error because of his vast, narcissistic nature.

So what, because if the economy and markets don't implode between now and November, he is likely to get another four years in the White House. Frankly, he ought to have been impeached for the single reason alone of his performance in front of the big, blind crowd of his cultish followers in Michigan precisely at the hour he was impeached. And the impeachment charges?

Well, the specific charges may not rise to the level of "high crimes and misdemeanors" unless you are a Democrat. There is little of concise specificity to the articles of impeachment in the opposition's point of view, and the opposition does dominate the U.S. Senate which is not going to convict Trump. It's all been just a lot more of Trump being Trump, a gasbag of ignorance and self-dealing.

He has nothing of merit worth celebrating so far, but if truth be told, the Democrats are not far behind aside from a handful of notable Congressional reps who have frequently been vilified by members of both parties. But to get how misguided Trump is, all one had to do was listen to him fulminate off the cuff and interminably before his Michigan fans. He rambled on unbelievably and in such a macabre way, it's fascinating.

Trump is the perfect expression of a country that seems to have lost its soul or has been losing its soul for the last 30 years or more. It's been a period when really nothing has worked out as expected, or at least not as it was promised. But yes, the wealthy have gotten wealthier, and the big corporations have profited, and fascism has slowly become the order of the day in America.

The "average" American barely recognizes the failures because the propaganda has been so intense and successful, it seems, from the corporate media, no thanks to Clinton who during his terms permitted media consolidation and full dominance by a mere five or so media companies.

The U.S. economy and markets are inebriated, an accident waiting to happen. False statistics can't convince everybody. The military and its nearly trillion-dollar budgets year after year have bought little but scorn and horror and death overseas and unsustainable debts at home that have never before been seen in all of history. The almost two-decade-long war on Afghanistan, for one thing, was never "winnable" and the Pentagon, Americans just learned this month, knew this when the war was initiated, but this was covered up.

Same with the Iraq war, except that if the goal was simply the destruction of a secular country, it succeeded. And so on in other areas of conflict such as Syria and Libya and Ukraine. It's possible to cite a much longer laundry list of what amounts to failed policies, and not just in the Middle East, but especially in the Middle East. Respect? The U.S. may have lost this forever given the magnitude of the various failures.

In truth, it's not just Trump (or Bush or Obama or the Clintons), but the entire country may need to be impeached and the payback has not even begun yet, but it's coming in the coming decade – first in dribbles as one can witness now but eventually in a flood of divisiveness and rancor and breakdown – which is why the sage among us have long counseled alleged enemies like Iran, despite the sanctions and more, to remain cool and thoughtful, to avoid war (if possible), to shore up its friendships and alliances because of all of America's detractors and enemies, the biggest by far maybe its own population like Trump's fans in Michigan this week who are wallowing in self-deception even if they are not "bad" people. It is terribly sad. Ignorance is tragic.

If it had a soul, America …

One is almost inclined to suggest that Iran, which has since the JCPOA was trashed, still try to reach out to the U.S. and ask: Tell us Iranians what you could do for us aside from trying to crush our economy and people. We are almost 90 million strong in one of the oldest countries on earth with a proud heritage and if you were capable of putting yourself in the shoes of others, you would understand that we don't take kindly to attacks and sanctions. But still, we want to know clearly: What is a FAIR quid pro quo to diminish the discord between us? Should we limit our nuclear capacities further?

Then you must resurrect the deal and drop the sanctions and then we can negotiate further and maybe go farther with that. Do you insist that we demolish what defenses we have against attack and walk away from our friends who are equally worried about your threats? In many respects, compared to your offensive capabilities, our defenses are miniscule but even so how can you expect Iran to drop them? Would you if you were in our shoes for the past 40 years?

Are we not to continue to recognize that your two allies in the Middle East, Saudi Arabia and Israel, continue to revel in war crimes and human rights abuses which, by the way, the entire world sees? Iran, as you know, has not attacked anyone aside from trying desperately to hold the line against further depredations by the Saudis and the Zionists against our neighbors. The Zionists, for example, with such influence in America have pushed so hard for support that America's response, aside from many billions of bucks, has been essentially to eviscerate free speech with anti-BDS laws in the U.S. and with your allies, like Britain and France, in Europe.

And what are you still doing in Syria? Please explain. Assad is popular and the Syrian Arab Army, don't you know, has virtually won the war against the terror unleashed by your foreign proxies like ISIS and al-Qaeda injected with your assistance into Syria. And what about the theft of Syrian oil – is that truly likely to win America, allegedly a great country, friends? Why President Assad now believes you are lying about the number of American troops or associates in Syria. The number of U.S. troops in Syria could be in the many thousands, opines a dismayed Assad, rather than the 1000 or 2000 or so the Pentagon claims are there. What is the truth? Can America TELL the truth?

The above might constitute a worthwhile, direct appeal to the Trump Administration by Iran: questions asked and questions answered coming from both sides, a basis for real talks that do not mean Iran has caved to U.S. imperialism but simply wants to discover what may be possible, what both countries can do, to reduce tensions because the world desires it. In any event, the greatest tragedy is that the U.S. has been rejecting the tremendous benefits, even in mutual trade, that would inevitably occur with a kinder, honest approach to Iran and its people.

Let the ICC do what it alleges it will

Dec 29, 2019

The sole country that truly is a threat to peace in the Middle East, as the world ought to realize by now, is Israel. The only country in the Middle East that might benefit in ANY way from another war is Israel, in part because it seems to thrive on warfare. War or the threat of it, in the Zionist mentality, permits maintenance of its territorial expansions and human rights crimes against the Palestinians and war crimes against others (given the de facto backing by Israel's benefactor, the U.S., and the Trump Administration).

It certainly seems, at least, that as much as the Zionists would like to start another war, especially on Iran and its allies, that there is no other polity in the Middle East that stands to benefit in any way from further war in the region, and of course, it is marginally questionable whether Israel itself would benefit, especially if it did not have American participation, and there is at least a small chance that it might not for a variety of both domestic and foreign policy reasons in the U.S. Trump and minions, despite the bluster, may well realize they don't have the assent of the American people.

Take American "allies" in the region: there is only one other U.S ally with any serious clout, and that is Saudi Arabia. The Saudis well know, given the still somewhat mysterious attack on oil facilities in the Eastern Province this past autumn, that their entire oil infrastructure could be wiped out by a cluster of missiles and drones. The reduction of that oil infrastructure could well foment revolution against the Saudis inside Arabia. Are they willing to risk any approval of the Zionists, and especially their own participation, in a big regional war led by Israel? When push comes to shove, this is unlikely. And the same goes for the U.A.E. They are all too vulnerable.

The Israelis, on Christmas Day no less, heard Israeli chief of staff Aviv Kochavi claim that Israel cannot permit Iran to have a military presence in Iraq, and that Iran has been transferring "advanced weapons" there monthly. (Whether this latter charge is true a layman cannot know.) Kochavi threatens to "target everything that helps in combat operations" against Israel anywhere in the Middle East, and particularly in Syria and Lebanon and Iraq, presuming there is a response anywhere against the Israelis. But of course, this makes no sense because it is and long has been entirely UNLIKELY that any country in the Middle East is going to start a war, beginning with offensive operations, against Israel. This latter assumption is just common sense: Israel is a nuclear power and also has by far the strongest conventional military assets in the Mideast. Even if most of the Arab countries in the Middle East could welcome the eradication of Israel, if not as a sovereign state, at least as a state AS IT HAS BEEN for decades, most would consider an offensive attack on Israel AS IT IS more or less suicidal. IF a regional war develops, it won't have been initiated anywhere but Israel. Again, this looks like common sense.

The danger, obviously, is a "mistake" of some sort by Iran or by Iran's allies or proxies that literally gives the Zionists (what they consider) a casus bello to initiate a war. So far, it seems, this has not occurred. Does Iran stationing forces or other military assets in Iraq or Syria constitute such a "mistake", or something that the Zionists can further seize upon to justify offensive operations? It's hard to say at this point.

Any sensible mind has to imagine that whatever Iran does (or has done to date), it must merely constitute only a threat of retaliation that might convince the Israelis NOT to initiate a regional war. Put another way, Israel is NOT threatened in fact UNLESS it initiates or starts a war. Why is it, it must be asked, don't the Zionists realize this and simply relax? They could. They could simply stop the threats and aggressions and enjoy what prosperity they have long enjoyed under the umbrella of American support, which is NOT likely to

Let the ICC do what it ...

go away significantly unless people wiser than most in the U.S. government now somehow manage to win in upcoming elections. People like, say, Bernie Sanders, a Jew no less.

It may be the case, as already said, that the Zionists are just flat insane with a lust for war, which has marked Israel's entire history. That they think the country literally thrives on war. In some respects it has thrived, but only to the extent that it has not suffered from it substantially economically or materially given the American backstops – except in the court of world opinion. But if they are insane, and there is good reason to suspect they may be, is this not alone a reason, in time, to imagine a future where Israel will increasingly be shunned and reviled and maybe even disempowered, where even many Israelis and Jews generally realize that militant Zionism is a mistake for all Jews?

Take the International Criminal Court's alleged and determination to begin to prosecute Israel for war crimes, or at least Israelis who have led war crimes in Gaza and the West Bank, the Golan and elsewhere. Even if Israel claims the Hague-based ICC has no jurisdiction over Israel, prosecution could still result in a situation where international arrest warrants against Israeli leaders like Netanyahu and many others could prevent them from traveling overseas! This alone, if it ever occurred, would likely be very effective in shifting world opinion even more against Israeli aggressions and apartheid conditions. Imagine, for example, people like Netanyahu can go nowhere except maybe Washington, and even if they go to Washington, they do so under a dark cloud.

In any event, it behooves Iran, especially given this new development with the ICC, to be extremely careful to avoid actions and moves that even if they are solely defensive, they don't give the appearance of aggression that can be seized upon by the warmongers. Maybe it would be smart to pull back some in Iraq or wherever Iran or proxies may be establishing defenses outside Iran? And letting the world know in no uncertain terms that Iran's primary objective in the Middle East is peace and the obviation of the vile sanctions that have hurt Iran's economy.

Trump may have given Iran an unintended assist

Jan 4, 2020

What with all the recent movements and protests in Baghdad around the U.S. embassy in the Green Zone resulting from the U.S. attacks on elements of Iraq's and Syria's national defenses, and then the blame game against Iran, it's no wonder that confusion reigns. And in Iraq the confusion is bleeding with U.S. attacks on Hashd al-Sha'abi (officially a part of the Iraqi army) positions and personnel in Baghdad and elsewhere. As of Friday morning the U.S. is only becoming more despised in Iraq and the situation there is explosive.

The Trump Administration seems unable to grasp the fact that the Iraqis who stormed the embassy perimeters were just flat angry at the slaughter of some two dozen of their soldiers or militia, the very people who had helped rid the country of most of ISIS and who, at least, seemed to have assisted the U.S. in this task. Hasn't that been the stated reason the U.S. troops are in Iraq, to help clean out the foreign terrorists? What, in fact, really accounts for the presence or reintroduction of roughly 5000 U.S. troops in Iraq a while back? It is or has become apparent that this was probably a lie, and observers know that over the past years there have been many instances of the U.S. actually shielding, funding and supplying ISIS and other terrorists not just in Iraq but in Syria, too, even if the U.S. at times also occasionally attacked ISIS.

But first one must address the anger at the U.S. now, and what is MOST remarkable is the failure of the U.S. time and again the understand why the Iraqi parliament may finally be obliged vote on whether to try to eject the U.S. military altogether. The anger now is cumulative, it seems. George H.W. Bush almost 30 years ago pushed Saddam Hussein out of Kuwait. An estimated 200,000 Iraqi citizens died. In the 1990's sanctions murdered some 500,000 Iraqi children, and then in 2003 George W. Bush invaded the country and murdered at least a million citizens and destroyed the country's infrastructure. The attacks this past week, allegedly because a single U.S. contractor died because of a missile attack from an as yet unknown source, just added gross insult to gross injury, and may have created a long-delayed tipping point. It has to be one of the most perplexing questions of this century: why Iraq has not for the past decade at least demanded a U.S. exit and the closure of the monstrous embassy in Baghdad?

The fact may be that the U.S. has been bound to screw up, and has and is screwing up, in the Middle East because its bottom line aim, aside from giving the Zionists carte blanche, has been perpetual chaos and conflict in the region, and in turn, the nurture of the U.S. economy with the maintenance of regional hegemony and arms sales. Given all the utterly bizarre things the U.S. has done, including the trashing of the JCPOA, there really is no other explanation. And maybe, at last, Iraqis fully realize this. Iran and Syria have known this clearly for many years.

Just at the moment when it appears some in the U.S. is angling more than ever to find cause to set the region aflame (and yet others may realize it cannot without grave consequences to itself and its allies), and m, ay have begun just that, in part because Iran has become increasingly influential, it is also quite possible that the U.S. is about to lose much of the Middle East altogether. This may begin with the loss of Iraq when and if a solid new government emerges that is widely acceptable across the diverse country.

Take, for example, the recent four-day naval military drills in the Indian Ocean and the Gulf of Oman between Iran, Russia, and China. It is the very first time the Islamic Republic has engaged in joint naval drills with two major world powers, and this despite the harsh sanctions. (At the same time Iran has also been trying to limit its economic dependence on oil exports.) This is an almost breathtaking achievement for Iran! And it points to burgeoning losses for the U.S. in the Middle East: more loss of influence and control. And the drills have also exposed, as never before, that even though Iran has been surrounded by on all sides by U.S. bases and an estimated total of more than 60,000 troops, these bases and troops are beginning to look like a U.S. liability because they are all so exposed to military retaliation whether by Iran or its Iraqi, Syrian and Hezbollah allies.

The U.S. seems to have just this past week moved the focus of protests in Iraq away from political corruption and the growth of Iranian influence to the obvious violation of Iraqi sovereignty. Make no mistake: it can be argued that Iraqis are far most likely to reject yet more American attacks on

Iraq and the American troop presence than they are to reject Iranian influence.

The U.S. may well have given Iran an unintended assist in the Middle East amid all the dangers. Trump may be a fool. He may be more or less incompetent with his even more foolish appointees like Mike Pompeo, but even in the U.S. wiser voices are saying that the President who earlier claimed he was going to drain the "swamp" that is Washington (and was probably elected on that promise and others) has actually become the swamp himself. He will lose the election next November if he starts another kinetic war, particularly a war on Iran, and in the recesses of whatever mind he may have, he must be aware of this. Note that after he threatened the Islamic Republic with dire consequences, and blamed Iran for the storming of the Baghdad embassy, he fast turned around a day later and said he was disinterested in starting such a war and appeared to back down. Sending yet more troops to the Middle East makes no sense to this very confused President.

It must be always emphasized: Allah's mercy and compassion

Jan 10, 2020

Amid the madness, one thing is indisputable. Trump and Netanyahu are joined at the hip in part because both face the prospect, however remote, of eventually winding up in jail. Trump has been impeached but getting him out of the White House before November is a stretch, Natanyahu has been indicted on multiple corruption charges. Both think they avoid jail as long as they are in office. They planned and executed the demise of Soleimani through their respective appointees alongside the Mossad and the CIA.

Worse, if conditions deteriorate even further between the U.S. and Iran, like into open warfare as prompted by the assassination of Qassem Soleimani and others, they may be even less likely to be fired ... until the publics of both the U.S. and Israel realize neither country can prevail over Iran and certainly not prevail over a Muslim world that maybe, at long last, has become galvanized to kick Western forces out of West Asia and perhaps beyond. To say with deeds, "no more Western imperialism!"

There are so many possible scenarios ahead after Iran, as it has promised, retaliates for the unwarranted attacks in Iraq on Soleimani and others. And what might be the ripest target for Iran's retaliation? The place from whence the drone that bombed Soleimani's convoy was launched: al-Udeid airbase in Qatar. Iran knows what's there and why it might be a ripe target. Moreover, if Iran does strike at all, and it seems it will, the world witnesses yet another impulsive action by Washington – retaliation upon retaliation (hardly an action befitting alleged (faux) "Christians" that also infest Trump's administrative ranks). If the U.S. then responds to whatever revenge Iran exacts, Iran will unleash the totality of its very specific military capability on the western shores of the Persian Gulf. Does Trump want to see the devastation of oil production facilities in Kuwait, Saudi Arabia and the UAE in addition to U.S. military and diplomatic facilities? The world economy would crater as oil prices would ascend to maybe $200 a barrel. Trump would lose big next November, but also consider that a crucial result of what the Trump gang has done in this nascent new year is the strong likelihood that

Trump will be voted out of the White House in November WHATEVER he does. If he does NOT go to war, the Israelis from afar and fifth column Neocons infesting Washington like cockroaches will likely permit Trump to be convicted on the impeachment charges put forth by the U.S. House of Representatives.

However, it must be said that Trump, unlike Neocons like Pompeo (also a crazy end-times evangelical!) and others around Trump, does not want a war with Iran.

But the murder of Soleimani and others virtually assures a war. So what now constitutes the red line in Trump's mind? Probably the killing of American troops by Iran in the Middle East. What did he expect, though, murdering Iranian and Iraqi soldiers? No retaliation from Iran? O, the contradictions boggle the mind! Through weakness of mind and spirit, it appears that Trump fell into the trap Netanyahu and his supporters inside Israel and the U.S. have long hoped to spring – a situation that makes war almost inevitable. But here is a wild speculation:

Two of the greatest and maybe the most important of the many attributes of Allah, the one God, are mercy and compassion. This is part of the sublime Sura al-Fatiha of the Qu'ran, and often appears elsewhere in the Qu'ran. Therefore, what if, and this is as fanciful and anything imaginable right now, Ayatollah Khamenei, Iran's Supreme Leader, came out and said: Iran is going to reserve retaliation for the death of Soleimani and others at the hands of the troubled Americans and Zionists. We will reserve retaliation and therefore obviate a probable response by the U.S. that would force expansion of a war that will engulf the entire Middle East and beyond, killing many people. But we will do so under these conditions:

that the U.S. come back to the JCPOA and eliminate economic sanctions on Iran entirely, and on other countries, it has hamstrung with sanctions. With that we can begin to jointly consider other ideas to reduce tensions of all kinds between us and others in the Middle East.

Why even suggest such a fanciful idea for Iran's leaders to consider? Because the idea shines a light on the glories of Islam and its divine message to humanity, and also on the Islamic Republic, but it also ensures and insures the amplification of what the Islamic Republic already has gained from the fact of the cruelties of U.S. imperialism and the insane murders of Soleimani and comrades in Iraq this past week: sympathy and empathy, both of which are often derived from the actual expression of mercy and compassion.

Protesters in Iran may be bolstering U.S. imperialism

Jan 13, 2020

From afar it can be upsetting to hear about protests at some universities in Iran, allegedly spawned by anger over the unintentional downing of the commercial aircraft near Tehran. One can understand the anger over the horrible accident of mistaken identity, but let's get real about this tragic event.

The most important to say is that if anyone blames the U.S. for the accident, they most definitely are not alone. In fact, even a candidate for the White House in November,

Tulsi Gabbard, a U.S. House representative from Hawaii and a veteran who has consistently opposed U.S. "wars of choice", has stated that ultimate blame must be placed on the U.S. She is not alone in Congress, as if to say, if Qassem Soleimani and others had not been assassinated, the aircraft would never have been hit by a rocket because a rocket would never have been fired. Which is true.

Iran's military would not have been in such a heightened state of alert over possible attacks by U.S. cruise missiles or whatever. That Iran was in such a hair-trigger state of alert says something quite positive about Iran's defenses, except that someone apparently made a grievous error and mistook the airliner for a foreign intrusion near Tehran. In wars or near wars, mistakes are legion. It's just terribly unfortunate THIS mistake occurred, especially after Iran had so carefully calibrated its superb initial response to the U.S. murders in Iraq. It is even possible the radar "signature" of the Ukrainian airliner might have been altered to appear as something different: the Israelis or the U.S. have the technology to do this, it has been suggested.

Protests, simply that they happen, are a healthy sign that a society that has not become so repressive and totalitarian that citizens are cowed by state power and don't express themselves. Anyone who was around and young during the Vietnam War, and also possibly subject to the military draft, engaged in massive protests and demonstrations against that war, and this was all to the good for they were a major factor in ending that monstrous bout of imperialism. Certainly, protesters in Iran have a right to be upset, but at the same time, Iranian leaders, after dithering for a couple of days while initial investigations were underway, did own up to the mistake and expressed great sorrow and remorse. Also, there are probably a group of hardcore dissidents in Iran that are encouraged by foreigners to stir up trouble whenever possible.

The U.S., by comparison, has never formally apologized for any of its horrendous foreign policies in the Mideast over many decades that took the lives of millions of innocent people. It never apologized for shooting down an Iranian airliner over the Persian Gulf, and former President George H.W. Bush said the U.S. would never apologize. (Iran actually is more accountable than Boeing has been, which built a defective 737 model and covered it up until well after two planes crashed, murdering several hundred passengers, and then recently allowed the fired CEO to walk away with millions of dollars in severance pay.)

But for now, at least Trump's popularity seem to be fraying. His only hope for reelection may be bringing the troops home from the Mideast. And what is most insufferable are his Tweets claiming that he has stood with Iranians since his Presidency began and that he is following protests in Iran closely, allegedly inspired by the courage of Iranians. A bigger lie is hard to imagine. Troop has not even stood for Americans in his stance on behalf of Netanyahu.

The primary point is this. It would be completely misguided for Iranians to think Trump cares about Iranians or Iran. One clear indication of this is just whom his administration has been backing for a desired regime change, such as the cultish MEK, which until a few years ago even the U.S. designated a terrorist organization. IF protesters in Iran imagine that by slamming the current government they may somehow usher in the fall of the Islamic Republic and a better government, they are sadly mistaken. The U.S. will exploit any changes in

Iran for itself, not for anyone else, as long as the U.S. is trying to wreck the Islamic Republic.

Never before has imperialism by the U.S. been more naked, aggressive, crude, transparent and self-serving. This is obvious regarding Iraq right now:

Trump, hearing the demands of Iraqis that U.S. troops leave, has not only refused to leave but has threatened the confiscation of more than a billion dollars in oil revenue currently located at the New York Federal Reserve Bank. This is nothing but blatant extortion, and European silence so far about the various U.S. threats suggest possible complicity or at least fear.

The U.S. has again become an illegal occupation force inside Iraq, as it has been in Syria, and will aim to do the same by force or by proxy to Iran if Iranians fail to remain united against U.S. threats come what may. So one must say to Iranians who protest too much: cast blame where it is warranted, not on your government which is trying the supremely difficult task of keeping Iran independent of U.S. control. The U.S. under Trump wants nothing more than continuance of militant "empire", control of oil resources and subjugation for foreign lands. There will be a time for disgruntled Iranians to address their concerns aloud, but only after external threats have been fully vanquished and the economy is once again thriving because sanctions are no more and the U.S. has lost what little support it still has in the Middle East.

Dignity, smarts and grace: that's Iran's performance of late

Jan 13, 2020

Who does Donald Trump and his gang of incompetents think they are kidding? One might suppose, or at least hope, that the only people are the "whites only" Bubba crowd who wear red hats with "MAGA" printed above the brim. These are the folks who show up at Trump rallies and get to hear the embarrassing 45th President blather like Robert DeNiro in his first big film hit, "Taxi Driver".

DeNiro played a young, disgruntled, lonely psychopath preparing to do some mayhem and psyching himself up in a narcissistic swoon while he stood in front of a mirror. Like the acting DeNiro, Trump likes to hear himself talk unsubstantially, he thinks he's still handsome assuming he ever was, claims he's a genius, etc. Joke of the century, maybe, but now that the immediate "crisis" is sort of over between the U.S. and Iran, it's time to survey the residual landscape.

One need not go over exactly what happened, what Iran did or did not do, what the U.S. did or not. Everyone in the world knows who was to blame, who started a close call with regional war if not worse, and it was not Iran.

In fact, Iran conducted itself with tremendous intelligence, thoughtfulness, dignity and sophistication under dire threat…whereas Trump and gang did exactly the opposite, in particular threatening to bomb Iran's plethora of cultural and historical sites (which to many ranks first in the world for quality, significance and often sheer exquisite beauty – part of the heritage of all of humanity).

By January 7th, it was over and at least in America, it felt like nothing had happened: the stock and bond market futures after a deep fall were blasting higher, Trump was blathering to a national audience and claiming he was going to impose yet MORE sanctions on Iran and somehow get NATO involved in the pressure on the Islamic Republic.

As for Iran, aside from the tragic plane crash that took scores of lives at Tehran, much actually had changed and no wider war had developed. In fact, one could argue that Iran handled itself so well that it got exactly what many Iranians, and particularly the government, wanted.

It received the likelihood that American troops are going to have to leave Iraq given the vote in Iraq's parliament. They will have to leave sooner or later There is no welcome any longer after the U.S. slaughtered Soleimani and al-Muhandis and others. (And if U.S. soldiers depart Iraq and the gargantuan U.S. embassy is forced to close, the U.S. troops in Syria are going to be awfully lonely in the oil fields east of the Euphrates. They will be forced to abandon Syria.)

Limits on Iran's nuclear program, given the crisis, were mostly dropped. No one was really adhering to the mandates of the JCPOA anyway, except Iran and the Europeans have been cowardly at best telling the Trump Administration to take a hike and also maintain their part of the quid pro quo for the deal.

After the protests resulting from the gas price hikes, the entire country, under grave threat and in the context of burying Soleimani with great honors, rallied behind the government and stopped for the time being worrying about whether women had to wear the hijab or who could attend sports contests in Azadi Stadium, and other issues. Given that Trump has just threatened yet more sanctions, it's quite likely that the 'assabiya' inside Iran and even with Iraqis, to use an Arabic word championed by the great Ibn Khaldun centuries ago, is not going to diminish anytime soon.

And no one is ever going to forget, in East or West, how Iran stood by its word and did exactly what it said it was going to do in retaliation. And it was done with such awesome precision and technical expertise that the missiles that hit at 'Ain al-Asad military base in Anbar Province and at Erbil in the north of Iraq apparently took no lives, which is almost a miracle.

It would seem that the American defense establishment over the past year now has some confirmed understanding about just what damage Iran could do around the Persian Gulf and out to the Mediterranean. And Iran barely used its most advanced defensive missiles.

The only disappointment remains with Trump: he should have dropped the sanctions and the threats and asked for renegotiation of the JCPOA…and apologized. He still claims his primary aim is no nukes for Iran, but this hardly is believable because he dropped the JCPOA and it had been a success because Iran had been faithful to it from the beginning.

The U.S. now: widespread thuggery

Jan 18, 2020

For those who remember a time when U.S. leaders and especially those in the White House appeared at least nominally dignified and worthy of some respect, the appearance now is one of outright immoral, widespread thuggery and its attendant ills like blackmail and murder, the latter for which Trump may be liable in the International Criminal Court provided Iran presents the case of Soleimani's assassination along with his comrades' demise to the court.

Donald Trump is an unfolding disaster for the entire world, and nothing he has done as President seems honorable. He has wrecked numerous Washington agencies, denigrated public education, shows no concern for the environment and so on. Nothing he did before he became President was based on honest dealing, whether in his personal or business life. This in not one man's opinion: the record is there for all to see. And he has neglected his campaign promises regarding foreign policy.

The most obvious question is that even while most of the world rejects Trump as an adequate U.S. President, slightly more than half of Americans may not – which tells one something about the caliber of the judgment of "average" Americans. One might be thankful for NOT living in the U.S. nowadays, despite the fact of relative prosperity, which in fact may not last much longer for a variety of reasons.

But here we witness the dean of West Asia correspondents from the West, Beirut-based Robert Fisk, writing this week that Iran's leaders at first concealed the truth about who and what downed the Ukrainian airliner near Tehran. The Iranian public rejected this concealment quickly and so the truth of the disaster was quickly exposed. Fisk suggest that Iran has been changed "forever", that no longer can Iran's religious leaders claim infallibility.

One begs to differ with Fisk's views. First, no one in Iran has claimed infallibility. Because none CAN claim infallibility without becoming quite fallible. This is akin to declaring one's self a god (if not the ONLY God) which is utter blasphemy. (Al-Hallaj, a Sufi in Baghdad in the 10th century, pronounced that he was "the Truth" in a moment of ecstatic spirituality, which at the time suggested he was calling himself "god". This did not go over well in Abbasid Baghdad and al-Hallaj was executed in 922.)

Iran's leaders did not dither for long in blaming themselves for the aircraft disaster, and it's worth noting that there are reports that there might have been American or Israeli sabotage of the electronic guidance signals and reporting equipment in Iranian airspace. In fact, this is probably the chief cause of the tragedy although it may take some time to prove and expose it thoroughly. Iranians need to go light on the government, in part because Iran's government has proven to be far more honest than the U.S. or European governments.

Great disgust, for example, must be reserved for the UK, France, and Germany, under the threat of Trump tariffs on the European auto industry, for in effect dumping the JCPOA this past week. It's one thing to do the wrong thing, but it's far worse to do the wrong thing out of cowardly failures to stand by commitments and abide by their terms. INSTEX was apparently a delaying tactic! Nothing more than a false promise to Iran. The entire Middle East must begin to look even harder north and east for reliable partners, to Russia and China especially, who are not threatening.

Iranians must understand that their government has done nothing wrong, and the U.S. demonization of Iran is madness. But it is largely because Iran is so resource rich, and this has been the case for many decades. If Iranians want to tinker with who runs the country and how, this ought to wait until external Western threats are history, and especially those of the U.S. and Israel. The threats against Iran's people re too great to allow any disunity.

Take Trump Administration spokesman Brian Hook describing how a new "nuclear deal" with Iran would differ from the JCPOA. In brief, that Iran would NOT be allowed to enrich any uranium, Iran's missile defense programs would be curtailed, Iran's alleged "regional aggression" (which has been defensive and requested by regional allies) will end. These demands are equivalent to Iran giving up its sovereignty and defenses entirely and are so arrogant as to be angrily laughable.

Maybe Iran ought to offer conditions for a new deal suggested by Hook? NO nukes permitted in the Middle East at all, liberation for Palestine, U.S. Navy barred from the Persian Gulf, U.S. troops out of West Asia and bases dismantled, and Western oil companies barred from Iran, Iraq, and Syria at least. And that's just for starters. Why is anyone supposed to pretend that a nuclear Iran is a threat to anyone as opposed to what it really is – a deterrent to more U.S. or Western and Israeli aggression?

Iran deserves much better than anything the West has meted out to it since the fall of Mossadegh. Sometimes ahead it will get much better for Iran. Fortune waxes and wanes. The problem, as ever, is how long it's going to take.

Iran's one strike may have changed Mideast forever
Jan 24, 2020

The JCPOA certainly seems to be comatose and dying. Don't blame Iran. Blame the U.S. first and then the E-3: Germany, France and the U.K. Can it be stated more plainly? No.

One should have no problem with Iran's reactions to shoddy treatment except that this is exactly what Sheldon Adelson, the casino magnate billionaire who has literally bought Trump and his gangsters and much of the Republican Party, has wanted, along with Netanyahu and the rest of the Zionists: that the JCPOA die and even that Iran might withdraw from the NPT and at least superficially, if not, in fact, seem to be pursuing nuclear weapons.

(On the other hand, it's not nuclear weapons that probably invokes the ire of the bloody Western "establishment" (led by the U.S.) so much as it is the fact that Iran has mastered the technology of nuclear energy and how to obtain its fuel from raw uranium.)

But why did they, the Trump gang and supporters, want this – the demise of the JCPOA? This is the haunting question because the desire never made sense. How much easier it is, though, to attack independent Iran if, falsely or not, propaganda can be blasted that claims the Islamic Republic is, finally, aiming to build a nuclear weapon given the sanctions it has sustained in the past year and a half plus and the slow demise of the JCPOA and lately Soleimani's criminal assassination?

And it is not only Adelson or others of his ilk, but many more in Washington, and it's no surprise they are almost all Zionists -- a people without honor but lots of lucre, the latter which Trump respects above all else. Trump, who has been impeached and is facing some sort of contrived "trial" in the U.S. GOP controlled Senate which will more than likely result in acquittal.

Still, Trump is only the third President who has ever been impeached by the U.S. House of Representatives. He will have that stain forever and it is ugly. But impeached for what? Illegally withholding several hundred million dollars he was by law obliged to ship to Ukraine in his attempt to try to get dirt on political opponents like former VP Joe Biden.

If the U.S. were a "normal" country (to use a Pompeo adjective who claims that Iran is not "a normal country") and not one that since World War 2 has killed an estimated 25,000,000 people around the world in its self-adopted role as hegemon, Trump would be up for impeachment for a lot more than manipulated funds. He'd be impeached for the cold-blooded murder of Soleimani and his companions, for one thing.

Soleimani, a hero across much of the Middle East for keeping the best part of the Mideast from falling to the ISIS goon-ocracy operatives, whom the U.S. mostly trained and funded with help from Persian Gulf Arabs and the Zionists and whom they also merely pretended to want to eradicate. How can it be clearer?

U.S. foreign policy has had one dominant aim at bottom during this century, and that aim has been too successful far too often: to sow and to create chaos and disorder everywhere it can to benefit the U.S. military industrial complex in perennial warfare for hegemony and the Zionist goons, who are every bit as useless and criminal as ISIS ever has been. It has not been a War on Terror but a war OF terror on those who disagree with the U.S. or just want to be left alone to prosper.

Moreover, and this has not been said often if at all: Aside from lucre, whatever inspired legions of men, mostly young and Arab but some Europeans and some Americans, too, ever to sign up for ISIS? (These males are, after all, mostly "losers" without prospects and far from being anything identifiable as "Muslim", they are no better than the "settlers" in the West Bank who also are "losers" who have been inspired by greed and crude, murderous incentives.) One easily could argue that for the ISIS horde, one big incentive has been that they can rape, literally rape, women and enslave them and murder their families and loved ones as they please, with impunity. Or just kill for the perverse pleasure of it, the same pleasure a bragging Trump apparently felt when he ordered Soleimani's murder, or that Obama felt when he expanded cowardly drone strikes all over the Mideast a decade ago.

If all of the above sounds too grim, there is better news.

Even if an Iranian pushed the button that sent two rockets into the civil airliner near Tehran, subterfuge by the U.S. or the CIA that forced this result has not been ruled out and may not be – ever. The fog of war is dense indeed.

Iran's precision strike on the U.S. airbase in western Iraq was a sublimely precise and masterful warning shot and retaliation for the murder of Soleimani and his comrades. And there was NO evident defense. This is a humiliation for the U.S. and allies. If the Saudis or the U.A.E. leaders have any sense, they now know that at the least their infrastructure of any kind can be wiped out. And the Israelis? They ought to realize that Dimona, just to name one site, can be destroyed if enough missiles are directed to it.

The Middle East will never be the same again because of what Iran has proven. That it has real, serious, defensive tools to help deter attack, and has had some 40 years to develop and refine those tools. The leaders of the Islamic Republic have been patient and thoughtful, but they have been let down by cowards: not just cowardly Trump in murdering Soleimani, but the cowardly leaders of France, the U.K. and Germany, too, given their failure to ensure that Iran reaped some benefit by staying in the JCPOA, which now even Iran may abandon for real.

The "Deal of the Century" is DOA, period

Jan 29, 2020

So in Washington this week Americans witnessed two criminals, Netanyahu and Trump, putting forth a Mideast "peace" plan where one side, the Palestinians, have no representation at all (nor a hand in crafting the proposals), and which must be a total embarrassment.

After 100 years of conflict since the Balfour Declaration gave Jews a faux, unilateral "right" to colonize Palestine with force and dispossess the indigenous inhabitants, nothing has been achieved to establish equity. Anyone who has bothered to study the history of the Mideast over the last century, whatever their original orientation may be, almost invariably comes to the logical conclusions that a tragic wrong has been done to Palestine and Palestinians. At first this was done for purely political reasons by British leaders, but since the 1940s, the colonization was seized upon by Zionists and their supporters as a "fair" reaction to the so-called Holocaust, except that it created a Nakba holocaust for millions of Palestinians, who had no hand in Europe's mistreatment of Jews.

There was always some hope that Washington might get around to dealing with some fairness and giving the Palestinians a break in the longer-term interests of fairness itself and some regional peace. You can forget this with Trump, and the irony and hypocrisy are enormous.

The "Deal of the Century" is ...

Trump by most all accounts is immoral, totally non-religious person. There is no aspect of his adult life that is not marked by lying, cheating and stealing, and this both in his personal and domestic life and in his business dealings. No one of such low or no character and paltry intelligence has EVER been a U.S. President until now. This is a President who, for one thing, refuses even to release his tax returns – because they are almost certainly marked by deception and fraud and corruption. This is a President who has told more outright lies than any other ever, and yet at the same time he has surrounded himself with many people who are alleged "Christians" or evangelicals, who are thus by inclination also Zionists. Why? Because Trump might not otherwise have any kind of political base – so he plays into the fears, delusions, fantasies and sheer ignorance of these people while pretending to have religious convictions of his own.

Zionists in Israel eat this up, pandering to Trump's weaknesses and his narcissism and desire to be "liked", and it goes beyond "liking": some have called him a quasi "messiah" who was elected President by a "god's" will to "save" the Jews who in fact are enemies to themselves ultimately. Trump is being played by people like Natanyahu – people who really at bottom don't care at all for or about the U.S. nor for its leaders, but are just seizing on opportunities to use and to milk the U.S. politically and financially and abuse people like Trump and others in an administration that is the most fervently Christian Zionist ever in the U.S. The Trump gang hasn't just dropped support for a two-state solution, it has moved U.S. policy to endorsing the reality that Netanyahu's right-wing government has created: an ethno-national state where Israel retains territories it illegally occupied in the 1967 war. This is a world where international law has been completely ignored, and it all began to grow much worse during Ronald Reagan's tenure in the White House in the 1980s. The one hope of late has been that the International Criminal Court in The Hague might condemn Israel and its war crimes and human rights abuses, as it claimed it might, but nothing has been done yet – in part because both the U.S. and Israel have been threatening the court with counter measures.

There was not a single Palestinian in the White House room where Trump announced the plan on Tuesday. But Sheldon Adelson and wife were there, and other hardcore conservative Jews like Ron Lauder and evangelicals like the self-proclaimed "minister" John Hagee. It was like a conclave of the demented.

Trump, according to Leith Marouf, a widely followed media consultant and Mideast expert who lives in Canada and in Lebanon, said that during the meeting Trump literally boasted about the "deal" and the assassination of Iran's General Soleimani. Marouf correctly contends that Soleimani's murder was for apartheid Israel, making this usurpation of Palestine more possible.

Meanwhile, the impeachment "trial" of Trump in the U.S. Senate continues, and even though more evidence of Trump's misdeeds could even be testified to by none other than John Bolton, it's still likely Trump won't be forced to step down, and even if he were, is Mike Pence any better? No, he seems to be dumber than even Trump and Mike Pompeo, if that's possible. Yet there must be some hope that Americans may be becoming less inclined to vote for Trump in November. Trump could lose the election, preferably, to Sen. Bernie Sanders of Vermont. There is a man of character.

Iran, under extreme pressure? Superb responses so far

Feb 5, 2020

To be quite clear, the bizarre creature who came up with the Israel/Palestine "peace" deal (that has been rejected most everywhere) is not very bright, and he is so waxen-looking that he belongs frozen in eternal silence in London's Madame Tussaud's museum. Except that he would not be acceptable there, even as a wax effigy, because he has never been good for anything.

That this guy, Jared Kushner, has any credibility at all is a miracle. He is a real estate slumlord and little more, whose sole claim to any knowledge about the Israel/Palestine matter is that, he asserts, he has read 25 books on the topic. Maybe there's something to having an undergraduate degree from Harvard, but his father, a convicted felon who spent time in jail, gave Harvard a sufficient amount of money to get his son into the university.

One need not write further about the proposed "deal". It's an abomination and even Israelis, some of them anyway but not Likudniks and settler extremists, oppose it. Worse, almost, is Trump's expanding ban on visits to the U.S. by Muslims, or people from more largely Muslim countries. This is a reelection strategy aimed at igniting right-wing nationalism and hatred amid his electoral base of lunatic fascists.

Adding to the misery is that the U.S. Senate, dominated by Republicans, refused to permit the calling of witnesses in

Trump's impeachment trial. But never mind on that. Trump's conviction was unlikely from the get go, EVEN THOUGH Republicans have essentially admitted the charges against Trump (regarding Ukraine) were valid. Thus the faux (no witness) trial actually exposed the GOP members of the Senate as being anti-democracy, anti even the U.S. Constitution. But this is actually a good thing, because IF Trump had been convicted and removed from office, the standing of Republicans might have been enhanced rather than diminished, and their re-election chances come November more secure. As it is, some long established sinecures held by Republican dinosaurs in the U.S. Senate, people like Sen. Mitch McConnell of Kentucky who has done tremendous damage to "democracy" in America, may not be reelected given the faux trial which still does not exonerate Trump from his misdeeds. Once Impeached, always impeached at least.

At any rate, Democrat voters may be on track to nominate the first Jew ever who has a shot at becoming President. This is remarkable and Sen. Bernie Sanders is more deserving than anyone in recent memory, and soon he may be the winner of the Iowa caucuses and the Democratic primary in New Hampshire, and then maybe more in South Carolina and Nevada – which could well sew up the nomination significantly, if not completely.

Sanders supports many, many good ideas: among those ideas are withdrawing support for Israel's apartheid, getting the U.S. out of wars of choice in the Middle East, perhaps even restoration of some accord with Iran and the dropping of sanctions. Sanders also wants Medicare expanded to all Americans, and the reduction of the role of big money in elections. It almost sounds too good to be true, and maybe it is, but the world could be surprised.

Except that the usual attack dogs, including Zionist Jews like Alan Dershowitz, a former Harvard Law professor who has become notorious for defending the guilty, including Trump. In his defense of Trump he may have gone too far, asserting essentially that Trump could do whatever he wanted if he thought his reelection would be "good" for the U.S. (which is an insane notion in any democracy.) But now Dershowitz is threatening to subject Bernie Sanders to the Jeremy Corbyn treatment using faux allegations of anti-Semitism if Sanders secures the nomination. But maybe such a strategy would backfire? Are Americans still so ignorant not to figure out the odious grip the Zionists have on the U.S.? The fealty to Zionism by the "establishment" has already half wrecked the U.S. this century so far.

One country that has so far played a lousy hand superbly well has been Iran. The missile attack on 'Ain al-Asad base in western Iraq in retaliation for the murder of General Soleimani was a thing of beauty for what it accomplished, and those accomplishment were many. Above all, it signaled to the world that Iran is no patsy, that it will defend itself, is afraid of no "superpower". The human toll at the base is still being covered up, too, by the U.S., and that toll is just right: no deaths, just enough human damage to suggest or forecast tremendous U.S. soldier carnage should the U.S. unleash an all-out war on Iran.

And those missiles! Such accuracy, which begs the question whether Iran had some assistance from Russia. Some use of Russia's satellite guidance system is likely. The Russians well know that if Iran is ever destroyed by the U.S. and its poodles, the next target will be Russia itself, and then on to China, which is groaning under the Coronavirus epidemic. Never has the world seemed more complicated or at risk, but it would be a mistake to literally believe so. Worse times there certainly have been.

Iran may be more "democratic" than the U.S. nowadays
Feb 14, 2020

Can it be more evident than it now is: that U.S. foreign policy is not "for" the U.S. or its citizens but for the Zionists.

The Biden Administration is jam-packed with Zionists, more so than when Biden served under Obama as vice president. There is apparently nothing these people won't do for the Zionist entity despite the fact that even Israel's leading human rights organization, B'tselem, has declared it a full-blown Apartheid state from the Jordan River to the Mediterranean, and "Israel" is reviled more than ever worldwide. In some ways, Biden's Zionist focus is worse even than under Trump, who was just primarily seeking supporters to salve his insecurities and boost ego and justify his narcissism.

Biden is a relatively cunning shill for the Zionists. He knows how Washington has worked traditionally (Trump had little clue). He is not at all, as Trump often seemed, an "anti-Semite" as witnessed through some of Trump's crude statements. Biden clearly has a vision of two huge military powers, the U.S. and Israel, lording it over West Asia and "securing" mutual "interests", the latter of which boils down to one thing: neither the U.S. nor Israel can be attacked in the region without reactive devastation, and both can continue to do as they please.

The Zionist lobby in the West, but especially in the U.S., is beyond gargantuan for power and influence. It can move policy in its favor easily and has long promoted the alleged interests of the greedy Apartheid state against the U.S. And Israel always avoids accountability for whatever it does. Just look at the confirmation hearings of Biden appointees in his administration. Discussions have centered on bashing Russia or China or Iran, and then questions about what appointees have done for the Zionist Apartheid entity. It's almost unbelievable and would be had this chicanery not been going on for decades.

Take for example Biden's appointment of General Lloyd Austin as secretary of defense. Austin may be a lot of things but one thing he is not by accepting the job and mouthing the things he has: he's not bright. His first call in his new job last week was to Israel's Benny Gantz, defense minister there. Both Austin and Gantz agreed that that the two countries needed to deal with "Iranian aggression". This is quite insane. What aggression? That Iran decimated ISIS in Iraq and parts of Syria by invitation? That it helped reduce other terrorists like al-Qaeda in Syria? That Iran has reasonably good and peaceful relations with Iraq and Syria now? Show anywhere where Iran has been "aggressive" of "destabilizing" except very, very occasionally in its own defense. Who by far has been most aggressive in West Asia? The U.S. Who has murdered millions of innocents in West Asia? The U.S. Who had underwritten vast Israeli aggressions in Palestine and Syria? The U.S. Etcetera. Do these points even have to be argued again? They are so evident.

And everyone in the world knows it is not Iran but the U.S. which hasn't lived up to the terms of the JCPOA and the U.S. must first drop sanctions before Iran is obliged to do anything else to return to the full terms of the nuclear deal. Meanwhile, whatever the Biden Administrations says about Iran consists of little more than pure lies and propaganda.

But consider what a longtime Jewish-born legal scholar, teacher, author and former diplomat serving in the UN, Richard Falk, has recently said about Iran. He correctly claims the Islamic Revolution in Iran just over 40 years ago turned Iran into a democracy. "There is no question that the Islamic Revolution brought about a drastic transition from the Shah's absolute rule taking the form of an imperial dynasty to the current Islamic constitutional order that has important democratic elements, including the periodic election of the President and members of the Majlis," American professor Falk said.

In addition, Falk recognizes that Iranian democracy is unique in the role it has afforded to Islamic authorities like Ayatollah Khamenei. Iran, Falk maintains, has managed to surmount a range of threats for decades given its social, economic and military advances.

Falk also notes that Iran in recent years has been an effective anti-terrorism force in its operations against ISIS, whom the U.S. has falsely claimed to be trying to eradicate in Iraq and Syria as justification for its continued presence in Arab heartlands. It's clear the U.S. and Israel have little aim but to ensure they have no challengers in West Asia.

Israel is clearly not a democracy. It never has been except exclusively for Jews. Half the people living west of the Jordan

River in historic Palestine have no rights at all. Iran may be a more effective, true "democracy" than even the U.S. is today if you push aside all the blather of the Democrats and Republicans, much of which is absurd and false like all propaganda.

Black Swans if not dangerous raptors are everywhere

Feb 15, 2020

One has to be cynical about the primaries run by the Democratic Party to choose a nominee to challenge President Donald Trump next November.

The only candidate by many accounts who has a chance to beat Trump (who was not convicted in the U.S. Senate after his impeachment because no witnesses, no thanks to the Republicans, were permitted to testify at the trial), is Senator Bernie Sanders of Vermont. Sanders happens to be the most consistent and honest of the candidates, but even if he gets into the White House he is unlikely to save "America" from the ultimate Karma of its ugly behavior over the past 30 years plus.

The best that Sanders or equivalent could do is to attempt a cleanup of the government and system or reform it so thoroughly that it's like starting from scratch: a world where paper fiat money simply cannot continue to determine and corrupt who wins and who loses in America, and where the

Military-Industrial Complex has lost its power to screw up U.S. foreign policy.

However, the Iowa Caucus last week was mismanaged badly due to internal corruption by the Democratic Party such that even though Sanders had a plurality of the vote, he was denied the limelight and a little-known challenger, one Pete Buttigieg, 38, may have picked up the most delegates. So, for now, no one of clear mind can trust the current Democratic Party leaders, or really, for that matter, either of the two major political parties.

Both political parties rig elections. When the U.S. castigates other countries such as Bolivia for alleged "voting irregularities" and then conducts a coup to install a right-wing, racist government that is disempowering indigenous people, one has to both laugh and cry: it's in the U.S., less so anywhere overseas, where alleged "democracy" has become almost a joke and power rests in the hands of corrupted, big money oligarchs and corporations that bribe politicians to do their bidding.

One of Pete Buttigieg's biggest supporters, for example, is Seth Klarman, a Jewish hedge fund billionaire who can't do enough for Apartheid Israel (like Adelson), while the candidate's only claim to fame is a Rhodes Scholarship. Otherwise, he is a power grubbing empty suit who dreams of escaping South Bend, Indiana, where he has been a lackluster city mayor for several years and also a "married" homosexual. An article allegedly from the South Bend newspaper from August 1998 appeared last weekend (and then quickly disappeared, as expected) reporting that a 16-year-old Buttigieg had been arrested for suspicion of murdering by strangulation five stray dogs just for kicks.

If this fellow (who was a U.S. soldier in Afghanistan for several months and doing some dirty work for the CIA) ever did become President, you can bet he is going to be murdering a lot more than dogs. You can't make this stuff up and American "democracy" has sunk far, far beneath Iran's, it would appear. Anyway, the first real primary in New Hampshire is ahead this week and it appears from voter polls that Sanders will win it, but it is possible that outcome could be corrupted by the Democratic party "leaders".

The sole litmus test for the Trump Administration of a claimed healthy U.S. economy has been the "stock market", which continues to hover at nosebleed, record highs. (The so-called economy for the past decade has done virtually nothing for average citizens, most of whom don't own stocks, but quite a lot for billionaires.) It all looks very similar to the U.S. stock market in 1929 during which pundits were claiming the market had reached a "permanently high plateau".

This was just before the crash that eventually knocked off 90 percent of the "value" of the market and led to the worldwide Depression of the 1930s. Trump is skating on very thin ice because the U.S. economy and the markets WILL implode. It's only a matter of time, and it MAY happen before the elections in November but Trump is desperate that it not since if it did he would not win a second term in the White House. It is quite possible that the spread of the Chinese Coronavirus worldwide and resultant economic dislocations may be the "Black Swan" that destroys the economy and thus the Trump Administration.

At any rate, if Bernie Sanders is the candidate opposing Trump in November and if by some lucky chance he should win the election, Iran could probably expect the end of sanctions, something like the resurrection of the JCPOA or similar, the end of the vast American military presence and wars in West Asia, the end of excessive U.S. government kowtowing to the Zionists' Apartheid regime, and maybe even the freeing of Julian Assange and others who have blown the proverbial whistle on American war crimes and malfeasance. That would certainly look and feel like nirvana to anyone of sound mind and heart after so many years of horror and cruelty meted out by various U.S. administrations in Washington.

America has not been helping itself

Feb 21, 2020

It's easy to get the impression that the people most set upon in the world now, really as never before, are the seven million or so people trapped in divided cantons inside historic Palestine with no civil rights, no vote, no official empathy and no resources to speak of except "samud", an Arabic term for something like gutsy endurance in the face of pain.

And reports are saying their overlords, Zionist Jews, another 7 million or so (who are stealing for Jewish-only "settlements" the land that Palestinian generations have owned for centuries) are being denied even the vaccines against the Covid pandemic that are being dispersed almost exclusively to Jews only. A few scattered people in the U.S. Congress are vaguely concerned about this, which is saying something. At least the International Criminal Court in The Hague is warming up to the notion of reviving efforts to charge Israel with war crimes and other abuses what with Trump gone, he who sanctioned ICC members over previous indications that court action was underway.

Perhaps most succinct were the words before Congress in 2016 of Michael Scheuer, a former CIA employee, author and adjunct professor at Georgetown University, regarding the U.S. role in this tragedy: "I'd dump the Israelis yesterday, but I suppose tomorrow would be better than nothing. Israel is possibly the single worst thing to happen to the U.S. since its founding. The entire "War on Terror" since 9/11 and the loss of millions of lives, as well as any remaining moral authority America had; the resulting destruction of the Bill of Rights; the trillions of dollars in debt resulting from the endless wars; crappy relations the Muslim world; false flag attacks on the U.S. which someday may go nuclear; these are all the fault of the "special relationship" in which the U.S. bends over and takes it from the Israelis every time with only the occasional protest for public consumption…. American has been CURSED by its support of Israel, and the curse will lead to damnation."

Strong words indeed, but true enough, except that no administration has had the courage to say these things even though one could wager that many in Congress who know anything of history since 1948 probably would agree…but only when they are no longer in government. West Asia's truths have gone unrewarded in Washington because those who speak it almost invariably suffer ostracism.

Now we have to witness a Biden appointment, Rob Malley (a West Asia expert who worked in previous administrations and now named the prime envoy focusing on Iran). He's getting smeared by the Neocon Zionist establishment in DC because he has been said to be too "soft" on Iran and not enthused enough about Israel. One can say this again: "Israel" will be the death of the U.S. as any kind of respected nation worldwide. Malley is probably the best person for the job according to respected commentators outside the "exceptionalist" mob of fools.

Obviously, the question now is whether the new Biden administration will ever challenge the Zionist hardliners. Don't bet on it unless Israel attacks Iran unexpectedly…and drags the U.S. into a fresh war that neither can win unless carnage and destruction are the sole aims. Note how fast Netanyahu has turned his back on Trump, who kissed his rear end for four years. Netanyahu has been making deals with the Chinese (another alleged U.S. "enemy" of sorts) but also cozying up to Biden's administration and cabinet appointments where Zionists dominate.

For now anyway it appears that the Palestinians are being totally forgotten, heaved into oblivion, in part because many have simply become exhausted by over 70 years of their struggle for human rights and political voice. The Biden administration must understand that pushing U.S. hegemony and exceptionalism and not multilateralism necessarily involves tensions with Russia, Iran and China.

Yet, importantly, the U.S. is sharply divided and in horrible shape financially. One side is still glommed on to the immoral buffoon who is threatening to start a new political party, while the other side is lined up behind senile Biden who is surely taking his talking points and orders from Deep State others. Even billionaire Ray Dalio, the leader of the largest hedge fund in the U.S., Bridgewater, has said this month that a civil war could unfold inside the U.S.

The answer for those who truly care about justice and democracy and better foreign relations? More "samud", more patience. America has been all about wrecking itself this century. And it's showing like never before.

America is not immune

Feb 28, 2020

One of the more absurd claims is the assertion by a kook rabbi in Israel (where there are many of the same ilk) that the coronavirus (Covid 19) that is sweeping across the world won't halt creating its trail of devastation and dislocation until the so-called "third temple" is built in East Jerusalem, presumably atop the rubble of a destroyed al-Aqsa mosque and the Qubba al-Sakra. This rabbi, one Aryeh Lipo, a "religious studies" teacher who is a Likudist, apparently gave a lesson on the Haram esh-Sharif with a bunch of other unwelcome Zionists saying a "third temple" is a powerful cure for the coronavirus pandemic which now even Iran is struggling to corral and eliminate.

Better this kook might have suggested that the most damaging virus in the Middle East and beyond is Zionism itself, which is the deep root cause of most all the various conflicts in West Asia spawned by Israel and its U.S. partner in the Trump administration and by previous U.S. administrations in the Middle East? Lipo said he was sending up a prayer for the "healing of the entire world", a joke if ever there was one and equivalent to giving a murderous psychopath a loaded UZI machine gun.

At any rate, the virus seems to be just beginning its spread, and one Harvard University epidemiologist has said that it could infect 70 percent of the world's population before an adequate vaccine exists, which has been estimated anywhere from six months to more than a year away. Currently, the only possible palliative that may have some very modest promise is infusing some blood of those who have survived and recovered from the virus into those who are ill since some antibodies may be present there.

In the U.S. where the virus has not yet widely disseminated itself in the population, and this may not occur until later this year, there exists the potential for chaos such as one can read about in China (and other countries, like South Korea, rising). The financial markets are just beginning to reflect the threats of this disease with the stock market finally trending lower and possibly about to crash, an inevitability that existed before the virus emerged but which the virus has undoubtedly speeded up.

In a move that has become acutely important this year in the U.S., the citizenry is learning that in 2018 Trump fired the entire then existing chain of command for a response to any pandemic. This president apparently thought, as with so many other now fired remainders from the Obama years, they were not loyal enough to him.

While Trump continues to claim that the virus is something like a marginal, minor irritant to the country that is not going to get out of hand, it's almost as if he does not want his fellow Americans to know of, or even do much about, this critical issue threatening not just Americans but the entire world with radical disruptions such as we are now seeing in China, where hundred of millions of people can't go back to work for fear of infecting many more people and deepening the already deep dislocations. China has been paralyzed and nothing like it has ever been seen before on such a scale.

Worse, economic and business supply chains are being broken willy nilly, and the U.S. in particular is at risk for, dare it be said, an economic Depression not seen since the 1930s. Procter and Gamble, one of the largest U.S. consumer supply companies with many thousands of products, asserted this past week that the production of some 17,000 items it sells could become unavailable because many of the critical components of its goods are dependent on failing production in China. It probably was a grave mistake that U.S. companies, in the pursuit of higher profits from cheaper labor in Asia, were allowed to offshore production over the past 20 years especially, hollowing out U.S. industry along with the "financialization" of the economy where Wall Street paper pushing has become the dominant economic activity.

Of particular note right now is Senator Bernie Sanders' victories, so far, in the U.S. Democratic primary elections for the nomination to run against Trump in November. These victories, which make him the front runner for the nomination, have appalled the Democratic Party establishment and the entrenched main street U.S. media, who have been banking for their continued provenance and power on the status quo in all its ugly ramifications through rival candidates such as, for example, billionaire former New York City mayor Michael Bloomberg, who was slaughtered in a recent "debate" by another rival for the nomination, Elizabeth Warren.

Bloomberg, a Jew and a Zionist, has already spent the obscene sum of half a billion dollars on his campaign, but this is a piddling amount given his fortune of an estimated $60 billion. Bloomberg is everything Bernie Sanders abhors given Sanders' posture as an alleged "socialist" who wants to raise taxes on people like Bloomberg and reform the health care system to make Medicare available to all Americans. Sanders, another Jew, also wants to make Israel more accountable for its crimes and give the Palestinians a fair shake, and many Democrats obviously agree with this notion and other various reforms that Sanders advocates, especially for the forgotten middle class and workers.

Probably with some accuracy if Sanders were to be elected President, a possible miracle, the economy and markets would suffer, but it's likely they are going to suffer anyway even if Trump is reelected. The money printing and more does have diminishing economic returns, not to mention the debasement of the dollar towards oblivion. America is just on the verge of a huge crisis that may be delayed but cannot be stopped. The coronavirus just quickens the pace of a lambent social, medical and economic disaster this year or next.

Javad Zarif's brain should be duplicated at the U.S. State Department
March 4, 2020

Javad Zarif's brain should be duplicated ...

Javad Zarif is so correct, saying that the U.S. never should have invaded Afghanistan (nor should the U.S. have invaded or attacked or sanctioned so many countries since World War 2 for that matter.)

But one must be reminded of what former U.S. Secretary of State Madelaine Albright suggested years ago: that given the fact of the existence of the U.S. military's might, it ought to be U.S.ED for something, as if that could be good excuse for shattering countries and cultures that are not American, and murdering millions of people. This has been done repeatedly especially since 9/11.

Albright, a Jewess of questionable merit for the jobs she has attained (unless a doctoral degree is worth mention, or later that she was the first U.S female who became the top U.S. "diplomat"), also said that the demise of some half a million Iraqi children in the 1990s when Iraq was under U.S. sanctions imposed by President Bill Clinton was "worth it". This occurred largely because the U.S. prohibited the import of chemicals to make Iraq's water supplies free of bacteria and other pathogens. (Just imagine having to drink from the Tigris River flowing through Baghdad after the river arose in Turkey for starters and flowed south over 1000 kilometers.)

Albright was also awarded the Presidential Medal of Freedom in 2012 by another President, Barack Obama. Why is anyone's guess! But U.S. Presidents of late have been inclined to award unindicted criminals or criminal minds big awards – Trump just gave the same medal to a vicious right-wing radio personality, Rush Limbaugh, whose verbal stock in trade has been racism, misogyny, far-right politics, and sheer banality.

Maybe Trump felt sorry for Limbaugh who announced he had Stage 4 lung cancer, but he'd have done better sending him a mere note of condolence on toilet paper? Trump cheapened the so-called Medal of Freedom badly, in the same way, perhaps, that the Nobel Peace Prize has been cheapened in this century, particularly by its award to Barack Obama in the early stage of his reign and who later never did anything of note for peace, particularly in the Middle East where his administration soon sparked the destruction of Libya and Syria by terrorists.

But again, the truly honorable and honest Mr. Zarif is so correct. The U.S. never should have invaded Afghanistan, he said, except as others may note that Usama ibn Laden, the alleged mastermind of the 9/11 attack, was allegedly there, and yet to this day no one has ever come clean about all the actors who were involved (the CIA, the Mossad, the Saudi leadership?) in the planning or execution of the attack in Manhattan.

But now we have the spectacle of the U.S. signing a peace deal with the Taliban. Trump HAS lived up to one of his campaign promises, which was to pull the U.S. out of Afghanistan, where to date more than $2 trillion has been spent, no real U.S. friends were ever made, and many thousands died. Imagine what $2 trillion could have done to solve real problems and make real friends in Asia, no war-making permitted. Imagine the friends the U.S. could make in Iran if the U.S. dropped and then apologized for the hideous economic sanctions and realized that friendships with Iranians could be far more profitable and beneficial than propping up a racist, Apartheid regime in what is still called Palestine most everywhere.

Zarif has said, also correctly, that the U.S. "surrendered" to the Taliban after years of "humiliation". And again correctly, that the U.S. is and has been THE problem in West Asia, which eventually it will be forced to leave altogether. Inshallah. But what Zarif has failed to mention is just this: that the U.S. Military Industrial Complex and its many corporate and contractor minions, which President Eisenhower warned about in 1960, have gotten rich murdering faraway foreigners and stealing control of resources since the 1950s…and the U.S. today has become virtually bankrupted, too.

Indeed, it is the recognition of horrific policies that have not benefitted most Americans that underscores Senator Bernie Sanders' bid for the Democratic Party's nomination for the Presidency in November. He seems to be the front runner currently, but his competitors are trying to ensure he will not be nominated … against the will of most Democratic Party and independent voters together. This is a travesty. The screaming question is why do party members oppose Sanders, who is claiming he cannot beat Trump when he is the best of the candidates against Trump? Partly the answer is that Sanders' economic programs may not work, but that not the prime reason.

Simply put, those of the "Establishment" so long established in positions of power and with reams of perks and privileges increasingly not available to average Americans, whose fortunes have been in decline for half a century since the Vietnam War, cannot conceive of giving up their power. Indeed, it has been noted that the privileged, enjoying great relative prosperity, would often sooner engineer their own destruction through their own rigidity and blindness than giving up even a small portion of their perks for the greater good.

With solidarity, Iran will pull through

Mar 9, 2020

Some 70,000 Iranians and veterans whose health was damaged by chemical warfare and who are still living with injuries caused by Western chemical agents supplied to Saddam Hussein in the 1980s are reportedly at extreme risk of dying from the Covid 19 virus, and some of these veterans already have been struck down in Iran.

Also, a disgusted Iran native, an academic at Princeton University in New Jersey, points out that an organization called "United Against Nuclear Iran" (UANI) has long been leading efforts to pressure companies to stop doing business with Iran. Lately, pressure by this organization has been directed at major pharmaceutical companies to halt any business they have with Iran under what has been dubbed "humanitarian exemptions" given the fact that Iran has already been hard hit by the spread of Covid 19.

A sane person can't make this stuff up because it goes parsecs beyond ANY sense of a "humanitarian" spirit and, you guessed it, the primary funders of this group are none other than billionaire Jewish Zionists like Sheldon Adelson and Thomas Kaplan. Other names that have been or remain associated with "United Against Nuclear Iran" are individuals (to name just a few) such as former U.S. Senator Joseph Lieberman, Dennis Ross, Richard Holbrooke, John Bolton, and even Mike Pompeo -- all prominent people and Zionists who have been involved through various postings at one time or another in setting U.S. foreign policies.

Major companies (among others) allegedly urged by UANI to halt whatever business they do with Iran include Bayer, Pfizer, Eli Lilly and Abbott Laboratories at a time when the legal channels for humanitarian exchange are not apparently providing enough medicines and related goods to help Iran alleviate the sufferings of Covid 19 victims and to halt the viral spread inside Iran.

The ultimate absurdity is that UANI claims it cares about the Iranian people. But this and similar claims by the Trump Administration and by others associated with crafting cruel U.S. policies now and in the past towards Iran have been lies and subterfuges aimed largely at encouraging Iran's citizens to foment discord inside the Islamic Republic. The policies of the Trump Administration and its minions and supporters towards alleged "enemies" (including other countries like Syria and Cuba and Venezuela, etc) must ultimately be carving out a special place in Hell for these immoral actors.

However, it may also be the case that more prudence in U.S. policies towards Iran could emerge as it becomes harder for the Trump gangsters to rationalize its ugly sanctions especially at a time when there is a strong need for relief from those sanctions given the viral assault. One observer has pointed out, for example, that former President George W. Bush, who falsely branded Iran as part of the absurd "axis of evil", still sent loads of medical supplies to Iran when it was hard hit by earthquakes in 2003 at the same time he was invading and destroying Iraq.

In any event, in the U.S., the status quo is falling apart and not just because of the Covid 19 threat (which is accelerating exponentially in the U.S., too). For one thing, Trump has been forced to "eat crow" because the economy is on the verge of what may become the worst recession ever, and his beloved "stock market" is gyrating downwards and giving the lie to any claims he has made that the U.S. economy has EVER been really healthy since the recession of 2008 and 2009, the deepest to date since the Depression of the 1930s. Since 2009 the Federal Reserve Bank has engineered a debt-fueled binge and fiat money printing the likes of which has never before been seen anywhere and which has been bound to eviscerate in time U.S. pretensions of economic health and leadership.

Given what's ahead, it is unlikely Trump can enjoy a second term in the White House IF, and this is a big if, the Democratic Party can manage to nominate popular Sen. Bernie Sanders.

Currently, former VP and current Senator Joe Biden have been elevated as the likely nominee with some ill-gotten primary victories, but evidence has already emerged that he is senile and probably incapable, if honestly prevailed, of literally serving as POTUS. in anything but name. In a recent campaign appearance, he managed to confuse his sister with his wife amid other embarrassing verbal gaffes. The long corrupted Democratic Party leadership will destroy the Party and ensure Trump's election for a second term if Biden faces off with Trump next November. And if Trump is reelected the prospects for real America democracy and any leadership in the world are more than probably doomed.

Trump, it seems likely, is finished politically

Mar 17, 2020

On March 13, a "Friday the 13th" by the way, a date in the West anyway often considered to be full of bad news, bad luck and bad omens -- a superstition to be sure – U.S. President Donald Trump was ebullient and bragging that the U.S. stock markets had one of its best days ever. The U.S. equity market climbed almost 10 percent on the 13th after a previous several days of what can only be termed a serious mauling by the proverbial "bear". No, the U.S. equity market did not make up its losses so far this winter, and in fact closed lower than the highs made just before the vicious recession of 2008-09 that affected the entire world.

What was really bad news on Friday the 13th for the world was more of the same – more evidence that the Trump Administration and much of the entire U.S. government is merely thrashing about destructively with no positive policies or agenda or the leadership required to stem the ongoing tsunami of the Coronavirus pandemic that is blossoming in the U.S. now exponentially, but also in many locations around the world and perhaps especially in Iran and points farther east in Asia. Furthermore, the relief rally in the markets are bound to be erased and then some, dramatically during this Spring season and beyond.

With Trump (and his gang), who have not a scintilla of real concern or empathy for a world in the grip of a dangerous, even murderous, grippe, it appears to be business as usual:

vilifying other countries, dropping bombs on other countries like Iraq and Yemen, supporting terrorists in Syria, denying aid to others – which in Iran's case would be the cancellation of the sanctions (which Iran has requested) and much, much more.

In the U.S. Trump has ordered some travel bans, for example forbidding citizens of the E.U. travel to the U.S., but not, notably, British citizens. Why? Some believe because Trump has private real estate, business interests, in Britain. (He always thinks of himself first.) But even so, health experts are saying the bans that have been enacted don't do anything much to halt the pandemic spread even in the U.S. It's too little, too late. It is predicted that maybe 20 percent of those who become ill with the virus will need hospitalization, and in most of those cases major interventions in intensive care facilities in U.S. hospitals, and there are not enough of such ICU beds, not enough equipment like ventilators in the U.S. to handle the predicted caseloads. Some experts have said that by early May U.S. hospitals will be literally swamped by ill patients and unable to cope very well, as may be occurring in Iran and some others countries now. I, for one, am hearing this, too, from a son, Dr. Sean Love, 33, who happens to be a "critical care" resident doctor at one of the top three hospitals in the U.S., Johns Hopkins in Baltimore. But is there anything at all positive about what is happening worldwide now?

For one thing, some leading writers are now claiming that Trump is finished and has little to no chance of being reelected in November. This depends, of course, on the degree and depth of growing perceptions about Trump's incompetence as well as his selfish myopia and his politicization about the suffering in other countries, particularly those countries that have a majority Muslim population like Iran.

Trump, it seems likely, is finished ...

This fact may well sum up the situation: the U.S. has been bombing Iraqis amid the virus outbreak while other countries, especially China, are delivering experts and medical aid and drugs and equipment to fight the virus. Mahan Air, for example, apparently delivered eight plane loads of aid to Iran from China, and that airline is under U.S. sanctions. And that's not all that China, the country hardest hit by a virus that may have been deliberately planted in the country by the U.S. back in October, is trying to do to assist. Iranians will never forget China in this regard.

But Trump may be finished politically, and that's important, claim some observers. Not only has he failed the American people in putting in place effective policies to halt the virus, but more and more Americans are finally realizing that he is unfit intellectually, temperamentally and morally to be President.

Even a few still lonely voices in the U.S. Congress like Muslim Rep. Ilhan Omer believe the U.S. ought to drop sanctions against Iran. A crisis always ultimately reveals such flaws as Trump has always possessed, not that it already hasn't been revealed since 2016 to discerning minds. Trump is a man of no character and no real leadership ability. He has always been little but a con artist, which is not news to Iranians especially.

Maybe, just maybe, this medical crisis sweeping across the globe is going to prove so devastating that it will reorder thinking generally, especially in the corrupted West: that humanity hasn't a chance of a decent future unless virulent nationalism and hegemonic pretensions are dropped and the species finally understands that cooperation and mutual aid are absolutely necessary.

Earth's non-human species enjoying diminished human activity

Mar 24, 2020

Reports are floating around that bigwigs in the U.S. Defense Department are discomfited if not appalled by Mike Pompeo's attempts to increase aggression towards Iran in the midst of the viral pandemic. Some voices are even saying that the assassination of General Qassim Soleimani has backfired and was a "mistake" because it has not snuffed out Iran's capacity or willingness to respond to U.S. aggression in Iraq and Syria and elsewhere.

Pompeo's "thinking" (if you can call it that) is that further assaults of any kind on Iran would bring Iran to the negotiating table or to its knees. One wants to laugh at this insanity...were it not so cruel and stupid.

And then one must ask, what's there to negotiate? Iran simply wants to be left alone and not bothered by the U.S. or any other country unless that country has something positive to offer Iranians in exchange for attention. Like, for example, an end to sanctions and the resurrection of the JCPOA. Anyway, amid this viral pandemic, the U.S. actually has increased sanctions on not just Iran, but Cuba and Venezuela, too. And others! But guess what. It's time for the world to defy U.S. sanctions.

Historians will use the actions of the Trump Administration, and especially Pompeo, to point out what must be seen as the personification of Evil. Pompeo himself may be becoming one of the worse mass murderers in history. He and his boss may ultimately be responsible for a million or more deaths in Iran, and even more altogether in other countries which have received no aid and not been offered any from the U.S. But lack of proper planning has made the U.S. unprepared for the pandemic, with hospitals in need of beds and equipment it does not have.

Trump and his administration are not just incompetent, but dishonest and immoral. There is no capacity for real leadership or empathy. A reporter last week in Washington asked Trump: "What do you say to the millions of Americans who are scared?" (given Covid 19 and the economic crash underway). Trump just insulted the reporter.

However, most of the world sees what is going on, and it would be some sort of miracle if after Covid 19 has gone into hiding and the illnesses abate that the U.S. has friends worth having anywhere.

The countries that are attempting to offer the most aid and medical assistance are China, Cuba and even Russia. Stricken Italy could not even get assistance from the E.U., of which it is a part, and are raising Chinese flags in some location in Italy – but not the flag of the E.U. And Israel is performing as it always does, abysmally: the Zionists got a shipment of 100,000 virus test kits from abroad with the help of Mossad. Of this shipment, it apparently gave 200 test kits to the 1.9 million Palestinians in Gaza and 400 kits to the three million natives in the West Bank. And the Zionists won't lift the sieges on Gaza or the West Bank natives.

But one can say that the literary wooden stake used to kill vampires is being driven through the heart of the vampiric U.S. and some of its allies, with the viral outbreak just being the immediate catalyst of an unfolding instance of pure Karma (which sadly is creating a lot of collateral damage). Consider:

The U.S. is broke. The Federal Reserve is printing up many trillions of fiat dollar "money" to "rescue", almost literally, ALL of the U.S. This is a Weimar event in the studied opinion of the sagest analysts. Hyperinflation can easily be the result of the death of the dollar and also U.S. power to inflict damage on other countries through sanctions.

The death of the U.S. military "empire" and the take down of its hundreds of offshore military bases may be unavoidable in the next two to five years. Where's the money to fund a military that spends nearly a trillion dollars a year? Annual budget deficits this year and next look bound to blow out to two or three trillion dollars of faux "money".

Real power, moral and economic and monetary, looks ready to shift to key countries like Russia, China and even in time perhaps Iran over the next decade. Saudi Arabia and even Israel appear doomed, bound to fail, not least because both countries are widely despised for their crimes against humanity and barbaric policies and arrogance.

Non-human species are getting a relative break from the aggravation of humans given the viral pandemic. Fish can be seen in the canals of Venice for the first time in decades. Rejoice!

The greatest financial bubble in history is deflating. Nothing will ever be the same again but real assets, not financial ones, will shine. Central banks have lost public confidence and the value of financial instruments, especially Western ones, is going to be reassessed by the markets like never before.

American society suffused with anger and violence: analyst April 16, 2020

American political analyst Martin Love is of the opinion that the recent shooting in the New York subway station mirrors anger and violence entrenched in American society.

"The facts include witnessing a society in the U.S. that is suffused with anger and violence," Love tells the Tehran Times.

"It's exactly what the Muslim historian Ibn Khaldun centuries ago warned against: the loss of 'group solidarity' – what he called in Arabic 'assabiya,'" he argues.

While there is no question that violence has been ramping up in big cities, Love believes that random violence is not solely confined to big cities in the U.S.

Following is the text of the interview:

Q: What are the implications of shooting at a subway station in New York City? Is the level of violence in big cities ramping up?

A: There are no mere implications, but there are facts. And the facts include witnessing a society in the U.S. that is suffused with anger and violence. It's exactly what the Muslim historian Ibn Khaldun centuries ago warned against: the loss of "group solidarity" – what he called in Arabic "assabiya". And random violence is not solely confined to big cities in the U.S. But there is no question that violence has been ramping up in big cities. Take last year. Last year one tracker of shooting incidents reported a total of 693 mass shootings in the U.S. 303 of the total allegedly resulted in zero fatalities. But over 700 people died all told and over 3000 people were injured. If one were to add in all gun violence, in which less than four individuals were killed, the numbers would be off the charts higher, and the numbers above only include those victims in the single year of 2021.

Q: Why are the American administrations unable to put a real restriction on gun bearing? Is the problem in regulations or in public culture?

A: The problem lies both in the absence of effective regulation and in the overall public culture in the U.S. Some U.S. states have even been loosening gun laws that prohibit citizens from carrying guns concealed or openly. This argument seems to be that those who would commit gun violence against others might be deterred if they thought law-abiding citizens might be carrying a gun and thus potential victims can defend themselves. Washington is dominated by big lobbies like AIPAC, which condones violence in Palestine against the natives where full Apartheid has taken hold, and the National Rifle Association (NRA), which has long advocated the alleged "right" for citizens to bear arms as indicated in the U.S. Constitution. It's an utter shame. The other problem is that most Americans are rather ignorant even though their votes are fervently sought by politicians, some of whom are willing "buy" votes by condoning ownership of assault rifles and handguns. And generally, U.S. foreign policies are violent. Feeding arms to the hapless Ukrainians now to keep the war going there to "bleed" Russia, rather than insisting on diplomacy and peace, is just one current example.

Q: How do you see the role of weapon businesses in hampering any process to restrict gun bearing?

A: Weapon businesses and manufacturers simply want to make money selling arms. That's their incentive to hamper the kind of legislation that would make weapon sales illegal. It's pure business for them.

Q: How do you see the role of public media in spreading violence?

A: One can hardly turn on a TV or go to the cinema in the U.S. and not be confronted with "entertainment" that includes a lot of violence. If the shows are not sci-fi garbage catering to teenagers, there are dark and ugly sagas of mayhem, social discord and quite frankly, insane characters. "Family" entertainment hardly exists any longer.

Q: Do you think Biden's policies to restrict gun bearing are efficient?

A: The alleged perp in the NYC subway shooting was a 62-year-old Black man who once he was identified turned himself into police. One assumes he did not want to get shot by police but the public waits to find out what his motivations were and more about him. It's a bit mystifying why this particular shooting incident, which has been deemed "terrorism" and for which the perp will face life in prison, has had such an impact because incidents like this have become relatively common. The Biden Administration has made some noises about tightening gun laws but Biden on this issue is out to lunch by not simply pushing laws that make some kinds of guns like the Glock 17 the perp used illegally with steep penalties and sanctions. Biden's Presidency has all but failed and the upcoming Congressional mid-term elections are likely to be a debacle for the Democratic Party. Fresh faces and leadership across the board for advocates of sane policies on so many pressing matters are sorely needed, and the GOP does not offer hope for change, and maybe worse. Biden is way out of his depth at almost 80 and is senile if recent press conferences are any indication of his mental capacity. As the great Irish poet W.B. Yeats wrote long ago: the center cannot hold, the falcon cannot hear the falconer.

Trump could "not have been more wrong" on coronavirus: analyst

April 18, 2020

American political analyst Martin Love believes that President Donald Trump has had a bad performance in handling the coronavirus crisis, saying, "He could not have been more wrong" on the pandemic.

"Spread of Covid-19 is occurring in the U.S. like in no other country," Love tells the Tehran Times in an exclusive interview.

Love says, "Some countries have managed the crises better than others, and most are managing their own crises better than the U.S. is currently doing."

Following is the text of the interview:

Question: Reportedly, people are queuing up in the U.S. to get free food. If true, what does this suggest?

Answer: There have been numerous reports of so-called "food banks" handing out basic food to those in need in the U.S. One recent report cited a four-mile long line of cars waiting to visit a "food bank" in the state of Illinois. I imagine people have lined up in places across the country for help because some 22 million people lost their jobs by some reports, and this is bad news because for a majority of the population few have much savings and many jobs created since the last economic recession were not high paying jobs and the so-called "middle class" in the U.S. has been reduced significantly in the past 30 years so while good, manufacturing jobs have been out sourced to countries where labor has been cheaper, like in China. The country is already in a deep recession and unemployment looks like it is going to eclipse the unemployment rates during the Depression in the 1930s. Some economists have predicted an unemployment rate in the U.S. above 30 percent. During the Depression in the 1930s the unemployment rate did not get above about 25 percent of workers.

"The risk of a serious fracture if not breakdown of American society has never been greater."

Q: Are these things the consequences of capitalism in which a very small percentage, or better say «one percent», keeps everything in its possession.

A: Every time there has been an economic recession in the past 20 to 30 years wealth has shifted to top five to ten percent of the U.S. population, and the gap between the 1 percent and all the rest is larger than it ever has been at least since the start of the Depression in the early 1930s. Capitalism under the "Neo-liberal" definition or practice of it has for the most part been a failure, as we are witnessing in the U.S. right now.

Q: Don›t you think that the weaknesses of capitalism are being laid bare more evidently in such situations?

A: Yes, and a socialist system seems at present to be the only way out of this economic mess for now, but it appears so far that most of the largesse from the creation of yet more trillions in "money" by the Federal Reserve Bank in the U.S. has once again been mostly directed to cover losses by the rich and Wall Street. Something is very wrong when the stock market goes up after recent market losses at the same time that unemployment rockets higher like never before. Average citizens have been offered a mere $1200 as a one-time emergency payment when what is needed is vastly more for the American people. The risk of a serious fracture if not breakdown of American society has never been greater. A country that maintains over 800 military bases across the world and spends almost a trillion dollars on military appropriations and cannot even provide a reasonable and inexpensive health care system that meets the needs of most Americans is insane.

"Capitalism under the 'Neo-liberal' definition or practice of it has for the most part been a failure, as we are witnessing in the U.S. right now."

Q: Socialism is being constantly attacked by that capitalists. However, in a country in which avaricious capitalism does not talk first, the public should enjoy a minimum standards of living, having a home (no matter how small it is) and have access to free healthcare. In view of such realities, don›t you think that the capitalism must be controlled?

A: Absolutely, and something has to give. It's hard to imagine how the U.S. can carry on when the so-called "American dream" has been put out of reach for so many citizens over the past three decades. The U.S. is essentially broke in some respects, and simply printing up fiat money in the trillions may result in hyperinflation in this decade ahead.

Q: What are the reasons that the Americans are purchasing record-breaking numbers of guns?

A: Some Americans like to think of themselves as rugged individualists for whom government control is considered anathema, and they seem to have an interest in owning guns. Others are criminals or psychos who get some sort of macho kick out of gun ownership. Others may simply be homeowners who want to protect their property. One reason for the purchase of guns is because the government frequently threatens to clamp down on gun ownership and therefore guns are sometimes considered prized possessions. The U.S. has incarcerated more people than any other country, often for minor offenses, and there is no question there is more crime in the U.S. than most anyplace else. The idea that ONLY the government or its agencies can own firearms is not popular.

Q: Also, do you think that the statistics given by the U.S. about Covid-19 victims are true, especially as officials in Washington keep accusing Iran of covering up the extent of the crisis at home?

A: Note that the spread of Covid-19 is occurring in the U.S. like in no other country. The number of cases is now well over 670,000 and probably much, much higher because so few have been tested for the disease. President Trump back in January utterly failed to prepare for the spread of the disease and suggested it was just something that would soon "go away". He could not have been more wrong. Iran, by accounts that many have read, has done a relatively better job containing the crisis even in the face of scant medical resources, because of sanctions.

A country that maintains over 800 military bases across the world and spends almost a trillion dollars on military appropriations and cannot even provide a reasonable and inexpensive health care system that meets the needs of most Americans is insane.

Q: Do you also believe that the world in general failed to contain the virus?

A: Nothing like Covid-19 has appeared in 100 years and the sole comparison might be the "Spanish flu" that wreaked havoc at the end of World War 1. Some countries have managed the crises better than others, and most are managing their own crises better than the U.S. is currently doing.

Q: What is your assessment of the handling of the virus by the Trump administration?

A: The Trump Administration has been a failure so far in handling the crisis.

Q: It seems that East Asian countries, such as Japan and South Korea, have been acting more successfully in containing the virus than the U.S. and European countries. What are the reasons?

A: This is quite true so far. Overall, the reason for it is that the U.S. has been preoccupied with maintaining its "empire" and even its equity markets and has not addressed the needs of most Americans. Some 80 percent of the U.S. population have not benefitted by the record equity valuations engineered by Wall Street and the Federal Reserve, because they don't own stocks. The notion of "trickle down" economics has been, if anything, a false concept since it was first instituted by the Reagan Administration back in the 1980s.

Q: How do you see the post-Coronavirus world?

A: This is a tough question. Huge changes are going to occur by necessity in many countries, and one would say especially, in time, in the U.S. — if the U.S. wants to maintain any kind of leadership in the world and any kind of decent standard of living for most of its citizens.

U.S. EXCEPTIONALISM IS FADING AT WARP SPEED

May 11, 2020

Americans, at least 80 percent of over 320 million souls, are getting walloped by one thing or another. They are having a hard time coping, and while the coping problems may be their own fault either from ignorance or a lack of broad perspective, what's going on is really not their fault. The United States looks like what it has often claimed other countries are, and often because of U.S foreign policies and war mongering: a "failed" or failing state. So, what is this?

A state "fails" when its political apparatus and its government no longer function properly and cannot meet public needs. It's failing or has failed when decisions made by the government cannot effectively address whatever problems may internally or externally exist, assuming the government has not yet lost its legitimacy. Failure can also occur when a country has lost control of its territory, or the government has lost its monopoly on the legitimate use of physical force. Failure can also be evident when the standard of living in a country declines to such an extent the decline threatens to destroy the entire government and literally to sweep away its presiding politicians, perhaps even to death.

But the time has not yet come for citizens and politicians of other countries that have been under attack or reprimand or sanctions to cheer the internal U.S. failures, if for no other reason but the fact that the U.S. government continues to wield the most dangerous and most powerful military force on the planet, and might tend to ramp up militarism to try to convince its alleged enemies to bow to U.S. pressures.

The cheering perhaps can come later when the chaos in the U.S. has become so evident and rampant that America must address its own problems before anything else and drop its pretense to "empire". This seems to be ahead in the coming decade. And that will be a welcome shift of attention even to a majority of Americans who, if anything now, are increasingly frustrated and frightened by burgeoning, current conditions largely fomented by governmental failures inside the U.S. Covid 19, which is more widespread in America than in any other country, is the catalyst but not the cause of the discontent and disillusion.

When Covid 19 began to hit the U.S. back in late February, there existed a host of underlying conditions that the virus has been exploiting relentlessly: a political class dominated by two corrupt political parties, a dysfunctional bureaucracy, a divided citizenry that has for years not been properly addressed. The mere fact that someone like Donald Trump became President, a self-centered man without much intelligence who has failed to mount a rational response to the pandemic, has been telling. The Trump Administration has presented no coherent responses or plans and failed to react wisely, and if it reacted at all, it has frequently been relying on other countries, even Russia and Taiwan, to send humanitarian aid and supplies to the U.S. to try to counter the viral spread.

In this century there has been one crisis after another in America. The first was 9/11/2001. The second was the recession in 2008 and 2009, in part the result of U.S. missteps overseas such as the Iraq War and other foolish, insidious military adventures. The recession just over a decade ago was improperly addressed. The government simply threw a wet blanket of monetary excess over the smoldering economy and the elite. This seemed to save the financial system when, in fact, it only laid the groundwork for the economic collapse now underway that has resulted in just over two months in some 33 million freshly unemployed workers and an unemployment rate that is pushing towards 1930s Depression levels of over 20 percent, and more inequality between the "rich" and all the rest than has ever previously existed. Trump is a President who has accomplished only one major legislative accomplishment, if you can call it that, which was to cut taxes radically for the wealthy, which only served himself and his cronies in business and on Wall Street.

So, for now, there is immense and growing pain for most Americans, and along with that immense frustration and anger. This in itself is bad enough, and it's a wonder the country has not so far been confronted with the kind of civic unrest that is occurring in some other countries, but it is most likely ahead as the November elections draw nearer. This is because it is so exceedingly difficult, especially for "average" Americans, to envision what the path beyond this current mess looks like, and how they can trust the government to do the right thing especially when there are no easy, painless answers.

For now, the "right thing" has seemed to be throwing trillions of freshly printed or digital "dollars" into the equation to staunch the economic bleeding at the top, and this certainly has softened but only very marginally the hard times faced by most Americans, half of whom allegedly have no or very little savings to fall back on. Meanwhile cumulative deaths from the virus are likely to reach beyond 100,000 this month and continue to climb this coming summer. But even worse, the entire economic/monetary system is likely to implode eventually because of the money printing, and just this fiscal year alone the U.S. budget deficit will probably be close to four trillion dollars.

Maybe the toll in lives was inevitable given the pandemic and Trump's failures to respond in a timely and effective way, but far worse, it can be argued, are the government's failures to respond to pleas for humanitarian assistance from the U.S. to countries such as Iran, and to other nations deemed de facto enemies of the U.S. like Cuba and Venezuela, Lebanon, Syria and others – many of which have in fact sent or tried to send aid to the U.S. and to other countries suffering under the pandemic strain.

This kind of failure in particular by allegedly the "richest" country will never be forgotten and perhaps never forgiven once this pandemic has subsided or when medical science has found a way to nullify the virus. One might opine that the U.S. may not for a very long time, if ever, be looked upon as much more than a fading rogue power that when it had the opportunity to appear and be a force for good in the world literally failed to change course and act like what it has merely pretended it has been, an enlightened democracy. American "exceptionalism" is fading at warp speed. And the irony is that most Americans, most of them totally disempowered these days, are not at all like the Trumps and Pompeos and their ilk in Washington.

The U.S. movement from prosperity to utter decay

May 25, 2020

Very few people in the West nowadays know or have heard of British General Sir John Glubb, but it is probable that some educated people in the Middle East know the name, and particularly in Jordan, Syria, and Lebanon. Glubb (1897-1986) was a soldier, author, and even a scholar of sorts who from 1939, until he was dismissed by King Hussein of Jordan in 1956, led and trained the famed "Arab Legion" as its commanding officer.

It's hard today to know what to make of Glubb, who was a kind of lesser latter-day T.E. Lawrence (who also was a British army officer with a kind of exotic fascination with the cultures and splendors of wast of Asia) at a time when Western imperialism might have seemed and should have been on the wane, except that it was not at all, finding its most odious expression in the Zionist infestation of Palestine over the last 100 plus years with gobs of British support initially and later especially with U.S. support (and corruption).

Glubb was not entirely trusted by thinkers in the Arab world and it was claimed that he considered giving Palestine away to the bloody Zionists if could have retained a small corner of the country for himself. There is no question he also served his ultimate imperialist masters in the British military. And tellingly, he named his son "Godfrey" – after Godfrey of Bouillon, who happened to be in 1099 for a year until his death the first ruler of the so-called Crusader Kingdom of

Jerusalem. (Might he have been remembered more fondly if he had named his son Salah ad-Din? One would imagine so.)

What can anyone make of the country, for recent examples, that set eastern Syria's wheat fields aflame with military flares to try to starve Syrians, or ran a legion of Cuban doctors out of Ecuador sent there to aid in the battle against COVID 19, or gave its assent to the racists in apartheid Israel to annex most of the West Bank against all international laws? But Glubb was not a bad writer even if he was not a great one, and perhaps recalling from his studies and experiences the example at least of the very finest early social historian and theorist, Ibn Khaldun (d. 1400), who discerned patterns in the rise and fall of countries, societies and empires, Glubb also came up with an explanation of what happens in failing societies and polities. Failing societies and polities like the United States has become in the past decade since the last economic recession in 2008-09.

Glubb wrote an essay in 1978, brought to this writer's attention by Charles Hugh Smith, in which he noted the progression of polities and societies from an Age of Pioneers, to that of Conquests, to Commerce, to Affluence, to Intellect and finally to the "age" the U.S. and some other Western countries find themselves in now – an age of Decadence. This last period happens to be, Smith correctly notes, one of greed, corruption, political fractures that cannot heal, moral decay, frivolity ("bread and circuses" as in the Roman Empire), and gross materialism.

Regarding the United States, these different "ages" appear to have progressed over the last 150 years and the one of "Decadence" is indisputably in full and rotten flower now. And this seems most apparent in the economic sphere where you have a private bank, the Federal Reserve, literally creating money in the trillions and trying desperately to throw it around to maintain what is mostly faux economic health which, ironically, is precisely undermined by the Fed's actions to save the system (and it has no other tools at hand but money printing) where debt has expanded and is expanding to such an extent that the world has never before seen anything like it. The inevitable, historical trap of excess spending, arrogance, presumptions of eternal "growth", warmongering and more has arrived in spades. And there is no apparent way out.

All this is pretty obvious to most history-minded observers despite the propaganda and bluster to the contrary, but why mention the obvious now? Because it presents a good lesson and a warning to other countries and especially those countries under attack by the U.S. either militarily or through sanctions (as in the case of Iran) in the mistaken U.S. belief that bringing other countries to ruin somehow enhances and guarantees continued power and prosperity for the U.S.

This is to say and insist on leaders of countries like Iran to try to avoid at all costs the mistakes the U.S. is in the process of making now. To avoid arrogance and presumptions and to embrace humility and above all boost efforts literally to make sacrifices for the benefit of its weakest citizens and the citizens of its allies real or potential whatever current circumstances may be.

As for the U.S. under Trump and earlier under Obama and Baby Bush, actions have done little but create enmity and certainly have not bolstered U.S. credibility, power, or popularity. What can anyone make of the country, for recent examples, that set eastern Syria's wheat fields aflame with military flares to try to starve Syrians, or ran a legion of Cuban doctors out of Ecuador sent there to aid in the battle against COVID 19, or gave its assent to the racists in apartheid Israel to annex most of the West Bank against all international laws? Examples of such actions are so numerous that it's a wonder that the U.S. has ANY friends, not to mention the carnage unleashed in unnecessary wars this century. And the further wonder is that American leaders by and large fail to realize how destructive they continue to be … even to themselves ultimately.

Martin Luther King was right : The earth does bend towards justice

June 29, 2020

Back 65 years ago when television was in its childhood if not infancy in the U.S. one TV game show had contestants going for a grand prize of $64,000, which in those days was a tremendous sum of money (not any longer, really), so any big issue or question that had not yet been resolved gave rise to the common cliché of "the $64,000 question" as to how it might pan out.

Another regular television drama series back then featured the surprise award of a million bucks to some lucky fictitious family that had been deemed exemplary by a character named "John Bearsford Tipton" (a name literally created to suggest wealth!), a generous fictional multi-millionaire who sent his agent to announce the award. It was all innocent fun to see lives suddenly transformed to extreme good fortune, how they reacted, how suddenly grateful the family became.

The spark of the murder by Minneapolis police of a Black man in May, along with other incidents of racism and racial abuse by the militarized police, has awakened many Americans this past month to the degree of their repression, and change is definitely in the wind, but it's going to take a long time before real change takes hold while the battle lines are more or less clearly drawn. This TV menu sampler was well before big lotteries sprouted, in part to raise taxable revenue for various state governments in the U.S. Nowadays, U.S. network television features reams of crime, corruption, violence, and mayhem, plus "news" programs heavily slanted and propagandized to one side or another of the political spectrum. Evil characters abound, and often they are foreigners, say "Arabs" or "Iranians" for example, or other Asians farther east, or Africans and poor citizens of Latin America.

One question obviously is whether human nature or at least American human nature, has over the course of several decades become so badly corrupted and purged of sweet innocence and benevolence to be confronted in the media with such dreck and social illness. Frankly, it's hard to imagine that human nature has EVER changed so dramatically anywhere.

One possible answer is that the rise of such sorry media "entertainment" possibly corresponds with the blatant, in-your-face rise of U.S. "imperialism" and its notions of U.S. exceptionalism, especially since the fall of the Soviet Union when American "leaders" got it in their corrupted heads that they could rule the world militarily and economically and cast foreign peoples and cultures that have objected to U.S. "imperialism" in action as simply some objectionable "other" that had to be dominated, reduced and demonized for the benefit of an ever narrower, very wealthy U.S. "elite". Now, remarkably, with recent administrations in Washington, and especially Trump's, the "other" has been expanding to include many Americans, too: the entrenched poor, people of color, immigrants, religious minorities such as Muslims and virtually anyone at the mercy of the almighty government.

The spark of the murder by Minneapolis police of a Black man in May, along with other incidents of racism and racial abuse by the militarized police, has awakened many Americans this past month to the degree of their repression, and change is definitely in the wind, but it's going to take a long time before real change takes hold while the battle lines are more or less clearly drawn.

At one extreme is the potential for real "revolution" similar to Iran's revolution 40 years ago, which is still unlikely, and at the other are years of seeming decline, chaos, and adjustments where very slowly better, fairer, brighter Americans somehow begin to get their hands on the levers of power at least at the local level and begin to reject business and government and various social ills as too long evident catering to the few, as it has been becoming for over 30 years.

This latter evolution at least has a certain inevitability about it, so in some respects, if much of the rest of the world can avoid precipitous actions that could ignite further U.S. hostilities whether wars or more attempts to strangle countries with sanctions, there is some reason for optimism and hope in the longer run. Racism is real in the U.S. and always has been since America's inception even if many have attempted to reject and expunge it. And racism is part and parcel of imperialism, so if imperialism dies, so too perhaps does rampant racism.

The fact is that current attitudes and policies at the top of the U.S. "establishment", or many of those found in Trumpism, in the GOP and also in parts of the Democratic Party, probably cannot be pushed much further and will likely be forced to recede. The narrow "establishment" seems to be slowly losing the very means to continue to project itself not just at home but around the world. There are hordes of factors, not least of which is that the U.S. is fast losing what popularity it has had, alienating even some of its Western allies in its overweening efforts to maintain power and control.

One case in point are U.S. efforts to kill Germany's access to ready and inexpensive energy supplies from nearby Russia via Nordstream II, which after a year of sanctions and delays will probably be completed by the end of this year. Another factor among others may be inherent in Iran's courageous push-back against U.S. sanctions and threats, this seen lately in Iran's shipments of fuel and oil field supplies to beleaguered Venezuela. And it's obvious China and North Korea and others are going to try to stand strong against U.S. diktat and aim at a minimum to carve out some breathing space between themselves and U.S. imperiousness.

But perhaps the biggest factor is simply that the U.S. has been living way beyond its means since the Vietnam War, and when it went off any semblance of a gold standard in 1971 and the U.S. dollar became purely fiat (along with every other currency), U.S. debt and money printing have become so enormous that the dollar simply cannot maintain its grip on the world's financial architecture much longer, probably not for another decade at the most. Some kind of major "reset" is ahead, and it's a reset that will include the loss of U.S. financial dominance, and thus its ability to project so much economic and military power.

One can even thank the wild emergence of COVID 19 and its mismanagement by Trump, where fiscal deficits are now set to expand into the several trillion unless the U.S. drastically reduces spending, which in itself will dramatically change American life, bending towards initial poverty, like nothing else. The other "bending" was cited by Martin Luther King before he was assassinated decades ago: that the human world no matter what in the long term, to its credit, "bends" towards justice.

An assassination has made a dark Mideast darker than ever Nov 30, 2020

Joe Biden's up and coming "climate" czar John Kerry has claimed the reason Russia came to Syria's aid several years ago was because ISIS was threatening Damascus. And he also more or less admitted to the U.S. role assisting ISIS because the U.S. thought Syria might thus be brought to the negotiating table. But what has been most elusive in this carnage, a decade long in Syria that continues with Zionist strikes on Syria that have gone unchallenged by the U.S. and the EU, is an adequate explanation as to why Syria under popular Assad ever constituted a real threat to anyone in the Middle East (West Asia). Was it a threat because Syria has long hoped that the Golan would be returned to Syria? Not likely. Or that Syria has long condemned Israeli apartheid and land theft? Not likely.

The answer actually is quite simple. The U.S. and the Zionists want to remain dominant in the Mideast (West Asia), and so the aim is to reduce sovereign countries to vassalage and penury. Already the world in this century has seen millions of innocents murdered in the region. And the assassination on November 27 of one of Iran's top nuclear scientists, almost certainly by Mossad or its proxies, really has very little to do with a nuclear weapons program in Iran that in fact does not exist.

Here's the problem: expertise with nuclear science and even its use for energy and medicine, even when it's not directed to weapons specifically, gives a country like Iran the potential nuclear weapons. The JCPOA was and remains, if only it would be resurrected by a U.S. return to the deal and the elimination of sanctions, an effective bar to a shift of Iranian nuclear expertise to weapons. The mere fact that the U.S. scuttled the deal bares the Trumpist aims: incite Iran to respond as a pretext for a U.S./Israel/Saudi/UAE war on Iran.

As to who was behind the killing of one of Iran's top scientists (again), one highly respected writer, who before retirement worked at the CIA for over two decades wrote a private message to a friend on the 27th: "Yes this is one instance where it (the assassination) begs to be credited to Israel, but in reality I am sure it is Trump/Pompeo who ordered it...and more is coming."

If this ex-CIA employee is correct about "more is coming" between now and Biden's inauguration, one can only literally pray that Iran's leadership has the resolve and strength not to respond to the provocation of November 27 or any other provocation that would be used as pretext for war, at least not between now and January 20 when Biden is supposed to become President based on his apparent, resounding election win.

Iran has shown remarkable restraint, and the world knows it, for a very long time, a time measured in decades. In the U.S., too, one also must wonder if Trump's aggressions, if they do result in a war, might be a war staged as a ploy by Trump to declare a "national emergency" and suspend Biden's move into the White House come January 20th. This is a question that must be asked, since Trump and his gangster administration seem hell-bent with trying to nullify the election by any means possible.

It has been said that it is "always darkest before the dawn". It's hard to imagine a darker moment in the Middle East (West Asia) than now. Netanyahu and the Zionists are doing more damage than ever in the West Bank, planning more settlement expansion and destroying Palestinian property with extreme prejudice. The faux "peace deals" with the corrupted Arabs along the Persian Gulf have nothing to do with peace, but largely involve arms sales to frightened Arab regimes whose economies are not doing well. The Nobel Peace Prize is even begging to be abolished what with the nomination of Netanyahu and the UAE's despot for the prize.

It is almost unreal, or surreal, how dark things have suddenly become. It would be strongly in Iran's favor if the Islamic Republic does not overreact to the provocations at this time and save their responses for a day when the U.S. and its horrific allies have been badly weakened by their ignorance and spite. That day is coming, someday.

The U.S. and allies have done little but inflame West Asia Dec 5, 2020

Heiko Maas, Germany's foreign minister, must be crazy, literally. Or just a blind twit, like so many others in the "Western" establishment of lily-white bigots, racists and Christian imperialists.

The king of them though happens to be Mike Pompeo, the soon to depart Secretary of State in the U.S. who allegedly has his eyes on the White House in 2024. These two and people like them with their rabid policy announcements and ignorant fantasies try to give the impression of aiming for something positive and calming to a world and especially to a Middle East wracked by discord, but in fact they and their kind are doing just the opposite. "Inflaming" might be the best word for what they do and have long done.

Consider what Maas said about Iran this past week: "A form of nuclear agreement is needed, which also lies in our interests. We have clear expectations for Iran: no nuclear weapons, but also no ballistic rocket program that threatens the whole region. Iran must also play another role in the region." He is correct that a nuclear agreement is needed, if for no other reason than Iran is suffering under sanctions and they must be lifted, but what (the Hell) is wrong with the JCPOA which was working just fine and Iran was fully compliant with it? Nothing, except the overweening hypocrisy, bombast and arrogance of people like Maas and Pompeo.

Germany, for one thing, did not fulfill its role under the JCPOA after Pompeo and Trump withdrew from in, and the other signatories also did not. They all should have slammed the U.S. and imposed their own sanctions on the U.S. and continued trade with Iran. It was all talk and no action. And then Maas mentions Iran's missiles which have been used just once after the esteemed Soleimani and friends were assassinated in early January this year. That against the U.S. airbase in Iraq, and allegedly no one was killed but damage was pinpoint accurate. With a relatively tiny military, how else has Iran had any deterrence except through its missile programs? So far, at least, missiles have kept enemies mostly at bay. Demanding that Iran lose this deterrence is like asking a man to walk across Antarctica buck naked and expecting him to survive even the first kilometer.

It (Germany) even supplied Israel with submarines that, with no evident objection by the Germans, Israel has armed with its own nuclear bomb tipped missiles.

And also consider Germany's claim, to cite just one idiocy, of offering Israelis Covid vaccination medicine…but not half the population west of the Jordan River, the beleaguered Palestinians! Germany, it seems, 75 years after the end of World War 2, remains all hot and bothered with guilt over the Holocaust. It even supplied Israel with submarines that, with no evident objection by the Germans, Israel has armed with its own nuclear bomb tipped missiles. And all the while Zionists are carrying out a slow genocide of their own against Palestinians, also to no objections by Germany.

Such facts just about Germany's postures, not to mention the longstanding U.S. foolishness, underscores the absolute rectitude of Iran's insistence that the JCPOA, if anything is to be done after Biden enters the White House, be reinstated as it was and sanctions lifted and THEN Iran backs off from its uranium enrichment activities. It seems reasonable to presume that Iran, after a year or two of calm, may (or may not) also then consider some slight marginal modifications to the JCPOA to satisfy the perennially dissatisfied Western powers that still might be freaked out that Iran has ANY nuclear expertise at all. But trust, which has been utterly shattered by the U.S. especially given its dishonesty and incapacity to abide by carefully crafted deals and treaties.

Also, it's worth mentioning what Iran has long and correctly advocated: the removal all ALL nuclear weapons from West Asia. This above all makes the most sense, for it obviates Iran EVER building a nuclear weapon because, simply, none are lurking elsewhere in the region to threaten the Islamic Republic. But of course, and sadly, the greatest threat to accord, and fomenter of discord, regionally for over 70 years has been Israel, and Israel is for now anyway not likely to become a country doing anything good in the Middle East (West Asia).

For example, on Friday past, one could read that yet another Palestinian child in the West Bank, a lad of 12, was shot and murdered by the IDF. This sort of crime seems to happen almost weekly in the Occupied West Bank or in Gaza. In a reasonable "West" just this ONE murder ought to have been roundly condemned by the U.S., and Germany and their allies, and some sort of sanctions imposed on Israel given the frequency of such outrages. But no, not a whisper of condemnation and let's face it, the Zionists want the annexation of the entirety of Palestine and more, like the Golan. This has at bottom been the aim since 1948.

As for Iran "playing another role in the region" as Maas suggested, what might that be that it did not already well play under the formerly intact JCPOA? Iran's intentions were peaceful, obviously, and whatever problems Iran has had internally and socially, the country has long been absolutely correct in at least hoping for justice in the Middle East as, at least, a prelude to getting its own house in better order.

Sustained and rare, honest goodwill by the U.S.D is its only salvation now

Dec 23, 2020

It would appear that the primary question regarding whether the JCPOA will be resurrected and sanctions dropped is on whose terms this might happen, if ever.

The best hope is that in some fashion the Biden administration, assuming it reaches the White House on January 20, apologizes in some way for Trump's unwarranted "maximum pressure" campaign against the Islamic Republic (perhaps ideally with reparations?) and re-enters the JCPOA as it was before May 2018. And this seems to be exactly what the Islamic Republic is insisting on, which to any level-headed person makes the most sense. On the other hand, the U.S. appears to be aiming for the terms of the deal to be temporally extended, and at first glance this does not seem like something that could not be achieved in time.

"In time" means that an extension modification may be possible, but not right away. Maybe not for a year or more because, after all, it was the U.S. that unfaithfully trashed the deal just as under Trump and Pompeo and other Neo-con-ish Trump lackeys it withdrew from a number of other international accords in fits of extreme arrogance and disrespect for other countries, in particular Iran.

It may be that over the last four years the U.S. reached the very apex of its imperialistic dementia in what has been ultimately a decades-long, futile effort this century especially to maintain its dominance and influence across the globe – a time when the U.S. has been relying almost exclusively on military depredations or threats of such and its craven, parasitic, world-despised "allies" like the Saudis and the Israelis. Whatever happened to the application of some goodwill and faithfulness to alleged or designated enemies of varying degrees like China or Russia, but especially Iran? It's been almost totally absent in the thinking and perverse strategies of Washington, and this absence or the effects of it are beginning to show more than it ever has in U.S. history.

Iran has not and never has sought special treatment from the U.S. or any other country but it has been subject to Western aggression, even regime change in 1953. Whatever happens, is this current decade, one thing has become utterly clear. The U.S. is in steep decline from where it was after World War 2 even if it remains a power that must be reckoned with if for no other reason but that an "empire" in decline, fast or slow, is still a dangerous one to those countries, especially those with natural resources and deep human capital, that want their sovereignty and independence respected no matter what. And Iran above all desires just that, it is so obvious.

Iran has not and never has sought special treatment from the U.S. or any other country but it has been subject to Western aggression, even regime change in 1953. (Whereas utterly dependent U.S. "allied" regimes like Saudi Arabia and Israel and a few others have demanded and received special treatments from the U.S. because otherwise they could not stand on their own legs and would quickly disappear without U.S. largesse or military protection at tremendous cost to U.S. citizens monetary and otherwise.)

Iranians know Iran's millennia of history and its manifold achievements and its variegated culture and it rightfully takes pride in itself however it has evolved over the centuries. Yes, the Islamic Republic as it currently stands may not be a "democracy" in strict, idealistic Western terms, and has its problems just like any other nation, but the U.S. itself is no longer a "democracy" if one compares it now to its own definition of what real democracy looks like!

And the downward slide of the U.S. into a non-democratic corporatist oligarchy has to be the greatest tragedy the U.S. has ever suffered in its relatively short history aside from the Civil War of the 19th century. A tragedy because the U.S. as powerful as it may still seem suffers a huge gap between the haves and the have nots, a Treasury that is virtually bankrupt, debts of such magnitude the world has never seen before anywhere, and a kind of moral rot that is eating away at the foundations of civil accord so deeply that many foreigners find the country laughable for its current pretensions and hubris. The recent election, allegedly of Joe Biden, and discord over the results is telling, for one thing.

Moreover, few worldwide have much respect any longer for what's left of U.S. world dominance – something that could have been obviated had the U.S. not turned itself into a military predator mounting useless and costly wars willy nilly that have merely benefited temporarily only a very few U.S. citizens at the top of the food chain.

One huge question now is whether someone like Joe Biden can begin to turn things around for America before it collapses. Given his proposed administration's appointments of many retreads from the Clinton and Obama years, a turnaround may not be in the cards but still those Americans at least who voted for Biden are hopeful. A good dollop of honest and sustained goodwill towards countries like Iran such that in time the U.S. might be trusted to a degree again may be just the correct formula for progress. And this in turn would have to involve less support, or conditional support, for the Zionists and the Saudis, to name two examples.

A view of the fractured U.S. by a non-neo liberal

Jan 19, 2021

As a long-time observer and with no stash of insider information and no affiliations with Power or powerful interests anywhere but who over 50 years has been on occasion in and out of the Middle East (West Asia) including several Arab countries and Apartheid Israel, one has at this particularly fraught time drawn a few conclusions even if they are not original.

For one, the U.S. now seems to be embedded in an irreversible, self-inflicted decline (from what it has been for decades as the world hegemon) ... unless Joe Biden and successors, if any are in future even possible, can manage to ignite positive perceptions of the country by positive deeds and realignments overseas.

The initial mistake after World War 2 was allowing the Military-Industrial Complex to expand to dominate the U.S. economy while broad U.S. industrial might narrowed and the economy became financialized. The Vietnam War was the initial gross debacle based on lies, and then along came the failures of Presidents Reagan and Clinton (witnessing the fall of the Soviet Union) to capitalize on its apparent world economic and military hegemony by choosing to attempt to amplify and boost both even further by unnatural, destructive militarism.

In the waning years of the 20th century, so-called leaders in the U.S. looking ahead saw that other countries such as China, a resurgent Russia, and others, even Iran, were beginning to assert their own economic power and influence and sovereignty. In the waning years of the 20th century, so-called leaders in the U.S. looking ahead saw that other countries such as China, a resurgent Russia, and others, even Iran, were beginning to assert their own economic power and influence and sovereignty. What might far better have occurred was the solidification of U.S. leadership by natural, humanistic, non-military means whereby the U.S. might have become a generous benefactor literally sharing finite leadership with others, especially rivals, in the realization that it did not have to dominate absolutely but could extend the stage to and with other countries in the knowledge that their own prosperity would reflect back on the U.S. and permit a shared world leadership to flourish, too. And where a balanced resolution of disputes dominated generally by order of, say, an empowered United Nations organization capable of enforcing peaceful and mostly positive, healthy relations between diverse nations.

At exactly the time, say around 2000, when the U.S. realized or projected that China and Russia and other countries such as Iran were likely to become bigger competitors for influence by virtue of their own advances and resources, the U.S. government literally began to go wild with paranoia and greed.

The immediate result then was 9/11 as most likely a staged event to justify the so-called War on Terror which itself has fostered a worse terror, particularly in West Asia, and which in fact has been and remains a bloody (and failing) effort by the U.S. to maintain exclusive dominance in world affairs. The U.S. came up with the insane notion, boosted by Zionist demands, that by destroying or trying to destroy a number of other Mideast (West Asian) nations, including Iraq and Libya and of late even Syria and Iran, it might prevail with its belligerent push for further dominance. The U.S. made or boosted alliances, particularly in the Middle East, with bad and equally sorry actors such as Apartheid Israel and Saudi Arabia, neither of which are "democratic" and which, along with some other countries, exhibit the worst of human impulses exactly at odds with alleged (and long unsupported) "American" ideals of fair play and behavioral decency. In Israel for example, B'tselem, that country's leading human rights group, has unequivocally and just recently labeled Israel a full-blown Apartheid state, not to mention Israel's continued attacks on its neighbors such as Syria.

A View of the Fractured U.S. ...

Thus we have arrived at 2021 and a world, and a West Asia, but especially the United States, in social and political disarray as it faces deep internal divisions that were embarrassingly unveiled on January 6 with the attempt by insurrectionists around the Capitol to nullify the November elections and ensure Donald Trump's second term.

Does Washington even understand a tiny bit what a joke the U.S. appears to be overseas a few days before Biden's inauguration with over 20,000 troops installed around the Capitol to try to obviate civil disorder and violence on January 20th in the wake of Trump's exit towards well-deserved oblivion? It must! This and other problems have given the U.S. aspects of a burgeoning Banana republic, not the leader of the so-called "free world".

Joe Biden, a possibly senile old man with a past checkered by earlier assents for bad decisions as a Senator and as a Vice President (like the wars on Iraq, and Afghanistan and the proxy war on Syria) is not likely to heal the divisions inside the U.S. going forward without the adoption of serious, overt humility, recognition and even apologies for the vast policy errors of the past 20 years along with a wholesale reorientation of the U.S. towards the honest promotion of true justice at home and abroad.

The U.S. has brought itself to a point where it teeters in many ways, including the financial, towards various forms of bankruptcy such that with any further misguided attempts to double down on failed policies to ward off a relative (if not absolute) collapse could make matters quite worse both internally and across the world. Israel, a chief U.S. ally, has been lately threatening that if Biden is successful in resurrecting the JCPOA, it will attack Iran on its own – counter to U.S.

interests. Iran would of course attempt to defend itself and it's unlikely the Biden Administration would have the courage not to join a war on Iran, which has in justifiable defense promised to react to any attack. This is the great danger of the U.S. having a faux ally such as Israel.

Not since World War 2 has humanity at large been so at risk, and one can posit largely because of the manner in which the U.S. has operated with arrogance and military pursuits in the past two decades especially. The historical (and still extant) stains of racism (and ethnic cleansing inside the U.S. in the 19th century) and xenophobia projected abroad has been in effect amplified further to a degree in the past years towards other people, other cultures, and other polities, especially during Trump's disastrous tenure in the White House. Average Americans of good conscience and reasonable intelligence tremble at the current situation. Had wisdom prevailed in recent decades it would not have to be so.

It's a wonder Iran has not ditched the JCPOA

Mar 9, 2021

Old man Joe Biden is showing a lack of fresh thinking more than anyone suspected he would, given his campaign promises, and this so soon in his own bizarre presidency. Some of his best promises have turned to dust.

It's a wonder Iran has not …

The promised $15 per hour minimum wage has been put on hold and Biden has not come out swinging for it as it seemed he might have last fall before his election although many Democrats in Congress have. (Given inflation in recent years, the true fair number for adjusted hourly wages is actually $24 an hour in the U.S.)

Even worse is the pass he gave to Muhammad bin Salman, the Saudi crown prince, whom the CIA with obvious evidence charged with ordering the assassination of Saudi journalist and Washington Post writer Jamal Khashoggi.

This matter is especially interesting to this writer because the biggest unofficial apologist for Saudi's medieval kingdom happens to be a former student in 1972 in Beirut at the fancy private school called International College, one 'Ali Shihabi.

Shihabi was around 12 years old in 1972, the son of a Norwegian mother and Saudi father. He did not look Arab. He was a blonde back then and widely traveled and rich. He even sported an expensive Rolex watch on his diminutive wrist and he wore Western garb. He was a fair student, too, at 12 in an English class but also somewhat full of himself. Later, he went to Princeton and Harvard Business School. And later still after time as a banker, he started something (now defunct) called the "Arabia Foundation", an alleged "think" tank but really just an operation apologizing for and defending the Saudi state. At any rate, he became and remains a slick, unofficial, and well-known pundit and "ambassador" of sorts speaking out positively for the Saudis in Washington. No doubt this is lucrative.

On the Khashoggi murder, he has been vehemently defending MBS. Right after the event in 2018 he claimed, aw-shucks, everyone makes a mistake from time to time. Lately, he is saying:

"The U.S. government went in and destroyed Iraq" and then he asks rhetorically who was held responsible for that? Shihabi has also just warned that if real pressure is brought to bear on the Saudis and especially MBS by the Biden Administration that Riyadh's displeasure with the U.S. would push the Saudis under MBS to look beyond the U.S. for support. Slick Shihabi also pointed out that China is already Saudi Arabia's largest trading partner. It's hard to imagine this is not a threat to the U.S.

Another notable Biden failure so far is his lack of formerly promised immediate movement on the revival of the JCPOA. So far the Biden gang and Iran have been stuck in a standoff, each declaring that the other should make concessions first. Of course, it stands to moral reason that the U.S. act first and drop the sanctions first since it was the U.S. that destroyed the carefully crafted nuclear deal, and not Iran. Of course, the Republicans are as usual saying that Biden must take a harder line and not lift sanctions until Iran agrees to broad concessions on its missile arsenal (Iran's sole serious defense against attack!) and regional military policies. Also, there are some Democrats in Congress who have aligned with Republicans on the Iranian issue.

The blatant truth is that the Republicans and the handful of Democrats who are bleating like sheep for a harder line against Iran are quite literally in thrall to Israel and the Zionists who don't want the revival of the JCPOA at all even if the world does. If you have to guess why then you need to be educated. It's because the Apartheid entity wants to attack

Iran eventually and it cannot if the JCPOA has been revived. It does not get any more complicated than this at the bottom.

The absolute truth is that the U.S. does not at all oppose tyranny nor human rights violations. The idea that it does is a complete myth. Yet this myth is believed because the U.S. has used it to justify wars, bombings, sanctions, and chaos for decades, and especially during this century. It's not difficult to look back since Worth War 2 and see how often the U.S. has propped up or installed dictators in other countries. This included Iran with the former Shah. So, what does the U.S. truly despise?

Countries and people who simply don't submit to U.S. commands and decrees. And this applies to polities where it does not matter how democratic and generally peaceful they are. All that seems to matter to become an enemy of the U.S. government is a failure to submit to whatever the U.S. demands. And this is quite simply insane. And one huge reason why the U.S. is becoming a failed and reviled country.

It's a wonder Iran has not said goodbye to the JCPOA and with great energy shored up its relations with Russia and China as a bulwark against attack by the U.S, and its criminal allies such as Saudi Arabia and Israel.

Martin Love: Pardoning Blackwater killers inexplicable

Mar 12, 2021

Martin Love, senior American journalist, says the former U.S. President's move to pardon Backwater contractors, who opened fired indiscriminately on Iraqi civilians in 2007, is not democratically justifiable.

Speaking in an interview with FNA, Martin Love said, "The pardons cement like few other U.S. actions an image of a lawless, cruel U.S. posture (or mental illness) that has often been witnessed and roundly condemned worldwide... . Trump has proven himself to be a vindictive, self-centered "leader" who has failed almost every test of human decency... He has demonstrated a racist bent his entire life. Trump IS a reflection of a demented American "exceptionalism" like few other Presidents have been."

Martin Love is an American author based in North Carolina. He is a longtime editor, columnist, copy editor and writer in major U.S. newspapers and magazines.

Below is the full text of the interview:

Q: Prosecuting the Blackwater contractors was to be in-line with Justice. Now, with Trump's pardoning them, do you believe justice is served?

A: Prosecuting and jailing a few of the Blackwater "soldiers" who without any justification whatsoever murdered 17 innocent Iraqis seems on a mere whim and wounded many more at the Baghdad roundabout in 2007 was one of the more heinous actions of the U.S. occupation of Iraq, but there were many others, including the torture at Abu Ghraib. That Donald Trump pardoned these killers is inexplicable. It is a reminder of similar actions against innocent civilians decades ago in Vietnam, in particular the My Lai massacre. But maybe the massacre in Baghdad and the pardons makes some sense in the twisted mind of Trump who has long demonstrated his hatred of people who are not Caucasian "Christians" (who are not golfers!) and, to boot, Muslims. If anything we have learned about Trump, he has demonstrated a racist bent his entire life. Trump IS a reflection of a demented American "exceptionalism" like few other Presidents have been.

Q: How do you believe Trump's pardoning Blackwater contractors is translated to the families of Iraqi victims?

A: We know from reports of the reactions of Iraqi families (whose kin were victims) to the Blackwater pardons that they are utterly appalled and mystified by Trump's actions which amount to a huge slap in the face of Justice. The pardons cement like few other U.S. actions an image of a lawless, cruel U.S. posture (or mental illness) that has often been witnessed and roundly condemned worldwide. The families of Iraqi victims did get some modest relief when a few of the Blackwater goons were prosecuted and jailed, and one can only wonder at their dismay now. It almost beggars belief that Trump pardoned them. But other pardons that Trump has granted to cronies and loyalists who were convicted of various crimes (but not murders) have also been questioned even by some Republican lawmakers in the U.S. Congress. These and other pardons were "legal" and Constitutional but they have been cited as a "misuse" of power, which they are.

Q: Neither the lives of African-Americans, nor the lives of Iraqis seem to matter to President Trump. Does this leave room for the U.S. to be looked at as a defender of democracy and human rights?

A: It is virtually impossible now for the U.S. to be viewed in the court of world opinion as an honest defender of democracy and human rights, but in truth this has been the case for a very long time especially since the Vietnam War which, like so many offensive aggressions by the U.S. overseas since the end of the World War II, were based on lies. Many Americans have been hoping that Trump in his last weeks in the White House might pardon Julian Assange and Edward Snowden, both of whom exposed U.S. government and military crimes. It is quite amazing that Trump has failed to realize that by pardoning just these two notable whistleblowers, he could have improved his legacy and been widely hailed as having done something positive at the end of his Presidency. But Trump has proven himself to be a vindictive, self-centered "leader" who has failed almost every test of human decency. One can also cite Trump's over the top support for Netanyahu and Zionist human rights abuses in Palestine as further evidence of his failure to brighten perceptions of the U.S. as a champion of democracy and human rights.

BIDEN AIN'T CUTTING IT SO FAR

MAR 26, 2021

Biden ain't cutting it so far …

On the surface, one might find it disturbing to have to read rumblings that the U.S. is in the too-long process of losing its empire and its privileges and hegemony and even the dollar as a viable and respected reserve currency. But the rumblings are probably true to some degree since they are popping up randomly like clichés and clichés always contain an element of truth or else they'd never have become such.

The U.S. still has over 800 active military bases overseas, the dollar remains the world "reserve" currency; the government is still handing out economic sanctions like a frat boy handing out condoms at a fraternity party of dipsomaniacs at a third-rate American university; the U.S. still has the chutzpah to demand that everyone heel to its diktat or else be slandered and vilified and made an enemy subject to "regime change" if not outright attack, and more. (But the U.S. only literally attacks smaller, weaker countries with natural resources for the most part, as bullies are inclined to do.)

One attack of note was not a military one when Biden, who has been called a crash test dummy, claimed that Vladimir Putin has no soul and moreover was a "killer". This is rather demented and hypocritical since the only killing Putin has managed of late it seems has involved terrorists of the worst kind like ISIS and al-Qaeda in Syria.

Putin responded to the crude charges by Biden saying that it takes a "killer" to know one but arguably Putin has done little but come to the aid of its long-beleaguered ally Syria and popular Assad and defend obvious Russian interests. Also, Biden is claiming that the referendum in Crimea was a sham and that Russia must give back the Crimea to Ukraine where Biden and his son reaped oodles of bucks in what was obviously a very corrupt engagement with Burisma, the Ukrainian gas company.

Anyway, the U.S. has been killing people by the millions especially in the Middle East (West Asia) for over three decades, not to mention five million Vietnamese long ago, more recently Libyans, Syrians, Afghans and many others, and never stops its threats against anyone who disagrees with it. Moreover, the U.S. has a collection of "allies" like the Saudis and the Zionists and the Emirate gangsters who have murdered over a hundred thousand poor people in Yemen and Biden has not yet done a darn thing yet to halt the war there. In Afghanistan, notably, Donald Trump last year, to his credit, was about to drag U.S. troops entirely out of that 20-plus year war but the Pentagon, according to a recent report, apparently engaged in some anti-Trump skullduggery that undercut his role as Commander in Chief and halted that move and now Biden is not doing anything yet to end that war.

Eisenhower was prophetic in 1960 when he warned that the Military Industrial Complex could sink the U.S., and while it has not sunk much yet, the MIC is pushing hard in that direction and may succeed this decade.

Consider, for example, what the U.S literally looks like today as a result of its decades-long catering to the MIC. The U.S. is the sole Western democracy now that does not have: universal healthcare, public universities that offer free or very low-cost educational opportunities to deeply indebted students, child care assistance to struggling families where both parents have to work to survive, and rational tax rates – especially on thousands of millionaires and hundreds of billionaires. Before Ronald Reagan was president marginal tax rates were 70 percent or more and "the rich" had to pay their fair share of the burden of government and the U.S. was far more viable and prosperous.

The net result of U.S. arrogance and militarism and greed is a federal debt burden soon to be over $30 trillion and climbing, huge current and forward budget deficits in the trillions ahead and worse, a U.S infrastructure that now resembles that of a Third World Banana Republic. And Biden plans to spend trillions more to rectify the infrastructure decay that's been ongoing for half a century while literally ALL of the Republicans and some Democrats in the U.S. Congress are dead set against ANY tax increases. But Biden has no choice but to try to push serious tax increases.

Indeed, the dollar has been hyperinflated by trillions of dollars printed by the Federal Reserve Bank out of thin air, but the U.S. Bureau of Labor's statistical compilations have been so mismanaged by dishonest inputs that they don't begin to reflect the real and expanding inflation rates currently and looming. Many economists are warning that U.S. "money" may eventually be destroyed by direct hyperinflation of living costs akin to what happened to German marks in 1923 when they could ultimately buy nothing. Back then wheelbarrows of paper German "money" could not even buy a loaf of bread.

Perhaps the saddest part of the U.S. situation overall is that most average Americans have been so dumbed down by propaganda that as dismayed as some of them surely feel right now they don't have a clue what to do, and maybe they literally can't do anything to halt the decline short of massive protests that smack of a revolution.

Really, one positive move would be to cut the budget for the Pentagon by two thirds and begin to address the real needs of Americans generally, plus tax increases on the rich and corporations. But this is not likely to happen as the U.S. has become little more than a cold-hearted military machine catering to worse "allies" who are not worthy of support given their own human rights records, especially in the Middle East (West Asia). One can only look in horror at what has been happening to the so-called leader of the so-called "free" world.

Huge whiffs of desperation in Washington now

Apr 4, 2021

How grand that China and Iran have finally formalized, after several years of waiting, a 25 year (and likely more) "strategic agreement" that's going to encompass not just trade and economies, but also cultural, educational, medical and other spheres, too.

It's all a part of what the U.S. despises most and is doing whatever it can to disrupt and halt – China's peaceful Belt and Road initiative binding, if not absolutely cementing, expanded trade and mutually beneficial relations across Asian countries at least between China up towards Europe. And to boot, Russia and China are closer in spirit than they have ever been before, and both countries are working hard to pull away from what reliance they have had on the U.S. dollar.

Meanwhile, especially of late, once can quite easily catch whiffs of desperation in Washington while the U.S. sinks slowly into a morass of its own making over the past three decades. The desperation is obvious. For example, there's the matter of the Nordstream 2 gas pipeline which is about 90 percent complete between Russia and Germany and the U.S. is desperate to stop it altogether and sell much more expensive LNG to Germany and Europe. Even a fool would wonder why Europe would ever buy the expensive gas if given a sound and reliable alternative supply, but again the U.S. is desperate to cast itself as Europe's protector, its Big Daddy, as it has been generally or claimed to be since the end of World War 2, and as well demonize both Russia and China as dangers to Europe and even Africa, and they are anything but that in fact. The slow transition underway to a New World Order frightens the bejesus out of Washington and its efforts to shore up its relevance by insisting that the "order" it wants to maintain or further impose makes sense in a world that aches for multilateralism and peaceful relations after 30 years or more of bellicose disruptions largely spawned by the U.S. and its alleged NATO allies.

What are those garbage assertions from Washington about a "rules-based" international order, as if it's a principled goal? One must ask, "what rules"? The U.S. in fact abides by no "rules" but its own arrogance where anything especially military goes and nothing at all is fixed and reliable and honest. The idea of a "rules-based" order sounds good on the surface but it's really just a sham which anyone with an IQ of 90 and maybe even less ought to perceive. What could be witnessed this decade is a U.S. that like the huge cargo ship Ever Given stuck in the Suez Canal temporarily, the U.S. could be similarly stuck and going nowhere permanently.

President Biden, in any case, had just put forth a rather lame notion that maybe the U.S. along with other countries create its own initiative to rival China's Belt and Road to prevent China from becoming more powerful than it already is with an economy that by some metrics already equals or surpasses the U.S. He claims that the U.S. must mount rival infrastructure projects with allies like the U.K. to assist countries like China has been doing. Is this idea going to take off? Not likely. One reason why not is because America's infrastructure is as shoddy as any Third World country and Biden must first attend to trying to upgrade the U.S., which does not, to cite just one aspect of it, have a single decent high-speed passenger rail line! Soon to be unveiled in Washington is an infrastructure plan costing several more trillions of dollars on top of the recent $2 trillion Covid relief outlays.

This is almost a joke because the U.S. is virtually broke with the Federal Reserve Bank literally conjuring up "money" out of thin air. It is, in fact, a race between getting anything done before the U.S. dollar and the U.S. itself virtually collapses into a burning dumpster of wildly inflated fiat "money" and broken dreams.

One must ask, how in the world can the U.S. accomplish much of anything positive unless the government raises taxes dramatically and cuts the Pentagon's budget by at least two-thirds, and closes most of its 800 plus military bases scattered across the globe? The truth is, it can't. A majority of the members of the U.S. Congress for one thing abhor tax raises because voting for them threatens their job tenure in Congress, and slashing the U.S. military footprint has long been off-limits for purblind legislators who mistakenly believe that military might is the sine qua non of U.S. influence and power. It's not, as China has demonstrated by not starting wars, and remember the U.S. has literally not won a war it has started or supported in decades, not even the war to topple little Syria and the Assad government there at Israel's behest.

Not to mention Vietnam, Iraq, Libya, Yemen, etcetera, unless "winning" constitutes mayhem, death, destruction, and chaos.

This latter concept of a "win" is something that Washington could never admit to because if it did the U.S. would destroy utterly what's left of its respect and influence overseas. Already the U.S., to cite just one bad move, is backing away from its agreement with the Taliban in Afghanistan to pull out troops in May. Australian writer Caitlin Johnstone put it most succinctly when she wrote recently: "U.S. intelligence agencies have warned the Biden Administration that if the U.S. withdraws its military presence from Afghanistan under current circumstances, the nation would be at severe risk of falling under the control of the people who actually live there."

Zionism is the Ebola virus of American political afflictions

Apr 16, 2021

A Palestinian boy is shot in the eye by an Israeli sniper with a rubber bullet, and loses the eye, while he is browsing in a food store. A Palestinian grandmother is run over and killed by a "settler" for no reason. A man is released from an Israeli prison after more than a decade of solitary confinement, but when he arrives home his mind has been so scrambled that he does not recognize any of his relatives, including his mother.

Every single day one can read of one or more fresh atrocities by the only Apartheid state on earth. After nurse Rezan an-Najjar was shot and killed near Gaza's fence with Israel by a sniper, the Israelis claimed few shots were actually fired and none directly at her, so it was not a random stray bullet that killed her. This assertion by the IDF actually supports the fact that she was targeted. And so on.

Back in the U.S. these stories go almost unmentioned by the press, and ever more commitments are made to Israel. More money, more (im)moral support, more lies and obfuscations, more insanity. And it never stops. It can seem like the U.S. has no friends since it only seems to court and support the most outrageous, undemocratic regimes in the Middle East (West Asia).

About this recent attack on Natanz, Biden is silent when he ought to be outraged because it could mess up the JCPOA revival that he is trying to push. President Biden meanwhile intends to give back some of the funds taken away by Trump, arguably the worst President in U.S. history, to UNWRA and the Palestinian Authority. But make no mistake, it's aimed at giving the PA, and feeble "leaders" like Mahmoud Abbas more wherewithal to amplify collaboration with the Zionists to further suppress the millions of Palestinians west of the Jordan River. Palestinians are supposed to have an election this year for a parliament of sorts, as they did earlier this century, but one can bet the election won't be honored because, as likely, some of those who will be elected to represent the Palestinians will not be, well, kosher. They may even be devotees of HAMAS or some other resistance faction.

Also, and frankly it's better than the nothingness of Trump, the Biden regime alleges it will rejoin the JCPOA and drop at least some of the economic sanctions that Trump imposed on Iran. But Biden in his fog may recognize just one thing clearly: the U.S. is in no position to kick off a war with the Israelis against Iran, something the Zionists fervently want or else they would not object to ANY measures that would oblige Iran to scale back its peaceful nuclear advances, and especially its uranium enrichment activities. To try to spoil the emerging JCPOA revival, the Zionists (again) attacked Natanz, this time by screwing up its electricity feed. The actual extent of the damage is so far not publicly known

About this recent attack on Natanz, Biden is silent when he ought to be outraged because it could mess up the JCPOA revival that he is trying to push. (And, by the way, deep gratitude to Russian warships which allegedly escorted some Iranian tankers leaving the Suez Canal to supply Syria with badly needed energy supplies like gasoline.) Of course Biden, if he had more marbles, would call a halt to the war on Yemen and as well end the U.S occupation and theft of Syria's oil and wheat production areas east of the Euphrates.

Biden and company really are severely schizophrenic. One the one hand, the Biden gang seems to want less chance of a lambent, new war in West Asia that the U.S. cannot afford, but on the other hand it's slamming China (obviously worried about growing alliances between China and Russia and Iran and the advances of the Belt and Road initiative and also Taiwan). But at the same time it's telling the corrupt Ukraine puppets that Russia must give back the Crimea and allow resupplied Ukrainian forces to mount fresh attacks on the Donbass. This could incite a world war. Russia is no pushover.

To try to spoil the emerging JCPOA revival, the Zionists (again) attacked Natanz, this time by screwing up its electricity feed. What the world witnesses here and there is a desperate U.S. which literally has been defeated by the Taliban in Afghanistan and can't quite admit it and leave quickly when it's evident to all. Even Syria under popular Assad, mightily damaged, still stands tall against the terrorists who flooded the country over the past decade. And the Houthis have done remarkably well against the Saudis and the Emiratis.

The biggest question is why the various U.S. administrations persist and have persisted for so long against countries which, like Iran and others, far lesser countries, are NOT a danger to the United States or to the American people and never have been. If anything, these countries have merely challenged the horrific idea pushed by Zionist American Neocons of U.S. "empire" and their insistence on "full spectrum dominance" over the entire globe, something which has virtually bankrupted the U.S. and created widespread chaos.

If all a country can project to control other people and countries is potential force to instill fear, control does not truly exist – just the temporary chimera of it.

And does one have to guess why this concept of world dominance by the U.S. has been and remains so important to Zionists who infest government and Wall Street and advocate for it? The answer may well be because such dominance (and it needs constant provocation and attention and upset to maintain) provides a huge shield behind which bloody "leaders" in Israel like Netanyahu and Benny Gantz and others can continue to enact a kind of bloody slow dance of human and cultural genocide against the Arabs of Palestine and take the entirety of historical Palestine and expel all non-Jews. This shield limits visibility towards the things the Zionists are doing to others – very bad things.

Emptying Palestine and filling it with anyone nominally a "Jew" (Ethiopians who are ill-treated in Israel are lately being sent to the West Bank to modify its demographic character!) has always been the ultimate aim of Zionists who early on were actually anti-Semitic. This was expressed over a century ago by Theodore Herzl even and a bit later by Vladimir Jabotinsky, the spiritual and intellectual leader of Zionist radicals and revisionists before 1948. (Netanyahu's father served as Jabotinsky's secretary.)

U.S. support for Zionism, amplified this century especially while the U.S. has been losing its luster (probably beginning with the loss of the war on Vietnam) will sink the U.S. such that it WILL become a failed state if it's not one already just hiding behind a proposed, obscene "defense" budget of $753 billion for the coming fiscal year. It's a tragedy for most Americans like no other but not understood yet by many given the propaganda suffusing the U.S. mainstream media.

War is not the solution but

patience is

Apr 27, 2021

If ever a nation was severely stuck between various hard places, the U.S. is it, and the only blame that can be meted out is to the U.S. government and the Federal Reserve Bank after several decades of mismanagement and bad policy.

Anyway, last week, several hundred Zionist settlers in Palestine went on a "wilding", storming through parts of East

Tehran Times

Jerusalem where they assaulted anyone without a yarmulke, any Palestinian, causing serious damage and scores of injuries to the natives. It was one of the worse expressions of racism and Jewish nationalism seen in some time, but this happens on a lesser scale all too frequently. It has become evident they want to take over al-Aqsa and expel even more people from their homes in Jerusalem to install themselves illegally there. The U.S. did respond, but very tepidly, and did not condemn the mob actions outright. The mob chanted "Death to Arabs". Of course, the U.S. has long been complicit, because a harsh word against the Zionists and making aid to Israel conditional is not yet likely. Consider this to understand it better:

Say one is a 32-year-old living in Brooklyn in a rundown apartment and working some night shift in a New York warehouse driving a forklift and has a wife and kid both of whom are difficult. And being a Jew, he suddenly discovers life could get a whole lot better with a fresh identity as a hardcore Zionist because the Apartheid entity will give his entire family airline tickets on El Al and a nice, newly constructed apartment on a hill in the West Bank on stolen land with a great view. And to boot, the family gets to carry around the latest military rifles and be a part of a colonial enterprise anointed by Yahweh, which in effect means Yahweh has in effect anointed this young man, too. Since he has long and ignorantly considered himself better than any non-Jew, it is now going to be confirmed vastly to him because he gets to do whatever he damn well pleases and can even kill the poor people with impunity in an ancient village near the settlement just because! Life seems golden suddenly. No more worries and it's all virtually free. What an inducement this is to abandon squalid Brooklyn! How wonderful the new identity! No more a mere schmuck but a member of the Army of Yahweh and he's backed by a couple hundred nuclear

War is not the solution but ...

bombs, too, in a country that declares nothing and does not abide by any rules at all.

This, essentially, is what the world has to deal with given the Zionists. People no better than members of ISIS and in some respects worse as terrorists. And they are creating problems not just in the Middle East (West Asia) but worldwide, and especially in the U.S. One must honor the Islamic Republic for resisting and condemning overtly the Apartheid entity. The paucity of resistance and wide support in U.S. government circles is or will be the end of all respect for America someday.

America is beset by many problems, but maybe the biggest is an indoctrinated population leading them to passivity and ignorance. Many believe themselves to be the "free-est" people on earth, but in fact citizens are taxed and garner no substantial civic benefits in return while the Military-Industrial Complex and the immensely rich continue to profit enormously. And the MIC literally has become the economy, because the country produces little while most goods are supplied from overseas, and especially from China.

Perhaps one big reason average American think they are free is because they get to own guns, with which random carnage has become an almost daily event. Make no mistake, the U.S. is in steep, irreversible decline with a virtually broke Treasury dependent on fiat dollars printed in the trillions by the Fed. It's hard to imagine the U.S. will not lose the dollar as the primary world reserve currency this decade and as well it's "empire" of hundreds of military bases across the globe and also the country's capacity to dominate anywhere. The absolute KEY to countries like Iran is patience and the avoidance of war, for the U.S. government has long been making all the wrong moves overseas and at home, too.

Iran has shown tremendous restraint aside from reminding its enemies very occasionally that it does have defensive capabilities. And Biden is not the solution, but he IS a far better and more popular President inside the U.S. than Trump. (Many in the U.S. are just waiting eagerly for indictments against Trump that may land him in jail eventually.)

Overall, it's unfortunate that most Americans will not wake up to the dangers of its own governance and past misdeeds spawned in Washington, as much of the rest of the world already has, before loss of faith in the U.S. promoted by some further madness comes home to roost further on average U.S. citizens. At that point there may be some sort of "revolution" or a vast anger that is likely to make the situation even worse for a while unless enlightened leaders come to the fore and manage to settle the U.S. into a full acceptance of a multipolar world where cooperation with other countries, and especially alleged "enemies" who have demonstrated patience, emerges.

Escalations in Palestine designed by Netanyahu to keep him in power: analyst

May 18, 2021

Martin Love, an American political analyst, believes that the ethnic cleansing of the Arabs of Jerusalem is a plot designed by Netanyahu to save himself from corrupt charges.

"The escalation in Palestine, beginning with the assaults and ethnic cleansing on the Arabs of East Jerusalem in Sheikh Jarrah and around the al-Aqsa and Damascus Gate were in some part designed by Netanyahu to keep him in power for a while longer," Martin Love tells the Tehran Times.

The neighborhood of Sheikh Jarrah has become the centerpiece of belligerent fighting between Israel and Palestine as Palestinians rallied around residents to resist the Israeli settlers encroaching on East Jerusalem.

Unrest in East Jerusalem has been on the rise since the beginning of Ramadan on 13 April, after the Israeli authorities installed metal barriers outside the Damascus Gate, blocking access to a public area for Palestinians.

"The escalation and bombings and killings of Gazans is a way for the Zionists to buy more time before they may be forced to change any policies," Love adds.

Following is the text of the interview:

Q: How do you evaluate the recent escalation in Palestine?

A: The escalation in Palestine, beginning with the assaults and ethnic cleansing on the Arabs of East Jerusalem in Sheikh Jarrah and around the al-Aqsa and Damascus Gate, was in some parts designed by Netanyahu to keep him in power for a while longer. This has been a cynical game for some time since he cannot be fully prosecuted and jailed on a variety of corruption charges as long as he holds office. But he and the Zionists probably did not expect what appeared to be a general Palestinian uprising on both sides of the Green

Line, especially in Gaza with many volleys of more effective homemade missiles raining on all parts of central Israel. The escalation and bombings and killings of Gazans is a way for the Zionists to buy more time before they may be forced to change any policies, but this time they may have miscalculated because it is possible Palestinians are not going to quiet down and chaos could prevail west of the Jordan River virtually forever until the Occupation ends. One would hope the PA would be thoroughly dismantled and Abbas exposed for what he has long been – a quisling.

"A person would have to be blind and deaf to not to know that Israel and the support of Israel by the U.S. is the real block to calm and peace in the Middle East (West Asia)."Q: Israel says Iran is a threat to West Asia while we see Israeli sabotage operations against Iran and killing people in Palestine. Who is the real threat?

A: Iran has never been an active threat in the Middle East (West Asia) unless one considers a prosperous Iran a threat that makes no sense. Therefore, we see decades of attempts to not let Iran prosper, to undermine the Islamic Republic by the U.S., the EU, and of course, the Zionists. A person would have to be blind and deaf to not to know that Israel and the support of Israel by the U.S. is the real block to calm and peace in the Middle East (West Asia). Imperialism and Colonialism have one aim: to divide and conquer. The divided part is not currently working very well, if at all, in Palestine for the very first time since the Nakba, it seems. The PA and Abbas must be obliterated. It has been a past century of utter SHAME that Muslims across the world have so far failed to come together and work together towards shared benefits. The Islamic Ummah must rise and prevail.

Q: How do you see Western media cover when it comes to conflicts in Palestine?

A: The mainstream Western media, particularly the New York Times and Washington Post, are still spouting the same garbage about Palestine and Iran and the Middle East (West Asia) generally. It is so predictable and ignorant. However, there are a few fair media outlets in the West and a handful of superb reporters and thinkers and writers, even a few in the U.S., who do understand the real dynamics underway and are not afraid, to tell the truth. More and more, we will see this going forward as more Western citizens wake up to the realities in the Middle East (West Asia). One big problem is that Americans and Brits and others generally have been dumbed way down by the usual media gibberish and propaganda that they understand very little.

The concern today is that President Biden, perhaps senile but certainly under the Zionist influence, is still saying what we have heard so often when "Israel" has erupted in violence: "Israel has a right to defend itself." But by murdering civilians in Gaza and the West Bank? What a joke that is.

Q: Why do successive administrations in the U.S. try to turn a blind eye to Israeli crimes?

A: Successive U.S. administrations are corrupted by their members' own ignorance, various Israel lobbies like AIPAC, and money. It is totally corrupted. AIPAC, for example, should be registered as a foreign agent liable to taxes in the U.S. One can posit that this corruption of governance could be the end of the U.S. influence eventually.

Q: How could Israel label its critics with anti-Semitism to marginalize them?

A: Anti-Semitism is a powerful concept when applied to others, given the Holocaust and so many references to it. Practically anyone who has advocated for the end of Apartheid has been smeared as anti-Semitic when all they have been against Zionism as a corrosive, criminal ideology. The conflation of Judaism and Zionism is utterly absurd, and many Jews in Iran would tell anyone if they were asked. Even Jimmy Carter has been called an anti-Semite for nearly 20 years! Most all decent journalists and writers focusing on the Middle East (West Asia) have been called anti-Semitic at one time or another. This is another crude absurdity. It is a ploy that is losing its effectiveness nowadays. It is worth saying that Western governments that continue to spout the usual platitudes about "Israel" are slowly losing credibility even at home. But the process has been way too slow and many continue to suffer as a result. Zionism is failing, will fail.

Imagine what Gaza could become if the siege were lifted
May 26, 2021

Words are not sufficient to describe the horrors of what "Israel" (and the U.S. as an enabler) have done in the last two months around al-Aqsa, Sheikh Jarrah and across Palestine, and then Gaza for almost two weeks.

Imagine what Gaza could become if ...

The price paid for the shift in worldwide perceptions about what the "Israel" actually is (a rabid Apartheid state!) has been horrendous for Gaza and across Palestine. Gazans celebrated a possible pyrrhic victory of sorts because not only were the Zionists forced to call a ceasefire but there have been profound changes in public perceptions even in the U.S. about how insidious and out of control Zionism has become and long been.

But it has not solved the problem because as soon as a ceasefire went into effect Netanyahu had managed to stay in power with the cancellation of a possible new government, avoided the resumption of his trial on corruption charges and worse has continued doing the very things that prompted a rain of bottle rockets over "Israel" with a resumption of military and police raids on al-Aqsa, hundreds of arrests including murders and further efforts to ethnically cleanse Sheikh Jarrah of Palestinians with other Palestinian neighborhoods in Jerusalem lined up for the same treatment eventually. And Biden and Blinken did almost nothing about the carnage: they let it continue for a while until the demanded ceasefire went into effect.

For now, despite alleged promises by the U.S. to help rebuild the bombed infrastructure damaged in Gaza, Secretary of State Tony Blinken is headed to Israel and other countries for what? In the West Bank he is going to consult Mahmoud Abbas for one thing (who if not an outright quisling hardly gives Palestinians effective leadership and is the wrong person to talk to about anything). Blinken ought to be trying to go to Gaza, too.

As for Hamas in Gaza now, they literally cannot respond to the same Israeli moves that caused this most recent war on Gaza because they are probably running low on those home-made rockets even if the organization has managed to garner some modest praise and support across the world. Moreover, the Zionist defense establishment and Netanyahu has proclaimed that it will hit Gaza even harder if Hamas does anything now. Also, in Israel, the government has done nothing to reign in the right-wing mobs of "settlers" who now are openly calling for the razing of the lovely al-Aqsa shrine, Islam's third holiest site. If al-Aqsa ever did fall, one would probably be looking at complete war in West Asia. All those "settlers", including many Americans, would flee, cowards that they are looking for freebies in the West Bank with U.S. support.

If there has been any kind of "victory" for Palestinians, it resides solely for now in the awakening of public perceptions about Zionist Apartheid everywhere which may, in time, have an impact. The BDS campaign is bound to expand mightily and the ICC is definitely going to charge "Israel" and its craven leaders with numerous war and others crimes. But the court in The Hague has been way too slow mounting its prosecutions.

But there is another aspect of this crazed situation.

The two million Palestinians in Gaza have long ached for relief from the siege (and their martyrs abound, including almost 70 children slaughtered by IDF bombs this month). Real relief, however, is not likely to arrive anytime soon even if there are repairs to the damage done, but if it ever arrived, consider or imagine what Gaza might become if the siege were lifted.

Imagine what Gaza could become if ...

This is something that the Zionists fear and despise and actually, prospectively, are extremely jealous of ever seeing. Gaza, if it could revive its port and repair its airport and other assets, could become a prosperous relative heaven for Gazans and for curious tourists from all over the world wanting to understand better Palestine and its people and history while enjoying Arab hospitality which the Gazans could deliver like few others. It's not hard to imagine even Americans wanting a taste of the Middle East and especially a look at a (then former) victim of Zionist aggression (that stood tall despite the Israelis). If travelers had to choose between visiting a discredited Apartheid regime and an inexpensive beachfront Gaza, even if only for purely educational purposes, Gaza would be the place to go.

But the Zionists above all want to crush the Palestinians if not eliminate them altogether and give them no quarter for what could be a magnificent revival given their own creativity and industrious ways that have existed for generations.

The sole hope for now that has any chance for success is a burgeoning condemnation worldwide of Apartheid and its aggressions. One day, perhaps, even candidates aspiring to become a part of the U.S. Congress will be judged in part on their postures towards Zionism

Zionists are a one trick pony called VIOLENCE

June 9, 2021

One must slide reluctantly into masochism to stay informed. Cruelty, chaos, criminality and insanity reign. And smack in the center of it all is America and its sidekick or dominatrix, Apartheid Israel.

It seems clear Netanyahu and other Zionist "leaders" in Likud and in smaller parties farther to the right are ramping up the ethnic cleansing and mass arrests of Palestinians like rarely before in what may be an effort to spark a regional war. Netanyahu does not care whom he hurts or kills: he just wants to stay in the political miasma that is Israel now with all its abusive criminality and arrogant assaults on international law and human rights. This can only get worse since the Zionists know nothing and aim for nothing but what they have always been about for over 70 years: violence against Palestinians and non-Zionists amidst land grabs and ethnic cleansing.

That possible war may be just the thing that scuttles a new coalition government in Israel and allows Netanyahu to remain as PM for a few days longer, and avoid prosecution and jail on corruption charges. Yes, Hamas launched the tiny rockets in May in response to invasions of al-Aqsa and the ethnic cleansing in East Jerusalem, but Hamas is likely spent for now and just trying to clean up the mess the Israelis made on Gaza and bury the dead. This must be a calculation by the Zionists who are proceeding with the same moves that caused

Zionists are a one trick pony ...

Hamas to respond to the Israeli violence at al-Aqsa and in Sheikh Jarrah in East Jerusalem.

Hapless and foolish Joe Biden anyway has promised the Zionists a complete restocking of the "Iron Dome" defense array which proved to be like Swiss cheese. One can only imagine how badly the Zionists would fare if there were ever a regional war and Israel also had to deal with real missiles from Iran or from Hizballah in Lebanon in addition to Syrian anti-aircraft rockets, one of which recently went astray and landed within a few miles of Dimona. If such a widespread battle ever materialized one can also imagine other Arab countries might well join the fray on the back of potential popular uprisings in places like Saudi Arabia or Jordan or the UAE, but this latter may just be wishful thinking. Jordan anyway would be well advised to eject the Israelis in Amman now, and so would Sisi in Egypt, but then this is just yet more wishful thinking. And the so-called Abraham Accords could well be dismissed, too. One can only dream of a better world.

But the real achievement, despite the carnage, is the apparent and long sought unification of Palestinians against Apartheid and occupation, and just as importantly, what appears to be a worldwide awakening against the evils of the Zionists, who have been exposed and which no hasbara can eliminate. Americans also are waking up and there have been scattered suggestions that U.S. voters ought to reject those in government who have long caved to AIPAC and other Jewish lobbies for money and political endorsements.

As for Iran, which is anxiously awaiting the revival in some form, preferably original form, of the JCPOA, which Biden has promised to resurrect, there have been inside Iran some fiery explosions of late on industry or infrastructure, which one easily wonders may have been the work of Israeli sabotage trying to incite Iran. The new head of Mossad, one David Barnea, has already threatened new assassinations of Iranians and attacks on infrastructure, and the Netanyahu regime has been warning that it will do anything it can to scuttle the JCPOA. A unilateral attack on Iran's nuclear facilities? But that would likely be the end of the Zionist regime and one can also imagine many of Israel's absolute worst elements, the settlers in the West Bank who seem to be directing the IDF's moves in East Jerusalem and elsewhere in the West Bank, to return to New York or wherever they have come from. Again, a bit more of wishful thinking. But the world despises Zionism.

The worldwide shift in perspective on Israel emboldens Israel's enemies to persevere against the occupations, but so emboldened, the Zionists have no answer but further repression and violence, which shifts the perspective even farther against Israel. This is to say Zionism (unless it is redefined in practice as some benign movement) is doomed, and so may be Israeli Apartheid.

In addition, there are now modest hopes for better relations between various Arab countries and between Arab countries and Iran. Some sort of unity or at least a rapprochement between largely Muslim countries, Shi'a or Sunni, may be in the first innings. This includes between Iran and even Saudi Arabia while the current crackdown on Palestinians, including Palestinian citizens of Israel, is the largest in decades and it is doing no service to Israel. This has only strengthened Palestinian resolve. When will Muslims finally realize their real enemies are not other Muslims, but rather Western countries like the U.S. which for over a century have imposed war, division, imperialism and colonialism on various largely Muslim lands?

As for America, it has been claimed that the general political disarray between Trump supporters in the GOP and the Democrats may be pushing the U.S. into an environment where if voter suppression efforts continue, the U.S. may no longer be able to call itself an honest democracy. The GOP is racist to its core under any lingering fealty to Trump and Trumpism, just as the Zionists are racist.

A roundup: America continues to lurch from bad to worse June 30, 2021

America has become a malignant power without consequence given the ignorance and malfeasance of those in political power.

One would think that eventually the self-serving political "elite" in Washington would get their just desserts for deeds that go against rationality, morality, and common sense, and which now undermines the viability of the U.S. as a respected influence. Many people across the globe simply wait impatiently for the expected consequences of further U.S. decline, which have by some miracle been mostly held at bay for decades, especially in this century.

Joe Biden so far has offered no positive relief. Already, twice in his short term he has unleashed the military on illegal bombing runs in the Middle East (West Asia) – most recently an attack on Iraqi militias' stores and personnel along the Syria-Iraq border region, the very militias which aim to obviate the resurrection of ISIS in Arab heartlands. These militias, who paraded in Baghdad this month, are claimed to be proxies for Iran, which they are not except that Iraq and Iran are allies for the most part. The U.S. claims it wants to destroy the likelihood of any future random attacks on U.S. personnel in Iraq, but obviously the best way to do that is simply to withdraw the U.S. military from the region. This is just one of many moves that make no sense. The other biggest offense remains the U.S. posture of support towards Apartheid Israel.

Netanyahu, who was not popular with former President Obama, is not popular with Biden, who refused to call him for over three months after he became President last winter. Now, there's Yair Lapid and Naftali Bennett, and who knows how long they can survive with such a motley coalition government? Lapid anyway is trying to mend relations with Biden and the Democrats, many of whom have already begun to challenge Israeli Apartheid and change the narrative about Israel as being some kind of enlightened democratic polity in the Mideast (West Asia). Many liberal American Jews agree with the shift in the narrative, which is superb. Prominent Jewish commentators and writers like Peter Beinart have become outspoken in their hostility to Zionism and Apartheid.

Bennett as PM may not yet have done anything particularly dramatic, but he has continued to bomb Gaza (after the 11-day "war" with Hamas) occasionally and seems to have done nothing to call off the "settler" dogs who are ramping up ethnic cleansing in vital Palestinian neighborhoods in East Jerusalem and elsewhere in the West Bank, while the IDF protects this rabble of thugs, many of whom happen to be Americans.

Meanwhile, Nizar Banat, who has opposed the Palestinian Authority and Mahmoud Abbas for deep corruption and even complicity with the Zionists, was beaten to death by Fatah thugs leaving the Palestinians more divided than ever in the West Bank. Abbas has accomplished nothing for decades but make himself and his cronies relatively rich. He is nothing but a quisling. (This writer, living in the West Bank for several months in 2006, got a good look at PA "police" who are doing nothing for the Palestinian cause of liberation from occupation.)

But the most glaring example of Biden's retrograde action is his June attack on press freedoms and access to over 30 news outlets, like Iran's Press TV, in the Middle East that happen to be a part of the so-called "resistance axis" that has long been challenging U.S. imperialism, colonialism, occupations and murder. The U.S. clearly does not have an honest "free press" in the mainstream media with some modest reportage exceptions, and does not want Americans to have access to alternative points of view from other media outlets which in any case can't be entirely obliterated. Biden also ought to set free Julian Assange from charges that this month have been exposed as false and were in fact discounted by at least one primary perp who has changed his story. But Biden has no mind of his own, apparently, and his administration fears the truth.

It is also deeply ironic that Florida governor Ron DeSantis, an aggressive longtime Trump supporter who has been aiming to become president, has just announced that Israel is sending a team to Miami to assist with the clearance of the collapsed

Iran and the U.S. 2017 - 2023

Miami apartment building and the recovery of some 150 more bodies rotting somewhere in the rubble. Unreal! The very country that has wiped out homes and big apartment building in Gaza once again this spring and continues threats to "flatten" Gaza! DeSantis is actually more dangerous than Trump, because he is maybe wilier than Trump who is fading fast and likely to be indicted soon for various crimes, including the crime of ever becoming "President".

Meanwhile, Iran warns it is not forever going to negotiate the resurrection of the JCPOA, which makes sense. This revival has been stalled for too long, probably because the U.S. wants to add additional restrictions on Iran's capacity to defend itself and Iran has correctly refused. It's a wonder Iran has not already withdrawn from the JCPOA under the elected President Raisi who has been called a "hardliner". The U.S. must own up to its foolishness. It was precisely because of its withdrawal from the accord in 2018 that "reformists" were largely demoted and excluded as candidates for the Iranian presidency. Did the U.S. fail to realize that after Trump canned the U.S. participation in the nuclear accord Iran would circle the wagons? How moronic is this oversight by Washington? Very. Thoughtful minds wonder why Iran can't successfully carry on building its alliances with over half the world's peoples in Asia and not literally be bothered by U.S. sanctions.

So, in sum for now, there is regression from assured peace in West Asia even as Iran has reached out to neighboring Arab countries to establish better relations.

America is still headed for a material collapse eventually

August 5, 2021

Some Americans, but far too few, want to know how Barack Obama gets to plan his upcoming 60th birthday bash this month on his 30-acre oceanfront estate on the island of Martha's Vineyard off the coast of Massachusetts.

There are 475 confirmed guests set to show up who will be catered to by a staff of some 200 people at the estate which the Obama family bought for $12 million right after he left the White House. One can imagine the party will cost close to a million bucks. And this for a president who was primarily a "social worker" before he became president?

One can recall that, in contrast, when Harry Truman left the White House and President Eisenhower took over in the early 1950s, Harry left his job in Washington and he and his wife drove home unescorted to Missouri where he had long maintained very modest family home.

Those were the days when the U.S. really was at the top of its game, and quite prosperous with a thriving middle class. Back then, too, the U.S. was THE respected world power. Eisenhower, a celebrated U.S. general in World War 2 who along with his peers was instrumental in helping defeat Nazi Germany, turned out to be a solid president. Just before he left office after eight years he gave his now-famous speech warning about the dangers of what he called the "military-industrial complex" becoming too big a factor in the development of the country and potentially leading to all sorts of horrors, as it so amply has since the mid-1960s and the start of the Vietnam war debacle. Eisenhower was never interested in buying a $12 million estate, unlike Obama.

But the question remains HOW any president unless they were already filthy rich by inheritance like JFK or the two Bushes, and very much like many in Congress nowadays, manage to become very wealthy on relatively modest salaries while in office and especially after they leave office. The answer quite simply is rampant, obscene corruption. Favors did to so-called elites and special interest groups such as AIPAC and even the military while in office have resulted in huge rewards after they are retired. The Clintons are another case in point and so are many in or out of Congress today. Nancy Pelosi, who leads the Democrats in the House of Representatives, is another example.

So what the U.S. has become is a society of the haves and have nots like never before, and the results of this, including the decimation of a middle class and even industrial enterprise because of off-shoring to China and other countries, is a country that is unraveling socially, spiritually, economically and infrastructurally.

Biden has pledged to "bring back America" but already he has failed to live up to scores of campaign promises and America so far is not "coming back" except as a bigger threat, along with horrifical allies like the Zionist Apartheid state and the Saudis, to name just two.

But one really needs to ask just one question: What can you say about a country that has spent trillions of dollars over the decades since World War 2 building and often upgrading several THOU.S.AND nuclear weapons? (When, presumably, a hundred or so of the barbarous bombs, which ONLY the U.S. has ever used unnecessarily – twice on Japan in 1945 – are certainly sufficient as a threat to rivals such as the USSR was, and could easily destroy civilization.)

Indeed, one can say U.S. governance has been on the wrong path, at its peril, for decades just as Eisenhower warned against. The U.S. has eroded at home and not served its citizens well overall, especially in the current century. Many realize this in the U.S. but far too few citizens understand exactly why and their scrambled reactions have often been absurdly counter-productive and severely fracturing to the social fabric and proper governance and respect from abroad.

The biggest "tell" pointing to the decline of the U.S. as a respected power seems to be this: the government has literally not been able to change directions under ANY president or party since Lyndon Johnson's reign. Yes, for example, Biden has or is pulling the U.S. out of Afghanistan but that's only because after 20 years and trillions spent and some 3000 grunts killed and more than 20,000 maimed the U.S. was utterly defeated in its war there. It's not because of a marginal change in direction.

So the question remains what action modest or big COULD signal (before some sort of deep collapse occurs) the beginning of a real change in direction for the U.S. internally and abroad? Here's a list of candidates, some of them seemingly minor, some major. 1. The U.S. lifts all the sanctions on Iran and restores the JCPOA with guarantees it cannot be canceled again as Trump and Pompeo did. 2. Makes aid to the Apartheid Zionist entity conditional on how it treats the Palestinians, half the population west of the

Jordan River and forces the entity to lift the siege on Gaza. 3. Slashes the obscene Pentagon budget materially. 4. Halts the rampant use of "sanctions" and lifts them from Cuba and Venezuela and other countries where deployed. 5. Raises taxes significantly for the billionaire and multi-millionaire "elites". 6. Legislates Medicare healthcare for all citizens. 7. Raises the minimum wage for workers. 8. Cancels most of almost two trillion dollars in student debt. 9. Enacts strict environmental standards, many of which Trump trashed. 10. Dismantles unilaterally 90 percent of nuclear weapons. 11. Stops prosecutions of whistleblowers like Julian Assange.

Any one of these moves, however small (and none of them cater to the long-entrenched "establishment") could be seen as a breath of fresh air for most all Americans and many others overseas. Sadly, for now, none of them are likely to happen until AFTER some sort of material collapse of the U.S. given the long road of bad governance the U.S. has been on. And as well, this ought to constitute a warning to other countries that seem incapable of changing directions themselves.

The U.S. empire is slowly disintegrating

August 28, 2021

Anyone in America with eyes to see and read and ears to hear cannot honestly conclude anything but that the U.S. is in decline. Its leaders during the past 30 years at least have presumed a kind of negative "activism" across the globe is good policy, but now the chickens as they say are coming home to roost and blowback is apparent most everywhere, but for now especially so in Afghanistan.

Negative "activism" primarily revolves around military overreach, trillions spent on the Military-Industrial Complex, Neocon-promoted wars, horrendous sanctions on other countries like Iran, bullying and more. Keep in mind the U.S. has not literally won a single war, or achieved any kind of strategic war objective (that made sense) since the end of World War 2. But the number one ill is state-sanctioned murder by the U.S. military, its proxies and its alleged allies especially in West Asia, of which there are only two of major note it seems: Saudi Arabia and Apartheid Israel, both of which are at the bottom of any list of favorite nations. The U.S. is no longer "the leader of the free world", as it has alleged for decades, because it has denied freedom to so many countries under its heel and made so many lives miserable, including Iranian lives.

Even little Norway, for example, notes this decline when its University of Science and Technology this month advised its students overseas to return home, and counseled: "This applies especially if you are staying in a country with poorly developed health services and infrastructure, for example, the U.S.A." Thus it is becoming increasingly apparent, quite aside from the debacle in Afghanistan, that the U.S. is flailing and struggling relatively at least, and President Biden is not to blame. He did the right thing halting the U.S. war on Afghanistan, which went nowhere for 20 years. If anything, Biden is fast becoming the victim of delayed but increasing blowback for bad policies over decades. And moreover, evidence of what appears to be cognitive decline suggest a bad outcome before 2024: that he will be replaced by VP Kamala Harris whom few Americans believe has the sensibility or smarts to become an effective president. Then the question looms how she could ever win a full term as president in 2024, and who might replace her in such a divided country where the Republicans seem bound to support a candidate even worse than Donald Trump – one who could well double down on the same belligerent policies of recent presidents that got the U.S. into the expanding jam it is in now.

This writer anyway has often, over the past four years, counseled simple "patience" to U.S. adversaries such as Iran, and the crushing part is that Iran never had to become a U.S. adversary except that U.S. policies has taken its marching orders from faux allies like Apartheid Israel and the Saudi regime. At least Biden continues to claim the administration desires the resurrection of the JCPOA, but as time marches on and Iran incrementally regains its footing and cements more goodwill and partnership deals from its near neighbors like Russia and China, even Iran may well begin to conclude that the JCPOA wanes in importance for the Islamic Republic as a necessary component of revival.

The greatest act the U.S. military is performing in Afghanistan and did perform in any other country it has literally struck since World War 2 is simply to leave. Dynamic Vietnam cleaned up the mess the U.S. made there and eventually Afghanistan will clean up the mess the U.S. made there even if it only reverts to its ancient ways of life in relative poverty. However, it is a country rich in some mineral resources, if not oil and gas like Iran, and China, in particular, is bound to step in and help Iran's economy in coming years with trade for its own economic juggernaut.

Meanwhile, VP Harris on a trip to Asia this month asserts that the U.S. "is still a global leader". Really? If one looks at various aspects of conditions inside the U.S. it's not at all leading in terms of the relative overall health of its citizens in many areas. Note that Harris did not say the U.S. is still THE global leader, but maybe just one of several and even that is questionable now. At best, what is ahead for the U.S. are years of penance for its policies internal and external over the past 30 or so years. "At best" because refusing penance and reflection and change will only dig a deeper hole than Afghanistan demonstrates.

Worth noting is that after the somewhat similar debacle and exit for the U.S. in Vietnam in 1975, hardly a dent was made in U.S. global dominance and various administrations continued to indulge in coups and wars and sanctions for decades as if killing some four million Vietnamese did not matter. But this time it's different.

As a hegemonic power with its military and economic "empire", the U.S. may be on its last legs. The world has changed dramatically since 1975. Some observers in Asia are even saying the 500-year-long upsurge of Western power and expansionism and colonialism and imperialism is fast dying, giving way to developments all across Asia led by China.

Something like Astana can be helpful for Afghanistan: analyst

Sept 2, 2021

Martin Love, an American political analyst, believes that an initiative like the Astana process can be an efficient mechanism to restore peace in Afghanistan.

"Spitefulness won't help anyone, not even the U.S. and its allies. Something like Astana could be a positive move," Love tells the Tehran Times.

U.S. exit from Afghanistan has raised concerns about the stability of this country as a pivotal point in the region.

While some political observers predict that the Taliban will commit violence against its people, others believe that the Taliban have changed and they are ready to contribute to establishing an inclusive government.

"Peace in Afghanistan is in my view entirely a function of whether the Taliban holds to its assertions that it is not the same Taliban of 20 years ago, that it will be or become inclusive, that it won't treat its subjects badly, that it will adopt the reforms it says it has internally and as well reached out to neighbors or other Asian countries for assistance and relatively 'normal' diplomatic relations," the American analyst notes.

Following is the text of the interview:

Q: How do you evaluate the U.S. withdrawal from Afghanistan after a two-decade war?

A: There is no other way to characterize the U.S. withdrawal from Afghanistan but to say it has been chaotic, poorly organized and absolute Hell for those wanting to leave a country set to suffer even more after 20 years of occupation and warfare. The sole defense for the Biden Administration is that the Taliban was not expected to take over so quickly, but that's an indictment of the U.S. "intelligence" apparatus which has shown no intelligence whatsoever. The withdrawal is an absolute stain on perceptions of the U.S., worse even than the withdrawal from Vietnam in 1975 which was chaotic enough after the NVA took over Saigon. The sole upside of this debacle is that the U.S. may think more than twice about even invading and trying to occupy another country again, assuming it even could afford such a move.

"Afghanistan exit is an absolute stain on perceptions of the U.S., worse even than the exit from Vietnam in 1975."Q: Do you think Afghanistan's neighbors can present an effective initiative to restore peace in the country?

A: Peace in Afghanistan is in my view entirely a function of whether the Taliban holds to its assertions that it is not the same Taliban of 20 years ago, that it will be or become inclusive, that it won't treat its subjects badly, that it will adopt the reforms it says it has internally and as well reaches out to neighbors or other Asian countries for assistance and relatively "normal" diplomatic relations. This of course remains to be seen. The adjustment to any new regime in-country is difficult, especially for Afghanistan's citizens, who eventually must be led in such a way that Afghanis ultimately welcome rule by natives and begin to feel like it is out from under the thumb of Americans and NATO oppression. But this can be helped by other countries. It has been suggested that the U.S. maintain its embassy in Kabul and offer assistance to the new government, with no strings attached. But it's anyone's guess whether the U.S. has the wisdom to accept all the changes. Spitefulness won't help anyone, not even the U.S. and its allies. Something like Astana could be a positive move.

Q: What are the implications of withdrawal from Afghanistan for U.S. Arab allies? Can they rely on America in times of crisis?

A: U.S. Arab allies are watching closely, as they must. Is the U.S. a reliable ally? Can it be trusted any longer? We know for one thing that the U.S. seems to want to shift its focus from the Mideast and West Asia to confront the rise of China and Chinese influence. There is reason to assume that the Belt and Road initiative to bind together West Asian countries and others in the region like Iran in mutual trade relations and more is probably in the offing. The U.S. has been trying for 20 years to preclude various accords suggested by China and its current Russian partners. Absent another war in Asia this is something that's likely to fail and this failure is a good thing for peace in the region. One may be able to view the U.S. exit as a critical turning point and the beginning of the end of the hegemonic Empire the U.S. has tried to build and maintain since the dissolution of the Soviet Union. The divide and conquer meme by the U.S. must be blocked finally at a time when the U.S. itself is in political and social disarray.

Q: Don't you predict a civil war in Afghanistan?

A: There is one notable pocket of objection and resistance to the Taliban in Afghanistan and maybe others of less importance. However, I do not expect a civil war. But this is contingent on the Taliban acting in such a way that it does not alienate Afghanis further as they adjust to the new government. And international assistance, too, is virtually required to help make sure civil war does not erupt. One thing seems certain: if conditions deteriorate badly, it is very unlikely the U.S. would attempt to re-invade and occupy Afghanistan again. The U.S. public, generally as much as it may condemn Biden for the exit and the horrific way it has been managed, will not support more American adventurism and imperialism especially there. Biden is in enough trouble as it is.

Q: What are the main misconceptions by American leaders?

A: American leaders have been stuffed with hubris and exceptionalism notions for far too long. Americans are waking up to the unsustainable aspects of it all, are tired of Neocon-inspired wars, and struggling enough with their own problems in a declining Imperium such as a weak economy, monetary malfeasance, inflation, Covid, rising poverty and other ills. The primary misconception is that the U.S. can solve problems and make the world a better place, but it cannot do this with military moves, and this has been proven especially of late. The U.S. has shot its wad and the only thing that can make a difference now is a strong humanitarian focus that is real and not a false one wrapped in military misadventures it really cannot afford any longer. Vast profits have been made for the wrong people for far too long, In Afghanistan, the U.S. did very little to improve conditions for Afghans. The infrastructure there remains mostly as it has been forever primitive, despite a two-decade-long occupation.

As the U.S. "empire" frays, there is Zubeidi and his colleagues
September 15, 2021

It has been reported that Zakaria Zubeidi, one of the four of six escapees from maximum security Gilboa Prison in the West Bank who was recaptured by Zionist thugs, has been admitted to an ICU at an Israeli hospital after repeated rounds of torture that included breaking one of his legs and then hanging him upside down by his broken leg, among other atrocities.

As for the two escapees who have not yet been recaptured, it has been suggested that one of them MAY have been able to cross into Lebanon, given some unconfirmed evidence that someone may have figured out a way to cross the border. But this may just be very wishful thinking.

It anyway goes almost without saying that the Apartheid state is the world's greatest sponsor of terrorism (not Iran or any other country), and this has often been the case ever since 1948 when Zionist terrorists perpetrated the notable massacre of hundreds of innocent Palestinian villagers at a place called Deir Yassin near Jerusalem in an effort to so frighten Palestinian natives that they would leave their homes and become refugees. 800,000 Palestinians did become refugees back in 1948 and many Palestinian villages and towns were emptied and then wiped from the maps of what became "Israel".

Zionist terrorism has been rampant ever since 1948 and one only has to look at what the IDF has done to Gaza repeatedly and many more Palestinians across the Middle East including more massacres such as at Sabra and Shatila refugee camps near Beirut and beyond. Not to mention the fact that some observers have been convinced that Zionists may have also been at bottom responsible for 9/11 in New York City even though it is clearer some Saudis were, and 14 of the aircraft hijackers who plowed into the World Trade Center were Saudi citizens.

Max Boot, an American Zionist Jew and commentator, and apologist claimed this week that the American "global war on terror" over the past 20 years has been a huge success. Why? Because he says, there has not been another 9/11 and that by one count a mere 107 people have been killed in jihadist attacks in the U.S. since September 11, 2001. And half of them are accounted for by carnage at a Florida nightclub. Boot has it all wrong.

Because the U.S. had enormous world sympathy after 9/11. (Boot adds that more Americans are dying of Covid 19 every two hours than died of alleged Islamic terrorism in the past 20 years.) The U.S. did not capitalize on the sympathy it had, but as everyone knows went on to launch or support various wars that have killed millions of people and destroyed any pretense the U.S. had as a fair arbiter of disputes anywhere. U.S. greed and war profiteering have been the norm ever since, and not one of the "wars" has been won, or won anything but the virtual bankruptcy of the U.S. financially and morally. Afghanistan is the current case in point. Are the chickens now coming home to roost? Some of them and many more to come back home in time. Boot among many others are nothing but shills for Zionists interests, suggesting that the decades-long U.S. fealty to the Apartheid state may well be the centerpiece of the ultimate downfall of the U.S.

The so-called "empire" affliction in the U.S. at least has been diminished this summer and at long last at least some in the current Biden Administration are waking up to the fact that "nation-building" by the U.S. anywhere is not a winning policy. Because, simply, the U.S. has been "nation-destroying" for decades reaching all the way back to the Vietnam War sparked by a false flag incident in the Gulf of Tonkin in the mid-1960s. Also, one could argue that the U.S. had long been even worse than the Apartheid state as the number one state sponsor of terrorism in the past 30 years, but on the other hand one has to dig deep and understand the deeper policies spawned by alleged U.S. allies like "Israel" that have led the U.S. by the nose to what some call "evil" foreign policies. The opportunity costs of the latter have been beyond enormous and increasingly reveal, even if too many Americans remain victims of propaganda of the sort that Max Boot has postured.

Iran and friends of Iran just need to wait a while for the day the U.S. currency implodes. At that time Allah only knows beforehand the troubles the U.S. will encounter affecting all Americans.

But back to Zakaria Zubeidi. One American Greta Berlin, who over a decade ago led with friends the "Free Gaza Movement" and literally broke the siege of Gaza briefly when she led a small boat that sailed into Gaza's harbor. She has offered up a short biography of Zubeidi and It's worth quoting:

Zakaria Muhammad 'Abdelrahman Zubeidi, 46, is the former Jenin chief of the Al-Aqsa Martyrs' Brigades and a "symbol of the Intifada". One of eight children, his father was prevented from teaching by the Israelis after he was arrested in the late 1960s for being a member of Fatah. He worked instead as a labourer in an Israeli iron foundry, did some private teaching on the side, and became a peace activist. The first Israeli Zubeidi had ever met was the soldier who came to take away his father away, leaving the mother to raise their children alone. In the late 1980s and early 1990s, during the First Intifada, Israeli human rights activist Arna Mer-Khamis opened a children's theater in Jenin, "Arna's House", to encourage understanding between Israelis and Palestinians. Dozens of Israeli volunteers ran the events, and Samira, believing that peace was possible, offered the top floor of the family house for rehearsals. Zubeidi, then aged 12, his older brother Daoud, and four other boys around the same age formed the core of the troupe. In 1989, at age 13, he was shot in the leg when he threw stones at Israeli soldiers. He was hospitalized for six months and underwent four operations, but was left permanently affected, with one leg shorter than the other and a noticeable limp. At age 14, he was arrested for the first time (again for throwing stones) and jailed for six months. At that time he had become the representative before the prison governor for the other child prisoners.

On his release, he dropped out of high school after one year. A year later, he was re-arrested for throwing Molotov cocktails and imprisoned for 4 and a half years. In prison, he learned Hebrew, and became politically active, joining Fatah. On his release following the 1993 Oslo Accords, he joined the Palestinian Authority's Palestinian Security Forces He became a sergeant, but left, disillusioned, after a year, complaining: "There were colleagues whom I had taught to read who were promoted to senior positions because of nepotism and corruption." He went to work illegally in Israel, and for two years earned a good living as a contractor for home renovations in Tel Aviv and Haifa. He was eventually arrested in Afula and, after being briefly imprisoned for working without a permit, deported back to Jenin. He became a truck driver, transporting flour and olive oil, but in September 2000 lost his job when the West Bank was sealed off due to the Second Intifada. On 3 March 2002, one month before the main assault on the refugee camp, his mother was killed during an Israeli raid into Jenin. She had taken refuge in a neighbor's home and was shot by an IDF sniper who targeted her as she stood near a window. She subsequently bled to death.

Zubeidi's brother Taha was also killed by soldiers shortly afterward. Aside from grieving for lost family members and friends, Zubeidi was greatly embittered by the fact that none of the Israelis who had accepted his mother's hospitality, and whom he had thought were his friends, tried to contact him. In a 2006 interview he stated angrily, "You took our house and our mother and you killed our brother. We gave you everything and what did we get in return? A bullet in my mother's chest. We opened our home and you demolished it. Every week, 20-30 Israelis would come there to do theatre. We fed them. And afterward, not one of them picked up the phone. That is when we saw the real face of the left in Israel." Losing hope in the Israeli peace camp, he joined the al-Aqsa Martyrs' Brigades, an armed wing of Fatah. Arna's son, Israeli actor Juliano Mer-Khamis, did return to Jenin in 2002 and looked for the boys who had been in the theater group. Zubeidi had turned to armed resistance, Daoud was sentenced to 16 years in prison for militant activities, and the other four were dead. In 2004, Mer-Khamis completed a documentary film about the group, Arna's Children. Israel tried to assassinate him four times.

In one such attempt in 2004, an Israeli police unit killed five other brigade members, including a 14-year-old boy, in a jeep carrying Zubeidi. On November 15, following Arafat's death, Israeli forces launched an incursion in Jenin to kill him, but he evaded them; in the raid, nine Palestinians were killed, including four civilians and his deputy, "Alaa". The raid uncovered an arms cache. Prior to these incidents, another attempt on his life had been made by a Palestinian; Zubeidi had his hands broken as a punishment. In September 2005 he declared that his group's cease-fire was at an end after Samer Saadi and two other militants were killed by Israeli forces in Jenin. Nevertheless, Zubeidi told a Swedish nurse, Jonatan Stanczak, that he wanted to re-establish his links with the Jewish peace movement. The way he spoke of Arna's project led Stanczak to contact Mer-Khamis and within six months they re-established the Freedom Theater in Jenin, which opened in February 2006. On July 6, 2006, the IDF attempted to capture Zubeidi at a funeral, but he escaped after an exchange of gunfire. He was on Israel's most-wanted list for some years until he handed over his guns to the Palestinian National Authority and accepted an Israeli amnesty. In mid-2007, he renounced militancy and committed himself to cultural resistance through theater. On July 15, 2007, the Office of the Israeli Prime Minister announced that Israel would include Zubeidi in an amnesty offered to militants of Fatah's al-Aqsa-Brigades.

In 2008, he was hired by Juliano Mer-Khamis (who was later murdered) as director of the Freedom Theatre in the Jenin refugee camp, where children could study theatre and experience the growing art and music culture surrounding the Palestine International Film festivals. On 28 December 2011, Israel rescinded Zubeidi's pardon. On 29 December 2011, Israel rescinded Zubeidi's pardon and Zubeidi stated to Ma'an News Agency that he had not violated any of the conditions of his amnesty. He was advised by PA security officials to turn himself in to Palestinian custody lest he be arrested by Israel's security forces. A week before Zubeidi was notified about the cancellation of his amnesty, his brother had been arrested by the PA. Zubeidi was then kept in detention without charge by the Palestinian Authority from May to October 2012. Zubeidi undertook to study for a master's degree from Birzeit University, where he was supervised by Abdel Rahim Al-Sheikh, Professor of Cultural Studies, with a thesis entitled The Dragon and the Hunter, that focused on the Palestinian experience of being pursued from 1968 to 2018.

On 27 February 2019, before he could complete his dissertation, Zubeidi was arrested again, on suspicion of having engaged in terrorist activities, and in May he was charged before an Israeli military court with carrying out at least two shooting attacks on civilian buses in the West Bank. Zakaria Zubeidi was at the Gilboa Prison since his arrest, and on September 6, 2021, he escaped from the Gilboa Prison in Israel's along with five other Palestinian prisoners. Five days later, on September 11, 2021, Zubeidi was caught near the Israeli village of Kfar Tavor. On September 12, 2021, Zubeidi was transferred from the site where he was being held unlawfully, to a medical center in Haifa for injuries sustained from torture and brutal beating by occupation forces.

It's not hard to say that Palestinians may be the bravest people in the world.

U.S. is stuck in post 9/11 power politics: analyst
October 18, 2021

American political analyst Martin Love says that the U.S. has been locked in the post 9/11 foreign policy. In contrast, Love says, China has preferred to focus on its economy and be away from wars.

"The U.S. literally seems stuck in foreign policies arising from 9/11 and some wise observers have claimed Biden has a complete lack of self-awareness that the world has moved on without the United States, which has been locked into a certain foreign policy mindset for two decades," Love tells the Tehran Times.

"Governments have been toppled by the U.S. and countries more or less destroyed and U.S. sanctions have taken a horrific toll, particularly in West Asia," the political analyst points out.

China has made every effort to improve its economy by establishing trade ties with Asian and African states. Some Arab states are also noticing that U.S. allies are turning to China as an alternative if Washington leave them alone in future crises.

"The Chinese have not started wars and patiently focused on their economy and relations, non-violent relations, with other countries. This path seems, in the long run, to ensure that China's influence in the Far East will grow on a net basis in coming years," Love notes.

Iran and the U.S. 2017 - 2023

Following is the text of the interview:

Q: Why doesn't the U.S. want to acknowledge China as a global power?

A: Since when has the U.S. acknowledged, much less cheered, the growing global position of any country that challenges U.S. primacy? This is the core of the problematic differences between China and the U.S. now.

Some have claimed the Chinese economy is currently bigger than the U.S. economy, and given Chinese efforts to garner allies across Asia and corral the region with economic agreements, especially through its "Belt and Road" initiatives, the U.S. sees China as a threat rather than any successful country that merits cooperation.

For a very long time, for one thing, the trade deficit with China has just expanded enormously, but this is not a fault of China. U.S. corporations offshored much of their manufacturing capacity to China and some other Asian countries over a period of three decades in the pursuit of profits through the use of relatively cheap Asian labor. The greed of U.S. corporations knows few bounds, and by most descriptions, the U.S. is in the grip of fascism and meanwhile most Americans are suffering economically while the top five percent of Americans are wallowing in untold wealth. China has also pulled back from helping support the U.S. It has sold billions of U.S. Treasury bonds and has pulled back from buying more. China may be in a position eventually to sink the dollar, too, as the world reserve currency. President Biden does recognize the problems. He has noted that U.S. infrastructure has fallen from the best in the world to the 13th. But just as importantly, he has said that America ranks

35th out of 37 major economies when it comes to investing in early childhood education and care and adds that the U.S. cannot be competitive in the 21st century if the country continues to slide. Thus he is trying to pass a bill amounting to at least $2 trillion to address the needs of average Americans but is getting stiff resistance from Republicans and even some Democrats in the U.S. Congress in part because this U.S. is sitting on almost $30 trillion in debt.

Q: Do you think U.S. allies in the Asia-Pacific region can help to curb China's influence?

A: The Biden Administration is trying hard to counter the Chinese in the Far East especially with military supports lately centered on Australia. As a result of these shenanigans, some allies, most notably France, have been angered by the U.S. deal with Australia to build non-nuclear submarines for Australia. In fact, there appears to be a growing distrust of the U.S. among many of its allies, or at least some questions about U.S. intentions.

The U.S. literally seems stuck in foreign policies arising from 9/11, and some wise observers have claimed Biden has a complete lack of self-awareness that the world has moved on without the United States, which has been locked into a certain foreign policy mindset for two decades. Governments have been toppled by the U.S. and countries more or less destroyed, and U.S. sanctions have taken a horrific toll, particularly in West Asia. Meanwhile, the Chinese have not started wars and patiently focused on its economy and relations, non-violent relations, with other countries. This path seems, in the long run, to ensure that China's influence in the Far East will grow on a net basis in coming years.

Q: How do you see Afghanistan's future after the U.S. withdrawal? Do you predict China will take the lead in Afghanistan's economic development?

A: China must and should take the lead in assisting beleaguered Afghanistan. Of course, Beijing worries about Islamic influence and unrest in western China. Helping the Afghans is critical not only for the success of the Belt and Road initiative but in helping China avoid a neighbor that could descend into anarchy, chaos and "terrorism".

The U.S. has made an utter mess in so many countries, and Afghanistan is a good example of that. It's unlikely the U.S. will be welcome in Afghanistan, but China may be especially if it does the right things to assist the country. The U.S. occupation of Afghanistan did very little for the country and its people and killed many thousands. This is why the Taliban won the war in large part. It's quite amazing, and the U.S. looks like a huge loser on many counts. The withdrawal debacle could well sink the Biden Presidency, but the gravest worry is that Trump, if he is not soon indicted and ultimately jailed, could come back to the White House in 2024. This is an indictment of many Americans' judgments!

Q: Do you expect any confrontation or exacerbation in the U.S.-China relations under Biden's presidency?

A: One could expect the U.S., given that the government now apparently sees China as its primary enemy of sorts, will not be constructive and exacerbate tensions if not start another war. But the latter would be insane, especially over Taiwan. There is great danger, not only for the U.S. and China but for the world.

Is the U.S. going to continue to insist on military hegemony worldwide and continue its bellicose postures? One problem is that the American economy has been so hollowed out that the Military-Industrial Complex almost has become the economy! If the U.S. begins to stress cooperation and recognize a multipolar world, then maybe humanity can be saved, and the environment, too, which has to be at the bottom the biggest problem facing humanity in the decades ahead. But the U.S. has been short on wisdom in Washington and big on arrogance and exceptionalism, and average Americans have long been afflicted by such.

Some observers have suggested that a sort of revolution COULD occur in the U.S. unless Washington and Wall Street wise up. Another related problem is that it seems the policymakers in Washington virtually demand that the U.S. create "enemies." Since the fall of the Soviet Union, the great unnecessary enemy has been some countries dominated by Muslims. This may be waning, and now China takes center stage, but China is no pushover. And one must not forget that the U.S. is virtually broke, and printing fiat dollars is undermining the monetary system.

Weep or not, America is beginning to hurt seriously October 24, 2021

In the U.S. there are signs of decadence almost everywhere nowadays. In the debasement of the dollar, in militarism, in the paucity of honesty and ethics, in mainstream media propaganda and even in educational standards and one could go on. The list unfolds like an ocean crossing tsunami.

Consider this, for example. Last August the Loudon County School board in the state of Virginia passed gender identity legislation to permit boys to use facilities for girls, and in fact a girl was raped in a bathroom as a result of this. If a boy identifies as a "girl" he can use the girls restroom in this county where the school board manages 94 public schools.

But of course the worst "policy" is giving a trillion dollars or so annually to the U.S. military at a time when the Biden gang asserts the U.S. is not currently and literally "at war" anywhere, having withdrawn from Afghanistan. Why? Decadence! At any rate the Tehran Times recently published an interview with an American analyst on some questions about China, and in light of that here's a further bit of information contrasting China and the U.S.

Laos was the most heavily bombed country in the world ever during the Vietnam War and that may still be the case now decades later. Laos is a very poor country that represents no threat to the U.S. And it certainly is no threat to China, which knows this and which has completed the construction of a high-speed railway in Laos for Laotians. No question that China is ascending across Asia, U.S. influence on the fast wane.

Can anyone of sound mind doubt that the U.S. eventually will get what it seems to deserve for the harm it has done worldwide as a crude and vicious military "empire"? Patience will prove it. The U.S. long ago tossed fair play, its cultural racism knows few bounds along with its arrogance and obtuseness, its environmental destruction is off the charts and support for Zionist Apartheid abroad and the lambent racism at home, especially by some GOP politicians, remains extant.

It feels like the U.S. may well experience a crescendo of consequences in the year ahead for bad policies abroad and at home over the past few decades, especially since 9/11. And few allies are going to weep about it if the dollar is further shunned and loses its reserve currency status, if the economy crumbles as it did in the crisis of 2008, if the various U.S. markets like stocks and bonds disintegrate and the wealth gap, the biggest ever in history in any country, expands further and more social chaos and division erupt.

Let what is happening, or going to happen in America, be a warning to other countries to avoid internal and external policies that at bottom harm their own citizens especially and even, ultimately, their elites in time. The great Arab scholar and social historian who lived in Muslim North Africa centuries ago, Ibn Khaldun, developed the concept of "asabiyya" which loosely means "group solidarity" as the key component of successful countries or political realms. When group solidarity begins to disintegrate, societies are weakened and eventually give way to challenges by stronger regimes which later, in turn, may fall apart, too, when they become corrupted.

This is exactly what the U.S. faces: a growing and intractable loss of social cohesion and national solidarity. Biden throwing fiat dollars conjured out of thin air in the trillions to the public is not going to heal this gaping wound, and efforts by Washington to use what amounts to fire hoses to douse the American citizens in propaganda about Iran or any other country is not going to work over the longer term. It's quite remarkable that even now some so-called political and thought "leaders" continue to assert absurd charges about Iranian intentions and deeds.

Even now, when an honest few Western journalists have clearly disproven that Iran's ally Assad in Syria used chemical weapons wantonly on its own citizens (who remain solidly behind Assad) as Syria emerges from a decade of destruction and death, the propagandists in Washington and some in the mainstream media continue to lie. The net result is that the American public has little clue what to think about many countries like Iran and Syria and dismay and ignorance prevail.

It's unlikely Iranians, beset by sanctions and threats from the Zionists and Washington and some other U.S. allies, are going to feel any sympathy for Americans whose unwise leaders have gotten the country on a downward trajectory, but Iranians should realize that the very policies that have damaged countries abroad have also damaged average Americans and they are marginally beginning to wake up to this fact. The faster this awakening expands, the faster things can improve worldwide.

A view from the peanut gallery in the U.S.

November 14, 2021

Few outside Iran's government probably know exactly what the country's leaders are primed to focus on around the alleged upcoming resumption of the JCPOA negotiations in

A VIEW FROM THE PEANUT GALLERY ...

Vienna. But a couple of smart commentators outside Iran in West Asia have claimed this past week that Iran will focus almost exclusively on trying to get the U.S. sanctions lifted so that it can again resume exporting oil widely.

At first glance, this suggests that Iran is not going to renegotiate the JCPOA, and this may be concerning but it's not – because the nuclear deal of 2015 which was adhered to faithfully by Iran was working until Donald Trump, completely captured by the Zionists, scuttled the deal in 2018 and the Europeans did nothing to try to work around the U.S. cancellation and the re-imposition of horrific sanctions.

Yes, the first order of business by Iran's leaders, and this is sensible, is correctly to insist on a return to the status quo prior to Trump's moronic and dangerous move. And demand that the resumption of the JCPOA cannot be canceled again by Biden or anyone else who becomes the U.S. president in 2024. The U.S. must show good faith and stick to it, and then, maybe, at the margin, some details of the deal might be modified in the future to satisfy the hardliners in Washington. Biden may or may not be keen enough to do what he should and what the world wants to see, but there are some pressures on him to do the right thing.

Consider for example the matter of rampant inflation in the U.S. and the West. It looks like a redux of the late 1970s, and oil prices could well get out of hand if they have not already and such prices ARE huge factors boosting inflationary forces. Saudi Arabia, for one, has not at Biden's request opened the oil spigot to lower prices to benefit the U.S. and tamp down inflation. The Saudis and its "allies" along the Persian Gulf are hurting these days especially so because they are close to losing the war on Yemen and it appears the Houthis are close to capturing the oil rich and strategic area around Marib. The Saudis have allegedly already spent some $300 billion or more on its war on Yemen and nothing has been gained. Indeed, if Ansarullah controls Marib, it could control all of Yemen and as well some of the most strategic waterways off its coasts.

As for the U.S., unlike around 1980 when Paul Volcker was Chairman of the Federal Reserve Bank, Washington literally cannot raise short term interest rates (Volcker raised them to just over 20 percent in 1980) because that would crash the entire economy and the capital markets and the U.S. debt load, approaching $30 trillion, would quickly reveal the U.S. to be utterly bankrupt and incapable of even paying interest expenses on its paper.

Meanwhile, the American public's perception of Biden's performance almost ensures he will not win a second term as President, and his VP Kamala Harris sports even worst popularity. She has the least popularity of ANY Vice President ever, and seems entirely incapable of doing an adequate job. The Democrats for now appear to be doomed not just in 2024 but next year when they could easily lose a slim majority in Congress. One litmus test was the Democratic loss of the election for the governor of Virginia earlier this autumn. The impending prospects of Democratic party losses ahead are frightening, not least because Trump, unless he is soon indicted for various crimes, could well run for POTUS. again in 2024 and too many Americans are just insane enough to give him a chance of winning the election.

It is no wonder Iran wants the U.S. to guarantee the perpetuity of a revived JCPOA no matter who gets in the White House in 2024.

Moreover, even while one hears that Apartheid Israel has ramped up military spending and alleged preparations for an attack on Iran's nuclear assets should the JCPOA not be revived as it had been (or maybe because it has been revived and the Zionists have always been against the nuclear deal), the U.S. to be clear is in no position to condone such an attack even while it could be dragged into yet another war in West Asia. If it comes to the latter, neither the U.S. nor the Israelis are likely to "win" a war on Iran. The collateral damage all across West Asia would be catastrophic for the U.S. at home and abroad and for the Israelis. As long said, Iran can easily become THE disastrous donnybrook of both countries and their allies.

One has to be impressed by what Iran did in attacking the U.S. air base in Iraq after Qassim Soleimani's assassination by Trump. There were pinpoint strikes on al-Asad air base with several missiles each carrying 1600 pounds of explosives. By some miracle or just careful calibration by Iran NO American troops died despite significant damage to the base. It was the biggest ballistic missile attack ever on the U.S. What the attack did was demonstrate Iran's military capabilities like nothing else ever has. A number of U.S. soldiers at the base suffered mental and some physical damage such as PTSD and oddly enough the U.S. has refused to give the soldiers U.S. "Purple Heart" awards to honor them for the "sacrifices" they suffered.

Biden, who has failed to follow through so far on many of his campaign promises to such a degree that many regular Democratic Party devotees are not keen on him, appears lost, incapable and perhaps doomed. Few Americans would applaud an attack on Iran by the U.S. or the Zionists. Empire of Chaos indeed.

IN TRUTH THE U.S HAS BECOME A WEAK AND THEREFORE DANGEROUS COUNTRY

December 5, 2021

Average Americans with any sense of what the U.S. government is doing, especially overseas, are generally horrified withal but have little found power to push change.

Take for example a recent assessment by the Pentagon of the validity of its force projections with some 800 military camps or bases across the globe. The Pentagon's conclusion this month is that it's all proper and sensible when it is clearly little but a gravy train for "defense" contractors to make bombs and other weapons and keep unemployment low in an economy that over the past 30 years has been severely hollowed out by the movements of industry to places like China and Southeast Asia. The "military industrial complex" has become all and more that Ike Eisenhower warned about in 1960 when he left the White House.

Take for example Biden's failures to enact a plethora of his campaign promises to aid the American people and also tamp down tensions with Russia and China and Iran in particular. And can anyone believe that an institute at Columbia University in New York recently issued a statement around the good chance that Biden may be too enfeebled to run again for the Presidency in 2024?

In truth the U.S has become ...

The Columbia University group opined that his Vice President Kamala Harris and the current Transportation Secretary Pete Buttigieg, formerly a not so great mayor of a mid-sized city in Indiana, would make a "strong ticket" on the Democratic Party side in 2024. Harris has the absolute worst ratings as a VP, some 25 percent approval, than anyone ever has. Buttigieg is literally a bizarre non-entity in Biden's cabinet who has little to none real experience on any topic of concern for anyone in any kind of power position in Washington.

It beggars belief that anyone hoping for a Democrat in the White House after the next election could stomach such a ticket. It's virtually assured to hand the Presidency back to the GOP and just maybe Donald Trump, who has not been indicted yet for ostensibly sparking the insurrection around the Capitol last January 6th, a day that will be remembered in infamy forever along with other Trumpian malfeasance.

The GOP and with Trump in the White House made horrific mistakes, the prime one being demolishing the JCPOA in 2018. A move which has recently been slammed as the absolute worst U.S. foreign policy error this century, right up there with Baby Bush's war on Iraq that commenced in 2003. And one must KNOW it was a huge error because even some Zionist Apartheid entity leaders have slammed Trump's and Pompeo's move in collusion with Bibi Natanyahu.

And even if one is not privy to the finer details of the current JCPOA negotiations underway in Vienna, a good many average Americans WANT the negotiations to succeed and this reportedly includes a majority of Jewish voters in the U.S. who are at the margin at least becoming dismayed and disgusted with the human rights abuses by the Israeli Zionists and the refusal of Washington so far to mount any kinds of effective objections to what's going on in the West Bank and Gaza. It's only fair that Iran's forty odd negotiators in Vienna are demanding (and focusing on) the lifting of sanctions the Trump gangsters imposed on Iran and also on firm assurances that IF the JCPOA is revived and there is a GOP White House in 2024, which is now more likely than not, that no one can re-do what Trump did in 2018 by essentially destroying what was the finest diplomatic achievement the U.S. has helped engineer in decades with its deal partners in Europe and including Russia.

Moreover, Biden of late has been trying to assert U.S. dominance not with any kind of goodwill and detente but by threatening both Russia around the Ukraine mess and China over Taiwan and its clear, general successes in challenging the U.S. on the economic front over the past couple of decades. It's no secret that matters have become so fraught with peril this autumn that an error on either side of the divisions could degenerate into a nuclear exchange.

As a now retired former CIA employee, Philip Giraldi, who is notable for his journalism and commentary and who visited Iran as a guest a few years ago says so well: "All this saber-rattling is despicable. Neither Russia nor Iran threaten the U.S. and there is no reason why the U.S. should be eager to defend Taiwan or Ukraine (and also Israel). China's military budget is miniscule compared to the U.S. and the only real threat it represents is as a competitor on world markets, where it is already dominant in a number of key sectors. The U.S. has to get off this global dominance militarism wagon but how do we do it when both major parties embrace it."

The truth is that the U.S. has become a WEAK country since it started so many unwinnable wars since the 1960s. It survives more or less in a cloud of desperation in Washington and mounting failures around its weakness, and so far its sole recourse has been militarism, as if that would revive U.S. standing and prospects. What would really stem the decline is peacemaking, but creative minds in leadership roles have been drunk on power and bullying.

S. Arabia and Israel becoming world pariahs: analyst Jan 28, 2022

American political analyst Martin Love believes that Washington has failed in West Asia and its allies are becoming world pariahs.

"The overall problem for the U.S. is that it is witnessing the birth of a multipolar world and does not know how to adapt any longer, or easily, to not being the sole hegemon, and the use of military power has failed both in West Asia and Southeast Asia (since Vietnam) And its allies like Saudi Arabia and Israel are fast becoming world pariahs," Love tells the Tehran Times.

While the U.S. is striving to expand its influence in East Asia, Latin America as Washington's backyard is progressively emerging from years of U.S.-backed dictatorships and right-wing governments.

Elected governments in Latin America and West Asia tend to adopt independent policies rather than following America's dictates.

"Several countries in the U.S. 'backyard' continue to try to defy the U.S. Nicaragua, Venezuela, Cuba and maybe even Chile with its new government and even Bolivia," Love argues.

Following is the text of the interview:

Q: How do you see U.S.-Russia's recent escalation over Ukraine?

A: Russia is not in fact "escalating" much except moving a lot of troops near Ukraine but still on Russian soil, but the U.S. and minions want to think it is escalating to justify sending arms to Ukraine and maybe 8500 troops to eastern Europe and thus raising alarms.

Whatever, it's a big distraction created entirely by the U.S., and daft Biden even allegedly threatened nuclear war, which I don't think has been done before since the Cuban Missile Crisis.

"Iran, China and Russia are continuing to develop and shore up their alliances in every respect at the same time that the U.S. begins to lose critical support in Europe for its postures." The escalation seems entirely on the U.S. side unless one believes Russia moving troops around on its own territory near or at the Ukraine border is any kind of real escalation. Sure, it may look like preparations for an invasion of some kind but it's hard to believe Russia would invade Ukraine over eastern Ukraine and its mostly Russian-speaking civilians whom the Russians do want to protect from attacks by Ukrainian forces. Rumors regarding Russian intentions, most of them anyway, are probably false. To demonstrate how bizarre Biden is: in a news conference Biden heard a question by a reporter asking about rampant inflation in the U.S., a concern for every American, and was heard commenting via a hot mic that the reporter was a "stupid son of a bitch". Rumors are all over the map over Russian intentions. One has it that Putin wants to replace the government in Kiev with one friendly to Russia. However such may be welcomed by Putin, the Ukraine government is a mess, as is Ukraine, and it is doing a good enough job harming itself. But it's hard to imagine Putin would take the bait and launch an invasion, as ever, the U.S. is desperately trying to stir up trouble. Biden was a leader promoting the coup as Vice President under Obama years ago.

Q: Do you predict NATO will surrender to Russia or it is going to surround it?

A: It depends on what is meant by "surrender" to Russia. Russia has not yet DONE anything that must be surrendered to. But in any case, if Russia invades Ukraine or crosses the border, it is going to be met with draconian sanctions and perhaps outright war, which will be a disaster for the U.S., for Ukraine, and for Europe. And perhaps for Russia also. Russians cannot forget what happened in Afghanistan years ago.

Q: What would be the U.S.'s reaction if another power tries to enter into its backyard or its sphere of influence?

A: Several countries in the U.S. "backyard" continue to try to defy the U.S. Nicaragua, Venezuela, Cuba, and maybe even now Chile with its new government and even Bolivia.

They all are tired of U.S. diktat over decades and just want to be left alone to develop as they see fit without the usual U.S. interference. There has been talk about Russia and China establishing a presence in Venezuela, assisting Cuba, extending the Belt and Road initiative of economic support to South and Central America. Moves by Russia and China to expand their spheres of influence may well occur or be occurring, but to be clear, it seems unlikely the U.S. can do much about this and are not going to invade Cuba or Venezuela one must presume. The U.S. does NOT itself have the power or influence it once had in its "backyard". But the overall problem for the U.S. is that it is witnessing the birth of a multipolar world and does not know how to adapt any longer, or easily, to not being the sole hegemon, and the use of military power has failed both in West Asia and Southeast Asia (since Vietnam). And its allies like Saudi Arabia and Israel are fast becoming world pariahs.

Q: Why is the U.S. insisting on entering other powers' spheres of influence like what we see in escalation with Russia over Ukraine and China over Taiwan?

A: The "why" is obvious. The U.S. cannot fathom losing its perch as the unipolar behemoth. It is scared and seems to lack the creative thinking necessary to maintain the degree of influence it has enjoyed since World War II. A frightened U.S. blusters and threatens, as it always has for decades, but extant military power isn't the key to maintaining real leadership across the globe especially at a time when the world is suffering a pandemic and its own economy and monetary system and the dollar are closer than ever to implosion. Some history is important: Germany and Russia built a gas pipeline that if it ever becomes operational it stands to benefit all of Europe. But then along comes the U.S. with its Empire in decline with interference and it tells Europe what it should do or not and Europe said until very recently "Okay". Now we witness Germany but also France and Italy balking at the U.S. demands which suggest U.S. arrogance, hubris and even incompetence to some European leaders. A former CIA employee who used to brief Presidents, Ray McGovern, has provided his own view, too, that "Godot (from Harold Pinter's play of long ago) is likely to arrive before Russia invades Ukraine!" Europe, in any event, seems to be wising up to a dangerous U.S. and the U.S. Secretary of State, Tony Blinken, seems well out of his depth and facing some rejection.

Q: How do you read new moves of Iran, China and Russia in inking strategic partnerships and exercising joint military exercises? Are they a reaction to U.S. interventionist policies?

A: Iran, China, and Russia are continuing to develop and shore up their alliances in every respect at the same time that the U.S. begins to lose critical support in Europe for its postures. Raisi had a very successful recent visit to Russia. Raisi told the Russians that Iran has been resisting the U.S. for over 40 years, and he was apparently well-received. Meanwhile, the U.S. has so far failed to give Iran guarantees over the JCPOA's sustainability. Part of the problem is that President Biden is casting about in all the wrong ways to regenerate support at home, where his approval rating is only about 30 percent, and also abroad. Iran definitely seems to be on the right track, looking East, and China, Russia and They are developing a new bank clearing network to compete with the SWIFT system and has potential member nations of the Shanghai Cooperation Organization and the Eurasian Economic Union on board with the idea. So far Biden's major threat is cutting Russia off from SWIFT, but some Europeans are aghast at the idea and know quite well that such a move would well sink Europe's and especially Germany's economy and as well ultimately harm the U.S. In sum, it's sad Biden never carried through on most of his campaign promises, even on the war on Yemen. His Presidency smells of utter failure after a year in the White House.

The U.S., aside from criminality, must be simply jealous of Russia

July 16, 2022

Sitting smack in the middle of the proverbial "middle America" one can only wonder what's ahead, and it looks no good.

The problems are legion: Joe Biden is grossly senile. He has headed to Palestine and Saudi Arabia to suck up to Muhammad bin Salman and to the ever-changing Zionist government. He wants more oil, he wants to steer MBS away from China, he wants to applaud and shore up the so-called "Abraham Accords" and he wants the Saudis to initiate formal ties with the Zionist Apartheid state. If MBS has any sense he won't agree. Moreover, it appears Biden will let the JCPOA fall by the wayside and not be revived, all at the behest of the Zionists, even while many countries are eager to see the JCPOA revival including European countries.

Worse is the Ukraine situation. It's fair to say, on the one hand, Putin should not have invaded Ukraine even though, as experts claim, he was mightily provoked by the U.S. last winter. The leading political science mind in the U.S., John

The U.S., aside from criminality, must ...

Mearsheimer at the University of Chicago, has often stated flatly and convincingly that the U.S. sparked the war in Ukraine, not the Russians. Yet the Russians fell into a trap BY invading: handing Europe and NATO minions full subservience to the U.S.

Meanwhile, the Biden Administration is utterly pleased about the war, and so is the Military Industrial Complex and the Pentagon inside the U.S. Many billions in weaponry and other support have been given to Zelensky. It's a proxy war that is verging on becoming a possible world war that could become nuclear. To say this is frightful has to be the understatement of this century so far.

Perhaps the only way out of this mess is for Europeans to revolt because they are beginning to suffer from high energy costs amid burgeoning paucity. There already exists social unrest in Italy, the Netherlands, Albania and elsewhere and by winter it's likely to be a huge factor that could destroy the EU as well as NATO IF a wider war does not unfold. It would be good to see the U.S. public begin to revolt, too. A poll last week of Americans suggested that only 10 percent of Americans think the U.S. is on the right track. And Biden's "approval" rating is a very weak 30 percent.

One thing seems assured: Biden won't be reelected in 2024, and both houses of the U.S. Congress will go to the Republicans this coming November. Especially as more lives are lost in Ukraine and Putin "wins" the war and Europe and maybe even the U.S.U collapses in some fundamental way. Frankly, it's hard to know who has been a worse President, Biden or Trump.

On the other hand, if one listens to some leaders in the EU (who seem to have betrayed their citizens with gobs of propaganda) have convinced too many so far in Europe that Putin is an imperialist and a monster, that he wants to recreate Russia's role as a super state, that he has designs on far more than eastern Ukraine. This perception is false however easily it is created in the public mind. Putin would never have invaded Ukraine, real experts claim, if the government in Kiev had supported the Minsk Accords giving the Russian speakers in Ukraine's east some autonomy, and also stopped Kiev's bombing and shelling that has murdered some 14,000 Ukrainian citizens since 2015 until the war began last winter. As well, Zelensky would have to have stated clearly that he had no desire for Ukraine to become a member of NATO. It does seem that much of what is happening in Ukraine since February has long been planned by the Neocons in the U.S. as the best outcome they could imagine in their attempt to destroy Russia as any kind of serious geopolitical competitor to the U.S. One may also opine that what motivates the U.S., aside from the drive to maintain world hegemony with its "allies", the worst of which has to be "Israel", is pure jealousy! Russia is a vast country with a surfeit of resources of all kinds that the U.S. would love to control. The U.S. dream is the "Balkanize" Russia and then more or less rape it. And many thousands of Ukrainians are paying the price as either dead or as refugees.

No one ever said getting to a multipolar world would be easy, but it appears to be ahead eventually. And there are some positive notes. The expansion of the "BRICS" countries to include new members, growing hatred of the U.S. worldwide, or at least outside the West, and China's continued ascension economically and politically. But above all a World War 3 must be avoided in this transition.

Maybe, just maybe, real change can happen

August 2, 2022

There seems little to cheer about in the U.S. and with its "allies" currently:

Climate control seems like it will not happen because maybe it can't happen and won't until it's far too late. Consider that the corrupted World Economic Forum has asserted that the personal ownership of automobiles must be curtailed radically or halted completely. What? The U.S., to cite one country, is entirely dependent on the automobile.

Its public transport is ancient, long neglected by government: so much spending on unnecessary warmongering during and since the Vietnam War that the U.S. is broke financially, its monetary system on the brink of collapse, its debt in the stratosphere…and still the U.S. government is prancing about as if it still owns the world and can do no wrong when the wrongs have been off the charts far too often.

Wars, often promoted by the U.S., have been springing up large or small. Ukraine is just one example and that's because the U.S. wants to break Russia and control its resources, or steal them, as it has already in other countries like Libya, Syria, Iraq, etc. The U.S. in its entire existence has only been at full peace for about 20 years: former President Jimmy Carter had said the U.S. is the most warlike country in world history.

Iran and the U.S. 2017 - 2023

The great intellectual Noam Chomsky has recently claimed that the U.S. mainstream media has during this century become more suppressive and repressive of "free speech" in the media than the Soviet Union was after the Stalin era. The net result of this? Honest journalists have been disappeared from the broadcast and print media in the U.S., with a few rare exceptions that almost no one gets to read and even know exist. The best U.S. journalists might be found on new outlets like Russia Today, though that can no longer be seen in the U.S., or even in al-Jazeera or in the Tehran Times for English readers. And 90 percent or more of U.S. citizens are woefully uninformed about what's really happening and why in a world that seems to be coming apart at the seams, even if or because many U.S. adults can no barely read English beyond a fifth-grade level.

U.S. allies, including countries in the EU, are some of the most debauched, detached, sorry "allies" anyone could conceive or even want to have. Saudi Arabia under the butcher MBS, who was shunned as a "little Saddam" by his classmates as a youth and often banned from the playing fields by his young peers in Saudi Arabia and was hardly seen as the future leader there. How in Allah's name did he come to govern Saudi Arabia as a dictator? That's a question for the ages. Indeed, it appears that in a number of countries or a collection of countries the worst faux leaders seem to rise to the top. Boris Johnson and now Liz Truss? Ursula von der Leyen? Vladimir Zelensky? And others. It's well-nigh unbelievable, but true, that these and others are corrupted leaders, vassals of the U.S. for the most part, not serving their respective people.

And then for now, there is the U.S. since 2000, but especially since 2016. George Bush? Even Barack Obama who started well but lost his mind six months after his inauguration and

Maybe, just maybe, real change can ...

his Cairo speech, quite likely under threat. Trump, who killed the JCPOA and gave the Zionists carte blanche, and who has lived a debauched life since his youth? Did Obama remember what happened to JFK in the early 1960s? Kennedy threatened to disband the CIA and even had second thoughts about the Vietnam War in its infancy, which in ignominy his successor, Lyndon Johnson, took beyond the moon, which effectively began to bankrupt the U.S. slowly. By 1971 his successor. Richard Nixon took the U.S. dollar off of the gold standard, debauching the dollar ever since as a store of real value by slow, and now ever faster degrees.

And now Israel, the U.S.'s number one alleged "ally" in Asia, is taking ethnic cleansing, land theft and murderous violence in Palestine to obscene heights, not to mention roiling the Arab/Muslim dominated world and especially Iran with threats of more violence even of the nuclear kind along with sanctions. What Arabs support Israel at all these days, or have ever? Not most regular, Arab citizens under the heels of filthy rich dictators as in the Persian Gulf area. Egypt is not much better under Sisi.

But this writer is merely pointed out a few of the most abusive negatives. What's the good news, if there is any?

A multipolar world is being painfully born. The U.S. is slowly losing its world hegemony and trying desperately in all the wrong ways to maintain it, further discrediting itself across the globe. Informed people in the U.S. see this. Joe Biden for example has the lowest approval rating of any President to date: a mere 38 percent of the population apparently. The possibly ascendent GOP is racist and fascist at its core for now. A third political party is being born at the margin inside the U.S..

Thus the entire world suffers but dreams of real change. The EU and even NATO could dissolve in this decade. EU countries have dispensed with sovereignty as mere vassals to U.S. demands. Europe has been taken down the primrose path by the U.S. but revolutions may be brewing there. And no one wins if the U.S. launches World War 3. Not even the U.S..

U.S. objections to anything in Iran are at bottom selectively hypocritical

September 18, 2022

Jake Sullivan, Joe Biden's so-called "National Security Advisor" is no unblemished government official. Merely spouting and supporting Biden's insane and misguided foreign policies across the board is bad enough. But still, he may have a point in condemning the untimely demise of Mahsa Amini, 22, an Iranian who allegedly was harmed by Iran's police when she was taken into custody for allegedly not wearing a proper hijab or maybe none at all.

Sullivan has called for an investigation of her demise. Yes, an investigation is proper, so nothing like her death happens again, although, admittedly, few, for now, know exactly what happened, and it's not impossible that the police did her no direct harm. But isn't it a reasonable thing to find out?

Yes, Sullivan, like most every functionary in the U.S. government nowadays, is a hypocritical monster. Why hasn't he and Biden, for example, absolutely demanded or instituted a formal investigation of journalist Sherrine Abu Akleh's murder by a Zionist sniper in Jenin in the West Bank last Spring? And she also happens to be an American citizen! So, on this basis alone, Sullivan, trying to score "brownie points" against Iran by bringing up the death of Mahsa Amini, is, by the contrast of only modest and maybe questionable merit by him at least. But not entirely so. Because if she was, as alleged by some, "beaten" by police, those who did the alleged deed ought to be held to account.

No young woman or girl should ever die for an improper dress if that's what actually happened. Just as no American should ever be beaten or killed by police in the U.S., as many innocents have been, and many of them who were murdered by police did not directly threaten anyone. In the U.S., this happens frequently, and once in a while, police perps are made accountable for such, but for sure, not often enough. And this matter in Iran hits on a personal level, too.

Personal because for years, I have been close friends with an internationally notable and widely respected and awarded Iranian journalist-photographer who, I hear now, simply wants to abandon her country when her country literally needs to retain talented artists and citizens like she had been. This incident involving Mahsa Amini has cemented her wish to leave Iran. And no question, there are many sages and talented Americans who want to get out of the U.S., too, for reasons of misguided government policies and repressions, including the repression of "free speech" in the U.S. that has long claimed to support it but no longer seriously does as once it did. Julian Assange's incarceration and possible extradition to the U.S. for accurate reporting is a case in point. (And the same can currently be said for the recent demise of "free speech" in Europe, too, especially over the matter of Ukraine and U.S. sanctions on Russia and any other country that objects to U.S. policies overseas.) Is the entire world turning into a totalitarian, fascist, global monster?

Islam, since its inception by Allah through the Prophet Muhammad in the 7th century in Arabia has always promoted a code of modesty for all people regardless of sex, and the hijab for females, as in Iran, can be described as just one of many possible outer manifestations of a person's inner commitment to worship Allah. And there is no question that a majority of Muslim females wear the hijab with pride in predominantly Muslim countries and often in the West, too. (I once had an adult Iranian student in a college class in 2000 who explained this perfectly well to me, and she made a lot of sense aside from being a top student.)

In fact, since the arrival of Covid 19 in 2020, I have often worn a mask in public locations to avoid catching the disease, even though I have been aware that it may not obviate illness. Nowadays, in public places like a high-end food store in North Carolina where I work eight hours every week, I have lately noted that maybe 35 percent so of customers wear a surgical mask. It's no longer required. But what have I learned about wearing a mask often in public: I like it! It's no burden at all. In fact, it affords a kind of personal privacy that can be compelling and pleasant. If I were a Muslim female, I could easily imagine wearing a hijab in public would likewise give me the same kind of modest, simple, and personal privacy.

The sole thing that may be "wrong" with the hijab in Iran or any other largely Muslim realm, instituted to one degree or another for many centuries in various locations as a way to demonstrate modesty in public as properly suggested by Islam, is the degree to which common "authorities", police or otherwise, in Iran or anywhere else may literally, and sometimes even harshly, punish females (or even males by grossly immodest behaviors such as nudity) who don't show basic respect to the Islamic concept of personal modesty and respect before Allah and to society at large. One could argue that the best way to deal with females in Iran who may be seen in public with no or an improper hijab is simply to have a conversation with them about their immediate motivations to discern what they are thinking and why, and at worse or at most, perhaps fine them very modestly, as if they had run a red light at an intersection?

In fact, given the moronic, hypocritical reactions people like Jake Sullivan, along with the organs of propaganda in the U.S., can demonstrate by throwing a blanket of condemnation over Iran or Islam, it's best that ANY Muslim country try to avoid feeding the propagandists in the U.S. government and its captured media. (And look at Saudi Arabia, a U.S. "ally", where females (and males) are treated far, far worse than in Iran and in most every other country on earth and given long prison terms even for Tweets critical of the regime and some of its policies. Does the U.S. object to such madness in Saudi Arabia? Sadly, no. Does it object to a cowardly Apartheid regime in Palestine where half or more of the entire population west of the Jordan River has no human rights at all? No.

Iran, it may be said, may sometimes appear to make too much of enforcing the hijab mandate, but frankly, this is no business of non-Iranians. Every deep culture has its own particular nuances and interpretations of decorum and expectations of citizens, and they should, in general be respected as part of a world that IS happily diverse and variegated. Critique ought to be solely reserved for the degree of harshness applied to enforcement, especially when such involves anything like hijab or dress code where there is no objective harm done by a female who may sometimes chafe at it, as in the possible case of deceased Mahsa Amini.

And the U.S. public, in any event, mirroring Washington's hypocrisy and warmongering and worldwide cruelty, has been losing many semblances of decorum and modesty and self-reflection as "leaders" march the U.S. towards almost inevitable societal and political disintegration.

Retribution is coming

December 2, 2022

Enlightened Americans were sad to see the Iranian soccer team underdogs 1 to the U.S. team. (For too long, since the ouster of Mossadegh by the CIA and the Brits in the early 1950s, the U.S. has maligned and tried to control Iran.) Sportsmanship seemed to have prevailed at the end of the match, however, with some of the opposed team members giving hugs to each other. That single goal made by the U.S. was an instance of luck even though the Iranians did not mount a particularly notable offense. But who is really losing this year and going forward: The West and particularly the United States. As an American, it may be hard to say it, but it's deserved.

Only after the U.S. losses are more of less completed and recognized will it be possible to empathize some with the

Retribution is coming December 2, 2022 …

U.S. or at least those Americans who long have warned that America has for decades been on the wrong track overseas and even often enough at home with the lack of real and beneficial leadership in Washington.

It's anyway closing in on payback time some might say for centuries of Western arrogance. But particularly for U.S arrogance since the 1960s and the Vietnam War. One can cast back to the failures of the U.S there and later in Afghanistan, Iraq and Syria especially. Even in Venezuela where sanctions have impoverished millions. Now, the U.S. is begging Venezuela to restart its oil industry and the puppet Guaido and his faux "government" in exile is all but dead. But failure in Ukraine is front and center now. The U.S. government, essentially taken over by Zionist-leaning Neocons and other ideologues in terms of policy, especially in the last three decades since the fall of the Soviet Union, have been utterly deluded to think they could get away with the chaos they have fomented. The best, clearest minds have seen it coming: retribution. And that has hardly just begun is this amazing year of 2022.

The Russians saw the potential for the current war's outbreak a decade ago and had been preparing for it. The stupidity of the U.S. to reject its promise to Russia NOT to expand NATO eastwards made this war inevitable. Financing what amounts to a Nazi regime in Ukraine with a paid-off clown, Zelensky, made it inevitable. The war could end in a few months, or it could drag on for another year or three in some fashion, but at what cost? The utter destruction of Ukraine as any kind of viable nation, handed off piecemeal to the proper Ukrainian patriots, not Nazis, in the Donbass, or to Poland and Moldova, etc.? (Of course, the ultimate cost could be the U.S. in desperation using nuclear weapons to have its way attempting to maintain a hegemony that for now is fading very fast.) And the arrogance does not stop: the U.S. and Israel conducting mock attacks just recently over the Mediterranean as if to destroy Iran's nuclear research industry? It's been reported that in Ukraine an electrician in Kiev rightly declared the war "horrible" and that it's only going to get worse unless the politicians from the Parliament in Kiev are lined up and shot. And more and more Ukrainians are allegedly claiming very quietly that a popular revolt there is necessary to stop the carnage.

But an even bigger problem looming for the U.S. is the potential loss of favor inside Europe. The protests across Europe against Russian sanctions and enabling to war to continue go largely unreported in the U.S. and Western media. One could almost predict the ultimate demise of the EU and NATO. People like Ursula Von Der Leyen, incredibly, see the destruction of the Nordstream gas pipelines as a GIFT to Germany while its economy goes belly up and bankruptcy and de-industrialization becomes the norm and meanwhile the U.S. rakes in huge profits selling high priced LNG and as well benefits from any relocation of German companies to the U.S. Already there are objections in Europe to the U.S. profiteering.

But the U.S. has virtually lost its unipolarity already. The world is increasingly shunning the dollar for one thing. The Chinese along with its Russian allies are ascending, making deals right and left, and even cancelling the indebtedness of small countries like Rwanda or, in effect, making friends all across the global south. And, of course, the BRICs are in the process of eventually taking on new, eager members not only in Asia but in South America, too. Sometime in the next decade there will also likely be a new, common trade currency deployed by the expanded BRICs that will be backed by a lot more than hot air and mere paper that cannot be sanctioned or stolen.

The biggest fly in the ointment for the U.S. and for some of its allies like the UK, propelling decline as a microcosm for all that ails the West, however, has long been the support for the Apartheid entity in Palestine. Even today most Americans do not understand what Israel is: not a "democracy" but a murderous gaggle of colonizers for over 70 years who have been spoiled by Western largesse.

Many in the West still think Israel is still, if it ever was anything but a mistake, some sort of noble cause: "O, the poor Jews who suffered the Holocaust" … who are no longer poor at all and have the Western media and most politicians in their grip, they horrified at the thought that they might be called "antisemitic" if they so much as lift a finger to throttle back Zionist and Apartheid crimes. But now it appears the Israelis have gone too far in reelecting Netanyahu, who is trying to escape trial for corruption and who to get elected by the slimmest of margins had to align himself with the followers of Meir Kahane. When he was alive Kahane was declared in effect racist scum by the U.S. and shunned. His followers may even be worse. What's really surprising is that Israeli media and tourists at the World Cup in Qatar have expressed dismay that when they were identified as Israelis they were shunned and harangued by others at the football games. That was refreshing, and also refreshing that at least a couple members in the U.S. Congress are suggesting a cut off military aid to Israel.

Iran and the U.S. 2017 - 2023

Soleimani was a great man. Period.

January 3, 2023

As an elderly American now, I have witnessed the apparent decline of my country in most all respects (except perhaps in military power) in to what appears to be an insane number of wrong-way turns since I was a youth in in the 1960s. It was with the Vietnam War that the pretensions or fact of "Empire" really began to take hold.

That was a war based on a lie in the Gulf of Tonkin just as all the other aggressions have been based on lies, in particular the war on Iraq beginning in 2003, which was anathema to Soleimani and gave rise to all sorts of carnage in the Mideast and gave rise to ISIS.

The "Pax" part of any alleged "Pax Americana" may have been mostly evident for those actually living securely in the U.S., but rarely overseas, and like many Americans who still have a brain I have been appalled by the bellicose actions of my government. I was horrified by the murder of Qassem Soleimani three years ago no less even though I knew not much about this lionized Iranian leader — except that what I saw of this general in the news suggested that if a military man could ever at bottom be a "man of peace", Soleimani fit that description. He appeared extremely smart and extremely warm and charismatic to anyone who took a close look, and he was not afraid of calling out "wrong way" turns by the U.S. which, of course, made him seem an enemy of the deeply entrenched Washington establishment which has long been built around hostility to any country or person objecting to U.S. pretensions of a dominance that spurned fairness and justice and basic respect for other polities and cultures.

Interesting or not, it's worth mentioning that I remember exactly where I was when I heard that President John F. Kennedy had been assassinated —a teenager in a study hall in a boarding school in Connecticut that Kennedy had also attended as a youth. And now Joe Biden recently opened up files about the Kennedy assassination, but not all of them. ALL of them apparently suggested that the CIA may have had a hand in the murder because Kennedy was opposed to the burgeoning, then potential war on Vietnam unlike his vice President Lyndon Johnson, and Kennedy may have also believed the CIA ought to have been disbanded. Real truths have always been hard to ferret out because lies have often been deployed to underpin the so-called U.S. empire. Propaganda silencing dissent back in the 60s was as rampant then as it remains today. No doubt the official posture about General Soleimani as some sort of U.S. enemy who seriously threatened the U.S. was pure propaganda. The U.S. for example pretended to be an enemy of ISIS, an organization it originally may have helped create in Iraq and Syria in opposition to Assad's Syria especially, but who in fact was the real and effective enemy of the ISIS scourge? Soleimani, who largely more or less defeated most of ISIS power both in Iraq and Syria.

What's largely unknown to most Americans is that before the U.S. invasion of Iraq right after the attack on the World Trade Center in New York, Soleimani and Iran actually worked indirectly with the U.S. and helped the U.S. subdue the Taliban and al-Qaeda in Afghanistan, groups which also constituted a threat to Iran as its immediate neighbor. This was reported even by the Washington Post. One might be hard pressed not to expect the U.S. to go after al-Qaeda whose leader Osama bin Laden, a Saudi, was holed up in Afghanistan, but of course nothing was done against other perps in Saudi Arabia. The U.S. attacked and occupied Afghanistan at least on the presumption the Taliban was in cahoots with al-Qaeda, which allegedly knocked down the twin towers and set off the U.S. military rampages across West Asia. The U.S. had some justification perhaps to go after Osama bin Laden, and Iran and Soleimani did assist in some fashion.

Some have opined that the assassination of the great general in Baghdad was a gross reaction of revenge to the fact that Assad survived the bloody carnage in Syria and remains in control of much of the country, except in the east where the U.S. is still stealing Syria's oil and wheat and has impoverished the country at large with that theft and other sanctions. The Russians and Soleimani literally saved Assad's Syria, which before the war there, despite having the Golan stolen by the Zionists, had been a relatively peaceful, self-contained country and largely self-sufficient and relatively prosperous by Mideast standards since 1973.

And the U.S. revenge factor is now playing out in Ukraine where the U.S. undeniably provoked Russia to attack and has seen that, albeit proxy, war as a means to hobble Russia and Putin, perhaps in part because of Russia's assistance to Assad among other issues. Well, digging a bit deeper, what country has been behind the U.S. wars on Iraq and the war on Syria? Israel, it can be argued, has been the prime underlying cause of every U.S. hostility in West Asia against countries that rightfully deplore Zionist aggressions, especially in the West Bank and Gaza. It's a good thing the nascent Netanyahu government with racists Ben Gvir and Smotrich in high positions in the Apartheid state has come to power. It's so extremely racist and selfish that even some members in Congress are sounding alarms, as well as some Israelis as reported in Ha'eretz, Israel's sole newspaper with at least some credibility and wisdom. This new government may be in time the key that forces a tipping point where Washington will be obliged to reject so much support for the Zionists. One can imagine that if Soleimani were still alive he'd be especially appalled again by the Zionists but might have some scintilla of optimism that things will get so out of hand and craven in Israel that change will come in time. Meanwhile Biden has recently killed hopes that the JCPOA may be revived and sanctions on Iran lifted. Scuttling the JCPOA has long been encouraged by the Zionists, perhaps because they know if it were revived, Israel could not attack Iran. It's hard not to believe that especially in this century Israel is at bottom the causative factor in so much chaos and carnage in West Asia.

But in any case, Soleimani was a great leader and a man of such charisma that he will never be forgotten. He had a smile and a twinkle in his eyes like few others have ever had.

"The Die is Cast" for the U.S.

January 21, 2023

This past week for an evening in North Carolina I had the pleasure of speaking briefly with Medea Benjamin and hearing her opine about Ukraine to an audience at a local church. A petite, elegant, straight talking Jewish lady, now 70, who for decades has been at the forefront of trying to explain to far more "average" and largely perplexed American multitudes and the world at large just what the U.S. government has been doing — criminally — across the globe but especially in the Middle East with its war machine over and over again, especially in the last 30 or so years but beginning primarily elsewhere Vietnam in the 1960s and 70s.

In this century alone the U.S. has already spent and wasted over $8 trillion dollars on making wars, killed millions of innocent people, virtually bankrupted the Treasury and turned the U.S. financial system into the largest Ponzi scheme ever. This is evident where, like soon, the government must raise the debt ceiling, a much repeated action, yet again simply to pay off outstanding Treasury debt by issuing newly minted debt with printed "money". If ever a U.S. President was correct in warning about the future, Dwight Eisenhower was the man in 1960 when he left the White House saying that the Military Industrial Complex, back then not nearly as vast as it is today, could become a danger to America at the very least.

Medea Benjamin came to North Carolina for a day to speak factually about the proxy U.S. war on Ukraine. She explained exactly what has been happening, and why, and especially that the U.S. Neocons actually started planning this proxy war a decade or so ago when it became evident that Vladimir Putin was pulling Russia up by its bootstraps and reviving at least a shadow internally and economically of what Russia had been when the Soviet Union was strong enough to limit to some degree if not grossly challenge the U.S. as the world's dominant nation.

Benjamin's core message has always been the futility of U.S. wars except for a small minority of people in the military and in corporations that feed the monstrous military complex and get rich in the process. She was asked by one person in her audience whether one of the biggest reason the U.S. has embarked on so much militarism this century is because the U.S. economy over the last 30 years or so has become so relatively hollowed out and de-industrialized that in many respects the "economy" has simply become largely one of military activity and production of arms by companies like Raytheon, Boeing and Lockheed-Martin plus all the countless smaller firms whose only viable businesses have been to support militarism? Her answer to this was more or less in the affirmative. And it's worth remarking that one reason the U.S. economy has been failing slowly this century is because U.S. corporations offshored much of its former industrial might to other countries with far cheaper labor, especially China, which in just a few decades has created something like a billion-strong middle class of sorts out of poverty.

For those majority billions of people outside the West whose disgust with the U.S. has been rapidly ascending for years, they have witnessed a China that has done relative wonders for its citizens and others without policies that amount to gross parasitism (and the afflictions of violence and crushing sanctions and, yes, arrogance and outright theft) that by now have have isolated the U.S. like never before and created enmity for the U.S. It's a wonder Europe has not yet gone its independent way while the Bidenists have aimed to de-industrial Europe and make it more dependent on the U.S. But many Europeans are protesting except you don't hear or see much about that in the Western media.

All the obvious reams of propaganda springing forth from the mainstream U.S. media condemning other countries like China and Iran and Russia for an alleged total absence of "democracy" must be a sad joke to well over half the world's people. Because in fact the U.S. where criticism of Washington is widely manipulated and suppressed by the media, real "democracy" has become but a faint shadow of what existed 50 years ago in the U.S. when, for example, millions of people repeatedly protested (with eventual success) the madness of the Vietnam War and helped end it finally in 1975. Consider that arguably the finest economist in the U.S. and one if the country's best minds, one Jeffrey Sachs who taught at Harvard and now presides at Columbia University, has become vehemently opposed the the U.S. proxy war on Ukraine and as a result stated this month that he can no longer place an op-ed article in a major U.S. newspaper like the New York Times or Washington Post.

Now, those Americans whose eyes are wide open like Medea Benjamin's await sadly the dangerous denouement for decades of belligerent foreign policy: the further decline of U.S. economic and dollar dominance and financial bankruptcy that is now and is going to crush further most all Americans like never before. For the people of countries like Iran, who don't necessarily want any innocent people anywhere "crushed", there is at least the relatively pleasant prospect that with gathering inevitability the U.S. literally will be incapable of meddling and making or supporting wars that much longer. (It will have to start tending its own citizens more if it can.) As Julius Caesar exclaimed when he crossed the Rubicon and headed to Rome with a Roman Legion of soldiers under his command in 49 B.C.: "The die is cast"… in this current case, for a U.S. ultimately emasculated and on the ropes.

The extreme danger is that, in a fit of pique at evaporating fortunes, insane U.S. "leaders" in the government and the Pentagon will drag humanity into a third world war that will utterly dwarf the two in the last century and involve nuclear weapons.

No one anywhere with sensibility and some knowledge can possibly not be alarmed. And Biden's and his administration's insistence (and by many in the U.S Congress, too) on not negotiating an end to the proxy war on Russia in Ukraine is the certain spark. They believe a competitive Russia will be destroyed.

For honest and concerned souls like Medea Benjamin who with great courage have tried to educate average Americans, Zelensky's lionized recent visit to Washington, and the subsequent suggestion put forth to place a sculpted bust of Zelensky in the Capitol building as some sort of hero, has to be the apogee of Washington's blighted mentality.

Zelensky is just as responsible, if not more responsible, for the destruction in Ukraine and hundreds of thousands of slaughtered Ukrainians. He could have brought the war to a halt last Spring, but then he was swayed not to negotiate an end by former British PM Boris Johnson and others in the U.S. and the E.U.

Such ridiculous panic over a darn balloon!

February 8, 2023

A rather large Chinese weather balloon drifted over the U.S. this past week. The Chinese really had no control over where it would go exactly. It could as easily flown over southern Canada and wound up over Nova Scotia.

This drift is quite normal however novel the incident was because winds high aloft usually flow from west to east. Washington called the big white balloon a dastardly effort to spy on the U.S. by the Chinese. One might readily suppose it was spying on the weather over the U.S., hit in recent days by an Arctic mass of very cold air said to mimic the temperatures seen on the planet Mars, a planet by the way named after the "god" of war. But in any case, the U.S. government went into a panic as the balloon drifted south eastwards over my home state, North Carolina, and the military finally shot it down over the coastal Carolinas for Allah knows how much-wasted fiat dollars. If the U.S. had really thought the balloon was "spying" it would not have waited until it crossed over the entire U.S. before the U.S military destroyed it. The wait was an attempt to build a case against China and the result was actually damaging to the Biden Administration's reputation and credibility, presuming it had much of that left to expire.

One has to understand the U.S. is in very bad shape, like utterly paranoid, when a darn balloon creates panic and becomes a geopolitical incident seized upon by the government as a means to call the Chinese an evil (or whatever) threat to the U.S. It's all quite risible, a sign of the times when the world suffers at the hands of the warmongers in Washington.

But in fact the U.S. is not doing well. It's deluded "leaders" are acting like petulant, spoiled children not getting their way — which they have become so accustomed to for decades that it has created blindness.

Such ridiculous panic over a darn ...

The Russians, for one thing, are said by the best observers to be "winning" the proxy war in Ukraine. And if and when Russia launches any suspected big offensive against the Zelensky regime it may spell the end of the war. The important Rand "think tank" which the U.S. "deep state" relies on for support and direction like few others, and which initially pushed the proxy war strongly, issued a paper recently which essentially indicated that Russia was gaining control and that it was time for negotiations with the Putin government. This constitutes a 180 degree turn in orientation by the Rand "thinkers".

With very few clear minds running the U.S. and its war machine, there exists at the margin and even in the Pentagon a few relatively enlightened souls who see REALITY which the Neocons, long in control of U.S. foreign policies, abandoned for bloody fantasies of perennial world domination. And as well, there is chatter that the Biden gangsters could be aiming to abandon Clown-in-Chief Vladimir Zelensky and giving the nod to Valerii Zaluzhnyi, who's been commander of Ukraine's decimated military. Word is that Zaluzhnyi and Zalensky despise each other, each blaming the other for battlefield losses. This inward turning against itself and peers is quite common wherever and whenever a regime is losing its marbles...or a war it provoked. Zelensky has been called crazy or crazed by those who heard a recent speech he gave.

The Russians, in any event, are likely to laugh at any U.S. gestures towards formal fresh accords over Ukraine. Since when has the U.S. not torn up treaties and accords like the JCPOA? Most of the world no longer trusts the U.S. government.

But more importantly, there is evidence that some erstwhile vassals of the U.S. are losing the scales over their eyes and beginning to show some courage and say "NYET" to the bullying the U.S. has largely been about since the end of World War 2 but especially in this century. This is a drift, like that drifting Chinese "spy" balloon, that reminds of what the great novelist Ernest Hemingway wrote a hundred years ago about how any bankruptcy occurs: "Two ways. Gradually, then suddenly."

The sudden part of a U.S. bankruptcy of confidence among other countries may be about to occur. And it's beginning to dawn on others, too. Confidence is most of everything and once it has been lost, it's gone forever. Instilling confidence, even in micro situations like in rearing children, is the most important thing that can be done by parents to insure at least some success in life. Iranian government "confidence" may be evident of late given reports that on the 44th anniversary of the Islamic Republic's victory, Ayatollah Khamenei allegedly approved mass amnesty and commutation of sentences for detainees in the riots initiated by the death of Masha Amini and subsequently provoked by the U.S. and the MEK and others. On this matter of loss of confidence between nations one can cite recent comments:

— The Turkish Interior Minister Suleiman Soylu recently told the U.S. "get your dirty hands off of Turkey!" Clearly, Turkey, a member of NATO, is losing confidence in the U.S. and its diktats. Turkey may well think the vague threat of a color revolution is imminent. With better relations with Russia, energy and food security for Turkey could outweigh whatever benefits may be provided by Turkey's inclusion in NATO.

— The top Hungarian diplomat, Peter Szijjarto, recently asserted that U.S. hegemony over the world is dying: "That era is over. The U.S. ambassador's views on Hungary are irrelevant. Hungary is a sovereign country." He accused the U.S. of trying to interfere in Hungary's internal affairs, because Hungary is not cheerleading the proxy war mounted by the U.S. in Ukraine against Russia.

This above is just an indication of what is beginning: a kind of revolution against further U.S. bullying wherever. Consider that China has not dropped a bomb on ANY other country since it had a brief war with Vietnam north of Hanoi some 40 years ago, and the Chinese economy is going to surpass the U.S. economy in a few years if it has not already. But the U.S. has pummeled numerous countries with a total estimate of some 500,000 bombs in the past 30 or so years and killed an estimated 25 million civilians. And finally, most of the globe is voicing what it could only feel and keep silent about until recently: objections to the so-called "rules-based world order" where, in fact, there are NO rules of any merit except "do as the U.S. demands" or else the U.S. tries to overthrow the objecting governments. It's long been for the U.S.: "our way or the highway".

And this is a tragedy for the U.S., and especially for the American people who have seen the U.S. spend its treasure towards virtual bankruptcy. For example, all the Russians and Chinese have to do is declare the trade currency they are attempting to create will be resourced backed, even by gold, and the dollar, the lynchpin of U.S. dominance for almost 80 years, becomes instant toast.

Did Sy Hersh's journalism spark an alien invasion?

February 15, 2023

What's happening is full on desperation at the eventual loss one way or another of even the shadow of hegemony by the U.S., NATO, and its alleged Mideast ally, Israel. And the desperation is only making things far worse, and for the U.S. and NATO countries, too.

What's happening is full on desperation at the eventual loss one way or another of even the shadow of hegemony by the U.S., NATO and its alleged Mideast ally, Israel. And the desperation is only making things far worse, and for the U.S. and NATO countries, too.

Seymour Hersh's expose of who destroyed the Nordstream gas pipes in the Baltic Sea is another classic of his, as were his exposes of Abu Ghraib in Iraq and the My Lai massacre long ago in Vietnam to name just two others. And the mainstream U.S. media is ignoring the report of the best investigative journalist in the past 50 years who (aside from Julian Assange), and who since Abu Ghraib, cannot get published in the U.S. like at the New York Times or even the New Yorker magazine where he once worked.

The U.S. government since Hersh's report on "Sub stack" media has been trying to deflect attention by channeling it to three or four instances of balloons or other objects (an alien invasion, UFO's) borne on winds crossing over the U.S. as if such constituted any kind of real threat to the country.

Breaches of U.S. sovereignty by the Chinese who, if the Chinese launched the objects, are scary? No way, but the government would have Americans think so. Even suggesting UFO's are aloft! If spying, the Chinese don't critically need to send balloons or whatever. They have an estimated 300 spy satellites in space some of which can allegedly read the license plates of cars and may be capable of even listening to phone conversations in the Oval Office in the White House.

What is particularly surprising is that given the Hersh report on Nordstream's destruction by the U.S., the German government so far has said NOTHING. And the loss of gas from Russia, cheap gas, is wrecking the once great German economy as well as Europe's. Aside from a few very scattered voices in Germany marginally ready to slam the U.S. for what President Biden and his Neocon advisors in the White House and State Department reportedly did, the Germans are acting like a bunch of SHEEP over arguably the greatest act of industrial and ecological terrorism since World War 2.

And Joe Biden's randy dementia was clear when he stood before the American people and delivered a State of the Union Address that claimed things in the U.S were just dandy? They are not.

And then there is the matter of the massive earthquakes in Turkey and northwestern Syria. Maybe as many as 100,000 people will be found dead when all the rubble is cleared. Biden has been weak sending aid to Turkey, but nothing for Syria where the U.S. occupies a third of Syria in the east, and has been stealing some 66,000 barrels of oil per day and burning Syrian wheat and even bombing aid convoys from the east. The draconian sanctions just add more misery and Biden has refused to lift U.S. sanctions. This, frankly, is yet another U.S.

crime amid many others. And don't get me started about the Netanyahu crime syndicates in Israel who are going wild in a de facto annexation of the West Bank and bombing Gaza, too.

The Palestinians resistance fighters ought to cancel throwing rocks and shooting pistols at the marauding police and IDF soldiers in the West Bank who have been raiding refugee camps in places like Jenin and Jericho. Almost 50, a least, innocent Palestinians have been shot dead by armed forces and settlers, too, since the start of the year. And the Biden Administration has said nothing. What might be a better answer?

The Palestinians should be sent scores of well calibrated sniper rifles with fine scopes and silencers attached. They know where to hide in the warrens of the camps. The cowardly IDF would think twice about raids in the West Bank!

But what does all this add up to? The U.S. under Biden has gone berserk like never before if you exclude the Vietnam War under Lyndon Johnson, which finished Johnson's political career. Provoking the Russians to attack Ukraine and all kinds of support for corrupt Zelensky…eventually spells the final end of U.S. as any kind of "leader" and even NATO's, and all hegemonic pretensions…provided World War 3 does not erupt and a war turns nuclear. A U.S. president who brings the world so close the nuclear war for whatever reason is simply not fit to serve anywhere and deserves to stand before the ICC in The Hague.

Someday a Day of Reckoning for Cruelties

March 1, 2023

The Zionists think they are winning. They are not. They continue to push their violence in Palestine too far. They are despised worldwide. It's one thing to be an idiot, but quite another to be a violent idiot. I remember a morning well years ago.

I was headed to Tubas in the West Bank where I managed to stay a couple months, helping at a school funded by a rich American Palestinian entrepreneur and scientist who lived in North Carolina and who had set up a school in Tubas, his birthplace, for children. Getting there was a bit of a bitch. There was an IDF "checkpoint" just to the west of the Jordan Valley. A Palestinian cabbie from Ben Gurion took me that far one winter morning in 2006. The IDF held me there for a couple hours, wondering who I was and what doing. My ride the 15 or so more miles to Tubas was waiting up the road. He was the headmaster at the school, which by the way survived only 18 months.

Soldiers stood and ambled about. Some Palestinian laborers had been detained by the roadside where they were forced to squat in the dirt. I went up to one soldier and I asked him, having a hunch: "Where are you from?" His English was good. He answered: "Israel", as if I were stupid. "No," I pressed the guy, a corpulent Jew. "Where are you REALLY from?" He hesitated a bit and finally said: "Brooklyn." I simply told him I had lived and worked in New York, not wanting to stir up more trouble. I was interrogated about what I was doing and where wanting to go. I told the truth. I also told him my ride to Tubas was a hundred meters away and pointed him out.

I was delayed and searched for another hour or so, but finally the soldiers let me go to meet the school headmaster, a very kind elderly gentleman in a ragged overcoat with an ancient little car. I scanned the checkpoint scene more and then noticed the most important thing to see there at Hamra Checkpoint that winter morning. Up on a hill off the road stood a man dressed in civilian clothes, carrying a rifle and a handgun. He was observing the entire scene like a vulture. It at least felt like he was in charge, even of the soldiers, some 20 of them at Hamra Checkpoint. Like the soldiers would defer primarily to this man in civilian clothes with the weapons if it were demanded.

The IDF finally let me go to Tubas. The headmaster drove slowly away and soon we were climbing up out of the Jordan Valley and soon arrived at his home in Tubas where his wife fed me and let me sleep on a couch on his porch there.

But I learned something interesting that morning. The man on the hill beside the road was a Jewish "settler" in the West Bank from some foreign place, probably the U.S. I imagined. And a couple hours later I heard that the IDF had sent out a patrol to bring me back to Hamra Checkpoint and disallow my visit to Tubas. But by that time I was inside Tubas town and they could not find me. And for two months I was "safe" in and around Tubas and even managed three weeks later to visit the famous refugee camp in Jenin, courtesy of the Palestinian Red Crescent, where scores of fairly fresh graves had been dug, the result of a horrendous, infamous raid on the refugee camp by the IDF.

Someday a day of reckoning for ...

But I never forgot the civilian with the weapons on the hill, the apparent "settler", and it was not difficult to realize that the "settlers" generally constituted the absolute core of Israeli designs on the West Bank: to force Palestinians out by making their lives so miserable that maybe they would just leave their country and become refugees once again.

The settlers have been wilding this year like never before. Killing Palestinians and destroying their property and with absolute impunity and hand in hand with their IDF protection in the background. The best (or worst) recent example of this was a literal pogrom in Huwara, a village near Nablus in the West Bank. Scores were injured and some killed, scores of Palestinian cars set on fire and at least a dozen Palestinian homes set on fire, too.

What makes the Jewish settlers in the West Bank from afar any better than the now diminished but still extant "Islamic State" terrorists in Syria and Iraq? Nothing. They are worse in many respects. (And Islamic State was, much against the Western and U.S. propaganda, often supported by the U.S. and may still be.

The worst tale I ever heard of the IS rabble involved attacks on the Yazidi communities in Iraq. A mother had become a prospective "sex slave" to IS goons. She refused the role. IS thus starved her for three days and then fed her a good meal. She ate her meal with gusto. But after she had finished she was told she had just eaten her baby, or parts of her child. One can hardly imagine anything so cruel.

So this degree of cruelty, whether fomented by IS or the settlers in the West Bank or the IDF or gangsters like Netanyahu or Ben Gvir or Smoltrich or others such as enabling supporters in the West in the U.S. is what not just the Mideast, but the entire world must deal with for the time being. The cruelties are likely to become worse for a while until vocal opposition becomes so strong around the globe that changes will finally be forced and the Zionists and others of their ilk finally have their day of reckoning.

sFew developments are as positive for the Middle East and the Global South than the agreement between Iran and Saudi Arabia to reestablish diplomatic relations. And better still is that the Chinese, after long discussions between the two countries with Chinese help, brokered the deal.

China has demonstrated what thoughtful efforts can accomplish, and it marks the demolition of the longstanding U.S. efforts to initiate and maintain divisions between major, predominantly Muslim countries, in this case the most important Muslim countries by far, one which happens to be primarily Shi'a and the other Sunni confessionally. What did lame and arguably demented Biden have to say when questioned about the fresh accord? He did not even mention the accord but made some silly comment about how good relations between some Arab countries and Apartheid Zionist Israel is a good thing! You have to bet that that he was taken aback by the agreement to open embassies between the Saudis and Iran sometime this Spring, for any enmity at all between Iran and Saudi Arabia has long been the keystone allowing the U.S. to lord it over Iran and to maintain threats and some dominance over the Muslim world.

One has to go all the way back to the early 1970s when the U.S., having spent many billions of dollars on the failed Vietnam War, realized it could no longer maintain any kind of monetary gold standard. The U.S. had an estimate 20,000 plus tons of gold socked away in New York and Fort Knox in Kentucky after World War 2 and for over two decades had more gold by far than any other country, and much of that had been stolen. But by the 1970s it was estimated that this mother lode of gold had been diminished by at least 12,000 tons, and real leaders like France's Charles DeGaulle especially had been demanding gold in payment for U.S. debts and a balance of trade issues. This was when the U.S. proposed to the Saudis that they sell their precious oil resources and other valuable, critical natural resources produced by other countries for dollars only and the entire world of oil exporters fell in line to collect PAPER. The quid pro quo? The U.S. said it would "protect" the Saudis militarily in exchange for its oil resources. Thus the world essentially shifted from a monetary gold standard to a U.S. financial paper standard.

No country had ever been so lucky as the U.S. to pull this shift off until quite recently. Not only could the U.S. buy real stuff with paper promises conjured as has been said literally out of thin air, but there was also the implied military threat that if countries like Saudi Arabia and Iran and many others did not comply with the U.S. demands to sell real valuables for almost nothing, they would be attacked. The weaponization of the dollar and the theft of reserve assets by the U.S. has been the coming disaster…for the U.S., where trust in the U.S. has all but evaporated.

One only has to look, for examples, at what happened to Saddam Hussein when he was threatening to sell Iraqi resources for Euros or some other fiat currency or maybe even gold. And there is the case of prosperous Libya under Qaddafi, too. Libya was targeted for destruction by the U.S. and its NATO allies in part because Qaddafi was alleged to be contemplating the creation of a Gold Dinar and spreading it across Africa as some sort of pan-African unit of exchange to settle trade accounts and more. And one must remember that IF a person happened to be a Libyan citizen, he or she lived in a society that under its government dispensed benefits to citizens like few others has ever done.

But what's happening now is that while the U.S. dollar has reigned KING as the world's reserve currency for decades and still is dominant to a lesser extent, it is losing what has been termed its "exorbitant privilege". The U.S. is going bankrupt by degrees, the dollar is becoming less and less an international monetary factor, and what has underpinned the U.S. empire (of chaos) is becoming increasingly irrelevant worldwide. Military threats by the U.S. and its "allies" like Israel become lesser real threats by the week.

In some respects what has been happening is tragic at least to average Americans, however much U.S. decline has become welcome by a majority of the world's population. The U.S. never had to become as it has been especially in his century so far. It could, for one thing, have been a benevolent behemoth but beginning with the Vietnam debacle in the 1960s and ever since the U.S. has accomplished very little but wildly sow discord in its efforts to divide and conquer and even steal resources from other countries that balked at U.S. foreign policies, warmongering and militancy. The U.S. has worked hard to divide the Muslim world, for one thing, and especially divide Iran and Saudi Arabia. And the Muslim world is one hugely important bloc of faith and achievements that can and will primarily prosper with a strong concept of unity of faith and cooperation despite any particular differences between Sunnis and Shi'as and lesser iterations or organizations of the what is at bottom deep respect for what the Prophet

Someday a day of reckoning for ...

Muhammad achieved in the seventh century in an Arabia then divided by warring tribes.

The very idea of a super" tribe" of Muslims, as the Prophet seemed to envision at the beginning, is a joyous concept like few others, because in history few civilizations have ever been so culturally and even at times politically brilliant, and also so generous and creative with its gifts to humanity over the long haul of some 14 centuries. What, for example, has American "civilization" (if one can use that term) ever offered humanity except its Constitution and Bill of Rights as a noble model of governance that has often been paid lip service and but not always profound, sure and steady enactment? The United States has been involved in some sort of war, whether internal or external for over 85 percent of the country's existence.

The major point here is that the U.S has all but lost its mind in the past 50 years in its overweening, arrogant and destructive efforts merely to dominate quite selfishly as the world's military hegemon, eschewing what China is demonstrating by stressing cooperation and expanded trade among nations and shared efforts to create a better, more peaceful planet.

Neither China nor Russia nor Iran has been running amok like the U.S., but solely trying to defend themselves from various predominantly Western attackers who are literally jealous of achievements which were bound to occur and blossom in recent decades. The U.S. economy's ills, which have been ascending for 30 years, cannot for example be blamed on China and Russia. Greedy Western corporations gave away much of its industry to China and Southeast Asia trying to capitalize on cheaper labor, wrecking what used to be a thriving and productive middle class in the U.S.

But still, the very best news of late is China's success in trying to eliminate the divisions between Iran and Saudi Arabia and getting them to ramp up diplomacy and mutual understanding. Yemen stands to benefit, too, for the conflict there has served no one but the U.S.

Dangerous times amid serious glimmers of real and huge, positive changes
April 2, 2023

It's difficult to be even a partially intelligent and informed citizen in the U.S. A kind of despair takes hold of one's psyche amid the blizzard of bad news around the Biden, Neocon Administration.

The country is deeply awash in incoherent, idiotic moves by the Democrats and some Republicans in Congress, and in blatant corruption so deep one wonders if the country can long survive as a reasonable, going venture. (Almost the same thing can be said about its chief and only "ally" in West Asia — Netanyahu's Israel — but that's another story and in either case, at least 70 percent of the world's population is about ready to say "good riddance" to both countries if ever it occurs.)

Consider first the remarkable developments beyond the chaos in Washington as February winds down. And this is the good news. China's leader Xi showed up in Moscow. Syria's

Assad visited the UAE with his lovely wife. She, apparently free of cancer, and diplomatic relations are being restored, following diplomatic restorations between Iran and Saudi Arabia and embassy openings ahead this Spring. Xi is presenting a plan to push a ceasefire at least in Ukraine and end the carnage. This has already been rejected by Washington! (And estimated 300,000 Ukrainian troops have died or been disabled. Maybe 40,000 Russian troops have been sidelined or killed in the senseless war provoked by Biden and his Neocon masters, many of whom are the very same ideologues, mostly Zionists, who played a big role in sparking the Iraq war among others 20 years ago. Ukraine, which had a population of some 39 million, has seen its population shrink to maybe 20 million as millions have become refugees in Europe.

The Arab/Persian/Muslim world may be waking up to the obvious benefits of cooperation and peace and more unity.

Representatives of 40 African countries also convened with Russian diplomats to bolster relations and Russia canceled billions in debts. Little Kenya decided to shun the dollar as a trade vehicle with China and other countries, and this is but one of other, smaller positive moves inherent in the rise of a multipolar planet which is well underway it seems. As one pundit remarked, it's possible that in the next few months more geopolitical and economic changes may occur that have not been witnessed in over 100 years.

But the fly in the ointmental salve is the U.S. and this if becoming more recognized around the world, even perhaps in places in Europe such as France where some observers smell "revolution", and get this, there has been some chatter in Germany about a repair and reopening of the Nord Stream gas pipelines, which the Bidenists destroyed last year but won't admit to.

Biden has proved to be so ignorant that he has driven Russia and China into a firm alliance, including Iran. Recall that since the 1960s a goal of U.S foreign policy was to align with China against Russia, or align with Russia against China depending on which country seemed like the greater threat! It's now likely that China and Russia will never be split apart again. Biden back in 1997 spoke about NATO expansion and the Russians told him they were threatened by it, and that it might force them into alliance with China. Biden (who has accomplished little in his parasitic career of any real merit while rising to the top of the Washington cesspool like a turd) at the time just literally laughed and said "Good Luck" with that. And now the U.S. also faces 16 countries that want to join the BRICS bloc, too, in defiance of the U.S. Is the world in dangerous times but in more promising times? You bet.

But even if much of the world suffers trying to create a fairer multipolarity amid U.S. threats of World War 3, the U.S. may be about to crash like never before into hostile divisions.

The Biden Democrats have become so desperate that this week, wanting a felonious indictment of former President Donald Trump, they may see the former President handcuffed and booked on a risible charge of having broken some law over a $130,000 payment to one former porn star named Stormy Daniels to shut her up during the election in 2016, she and Trump having been involved in a sexual escapade. While it's difficult to consider Trump anything but a self-serving narcissist, no President has suffered as much opprobrium as he did over the trumped up "Russiagate" scandal, which has been exposed as utterly false. One would think with all the garbage the Democrats have tried to find to indict Trump and insure he won't or can't run in the election in 2024 (if it even occurs), they'd have found something more damning than a personal out-of-pocket hush money payment to a women of ill repute. Some pundits are claiming that IF Trump is indicted, it will virtually assure his reelection in 2024 since so many Americans remain Trump fans and are beginning to despise Biden.

The top two contenders currently for the Republican nomination are Trump and Florida governor Ron DeSantis. Interesting it is that both men believe the proxy war on Ukraine does not serve U.S. interests. This fact alone ought to insure a Republican win in the 2024 elections over anyone the Democrats vomit up to run for office as it becomes increasingly apparent that the proxy war against Russia, and expenditures to support it of over $110 billion so far, have utterly failed to bring Russia to its knees along with the rejection of Putin within Russia.

In sum no person of any intelligence said the end of the "American Century" and its bloody empire would ever be anything but frightful and perilous for humanity. What is imperative is that average Americans wake up en masse and realize the Biden gang's sole aim has been to maintain American military and economic hegemony over much of the world for its elites, but none of this effort has benefitted nearly all Americans. At least it can be said that the Global South is rising and prospects exist with that for a better, more peaceful world whatever becomes of the U.S.

American influence is fast crumbling

April 9, 2023

The entire West is in dangerous turmoil.

This fact is quite aside from former President Donald Trump this week having to submit to arrest and felonious charges in New York City and some 30 plus counts of criminality over a hush money payment to a porn star in to keep her quiet over a brief sex engagement.

The payment occurred as Trump was first running for President, which he won, and obviously he did not want his improprieties as a married man to sink his chances to become top U.S. dog, literally. However, it remains questionable whether the charges against him have enough merit to put him behind bars, and anyway the Democrats are going nuts over the prospect that Trump might get nominated by the Republicans because he or almost any Republican is likely to win the Presidency again. Why?

Because Biden is arguably the worst President in American history.

The Neocons' stoking of the proxy war on Russia alone through Ukraine and through the Biden Administration worked, and it's a disaster, but the war actually was planned and began in 2014 with the fall of Yanukovich, the democratically elected but pro-Russian Ukrainian leader. The Minsk accords between 2014 and for a few years were a false hope for Russia and Putin, who only sought Ukraine's neutrality. False because while those accords, had they been enacted, would have totally obviated Russia's invasion of Ukraine last year. Even Germany's Merkel said the Minsk agreements were designed to give Ukraine time to build up its armed forces with billions of U.S. dollars and weapons for a war provoked by the U.S. The fake accords gave some hope to Russia for peace for a while and thus Russia had NO plans to invade or take Ukrainian territory or wipe out Ukraine's military. But they were a joke on Russia, and now the subterfuge has been backfiring.

It's all quite amazing like the few times in history when such tremendous and fast changes underway now challenge the entire world with shifts of influence, and raises the specter of World War 3 at least. One must say "at least" because the U.S. provoked a war with a nuclear power, not some relatively helpless country like Saddam Hussein's Iraq, or poor Afghanistan or prosperous but tiny Libya or Syria for examples. Behind it all is the U.S. determination to kill China's emergence as a truly great power and its Belt and Road initiative while the U.S. economy sinks slowly on the back of $32 trillion in debt and many more billions in unfunded liabilities. The blizzard of sanctions on important countries like Iran, not to mention Russia, have also been instrumental in sparking the changes underway. The U.S. has bit off far more than it is capable of chewing and enraged a majority of the human population worldwide, if not yet in vassal states in Europe or in Apartheid Israel, which may be falling apart with Netanyahu and his far right colleagues.

But Iran's leaders are quite aware of most of this.

Iran and the U.S. 2017 - 2023

What is interesting, if only by way of impressing on the world that not all notable Americans back what the Biden and his Neocon handlers have done, are people like Robert F. Kennedy Jr., the nephew of assassinated former President John F. Kennedy.

Robert Kennedy Jr., whose father was JFK's attorney general, suffered his father's later assassination in 1968. He has made a name for himself of late in fully opposing the way the U.S. handled (and may have even created) the Covid 19 pandemic. He has felt the vaccines against the disease were ineffective and a means for pharmaceutic companies like Pfizer to make billions of dollars on a vaccine product that was actually as dangerous as Covid 19 itself. For his medical posture Robert Kennedy has been strongly maligned by the medical and political "establishment". It's worth presenting, however, what he recently wrote about U.S. deeds over years and the blowback it has created:

"The collapse of U.S. influence over Saudi Arabia and the Kingdom's new alliances with China and Iran are painful emblems of the abject failure of the Neocon strategy of maintaining U.S. global hegemony with aggressive projections of military power. China has displaced the American Empire by deftly projecting, instead, economic power. Over the past decade, our country has spent trillions bombing roads, ports, bridges, and airports. China spent the equivalent building the same across the developing world. The Ukraine war is the final collapse of the Neocon's short-lived "American Century." The Neocon projects in Iraq and Ukraine have cost $8.1 trillion, hollowed out our middle class, made a laughingstock of U.S. military power and moral authority, pushed China and Russia into an invincible alliance, destroyed the dollar as the global currency, cost millions of lives and done nothing to advance democracy or win friendships or influence."

Even now far too many Americans don't buy Kennedy's views primarily because of U.S. and European mainstream media propaganda and wishful thinking. One must ask: How long will it take for a firm majority of Americans to realize he is correct?

Ruminations about the changes underway April 16, 2023

Any American voice may not count for much in most of Asia and especially in West Asia and that is quite understandable. Anyone in Iran or now in Iran's neighboring Arab countries have an unquestionable right to question Americans and the government in Washington for countless misdeeds over the last 30 years around divide and conquer policies and actions that have created rampant chaos and misery that never, ever should have been meted out by Washington and its allies wherever.

It was Vladimir Putin who really posed the question before the General Assembly at the UN clearly and unequivocally a few years ago in an address in New York when he pointed to the U.S. and asked one simple question: "Do you realize what you have done?" (Or been doing for many years.) One answer to this pregnant question by Putin is that maybe the U.S. was aware of what it had been doing but it did not give a damn. And for not giving a damn there is, this year and quite suddenly in parts of the world from which no great response was expected so fast and so soon. However, much responses have long been warranted and building under cover, it is happening: blowback and revolt rarely before seen so clearly, and unifications or reunifications few could have imagined.

Central to all the change that is underway has been the leaders of Iran and Saudi Arabia shaking hands this Spring and saying, as Putin would, "Nyet" to more division, and further, let's cook up some peace for a change. And not only between Iran and Saudi Arabia, but over Yemen and even with Syria, too, which will be invited to rejoin the Arab League soon after a decade of dismissal. The UAE is also playing its part. One can thank China's leaders, too, for pushing for peace between disputants this century especially in resource-rich West Asia. A multipolar world is taking shape, and leaving Washington in the foul dust of its hubris and arrogance and divisive warmongering like never before.

And a change of attitude is also breaking out among the erstwhile vassals of the Empire of Chaos in Europe. France's Macron returned from a visit to China saying that Europe must reduce its dependency on the U.S. which has deepened with negative results given the U.S. proxy war on Russia in Ukraine. And even in the German Bundestag demands have been made that Germany break its relationship of extreme subservience to the U.S. which is destroying Europe's economy.

This seeming revolution is like the massive amounts of snow that covered much of the western U.S. this past winter now in a thaw, like perhaps on Iran's highest peak, Demavand, racing downhill and picking up mass and speed. It's hard to find a place on the world map outside of, say, Australia or

Japan or S. Korea or Canada or much of Europe that is not now experiencing some exhilaration over the mounting and well-deserved rejections of fealty to all of Washington's demands.

People want to create and enjoy a broader peace they have not had in decades largely because of the U.S. They want to breath more freely. They want to focus on trade and mutual benefit and cooperation between nations of different cultures and religions. This is the real "Arab Spring" of slightly more than a decade ago and which fizzled out because of Western and U.S. rejections and power moves. What is now is or is becoming a potentially huge springtime of more unity and peace for much of the world. It's quite remarkable and it must not be blocked, must be pushed even harder whatever becomes of the U.S. in decline.

But no one and especially in the Persian/Muslim/Arab realms should be mistaken.

Because if much of the rest of the planet appears to be witnessing an awakening, or at least having already woken up and finally doing something real about their valid perceptions such as rejecting the dollar with some help from Russia and China especially, the same realizations are starting to burble up among many Americans, too, even though for now most are baffled and confused and way behind Iranians or Arabs leaders because of the mainstream media in the U.S. manufacturing consent, as Noam Chomsky has said for years, for Washington's international misdeeds and wars with reams of propaganda and misdirections and demonizations of others.

Further, this is not to say than ANY government anywhere is "perfect" and could not benefit from some reformations for its subjects, but it IS to say that the U.S. government pushing its militant "empire" for decades and bankrupting the U.S. people with debt and with over 800 military bases around the globe has, in fact, probably been the least perfect and the least healthy for humankind in recent decades.

The U.S. is on a suicide mission

April 23, 2023

The U.S. may be self-destructing in front of the world. This may be a good thing and no one will be blamed for it except Joe Biden and the Presidents and administrations that came before him after Ronald Reagan, each with their own miserable moves and policies after the fall of the Soviet Union in 1991.

In 1992 American political theorist Francis Fukuyama published a book in which he argued that humanity had arrived at "the end of history"! That the fall of the Soviet Union had resulted in the end-point of the evolution of ideologies and that "Western liberal democracy" had become the final valid form of human government. This bold, even stupid, assertion could not have been more incorrect. There exist a thousand reasons why he was insanely wrong but the major reason why Fukuyama's assertion was wrong was that ever since he wrote such the United States and its Western allies seized upon it not with any humility or care or consideration that humanity's ideologies and cultures have always been variegated and suited to various diverse populations and cultures.

That, plus other truths such as the one that ever since the early 1990s the U.S. has been sliding far away from supporting both real liberalism and "democracy" whether at home or even overseas. The U.S. has long been solely about bullying hegemony.

Regime change actions by the U.S. have nothing to do with liberalism or democracy, but have everything to do with installing governments in foreign countries that do the bidding of Washington. Ukraine currently is the most striking and dangerous example of this. In Pakistan for example the U.S. fomented the marginalization of former popular leader Imran Khan because he refused to support U.S. policies around Ukraine. There are myriad other examples of this kind of action, some successful and some that have utterly failed like, for examples, in Venezuela or Syria and even now in Russia via the proxy war on Russia in Ukraine.

And underneath that slide away from true liberalism and honest democracy has been such off the charts hubris and triumphalism in Washington that real democracy barely exists any longer in the U.S. and what's left is not "liberal" but a kind of radical totalitarianism. Retired Princeton University professor and political theorist Sheldon Wolin identified this when he called it not classic but "inverted totalitarianism" wherein corporations and elitist minions have corrupted true democracy by commodifying and exploiting every natural resource and every living being. This has led the U.S. in the direction of social collapse as citizens are manipulated to give up what liberties they had and their real, actual participation in government … even though most Americans are still often not even aware of what has been lost. The propaganda in the U.S. mainstream media has been absolutely intense and few Americans have time, if they have any time but to try to survive, to read beyond the mainstream, misdirecting headlines. It has also led the world to begin to reject soundly U.S. economic and military power such as it has existed and expanded since the end of World War 2. The Turkish Interior minister said it succinctly this week: "The world hates the U.S." Or is learning to.

The dire illness and ignorance of U.S. leaders leading to eventual self-destruction was well revealed this past week by General Mark Milley, the head of the "Joint Chiefs of Staff" of the U.S. military, when he opined that the U.S. military budget must be doubled if the outcome of the proxy war on Russia through Ukraine calls in to question the "rules-based world order" which itself is a risible joke and in fact has resulted in widespread "disorder". The "defense" budget in the U.S. is already nearly a trillion fiat dollars, larger than what the next nine or 10 countries combined spend on defending themselves. This alone is crippling the U.S. and leading towards total bankruptcy and social dismay and disintegration. If ever a U.S. President was correct in warning against the growth of the "Military Industrial Complex" or MIC in the U.S. it was Dwight Eisenhower in 1960 in his farewell address when he left the While House. And recall the MIC has not literally won any serious war since 1945!

The sole, now formal candidate for the Presidency in 2024 who is telling at least some truths that offend the establishment and may raise a spark of hope for the salvation of the U.S., however difficult this will be to achieve, is Robert F. Kennedy Jr., the nephew of JFK who was assassinated and who also lost his father to assassination (both murders with alleged CIA assistance) long ago just before and during the ill-fated debacle of the Vietnam War.

Kennedy announced his candidacy very recently in Boston and the mainstream U.S. media has already announced no likelihood for his success. (And this is because presidential elections are rigged and the primary media is hand in glove with the elitists and other powers that be in the U.S.) Among many other issues, Kennedy has come out against the dominance of the MIC with regards to U.S. policy and warmongering. Kennedy intends to run for the Presidency in 2024 as a Democrat, but he also has called for support from Republicans and the disaffected mass of independent voters who don't affiliate or identify with either of the two dominating political parties.

In any case, history has suggested this: desperate, failing empires such as the U.S. has become in the past decades have a habit of demonstrating suicidal tendencies.

Greed is the downfall of Western and U.S. power

May 19, 2023

The rare word "pleonexia" comes to mind. It means, simply, a psychiatric ailment of excessive, overweening greed that dominates the afflicted and determines most of what they are about, even as so-called "public servants" in government and who in fact rarely serve anyone but themselves.

Take for examples a few names among many: Barack Obama. Bill and Hillary Clinton. Nancy Pelosi. Joe Biden... and hundreds of other power brokers and politicians in the

U.S. in recent decades. Even young Alexandra Ocasio-Cortez. These people and many others have become filthy rich or just rich during their political careers on salaries that are quite modest by Wall Street standards at least.

Ocasio-Cortez just a few years ago was a young 20-something bartender in New York City before she somehow managed to get elected to Congress as a young "progressive" leader. Obama was in the past a "community organizer" before he became President, and so on with a variety of politicians. Ocasio-Cortez has dropped a number of her "progressive" postures and is now said to have amassed a small fortune of over $4 million which must be the envy of over 98 percent of all humans worldwide. How so for her and all the others? In one word, they all succumbed to "corruption" as alleged, faux public servants.

The most dangerous corruption at the heart of American governance has long extended itself to Washington's fawning over Jewish power and Apartheid Israel. Part of this particular corruption is a function of the fact that Washington has few alleged allies left in a rapidly changing world that is fast moving to more balance and multipolarity. But even if the trend to a multipolar world were not so apparent, there would be little change with regard to relations between the U.S. and Israel and that country's few supporters. For those with clear minds, and I have claimed this before, the end game of American influence and its Empire of Chaos has for decades been wrapped around its misguided, immoral fealty to the "only democracy in the Middle East" which has been anything but a "democracy" for 75 years.

Put another way, is there ANYTHING the U.S. has promoted in the last 30 years, various wars especially, that have not primarily been cheered and pushed by Israel and that country's overweening influence on U.S. politicians to protect the bloody status quo in West Asia? A hundred years from now when historians look back at the disgraceful evisceration of the United States as once a great nation, they most certainly will point to "Israel", a racist colonial enterprise and its demands, as the prime factor of erosion.

What the world witnesses now is the ultimate demise of the American financial system and the dollar, which in turn will in time severely limit the capacity of the U.S. "rules based" disorder to impose sanctions and war on others. The U.S. debt load is already well beyond effective management and unlike some other societies in the Middle East centuries ago there is no mechanism for periodic debt cancellation. The "pleonexia" or "wealth addiction" so rampant among Western elites has already led to vast corruption and to predatory and socially damaging practices which don't appear to have any hope of abatement. One of America's top three economists, Professor Michael Hudson, points out that in ancient Greek times the sage Socrates proposed that only non-wealthy managers ought to be appointed to govern society so that they would not become hostages to hubris and greed. But wealth addiction is very sticky and once wealth is acquired the maintenance and augmentation of it becomes an almost irresistible, primary aim of those few who have enjoyed it.

As for Israel and the United States joined at the hip for 75 years as a grotesque team of parasite and donor, both countries are doomed to eventual destruction unless they, in some crazed effort to carry on as they have for decades, literally spark a nuclear war with China or Russia or both as their mutual acceptance anywhere continues to wane. In this regard the joint, reinforcing policies towards Syria alone are beyond frightful.

Syria has suffered horribly for over a decade and it's hard to fathom why except that both Israel and the U.S. have wanted to destroy its government and supplant it with either total chaos or its own puppets. Greed for added wealth is clearly a big part of this. The U.S. has been stealing Syria's resources for years. The only real threat Syria ever constituted has been ideological objections to Jewish Apartheid and to the theft of the Golan as well as U.S. soldiers occupying parts of the country in the east and allowing the Zionists to bomb the country at will.

For the past 30 years the U.S. and its Western vassals literally have not done ANY public good, not even in their own countries. Above all, the West has not brought peace and prosperity, but only various wars and crises, and corruption and rot in Western societies. Some smart commentators have opined that the literal end of the West's ascent to world dominance over the past 500 years is finally ending as multipolarity takes hold.

Countries can rot like fish out of water — from the head down

June 7, 2023

Badly disposed homo sapiens inhabit every nook and cranny of the globe. There are enough of them, though they are a small, distinct minority, to make a soul sometimes feel ashamed of being one of the species. There is absolutely NO other species on earth that has done so much damage to other species and to themselves and to Nature for millennia as homo sapiens, and perhaps especially in the last couple of centuries as the earth's number of humans has swelled in Malthusian leaps and bounds. Among mammals, it's not even remotely possible to compare destructive human behaviors to the behaviors of other mammals because, simply, there is no comparison to be made.

Of all existing countries and cultures today, and since the end of World War 2 when the first and only couple of atomic bombs were unnecessarily dropped in 1945 at war's end over Hiroshima and Nagasaki, and in ever increasing degrees of expression, it is arguable that the United States has done the most harm, the most unnecessary harm, of any country.

This is not to claim at all that average citizens of other countries are "better" than 95 percent of Americans. The mainstream Western media this century especially has made it difficult for most Americans to be informed and most are not. But it can be argued that average citizens anywhere else are a lot "better" overall than that small minority of Americans who have at the top and have exercised power and control in Washington and on Wall Street and built for decades the extant but now crumbling so-called "empire" — even while many others have profited and enjoyed some personal, even selfish advantages and benefitted from the crumbs accruing to some U.S. citizens as simply lucky parts of the "richest country in history", including some so-called allies elsewhere.

Most of earth's population is waking up fast and trying to distance themselves and their countries from many things "American", and it's about time they did to limit further harm derived from U.S. arrogance and hubris especially since the fall of the Soviet Union but probably beginning in the 1960s with the unnecessary war on Vietnam that murdered millions. Many have spent most of their lives dismayed and confused sniffing out the rot that has seized the U.S. in ever increasing ways — politically, socially and economically — and it's worth noting that the rot of countries, as with dead fish, proceeds from the top, from their heads, downwards towards their tails and usually on a flood of lies and narrowly self-serving, mostly destructive actions and policies.

This progression of rot and dissolution has played out for millennia in various degrees in other societies, cultures and polities, but perhaps not so much and so blatantly as in recent decades with the U.S. This progression began in top leadership circles.

In the U.S. it can be surmised legitimately that Joe Biden will be exposed as the worst President ever, and the most morally compromised, but Donald Trump and Barack Obama and George W. Bush and Bill Clinton are not far behind given their own histories with war crimes and other ills.

With Biden the world is witnessing the fullest expression of insanity (and also senility) in a POTU.S., and this for several reasons, but perhaps especially because he and his overbearing Neocon bosses and handlers have literally brought the planet and humanity closer to nuclear annihilation than anyone else ever has with his provoked proxy war on Russia in Ukraine and his failure and refusals for a decade to negotiate a deal with Vladimir Putin to allay Russia's reasonable security and border concerns. All Putin wanted was the enactment of the Minsk Accords, which even Angela Merkel called a sham. And this solely to maintain U.S. hegemonic pretensions via the gross expansion of vassal European countries into NATO since the 1990s.

Biden himself became a millionaire during his long career slurping at public expense in Congress and by other means and later as Obama's Vice-President. And perhaps also his infamous son, Hunter, now 53 a professed drug addict, failed lawyer and all around opportunist who served on the board of Ukraine's largest natural gas concern, Burmisma, in recent years past, for which he was paid handsomely and did nothing. It has been suggested one reason Biden provoked the war in Ukraine may have been connected with his desire to bury dealings between the Bidens and possibly the most corrupt government anywhere in Ukraine. Hunter has also been under investigation for years for tax avoidance issues by the IRS. Nepotism works, it has seemed.

Father Joe has recently claimed Hunter "never did anything wrong", but the infamous laptop computer that Hunter lost control of or left behind by mistake in a computer repair shop is now strongly suggesting otherwise. It's full of incriminating business, finance and political e-mails and many hundreds of photos, the latter at least just now coming to light publicly, of

Hunter engaged in sexual escapades with a variety of people, apparently including underage girls.

The photos reveal some of the raunchiest pornography one might scrape up from the fetid bowels of the Internet. In any event, Joe Biden has done the bidding of his Neocon handlers but is not popular nowadays and a good majority of Americans consider him unfit for a second term in the White House. Corruption is rampant in Washington like never before. There seems to be a mad scramble among politicians and lobbyists to pad their personal wealth before the economy and financial system eventually collapse in a heap of debt that cannot ever be repaid.

Literally freakish times in the U.S. as decline accelerates
June 17, 2023

U.S. President Joe Biden recently hosted a party on the south lawn of the White House for transgenders. There were topless "women" there showing off. They had been males before surgeries and hormones transformed them into freaks. Is this at all important? In one sense only. The decline of the U.S. was on full display on the sunny lawn at the White House.

But meanwhile much of the world is suffering turmoil like few times in history, and especially since the fall of the Soviet Union. Who is largely responsible for this? There exists only one answer: the fading Hegemon, the United States. The government since 1991 apparently believed it had been gifted virtually ALL the marbles of power and full spectrum global dominance in the 1990s militarily and economically, and then successively made every mistake to whittle away at the advantages it had amassed. The rising Neocon cabal of Zionists in the U.S. State Department had gained tremendous influence on the direction of U.S. policies, and this was striking early on at the start of the new century with the disaster that the invasion of Iraq became, and as well the disasters in Afghanistan, Libya and Syria by terrorist proxies and NATO bombings.

But the mother of all interventions, this one by proxy with Ukrainian youths, is the one underway since winter 2022 in Ukraine where Ukrainians and NATO are at last meeting more than their match while Russia seems determined to achieve its goals of gutting the Ukraine military, de-Nazification and the neutrality of what in time may remain of lands under Ukrainian control. This is a kind of tragedy of deeds for the U.S. that historians will write about for decades simply because the U.S. offered anything but extensions of goodwill and measured cooperation. Incremental dissolution of the U.S. is now underway and quite literally, the U.S. cannot rectify itself and doesn't have the intellectual creativity to halt the slide.

One fascinating part of this while the U.S. slowly loses its Empire and control, and tries to destroy Russian power so that it can then attempt to go after China using the Taiwan question as its key focal point, is that no country, including Iran, that has been sanctioned or attacked by the U.S. seriously challenged the U.S. except with their own relative growing excellence and achievements especially in the economic sphere. Iran even today wants to revive the JCPOA after it was scuttled by Donald Trump. Increasingly, Iran does not necessarily have to rejoin any JCPOA with all the changes of national alignments occurring and evident erasures of divisions in Muslim world. And Iran was in the past no challenge to the U.S. except that after the Revolution led by Khomeini the country rightfully opposed Israel's Apartheid to this day Zionists still control much of U.S. foreign policy especially in West Asia. And one cannot exclude pure jealousy on the part of Washington, which cannot deal with its own self-imposed problems, blaming it on others. The U.S. has virtually bankrupted itself with its pursuits: war after war for 30 years. Neither Iran nor China has done anything like this, and economic problems outside the U.S. have arisen mostly from the weaponization of the dollar, which economist Michael Hudson, America's best, declares is fomenting rapid de-dollarization that will in time curtail the capacity of the U.S. to intervene militarily anywhere and likely lead to the eventual closure of most the country's 800 plus military bases across the globe. Even Treasury Secretary Janet Yellen admitted this week that the reserve currently status of the dollar was eroding significantly.

Also, but internally, the former U.S. President, Trump, was just indicted on felony charges this week in Miami for allegedly mishandling government documents. This is malarkey because the Clintons and Biden himself have done same. It's purely political. The sole way to get Trump gone is to convict and imprison him thereby excluding him from running for reelection in 2024. But this will backfire especially in 2024.

Interestingly, pundit Tucker Carlson, who is very popular and who was fired from Fox News this spring, is appearing again but now on Twitter with millions tuning in. He claims to pinpoint exactly the moment the so-called Deep State in

Washington decided to find a way to wreck Trump. February 16, 2015. Trump back then stated as a presidential candidate that the Iraq War was sold on a lie, that Iraq had never amassed WMD. Imagine that! He told a truth challenging the Neocon war agendas and he was not yet even voted into the White House. A rocky Presidency followed trying to fend off ejection by any means possible by the corrupt Democrats, but he was, to be clear, not without fault himself on many other matters, including Iran. Never mind, he merely told the truth about Iraq. In Washington disqualifications come from critiques or exposures of U.S. military crimes. Just look at what has happened for over a decade to Julian Assange. He's still rotting in Belmarsh prison in London and hasn't been charged with a crime and could well be extradited to the U.S. soon to face charges that would put him in a maximum security prison for life. And just for exposing U.S. war crimes.

Inimical to U.S. health, the greatest poison is the Neocon cabal

July 2, 2023

Remember the unguarded conversation the U.S. State Department's Victoria Nuland had with the then American ambassador to Ukraine, Geoffrey Pyatt back in 2014 when they were spending $5 billion in U.S. taxpayer funds to foment a coup in Ukraine and overthrow the elected pro-Russian President there? That conversation was world-widely noted for Nuland's infamous comment "Fuck the E.U." (She, long an arch Zionist Jewish Neocon, was making it clear to Ambassador Pyatt that nothing and no one mattered but the U.S. plans to control Ukraine and even the E.U. and ultimately bleed or attack Russia.)

The fine commentator Philip Giraldi, long retired from over two decades with the CIA, recently penned yet another excellent article of many for over a decade focusing on yet another Neocon, the now deceased former Secretary of State for the U.S. and also a Zionist, Madelain Albright, for whom the post office he uses near his home will lamentably be named.

Albright's lifetime signature comment was claiming the death of hundreds of thousands of Iraqi children leading up to the U.S. invasion in 2003 were "worth it" back in the years after Saddam Hussein had fallen out of U.S. favor. One reason so many children died in Iraq was because an embargo had been placed on Iraq which among their items barred the importation of chemicals to kill bacteria and other pathogens in Iraq's water supplies. Imagine drinking untreated water from the Tigris River!

Anyway, Giraldi writes in his recent article, this in the "Unz Review", that Neocons like Nuland for years and crones like Albright over decades had slowly infiltrated powerful policy-making roles in the U.S. government. He also cites a long article written by another Jew, Ron Unz (who founded and manages the website where writer Giraldi often appears) about the rise of the Neocons to achieve their control of U.S. foreign policies, and especially their advocacy of the Israeli Apartheid state no matter what crimes they commit. (Ron Unz, by the way, is a serious publisher of many truths, but even his website and the submissions therein are banned from appearing in many places including even Facebook where the average American might become better informed.)

In contrast to the often buried, honest, accurate and even brilliant articles that show up in nooks and crannies of the Internet, and that few Americans ever get to read because the pieces are not shoved in their faces with morning coffee as they head to work, we have the U.S. mainstream media suffused with clever propagandists supporting Empire and elites at any cost. Newspapers like the New York Times and the Washington Post are so full of it in the last three decades at least that they do not resemble what I recall they were when I was a youth when they were exposing crimes and especially war crimes in Vietnam and even lies about what caused the war on Vietnam. Take the current postures in the mainstream media about the Prigozhin matter in Russia. Consider The Washington Post as an example.

All eight of the Washpo's primary opinion writers reflected in their own words and nuances what Secretary of State Antony Blinken has said about the Prigozhin matter. That Russia and Vladimir Putin has been substantially weakened, that dangerous "cracks" have appeared in the Russian "facade" of unity and purpose and those "cracks" were already profound before the attempted Prigozhin coup d'etat. Blinken goes on the cite all the alleged "failures" of the Russian state under Putin's "aggression" on Ukraine. That Putin managed to bring NATO together, that he's gotten Europe to move away from Russian energy, to unite Ukrainians and so on. He adds that everything Putin and Russia have tried to do since February 2022 has been a failure and a serious strategic failure. Really? People like David Ignatius at the Washpo, decades ago a fine journalist with sources like few others, ought to be ashamed of himself nowadays because he is little more than an old, seasoned prig now raking in big bucks writing BS.

Put simply, most of the opinions and commentaries by Blinken and his followers at leading newspapers like the NYT and Washpo constitute little more than an organized propaganda campaign full of mostly lies and false innuendos about Russia's advances militarily and economically even since the war began. And Putin, he is said to be favored by 90 percent of Russians. As for Prigozhin, he was all alone in his mutinous effort. No one person and not a single group in Russia's government or civil apparatus supported him and he was fast vanquished to neighboring Belarus. He is lucky to still be alive and had Putin been less circumspect, he would not be alive.

It is anyway remarkable that almost no one, it seems, in power in Washington and in the mainstream media can even discern factual truths, much less tell them as they are supposed to do in the jobs they have. Most U.S. "journalists" are not. They are whores and shills to the powerful and one day this will become apparent to most Americans as it already is apparent to over half the world's population.

But back to Victoria Nuland. Back in 2014 with Ambassador Pyatt part of their conversation involved whom they would finger to become Ukraine's leader. This was one Arsenly Yatsenyuk who did serve for a while as Prime Minister. He lately revealed that he thought: "We killed our own country!"

All the earth is at risk

July 10, 2023

There have been announcements by some that when BRICS meets later in August it will announce the creation of a gold-backed trade currency aimed at replacing the dollar as the medium of account for trade among significant countries comprising over half the world's population.

This may mark a sea change in the world monetary situation since the end of World War 2 as the usage of this alleged new currency unfolds in stages over time. And additionally, some 30 or 40 countries that are not in the BRICS lineup as it currently stands are clamoring to join.

Old Joe Biden, who can barely tie his own shoelaces, is a tool of his advisors and his administration (filled with strident Neocons and Zionists) and has by some accounts made himself a world historical figure as a result: overturning by insane belligerent policies across the globe on steroids, and especially in Ukraine against Russia, much of any still lingering presumptions in Washington that U.S. economic dominance, already waning, can continue. One can argue that the administration is desperate because the most accurate observers have suggested that with the failure to date of Ukraine's much heralded offensive against Russia, that country's collapse later this year could occur. And Biden has upped the ante by his upcoming shipment of cluster munitions to Zelensky, allegedly because Western stocks of items like artillery shells are in short supply.

Iran and the U.S. 2017 - 2023

A couple of years ago Biden's former press secretary, Jen Psaki, speaking for Biden, asserted that cluster munitions were absolutely forbidden and criminal!

One can smell the rancid desperation now, and it is dangerous to all. World War 3 and the use of nuclear weapons has never been closer, and few Americans are knowledgeable enough to understand this current threat. Were they aware, Biden would be impeached and his entire administration shunned if not jailed in an asylum for cretins. After the ignominious U.S. exit from Afghanistan, and other failed military ventures over several decades, the psychopaths in the U.S. government seem incapable of accepting reality and they are putting humanity at extreme risk.

Russia and Vladimir Putin, whose sole aim was to establish Ukraine's neutrality after February 2022 and its exclusion from NATO (not to invade any other countries after the reduction of Ukraine's Nazis and military), MU.S.T appear to have some heroic qualities even though his attack on Ukraine was a dangerous gambit for Russia and may have best not have been launched given all the hundreds of thousands of victims, but IF the U.S. had not been so bent on Russia's destruction with its proxy war, Russia would not have invaded. One must also be aware of Putin's many accomplishments over the last 24 years for Russia's citizens. He is in fact the most liked leader worldwide, some say now.

Recall that after the fall of the USSR and its aftermath during the 1990s, Russia was supine, its political, economic and social situation wracked by many problems. Putin at Russia's helm has righted a moribund economy, its military clout, its many exports that include agricultural goods, and even its societal confidence, and he allegedly enjoys a 90 percent approval rating inside Russia. He reduced inflation, set up firm alliances (especially with China) and cooperation with other countries outside the West and much, much more. In itself, Russia's progress out of the depths of its troubles in the 1990s is something of a miracle that few other leaders could have engineered in such a short time. The U.S. and its vassals in Europe are clearly appalled by Russia's successes, or at least Russia's endurance, since Putin took over, especially since the U.S imagined itself after the dissolution of the USSR as having been handed all the marbles it had long sought — the effective reduction of Russia to a "has been" nation ripe for the pillage and the theft of its vast resources and its full emasculation as a rival. This was Russia before Putin. The proxy war on Russia in Ukraine (with a Europe that has all but lost its sovereignty and independence and its cheap energy supplies) is one result of the very dark pathology of Western rage, jealousy and envy while America and the E.U. wallow in bankruptcy and decline and ascending irrelevancy except as purveyors of violence and discord across the planet.

This is not to say that Russia has solved or eradicated all its challenges. In fact it had a major role in creating its largest current challenges around Ukraine by its Special Military Operation. This was an operation, still unfolding, that Biden, Washington and its Neocons gleefully welcomed both in fact and spirit because it gave the U.S. a literal pretext to try to destroy Putin and Russia on the backs of Ukrainians supplied with many billions in Western armaments.

No doubt the Biden Administration and its Neocons expected Russia to quickly lose the proxy war and retreat, but the opposite has occurred with Russia so far incrementally achieving its aims against the Zelensky regime much to the chagrin of Western imperialists led by the U.S. Hence, we now witness desperate Western escalations, such as the supply of formerly disavowed cluster bombs to Ukraine's unhappy army full of reluctant recruits or all ages.

The question now is whether the U.S. is going to provoke World War 3, which is not winnable by ANY party to the conflict because of the risks of desperate nuclear escalations. Given the lack of wisdom in Washington and its perverse desires to cling to hegemony, we have entered the most frightening time in modern history.

Avoid moral decline because the result is failure
July 17, 2023

America in the distant past had a shred of moral decency. Although Russia essentially won World War 2 against the Nazis and Japanese, even at the very end of the war which it rightfully helped "win" it stooped low to drop two atomic bombs on Japan over which it had already triumphed. Why? Because the U.S. wanted to send a threatening message to countries like the Soviet Union that the U.S. aimed to scare and dominate, not to mention the cruel punishment to Japanese civilians in Hiroshima and Nagasaki.

This was the beginning of America's steep moral decline and in some respects its amoral "empire". Only two years after the war ended the U.S. created the CIA, which has been up to no good ever since and may have even set up the assassination of President John F. Kennedy in 1963 and his brother in 1968. The next notable move, with help from the British, was to begin its still continuing pursuit of toppling other governments that simply wanted to own its own resources and be left alone, such as Iran which saw its elected Prime Minister Mohammad Mossadegh cast aside to make way for a puppet that Iran finally kicked out with its fascinating revolution in 1979. The list of countries attacked, governments toppled, citizens murdered, resources plundered and so on since Mossadegh's day is almost too numerous to list. But every major crime provoked by the U.S. and all of them mostly on false pretenses (Vietnam, Afghanistan, Syria, Libya, the former Yugoslavia and lately Ukraine to cite just a few of scores of U.S. interventions of various kinds on every continent, most often directly military) did not result in any kind of victory that the U.S. expected, even promised its citizens.

In fact, the REAL defeats of the U.S. after decades of interventions have just begun to occur in the past few years and will continue for many years ahead.

Many of these defeats are self-defeats marked by exhaustion and they are at last becoming apparent and are well deserved. Take Vietnam alone: the U.S. finally walked away realizing it was spinning its wheels and budgets in Southeast Asia despite having killed an estimated four million Vietnamese while Ho Chi Minh and his great general, Vo Nguyen Giap, stood firm. Vietnam today is a fast-growing land of superlatives still under its "communist" government.

Now, largely, Americans have to deal with Joe Biden and the Zionist Neocons to whom he is subservient and the proxy war on Russia through Ukraine and the Zelensky regime. One can say with that this proxy war debacle is one of the most stupid interventions by the U.S. and the last that the U.S. will ever be capable of mounting against its alleged enemies, in this case Russia. (Unless it ends up sparking a nuclear war especially in which case no one wins).

The recent NATO summit in Vilnius was a disaster, showing some fractures within NATO and marked especially by the refusal to offer a petulant and embarrassing Zelensky NATO membership "unless Ukraine defeats Russia", which is highly unlikely.

In the meantime, Russia's Putin has been extremely patient and focused on incremental war gains, largely because he does not want to go ballistic (but could) to crush Zelensky's Ukraine quickly. He does not want to spark the EU and the U.S. to enter the war directly with troops or whatever, or World War 3. Putin also apparently recognizes that Ukrainians are centuries-long Slavic "brothers" of a sort, minus the Nazis there.

From the beginning Putin has almost exclusively aimed to create a "neutral" Ukraine outside of NATO. It has been estimated that Ukraine has lost over 350,000 soldiers to date, and Russia maybe 50,000 (roughly the same number of U.S. troops that died in the Vietnam War.) But one would never know WHAT Putin's aims have truly been via only the mainstream media in the U.S., which has been suffused with propaganda, keeping most Americans ignorant and thereby allowing the war to continue so far. This was NOT the case during the Vietnam War, which ended in 1975: the U.S. government was largely exposed by a mostly honest primary media and young people in protest who had faced the military draft, which was abolished after the war for a "volunteer" force of severely dumbed down soldiers. So why has the U.S. media been dishonest about Ukraine? Corruption and maybe the realization that it cannot expose the truth because so many power brokers in government and elsewhere, the extant oligarchy, would be disenfranchised by an angry American public realizing that real "democracy" in the U.S. has been discarded over the past 30 years.

The U.S. mainstream media is desperate with lies
July 23, 2023

"For the U.S. and its NATO allies, these past 18 months have been a strategic windfall, at relatively low cost (other than for the Ukrainians). The West's most reckless antagonist has been rocked. NATO has grown much stronger with the additions of Finland and Sweden. Germany has weaned itself from dependence of Russian energy and, in many ways, rediscovered its sense of values. NATO squabbles make headlines, but overall it has been a triumphal summer for the alliance."

This above is what passes for "honest" commentary in the Washington Post. This is what the mainstream media in the U.S. essentially tells the beleaguered American people nowadays. If it were not such a raft of lies, it would be quite funny. It's nothing but lies. This demonstrates how corrupted the mainstream media has become as a cheerleader for the American hegemony and Empire. Perhaps it's obvious to say that losers often cling to any fantasy to convince themselves and others they are not losing. But consider.

Iran and the U.S. 2017 - 2023

The proxy war on Russia through Ukraine was long in the making. Especially since the coup in 2014 and actually several years earlier. All it required was the U.S. provoking Russia so rabidly that Russia invaded Ukraine and it did so last year primarily because Ukrainians under Zelensky had already murdered some 14,000 of its own citizens in Ukraine's east. Most of the dead happened to be Russian speakers.

Look at the Washington Post's assertions. Russia "rocked"? (The Russian economy is doing okay, two percent growth, ruble stable, and it has allegedly ample "supplies" to maintain the war effort on the Zelensky regime to neutralize Ukraine. NATO stronger? Not sure on that even with Sweden and Finland sucked in. There are some cracks in NATO despite the additions. Germany energy is secure paying multiples more for U.S. LNG especially? Sense of "values" recovered in Germany as it is de-industrialized when all Germany WAS doing was buying cheap Russian natural gas and prospering? "Triumphal" summer when it's clear the Ukrainians have all but lost the proxy war with an estimated 350,000 soldiers dead or defunct and the Ukrainian army allegedly low on ammo even after the U.S. and vassals sent them well over $150 billion in arms and ammo? This is much more than Russia's entire defense budget pre-war anyway.

The primary question now is what is going to take to force the U.S. mainstream media to tell the truth to the American people and accept reality: that the proxy war on Russia is the greatest failure of U.S. policy ever (worse than the wars on Vietnam or Iraq), having wrecked Europe, having helped bankrupt the U.S. morally and financially, having encouraged de-dollarization across the Global South and the imminent rise of BRICS plus with perhaps the addition of a gold backed trading currency, and above all the loss of U.S.

credibility, respect and even Empire. Not to mention what this is going to do to average Americans: significant loss of American living standards which have anyway been eroding slowly for decades. Certainly the highest water mark for the U.S. in the last century probably occurred in 1991 when the USSR had disintegrated, but successive U.S. administrations completely wrecked the advantages it had with this "gift" from Russia which had earlier overextended itself in Afghanistan, too.

As the American novelist and Nobel Prize winner Ernest Hemingway wrote in the 1920s about how bankruptcy occurs in a famous quote from his first novel — "slowly, then all at once". The U.S. as a whole has about reached the "all at once" phase in this process. But note that psychopath Neocon Victoria Nuland is going to South Africa just before the BRICS summit later in August. No doubt she will arrive with threats and above all try to kill any move by BRICS nations to create the alleged new trade currency which will de-dollarize much of the world's population and create high inflation in the U.S. as dollars return home, no longer needed. South Africa should NOT give Nuland a visa to visit. She is largely responsible for the Ukraine mess, too.

There is, however, one slug of good news and it may involve Apartheid Israel becoming accountable for its many human rights and war abuses. The International Criminal Court (ICC) in the Hague is allegedly set to unveil an online electronic platform to allow the Palestinians and other victims to sue the "Israelis" who commit war crimes. The platform will allegedly enable people to submit multimedia complaints to the ICC. But what the ICC ought to do is simply charge Israeli leaders like Netanyahu with war crimes and more, or better the entire country with the devastating crime of Apartheid.

If the ICC can create any charge against Vladimir Putin as it has done, who looks heroic to most of the globe, NOT going after Israeli leaders just shows total hypocrisy and the degree to which the U.S. and allies have "captured" the ICC.

****

The proxy war on Russia is the greatest failure of U.S. policy ever, having wrecked Europe, having helped bankrupt the U.S. morally and financially, having encouraged de-dollarization across the Global South.

One notable Palestinian sees no changes for now but "samud" will prevail

July 30, 2023

I have been to Jenin in the West Bank. This was in winter 2006. I visited the cemetery there and saw the graves of Palestinians, many who died from an earlier attack on the Jenin Refugee Camp somewhat similar to the one this summer. My host was the Palestinian Red Crescent in Tubas, some 30 miles to the southeast.

What I saw and heard in Jenin was appalling, but what has happened overall since the latest Netanyahu government came to power is worse.

One notable Palestinian sees no changes …

My host in the West Bank for several weeks in 2006 was one Dr. Adnan Mjalli, age 60, a medicinal biochemist and business whiz with a PhD earned in England as a young man. A Tubas native, he is currently running an investment firm based around a number of previous business successes both overseas and in North Carolina. He has a lavish, almost palatial home in Tubas where his extended family lives, and he may well be among the best connected and most successful of all Palestinians emerging from the West Bank.

Back in 2006 I barely made it to Tubas through Hamra Checkpoint in the Jordan Valley. After the IDF let me go on to Tubas after a delay at the checkpoint, they had second thoughts and sent out an unsuccessful patrol to find me. Then came those delightful weeks in Tubas where I helped out at a school, The American Academy of Palestine, that Mjalli had just established to serve children in Tubas and surrounds. The school, lodged in a multi-story building Mjalli owned in Tubas, was an object of harassment by Israel and the school was forced to close after three years of operation.

I was able to conduct a brief interview with Dr. Mjalli this past week. He called me over lunch in a restaurant in Serbia where he was on a business trip. I had not spoken with him in almost a decade:

Mjalli is well aware of what the current Netanyahu government in doing: the Zionist plan is simply to make life so miserable for the natives of the Holy Land that they will pack up and leave. He recognizes that things have rarely been worse, but he believes the millions of beleaguered Palestinians are NOT going anywhere and will continue to operate with their "samud" - their "steadfastness and perseverance" against Zionist aggression, oppression and violence. And that the scattered push back from Palestinians against the Israelis will continue. As for the unpopular Palestinian Authority under Mahmoud Abbas, he says it will probably survive nominally but remain weak and ineffective in addressing demands for Palestinian freedom and civil rights. He also suggests that the so-called Abraham Accords will limp along, if not expand.

Israel's current government is presided over by terrorists hiding behind government titles. Notably Bezalel Smotrich and Itamar Ben Gvir whom Netanyahu became dependent upon so that he could return as Israel's prime minister and also try to avoid trial and conviction for corruption charges earlier as Israel's leader. Lately there has been talk of some sort of civil war in Israel over the efforts by Israel's far right to emasculate the Supreme Court and essentially destroy ANY "democracy" in the Apartheid state. Dr. Mjalli claims a "civil war" among Israelis is unlikely but not impossible.

In sum, Adnan Mjalli had no breakthrough information to offer, no precocious surprising projections or forecasts about what's ahead except more of the same Apartheid until it one day just stops, and it will because it simply must. The Palestinians will carry on steadfastly with "samud" and if the Zionists try wholesale evictions like a second Nakba, the world will not stand for it, not even the U.S. government. Zionism is, after all, one of the greatest crimes ever.

Desperation threatens the entire world

August 8, 2023

There exist maybe five hands-full of good minds in the West with communications skills who say intelligent things about the U.S. war on Ukraine (and any other conflict they may address). One will rarely find their commentaries in the Western mainstream media which is exactly most all of what most Americans read, if they do read at all, and if they read at all they often just look at headlines and otherwise don't know much except in their specific jobs or about their families and friends and their ailing bank accounts.

This is to say that U.S. citizens are probably the most heavily propagandized people on earth, but they may be waking up some despite their subjection to tons of misinformation or none at all that question what Washington and its "empire" are all about (which almost exclusively is self-maintenance and wealth augmentation for an elite few.)

It's no joke about the American public's lack of honest information about the origins of the proxy war in Ukraine against Russia. Or misguidance about Palestine or Iran or other so-called "enemies" of the U.S. as it desperately tries to cling to a status quo of dominance despite decades of failures to seek peace and accord.

One could interview a guide in the meadows below Damavand Mountain or a cabbie in Qum and he or she would likely be better informed about issues beyond Iran than most Americans. But change may still be occurring marginally.

Matters are slowly coming to a head on a raft of issues. Joe Biden at least has been clearly exposed as both a corrupt money and warmonger of late as the most damaging POTU.S. ever, but accountability so far remains distant and the Democrats' focus on Donald Trump's misdeeds via various indictments has been and remain deflecting factors from Biden's crimes and recognition of the additional corruption of the U.S Department of Justice, the FBI, the CIA and so on under the current administration. This all has elevated Trump as the possibly winning contender for the White House next year if he is not jailed because, quite simply, many Americans are put off by what they consider a surfeit demonization and persecution even while they know Trump is no paragon of virtue. It's all relative in the self-seeking cesspool that is Washington.

Remember, by contrast, the downfall of President Richard Nixon, scuttled politically by his attempted cover-up of a break-in at the Watergate complex in Washington in the early 1970s? What Nixon did in trying to suppress information of the Watergate break-in in comparison to what Biden and even his recent predecessors have done looks like child's play, but back then U.S. did have a relatively honest media, and generally far more astute elected reps in Congress and in federal agencies. In the 1970s an estimated 30 percent of working reporters/journalists in U.S. media did not even have college degrees, but they were gritty and passionate to uncover truths as the famed duo of Bob Woodward and Carl Bernstein at the Washington Post demonstrated in uncovering the Watergate scandal coverup. Today, it's estimated that most all of staff at the New York Times have degrees…but 50 percent from Ivy League schools like Harvard and Yale. It's all about privilege and perks and rubbing shoulders with power, never mind any focus on serving the public.

One example of journalistic propaganda is Time magazine's recent publication of an article by three writers, one of them Frederick Kagan. Kagan and his relatives, including one Robert Kagan who is married to the infamous Victoria Nuland, are all Jewish and Zionist Neocons who are part of an aristocracy of sorts of warmongers who for over three decades have had a strong grip fomenting U.S. wars, notably the Iraq war and now the proxy war in Ukraine. Time magazine's article essentially argues for the continuance of support for the Zelensky regime, claiming that the current counteroffensive against Russia which began in early June has good prospects for eventual success, but there has been NO success to date for Ukraine. Good prospects are a lie.

Arguments by Kagan's covey of lunatics include assertions in Time magazine that Russia lacks sufficient troops in reserve and that the troops on Russia's layered defensive lines in eastern Ukraine are suffering from poor morale. This seems to be sheer propaganda, for the real morale problem is Ukrainian and Zelensky's forces are reportedly surrendering in batches occasionally if not just walking away from the long battle lines and giving up. For Kagan and others, they aim is to keep the war going and to avoid negotiations with Russia which is now the fifth largest economy in the world, surpassing Germany, as Europe sinks in its vassalage to the U.S.

If Russia continues to prevail, people like Kagans will be totally discredited along with the Biden Administration and most Congress critters. The world cheers for this outcome: an end to the war, even on Russia's terms.

Oddly enough, the Pentagon itself has since the war began tried to restrain somewhat the warmongers in Congress and the White House under Neocon influence. Top Pentagon brass rightfully fear a nuclear escalation and direct American involvement in the war with American and EU soldiers. And most Americans now, 55 percent according to a poll taken by CNN poll this week, of all places, do not want the Neocons managing U.S. policy overseas and spending trillions to murder people in faraway lands. Since the start of the counteroffensive this summer Ukraine has lost an estimated 45,000 troops and maybe 300,000 since February 2022 and many tons of all kinds of assorted, donated weaponry, tanks and vehicles. Ukraine is on Western life support, almost destroyed. Russian troops have suffered and died, too, but not in the same numbers as Ukrainians.

U.S. IMPERIALISM REMAINS VERY STICKY AND TERRIBLY TRAGIC

August 16, 2023

The inimitable Chris Hedges, who for years was the New York Times bureau chief covering the Middle East, and who lost his job at the newspaper 20 years ago because he opposed the U.S. invasion of Iraq, has lately written another masterful piece covering all the bases with regard to Apartheid Israel.

One need not re-describe what Hedges has on Palestine, but the only conclusion one can come to is that the current Israeli government intends to annex eventually all of the West Bank, give no relief to the two million plus Palestinians in

Gaza, and eventually drive out the remaining Palestinians in the West Bank, some three million, one way or another. For anyone who has been involved with trying to understand the Palestinian plight in recent decades, what Hedges relates is one of the saddest stories among many unfolding now. Iranians know this, too.

The other hugely horrific story is in Ukraine, and a potential new story now involves Niger which in a coup installed new leaders fed up with French colonialism there and in West Africa. Note that some 70 percent or more Nigeriens don't even have electricity for light bulbs, but France depends to a significant degree for its own power needs on uranium extracted on the cheap by and from Niger's poor. Also, of late, we have the imprisonment of Pakistan's popular Imran Khan, this is largely a result of U.S. demands to effectively bury the popular Khan from leading Pakistan. And this is because he objected to the U.S. proxy war on Russia in Ukraine. One also witnesses efforts by the U.S. to corral China both economically and politically with the focal point on Taiwan to ensure that it remains a U.S. vassal and does not re-join China even while the U.S. allegedly recognizes that Taiwan is in fact "Chinese".

The U.S. is even sending "cookie monster" Undersecretary of State Victoria Nuland to Vietnam soon to try to convince the Communist government in Vietnam to support the Biden Administration. Nuland failed in her recent mission to Niger in her opposition to that country's new government. She is likely to fail in Vietnam, too, whatever her precise demands may be. And there are other so-called diplomatic efforts in other countries to try to keep the U.S. "empire" intact, where compromise is not in the U.S. cards but simply arm twisting, threats, bribes and demands. It's obvious that ANY important country that does not obey the U.S. is a potential target for political and military turmoil. But the big enchilada nowadays remains Ukraine, with China, in the growing recognition of U.S. failure in Ukraine, the next target.

There is no question, regarding Ukraine, that the Zelensky regime has all but lost the much heralded "offensive" against the Russian forces in Ukraine this summer. This suggests the war in Ukraine could end by late autumn in some fashion but on Russia's terms. Even a few U.S. mainstream media outlets such as CNN have admitted to the U.S.-NATO proxy war's military failures.

No one can kill an obvious truth forever, not even CNN or other parts of the U.S. mainstream media, so the question is, what does a country do with truths that are staring it in the face? In the case of people like Nuland and Antony Blinken, Nuland's boss, and Jake Sullivan, a "national security" advisor to senile Joe Biden, they don't modify policies at all and carry on as if truths don't matter. They simply cannot conceive of supporting a geopolitical strategy where cooperation might prevail even now when it becomes a necessity because tensions could explode in a nuclear way.

Biden just this month authorized or suggested another $40 billion to push the bloody war further, according to James Rickards, an American lawyer, financial expert and author. The U.S. may already have committed some $200 billion into the overall effort to castrate Putin's Russia, Rickards says, and will brook no competition economic or military to U.S. dominance. And this is a financial environment where the U.S. is $33 trillion in debt and the annual interest on the debt is well over $730 billion. This expense will surpass a trillion dollars in another year, more than the entire U.S. "defense" budget which itself is insane. It's totally unsustainable but there you have it, another failure to recognize a truth.

Even Muammar Ghaddafi, who was sodomized with a bayonet and murdered in Libya, the most prosperous African country in his day, said this way back in 2005: "NATO is expanding towards Russia to reach and capture the gas, oil, coal and iron owned by Russia." Ghaddaffi went on in his long-ago speech vaguely foreshadowing his demise and the NATO/U.S. destruction of prosperous Libya, adding that the U.S. is in effect killing itself, claiming that the hour will come when the U.S. will collapse like the Soviet Union did just over three decades ago.

But none should make the mistake of failing to recognize that the U.S. has not seriously been about promoting "freedom and democracy" and especially goodwill, but about resource theft, dominance, control and rapine, all at bottom to try to make sure that the "empire" survives and thrives with little regard even for the longer term well-being its NATO allies in a de-industrializing Europe that has lost its independence and become dependent on the U.S. for table scraps of economic support.

GOP debate matters and two "winners". For now: Trump and Ramaswany August 27, 2023

Iran and the U.S. 2017 - 2023

Off the cuff one can say that most all of the Republicans who "debated" their candidacies on August 23 to become the GOP nominee for President next year in the U.S. are a bunch of clownish political hacks who have been on the political scene way too long for years in one undistinguished capacity or another and this was well demonstrated.

Former President Trump stayed out of the fray on Fox News, remains way ahead in polls of anyone in the group for the nomination next year, and at the same exact time appeared on Twitter where he was interviewed by Tucker Carlson in what turned out to be the most widely heard interview perhaps in all of modern history — scores of millions of people watched on Twitter. Not a single GOP candidate but one had anything smart to say, repeating the same old platitudes about American exceptionalism, reflecting disdain for all the damage the militant U.S. "empire" has done for decades — almost seamlessly since the end of World War 2 but especially since the fall of the Soviet Union in the early 1990s.

The candidate who did have the freshest posture was Vivek Ramaswany, a 38-year-old American of Indian parentage with a degree in biology from Harvard, where he was elected to Phi Beta Kappa, and a law degree from Yale University. He has also been an entrepreneur in various biomedical related business ventures and has amassed a fortune of nearly a billion U.S. (fiat) dollars.

Ramaswany was the sole candidate of eight seen on Fox News who called for the end of U.S. financial and military support for the Zelensky regime in Ukraine. Hallelujah to that! He asserted climate change is a hoax. He proposed to scrap the FBI and other federal agencies. He was combative and critical. Above all he asserted that Americans live in a very "dark moment" fraught with a cold cultural civil war in the U.S. that must be recognized and dealt with. He also said that if Donald Trump became the GOP nominee he would support him… despite Trump's several outstanding indictments for alleged criminality related to the January 6th, 2021, insurrection or the riotous behaviors in Washington after Biden was elected in 2020 in what may have been a rigged election, and for other alleged misdeeds. The bottom line of the dash for the GOP nomination so far and at its start is that Vivek is the most interesting of the Republicans and he has even claimed he likes Robert F. Kennedy Jr., a Democrat, and might support him if were not aiming for the White House himself.

There was no specific discussion during the "debate" of the Middle East or West Asia. Not a word about the extreme troubles in Palestine, but Americans have long known about Nikki Haley, one of the eight contenders at the "debate", as a fervent supporter of Apartheid Israel who has claimed the U.S. needs Israel even more than the Zionists need the U.S. This alone is hard to fathom but one can reliably bet the other GOP contenders for the nomination more or less agree with Haley's assertion. As for RFK Jr, he has said some wise things on the Democratic side, but one with any sense is inclined to discount him for his overblown support for Israel. Maybe he's afraid of his own possible assassination by Israeli interests? It's no secret to Robert Kennedy Jr. that the Zionists may have had a hand in the 1963 murder of his uncle, President John F. Kennedy, who objected to Israel becoming a nuclear power, and also a hand in the murder of his father in 1968.

As for Trump with his huge lead as the GOP nominee for the election next year, in his appearance with Tucker Carlson, he at least appeared unusually relaxed and not as shrill as he can often seem, and was clearly capable of discussion with Carlson and the capacity to put sentences together, unlike senile, demented Joe Biden who belongs in jail or a nursing home or an asylum.

The looming immediate question about Trump, who did huge damage as President with his unilateral trashing of the JCPOA and especially the assassination of the revered General Qasem Soleimani, clearly at the urgings of the Zionists, is whether Trump MAY have become wiser and more knowledgeable about foreign policies and the dangers of current and former U.S. policies in Asia to U.S. interests? Is he aware enough going forward that the U.S. has clearly undercut its welcome in the Arab world, that China and Russia have been driven together closely, that Saudi Arabia has begun to restore healthy ties with Iran and that overall, in effect, U.S. "divide and conquer" moves across the globe have spelled the erosion if not yet the complete end of U.S. influence in the Global South, including in South America?

Saudi Arabia, by the way, it has been suggested, is being bribed by the Biden Administration not to sell oil for anything but dollars and stay on the U.S. "side". With what offering? Is the U.S. offering Saudi Arabia and headstrong MBS nuclear technology and would the U.S. look the other way if the Saudis somehow created their own nuclear weapon?

For the moment, hail to the Saudis for joining BRICS and to Iran, too. Does this mean MBS will not be swayed by the Biden Administration? It does seem the "petrodollar" is on the way out given the BRICS expansion.

Americans: Prepare for life in a fumbling Third World pariah!
September 10, 2023

Headline seen in Zerohedge, an online news and editorial site, on September 2: "U.S. and Israel plan joint drills simulating attack on Iran"

Why such a waste in all respects? There is no reasonable answer. But U.S. foreign policies and actions for decades have had one primary push from behind: support for Apartheid Israel resulting in the wreckage of some countries in West Asia. Why? Because the American "Empire" is insanely jealous of many countries like China, Russia and Iran with all their human and natural resources as it and its allies ratchet down the crapper.

Nowadays is that rare period in history when narratives put forth by the U.S. to explain itself and its actions as if they were benevolences, especially overseas and for decades, are rapidly being peeled away to reveal evil intent. Same goes for European vassals of the U.S. France is one example and France is being rejected by West Africans for Neo-colonialism.

In the case of the U.S., which is losing and has lost respect all over the globe, a knee-jerk reaction is to "support" its few remaining alleged "allies" such as Israel. Israel, which is helping destroy U.S. standing anywhere except among Israeli racists, xenophobes and Zio-cultists. From a formal bloody inception in 1947-48 it should have been cancelled. The Balfour Declaration of 1918 was the initial mistake. Israel's creation was not merely some (cruel) expiation foisted on the Arab and Muslim world for the Holocaust, which was a German crime, but also a platform to extend now fading Western military and economic dominance.

One huge Nazi crime, the Holocaust, begat myriad more crimes through Israel's creation. And the Western governments sit idly by. And the very weird thing is that almost no one would have objected to Israel had it ever been aimed at the consolidation of a new, inclusive state in the Levant that truly would fast become a real democratic entity for all the people west of the Jordan River. Every decade since 1948 has seen the true visage emerge, the substance of the Zionist state, its skin peeled back to expose a monster enabled by the West. Not a single war or occupation by Westerners - not in Iraq, Syria, Libya and elsewhere - and even U.S. sanctions on Iran and others would have occurred had it not been for the core blight of efforts to maintain Apartheid Israel and give it a free hand with no serious Western objections.

The various moves against Iran beginning with the deposition of Mohammad Mossadegh are foul. Any condemnation or redress by mere apology by the U.S., say, of any of its moves leading to Apartheid Israel primarily (and yes, some other crimes overseas) present a huge conundrum to the U.S. and its Western allies. Because if the U.S. were literally to ADMIT to one stupid policy error and make some amends, it would have also to admit to all the other errors of the "Empire" during its construction and maintenance. As for NATO, which has had no reason to exist since 1990, it continues, but Europe is already in the economic crapper thanks to Washington, including destruction of Russian Nordstream gas pipelines.

Witness the incarceration and persecution of Julian Assange. Washington hopes he dies in prison. He may. The U.S. cannot simply free him to be with his family? He did nothing wrong as a journalist. He did what journalists ought to do. Were the Biden gang to free him, as the world demands, would it not be a self-admission essentially of all the other moronic moves the U.S. has made creating an obvious dystopia abroad and at home? This may be one reason among many explaining why Washington's hubristic dinosaurs remain obdurate and unyielding on so many issues. Take a single recognizably critical support out of a foundation and structures can collapse.

Rest assured in the next decade the U.S. will decline into some nearly Third World country if World War 3 does not turn the globe to ashes. Bad economics alone will do the trick. So will social unrest. $33 trillion in debt and climbing? Interest payments on the debt to surpass $1 trillion next year, currently about $750 billion? Inflation embedded in the system? The U.S. Federal Reserve has only two choices: kill the dollar or kill the economy with high interest rates, which will kill the dollar anyway. Will the U.S. have to default? Probably. Use of the U.S. dollar is fast fading. U.S. bonds are getting sold off, by Japan and China and others. The "Petrodollar's" days are numbered. Blame the deeply corrupt Biden regime. Pray the stumbling corpse does not try to run for a second term. His and past administrations have woefully imagined that they can continue to dictate to the rest of the world forever. Rare informed Americans are horrified, too.

Nuclear war can be avoided if the U.S. gets wise
September 18, 2023

From afar one gets the impression that Iran's fortunes are improving. The exchange of prisoners between the U.S. and Iran and the return of $6 billion stolen dollars to Iran is a positive. Iran also has joined BRICS, the Global South is more or less rejecting Western hegemony, Africa is pushing off French colonialism, and U.S. and Western dominance is unraveling some like never before since World War 2.

Europe is sinking into a self-inflicted economic morass and the U.S. is not far behind with its unsustainable debts built up this century especially. The U.S. has all but lost the proxy war on Russia in Ukraine, the Russian economy so far is doing okay, Putin remains popular and Russians in general are united in their own sovereignty with resolve. Apartheid Israel is a divided mess what with the incompetent Netanyahu government staffed with evil clowns, racists, and belligerents.

However, it must be said by this American observer from afar, that Iran could prosper even more than it may in future if it can dispense with any perceived oppression of its own population by its own citizens. Doing so is no threat to Iran's Islamic orientation.

But at this juncture here's a few prognostications with commentary.

Nuclear war can be avoided if ...

The worst President this century, senile Joe Biden now facing an impeachment inquiry in the U.S. House, is being pushed by important voices in the U.S. not to run for a second term. The Washington Post confirms this. He is likely to be forced to cancel his candidacy later this autumn or winter.

The bloody, ill-conceived and provoked U.S./NATO proxy war on Russia is likely to end early in 2024 with negotiations. But Russia will never abandon Crimea or the regions it occupies among Russian-speaking and leaning former Ukrainians in the eastern parts of Ukraine. They are Russians now. And a neutral Ukraine is imperative to Russia. The war is unsustainable but if NATO/U.S. enters the conflict directly that could spark a nuclear apocalypse. Russia will NOT permit a threat to its existence.

With respect to China, the U.S. cannot abide competition anywhere. (Huawei, one of China's leading hi-tech companies, is under attack again given fear of Huawei's latest 5G consumer mobile phones which have been supplied with a Chinese-made advanced chip after being cut off from buying them elsewhere. The U.S. House of Representatives has proposed sanctions against Huawei and SMIC, not only severing all commercial relations with them but also filing criminal lawsuits against their executives for managing to compete! This is beyond petty.

The U.S. has stationed an alleged 375,000 thousand personnel at 66 military bases in the Indo-Pacific region, and focused the U.S. defense budget for 2024 on China. It is pushing war with China on its gullible Pacific allies, too. This is waste on a gargantuan scale by a U.S. that is virtually bankrupt even without war. The Pentagon, playing war games from time to time, has concluded the U.S. cannot "win" a war with China, not to mention any war with Russia that cannot be won. As long as the U.S. maintains economic wars on competitors and even Europe, it will backfire on the U.S. economy. Expect more erosion of the dollar as a reserve currency.

Expect increasing military, social, economic, and political decay in the U.S. and vassal Europe. Ukraine is the last of militant U.S. imperialism on steroids, which is why it's so dangerous to humanity. Too many psychopaths in Washington remain, fewer in the general populating by the week. One must ask simply: what's wrong with a more peaceful world, one where competition is acceptable to spur innovation and the U.S. isn't the hegemonic beast throwing its weight around waging wars of choice, and none of them to date have "won" a thing but dollar profits for the Military Industrial Complex in the U.S. and for politicians. Average Americans also are in desperate need of attention and are suffering relatively. Corrupted Zelensky is coming to the U.S. and will appear at the UN in New York. Would that he were shunned and ridiculed there. He's coming to beg for another $24 billion atop nearly $200 billion already wasted and he's likely to get another lame infusion to prolong the bloody proxy war on Russia.

West Africa is likely to avoid a general conflagration and Nigeria probably won't be able to lead a war on Niger.

Robert F. Kennedy Jr. has threatened to leave the Democratic Party in his bid for the Presidency in 2024. Biden won't even give him as a candidate normal Secret Service protection and he faced a distinct threat of assassination last week. He or Vivek Ramaswany could win the 2024 election in a truly free and fair election, which the U.S. will never see again if the so-called Deep State has its way again. The U.S. has not really been a "democracy" of merit for many years.

The "American Century" is dying. Multipolarity is rising. No one can weep about this.

Iran and the U.S. 2017 - 2023

www.ingramcontent.com/pod-product-compliance
Lightning Source LLC
Chambersburg PA
CBHW050313240426
43673CB00042B/1394